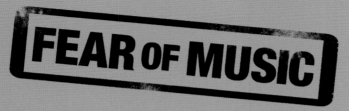

FEAR OF MUSIC

Garry Muholland was born in Islington, London, in March 1963. In May 1977 he bought the Sex Pistols' 'God Save the Queen', discovered discos and realised that being a pop star was his vocation. Fifteen years on and with no record deal in sight, he entered the world of music journalism. Despite knowing next to nothing about jazz, Garry became a jazz columnist for *Echoes* in 1993. He's now a club and radio DJ and has written on every genre of popular music for numerous publications, including *Time Out*, where he became music editor in 1998, the *Guardian*, the *Observer Music Monthly*, *Q*, and the London *Evening Standard*. His first book, *This is Uncool: the 500 Greatest Singles Since Punk and Disco*, was described by Tim Lovejoy as 'A bible for music fans' and by Julie Burchill as 'the finest book published this century'.

By Garry Mulholland

Fear of Music: The 261 Greatest Albums Since Punk and Disco
This is Uncool: The 500 Greatest Singles Since Punk and Disco

THE 261
GREATEST
ALBUMS
SINCE PUNK
AND DISCO

FEAR OF MUSIC

GARRY
MULHOLLAND

An Orion paperback

First published in Great Britain in 2006
by Orion
This paperback edition published in 2007
by Orion Books Ltd,
Orion House, 5 Upper St Martin's Lane,
London WC2H 9EA

An Hachette Livre UK company

10 9 8 7 6 5 4 3 2

A CIP catalogue record for this book is
available from the British Library.

ISBN 978-0-7528-8243-7

Printed and bound in Spain by Cayfosa Quebecor

The Orion Publishing Group's policy is to use papers that are
natural, renewable and recyclable products and made from wood
grown in sustainable forests. The logging and manufacturing
processes are expected to conform to the environmental
regulations of the country of origin.

www.orionbooks.co.uk

For Linsay

ACKNOWLEDGEMENTS

As with my first book *This Is Uncool*, the major source of information used in the writing of *Fear Of Music* was Martin C. Strong's *The Great Rock Discography*, in this case the seventh edition, complete with foreword by the late John Peel, and published by Canongate. It's very simply the broadest, wisest and most trustworthy rock reference book in existence.

For the double-checking of UK chart positions and release dates, I used the third edition of *The Complete Book Of The British Charts* (Omnibus Press) by Neil Warwick, John Kutner and Tony Brown. For double-checking US chart positions, I used the online *All Music Guide* at www.allmusic.com. *All Music* is also an invaluable – and free – resource for artists' career details and reviews. The other online resource that took on increasing importance as the book progressed was the internet encyclopedia at www.wikipedia.org.

From there, I just need to acknowledge and express my gratitude to the writers of the books and magazine features, plus the websites and individuals, who contributed vital info on the entries listed below. They are:

David Bowie/Low and "Heroes" – 'Trans-Europe Excess' by Stephen Dalton and Rob Hughes, published in Uncut Take 47, April 2001

Kraftwerk/Trans-Europe Express – 'Kraftwerkfeature' by Lester Bangs, from *Psychotic Reactions And Carburetor Dung* (Vintage)

Fela Kuti/Sorrow Tears And Blood – *The Penguin Encyclopedia Of Modern Music*, edited by Donald Clarke (Penguin)

Elvis Costello/This Year's Model – 'Horn-rims From Hell' by Nick Kent, from *The Dark Stuff* (Penguin)

Dr. Alimantado/Best Dressed Chicken In Town – www.green sleeves.net

The Smiths/The Smiths and Hatful Of Hollow – *Morrissey & Marr: The Severed Alliance* by Johnny Rogan (Omnibus Press)

Hüsker Dü/Candy Apple Grey – *Our Band Could Be Your Life* by Michael Azerrad (Back Bay)

Various Artists/Retro Techno/Emotions Electric – Sleevenotes from the 1991 vinyl edition by John McCready

Cornershop/When I Was Born For The 7th Time – Interview by David Fricke for *Rolling Stone* magazine, October 1997

Belle And Sebastian/If You're Feeling Sinister – Chris Geddes

That just leaves the more personal thanks. Big shouts to Garri Raynor, Manish Agarwal, Sharon O'Connell, Andy Fraser and Ian Preece for lending me precious albums to listen to before making my final list, and not complaining when they didn't get them back for over a year. Ian Preece deserves more than a special mention: as the editor of both *This Is Uncool* and *Fear Of Music*, his incisive cuts and faith in my writing are the reasons why I've written two books I'm proud of. Ian has also shown the patience of a saint throughout the somewhat fraught gestation of *Fear Of Music*, and for that I'm doubly grateful. The same gratitude, for the same reasons, goes to my agent Robert Caskie. Stand-up guys, the pair of you.

That just leaves two more people who know how crucial they are to the existence of this book. Thank you, Julie Burchill, for support above and beyond. And finally, to my wife Linsay, to whom this book is dedicated. Cheers, Dollface. Again, and always.

If you have any comments or observations on, or corrections or critcisms of *Fear of Music* you can reach the author on Garrymul@aol.com.

INTRODUCTION

When I'd finished *This Is Uncool* – my book concerning the 500 greatest singles since punk and disco – the last thing I ever envisaged doing was writing a follow-up. Particularly one about albums. I had, after all, made a big deal of the fact that, in contrast to perceived critical wisdom, singles were far more important than albums in the Great Pop Scheme of Things. It was readers of *This Is Uncool* – those generous enough to praise me for it personally or by email – that changed my mind. 'When are you gonna write one about albums?' they repeatedly asked. The only convincing negative reply would've been, 'I don't want to.' But I did and do. *This Is Uncool* feels like unfinished business.

This Is Uncool was an attempt to get music criticism . . . ugh, let's try again . . . talking about and loving music away from the rockbloke nerds and their obsessive cataloging of the minutiae behind 'proper' albums, and put it back where it belongs; in the shared memory of pop lovers who have other things going on their lives – lives often illuminated by a song, a chorus, a beat, a lyric, a dance, a soundtracked memory. By arranging what I believed to be the 500 greatest singles since punk and disco in chronological order, I hoped to tell a tale – both personal and general – about where pop has taken us, and why. By choosing singles I wanted to elevate the radio moment above the bedsit chinstroke, and by choosing the period enjoyed by the young(ish) generation, make an argument for pop culture that isn't choked at birth by an overbearing reverence for the 1960s, particularly The Beatles and Bob Dylan. The plethora of list TV shows that cover the post-punk/disco period seem to glory in a glib form of self-loathing, with even nostalgia for the things we loved – and especially things that attempted to matter in some social or political way – filtered through a constant kitschifying dismissal of our own culture as something to be ridiculed. *This Is Uncool* was a kind of response, based on the belief that the things we made, consumed and remember do matter, because to dismiss that is to dismiss the stuff that's made us what we are. The end result of this is a refusal to discern between the huge emotional and intellectual resonance of great pop, and the stultifying cynicism of bad pop, as if the only thing that matters is whether it sells or not. Which, I guess, is what happens after several years of watching bad things prosper and good things disappear. It's either shrug, wink knowingly and celebrate your own rubbishness, or take the time and trouble to find out where the good things disappeared to. The readers who enjoyed *This Is Uncool* were those who weren't ashamed of loving music and its surrounding culture, and despised the shallow version of irony and cruel gossip that passes for pop cultural discourse in twenty-first-century Britain.

But a book about albums has to be different. Entire albums don't slap you in the face when blasted out of a radio in the hairdressers. You have to buy them (well, less so in the wake of internet file-sharing and downloading, but you know what I mean), listen to them, and form a deeper relationship with them. Singles can just be fuck buddies. Albums expect to be partners for life.

Even though the singles market has collapsed and pop's discourse and commercial success is dominated by the long-playing record, it's rare for anyone to find an album that they choose to listen to over and over again, from beginning to end . . . and I don't mean as background, but to truly listen to. The reasons why we all love the iPod and burning our own mix CDs is not just about the ease and convenience of new technology. It's about our yearning to go back to singles culture in the wake of 70-minute CD albums that obscure the five good songs with answer-machine messages, portentous self-mythologising interludes, interminable ambient jams, or that nightmare of our post-hip hop world, the 'skit', which manages to combine all of the above with either naff preaching or gratuitous hatred of women/queers/anyone who doesn't want to give the artist 'love' (whatever the hell that could mean, except money, in this context), and does it so often that putting your CD on shuffle ends up producing some form of bad experimental radio play. As albums have got longer, the pressure on artists to make songs that have any point has actually receded. No wonder even non-nerds are keen to prune the fat and use their gadgets to create their own albums.

But all that means is that, when an artist does make an album that takes you on a journey into their world, and compels you to keep going back, they must be among that rare breed who take this pop stuff seriously outside of money and fame, and therefore should have their work picked out and praised to the heavens for having the heart to see art as an end in itself. The more I thought about this, the more I wanted to write about those records, the sort of sets of songs where you end up knowing the exact amount of time between each track, so completely do the hills and corners of the musical journey impress themselves upon your consciousness.

The title for this, a list of the greatest albums since punk and disco, comes from the title of an album by Talking Heads, but also from an interview I did with Tim Lovejoy, producer and presenter of a daft, inspired Saturday-morning football show on Sky Sports called *Soccer AM*. The interview concerned the music he and his team chose to backdrop various football highlights, games and comedy skits, which

seemed to be everything British radio wasn't capable of anymore. Robbie Keane scores yet another impudent masterpiece of a goal while The Velvet Underground tell you they're beginning to see the light, or 50 Cent asks you to party like it's your birthday, or a record you've never heard before illuminates the moment when ball bulges net. That sort of thing. Such a simple idea – watching poetry in sporting motion, backed by a brilliant range of music from vintage rock 'n' roll to kitsch MOR, from hip hop to youth-club punk, from ancient to not even out yet. The filter they used was quality rather than genre . . . and the fact that the programme was so successful, and that the music content was becoming increasingly influential, seemed to fly in the face of music radio and TV wisdom where every music radio show or TV channel's playlists are shrunk to fit the tastes of people who want to hear the same kind of music for hours on end.

So Tim was successfully rebelling against 'niche', and playing a wide variety of great music on his football show, but . . . I recalled that when he'd first taken over the slot in the mid-'90s, he'd played a predictable diet of dadrock – you know, indie rock for blokes. Oasis, Stereophonics, Travis, Ocean Colour Scene . . . that sort of thing. I asked him why. He answered, without pause, 'Because I was scared of music.' Excuse me?

'Because,' Tim explained, 'in this country, if you're not a music expert with all those classic albums listed and whatnot, your opinion of music isn't supposed to count. I mean, I don't like Van Morrison's *Astral Weeks*. I don't like The Beatles. So it took me a long time to get the confidence that I could just put on a record 'cos I liked it. I was scared to have an opinion.'

This stuck in my mind when I was thinking about this book, and about everything else I was writing. This pantheon we've (and by 'we', I mean rock critics) invented that gets trotted out in magazine Best Of lists over and over. This very white, straight, male view of rock history, whereby a 1967 Beach Boys album that doesn't actually exist (it's called *Smile*. Brian Wilson went nuts while making it) is seen as a more classic album than anything you've bought, laughed at, danced to, fallen in love with this week. Especially if you happen to be a girl and suspect that Beach Boys outtakes aren't very sexy, when BEING SEXY IS POP MUSIC'S JOB. Where not liking Neil Young is seen as evidence of not being clever enough to 'get it'.

Critics turned jazz into academia. If we're not careful we'll turn everything previously thrilling, irresponsible and gloriously, stupidly shaggable about pop into one enormous library of alphabetised lists of private ponderings on the meaning contained within Bob Dylan's bum note at the beginning of the thirty-fourth bootleg version of 'Positively 4th Street'. Music is a social thing, based almost entirely around dancing, copping-off, drugs that make you love each other, romance and the belief that if you just shake uncontrollably to this beautiful noise in a roomful of beautiful people right now, then your lousy job/debt problems/marriage/friendships/life will simply cease to be. Until the next beautiful noise begins, or the dream ends. This is what pop does for us.

So I figured, yes, the 261 greatest albums since punk and disco. No niches, no completism, no problem with the argument that Bow Wow Wow's *See Jungle! See Jungle! Go Join Your Gang, Yeah. City All Over! Go Ape Crazy* is a better album than Radiohead's *OK Computer*, because it so obviously is. Of course, acknowledged classics by the Sex Pistols, Bowie, Costello, Blur, Public Enemy, and, indeed, Radiohead will be in there. But so will Defunkt, Kathryn Williams and Son Of Bazerk, because these records are extraordinary and say huge things about us and about music, and a record doesn't have to be popular to be brilliant, just in case you thought that's what I was getting at. The music business is more about luck than all the endless talent contests and Executive Producers would have you believe, and if these artists had had some, then we'd perhaps be boring ourselves shitless about their 'classic legacy' or something, instead of the bloody Beatles. Again. And 261? That's simply the exact number of records I wanted to write about. No need to round up the number, and definitely no need to boil down

the list when we all know that brilliant singles far outnumber brilliant albums, and that those brilliant albums scream their superiority over the humdrum majority, as soon as you begin to sink beneath their surface and become fascinated – even changed – by what they have to say.

There will also be a smattering of what has become a total no-no in learned discussions of best albums ever: Greatest Hits collections. That's right. Partly because Roxy Music's *Greatest Hits* is one of the biggest things that ever happened to me, but mainly because the Best Of set is often an artist's best collection of fun, entertainment and song and dance numbers, and therefore is the record we most often get out when we really want to enjoy listening to our favourite band. The idea that these are somehow not proper albums goes back to this odd notion that we should like the band's double concept album more because that unlistenable fifteen-minute meditation on root vegetables or the everlasting pain of being healthy, wealthy and never having fought in a war is good for us. If you don't eat your self-indulgent album-filler greens you'll never get any singles dessert. No wonder they call it dadrock.

So – 261 albums, set out in similar fashion to *This Is Uncool*, in chronological order but with any discussion of wider social context or events of the day included in the essays, rather than prefacing the year's albums. The starting point is the debut album by the Ramones, released in July 1976. The list closes at the end of 2003, simply because it takes at least 18 months to decide if any record truly stands the test of time or not.

Hopefully, like *This Is Uncool*, it will tell some kind of story of how we got from the Ramones to OutKast. It will also attempt to draw up some kind of alternative aesthetic for British pop culture – a set of impulses, influences and musical insights that are not forever apologising for not being old enough to remember – or be in – The Beatles.

But mostly, it will be an argument against Fear Of Music. This stuff is not rocket science. It's just the soundtrack to our lives.

1976

RAMONES

RAMONES
PRODUCED BY CRAIG LEON AND T. ERDELYI
SIRE/JULY 1976
UK CHART: DID NOT CHART
US CHART: DID NOT CHART
KEY TRACKS: 'Blitzkrieg Bop'; 'Judy Is A Punk'; 'Now I
Wanna Sniff Some Glue'; 'Beat On The Brat'; '53rd & 3rd'

The first thing to 'fess up to is that the debut album by New York's Ramones was not a personal Year Zero. I didn't spend the rest of 1976 trading in my purple loons for Levi drainpipes, informing friends that I wished to be known henceforth as Dee Dee, and hollering 'HEY! HO! LET'S GO!' at passers-by. In truth, I didn't hear this weird, runty, luminous thing until after I'd digested the Sex Pistols and The Clash, and convinced myself that punk rock was actually left-wing politics backdropped by savage power chords. But there's no doubt at all that this is the record that redrew the boundaries of both the rock and pop album. The fact that Ramones did this without ever charting anywhere only adds to the allure, and the mystery, of its instant influence. Plus, as a handy bonus for kicking off a book about albums, the Ramones occupy the unique position of being a group entirely based around worship of the radio pop single who just happened to only make complete sense over the length of an album.

The most obvious way to describe the Ramones is to say that they sound like The Beach Boys reduced to base elements. But this would imply that Johnny, Joey, Dee Dee and Tommy were crude, which, unlike the vast majority of musicians who leaped at the chance offered by the four's basic musicianship and catchy songs, they weren't. So many have tried to play thrashed-out power chords like Johnny, and failed to build that perfect wall. And no one has ever sung like Joey, whose nasal moan captures androgyny, shyness, fear and the eternal blight of geekdom so well that what could have been another macho form of rock becomes some

kind of third gender exercise in both pain and defiance. What this album said to everyone who heard and loved it was not anything so mundane as 'anyone can form a band', but, that any apparent loser and society reject – any punk – with a true idea of who they are, and an utter refusal to hide it, is allowed to make their stand, in any way they see fit. It revealed a geek army. And it insisted, obviously and secretly, that The Bay City Rollers mattered as much as The Shangri-Las, who mattered as much as Iggy Pop – who all mattered more than Rod Stewart and Supertramp and . . . well, you know, that stuff before punk and disco which we've all forgiven to some extent, but still has to be put out on compilations called Guilty Pleasures because Ramones taught us a lesson about what rock and pop really were.

Of course, although the Ramones have been rendered both classic and cuddly by the passage of time, there are unlovable things on this first album. 'Loudmouth' appears to advocate beating up a woman who talks too much for Joey's liking. And 'Today Your Love, Tomorrow The World' appropriates Nazi imagery so neatly that it cleared a path for punk's intermittent flirtation with fascism. Excuses? Well, the Ramones never bothered to make too many for themselves, and Johnny, Joey and Dee Dee are all dead now, so I can't do better than the on-record, 'it was an art statement' or 'it was a metaphor for rock'-type platitudes they left behind. What I can say is that the Ramones, who were bored Forest Hills suburban twenty-somethings rather than Manhattan sophisticates or teen prodigies, opened up a hole with this album's sublime, strange noise in which they could pour their nerdy, frightened obsessions with Vietnam, *The Texas Chainsaw Massacre*, rent boys, sniffing glue, cruelty and violence and being endlessly rejected by girls far braver and more reckless than they, and then covered that hole up with so much truth and bluff, power and prettiness, contagion and thrust, that you could only look into its fourteen songs in twenty-nine minutes and see your own private obsessions and worst-case scenarios, and then . . . laugh. And jump around, play air guitar, sing through your nose

RAMONES/RAMONES

and, probably, certainly, for better or for worse, form a band.

The simple things, you see, are all complicated. That's why there's no substitute for the first album by the Ramones.

THE MODERN LOVERS

THE MODERN LOVERS
PRODUCED BY JOHN CALE, ROBERT APPERE AND ALAN MASON (REMIXED BY GARY PHILLIPS, MATTHE KING KAUFMAN AND GLEN KOLOTKIN)
WARNERS/OCTOBER 1976
UK CHART: DID NOT CHART
US CHART: DID NOT CHART
KEY TRACKS: 'I'm Straight'; 'Old World'; 'Roadrunner'; 'Pablo Picasso'; 'Someone I Care About'

But before the Ramones there was The Modern Lovers, and the one and only album by the original line-up of that band did invent punk rock. Oh yes. Not The Stooges nor the MC5 nor The New York Dolls, nor even the Velvet Underground, who The Modern Lovers had copied so well they even got The Velvets' John Cale to produce them. Nope. The Modern Lovers: the true missing link between the avant-thug experiment of your arty type, and the blithe naivety of your suburban garage band.

To keep the history bit brief, The Modern Lovers were Jonathan Richman, Jerry Harrison, Ernie Brooks and David Robinson, four bony geeks from Boston, Massachusetts who loved basic '60s garage rock 'n' roll, The Doors and aforementioned Velvets. They were discovered in 1972 by veteran music-biz jester Kim Fowley, and signed to Warner Brothers, who arranged the session with Cale. The major record label did what any sensible business would do when confronted with something the mainstream didn't want to hear – they dropped the band, and shelved the tapes. Why? We'll get back to that.

Anyway, one song from the sessions somehow entered the underground, became a legend, a bootleg, a cult. It was called 'Roadrunner'. 'Roadrunner' was everything that rock was not from 1972–76. It was droning and minimal yet irresistibly catchy. It had pure pop heart. It sounded innocent but anthemic. The singer drawled instead of screeched or crooned, and the song was about nothing more than driving around listening to rock 'n' roll. It seemed '50s-nostalgic, but spoke of its love of 'the modern world', and anyway, the music was art-buzz, not Elvis-lite. Best of all, any fool could learn to play a song that hardly bothered with the third chord, and because the song was great, the band would sound great. Mid-'70s-rock's main message was, 'You'll never be able to do this.' 'Roadrunner' shouted, 'Everyone can do this!'

So, in 1976, a smart US indie label called Beserkley tracked down the band, bought the tapes from Warners, and brushed them up until they became an album, released four years after its recording. It gave Richman, a music journalist, the music career he craved, even though Harrison

had joined Talking Heads and Brooks had joined The Cars. But, for the few who bought it, it was a dirty great sign saying, 'Walk this way'. For, would you believe … 'Roadrunner', the future rock standard, wasn't even the best song on it.

I was going to write at great length about the wonders that are 'Old World', 'Pablo Picasso' and, especially, 'I'm Straight'. The latter, I'm convinced, is The Thing Of Things, the moment where morality crashed into rock's diseased decadence and exposed the lie that was hippy hipness, that someone pointed out, with anger tempered by compassion, that the '60s counter-culture had created nothing more than a generation of drug-fucked cowards who 'Can't take this place/And take it straight'. Take the song straight, as delivered to the girl Jonathan wants, or take it as a metaphor for everything wrong – still wrong, frankly – with the rock side of the music biz, it still makes me want to get up and cheer every time I hear it.

And there's more information in the way Jonathan drawls the words 'hippy Johnny' than I have space to do justice to.

So why had Warners passed? Well, the simple answer is in the chart placings above … even in 1976 hardly anyone bought it. The deeper answer is this: Warners had signed a rock band who'd written the first great songs about what a piece of shit rock was. Not rock 'n' roll, that beautiful, urgent, furious, lovelorn, direct, animal, groove-heavy, panicky grasp for Now that had changed the world infinitely for the better. But rock, that fake blues, self-pitying, white, dishonest, flashy, grooveless, blokeish, reactionary and self-absorbed bunch of jiveass corporate soft-porn that had had the roll removed and replaced with suck-my-dick misogyny and misanthropy. Richman just laid waste to this waste and reclaimed rock 'n' roll for the good-hearted geek. It sounded like Buddy Holly if he'd been born ten years later and made head barman at Warhol's Exploding Plastic Inevitable.

Suffice to say, if you don't know this record and you love music by the Ramones, the Sex Pistols, The Fall, Talking Heads, Elvis Costello, Echo And The Bunnymen and the Jesus And Mary Chain – to name just the most obviously influenced – then you should get this record and hear why the best rock 'n' roll rebels against something more fundamental than our long-suffering parents, and why no one ever called Pablo Picasso an asshole.

SONGS IN THE KEY OF LIFE

STEVIE WONDER
PRODUCED BY STEVIE WONDER
MOTOWN/OCTOBER 1976
UK CHART: 2
US CHART: 1
KEY TRACKS: 'As'; 'I Wish'; 'Village Ghetto Land'; 'Have A Talk With God'; 'Black Man'

There's a moment on this record which never fails to freak me out … in a good way. It's in funk monster 'I Wish', and comes just as the second verse struts off into the bridge. Stevie's just recalled his Ma telling him not to go outside, and as the band lay heavy into the change, this fucking noise rears up and out of the mix … like a finger wagging, or maybe a dirty, sweet impression of teen boy rage. It throws everything up in the air, taking Wonder from safe nostalgia about his childhood to imminent, nervous, hormonal danger, in one flail of bass. Sure, bassist Norman Watts just picks a note and wobbles it. But from such moments genius comes, because this split-second flinging of grit into the face of the past gives the truth to the misspent youth lyric, which helps gives the truth to all the la-la-love and God-bothering of Stevie Wonder's epic double album. After all, if you call your album this, even Steveland Morris, a man-and-boy hit-maker for thirteen years by this point, has to step up to the plate and find that key.

Songs In The Key Of Life locates a lost chord by providing twenty-one songs that are not just about one man's life, but anyone's. And, by that, I don't mean that everyone has necessarily experienced everything Wonder sings about. I mean that his vision, lyrical commitment and sonic palette are so strong here that, if you've never lived in a ghetto, 'Village Ghetto Land' makes you feel it. If you've never been religious, 'Have A Talk With God' makes you understand why people are. If you've never felt that love conquers all, then you have to pick a fight with 'As' to win your argument. And if you think that rock stars delivering obvious history lessons is dull and worthy and pretentious, then check out 'Black Man' and wonder whether music's greatest strength is telling you what you should already know in a way that makes old news into brand new information, ready to stick, ready to be used.

One of the odd things about . . . *Key Of Life*, rarely mentioned in the rush to canonise Wonder, are the portentous, gibberish sleevenotes. I should quote here to prove my point, but it seems a bit rude and smug, really. I suspect that's why they exist – no one wanted to tell him how awful and incoherent they are. One can sympathise. 'Um, Mr Wonder, these sleevenotes . . . I wonder if I could suggest some improvements, you know, just to make them simpler for your simple fans. What's that? Have I ever written 'Superstition' or 'Livin' For The City' or 'Uptight'? Yes, Mr Wonder, see your point. Fuck off? Of course – how off would you like me to fuck?' Must be a bastard working with a genius.

Still, you would get to be involved, somehow, with 'Joy Inside My Tears', with its queasy seaside synth, testifying vocal adlibs, 'Hey Jude' repetition, and casual blend of soul and rock balladry, which provided the template for every ballad Prince ever wrote. You would get to hear 'Another Star' invent Basement Jaxx, and to bawl your eyes out before the rest of the world when you hear 'As' use a definitively swinging kind of gospel to put us in our small but vital place amongst nature, history, the universe and everything. You maybe got to be amazed and moved when Wonder – who would never come close to making a record this good again – took four amazing songs which couldn't make it onto the original double vinyl and would form the backbone of any other artist's follow-up, and insisted that they be put on a bonus EP. So now, in the CD era, 'Saturn', 'Ebony Eyes', 'All Day Sucker' and 'Easy Goin' Evening' are the accepted end of . . . *Key Of Life*, right and proper and where they ought to be.

'Isn't She Lovely' and 'Sir Duke' are also where they ought to be. These cheesy hit tributes to Wonder's sprog and Duke Ellington should make me kind of nauseous, but they don't because . . . they're part of *Songs In The Key Of Life*. It just wouldn't be the same without them, like lamb without mint sauce or Bowie's career without *Tin Machine*. *Songs In The Key Of Life* sets the tone for what all the albums in this book are; journeys that have potholes and leaves on the line, but still journeys in themselves, which maybe resist you doing your own computer edit, because, in these cases, you know that the artist has taken you somewhere, and you'll take the rough with the smooth. The extraordinary run of '70s Stevie Wonder albums is all about those wonderful journeys, and heads off a debate about why he was never great after this, because, hell, he did his bit.

Every soul, hip hop and R&B-based pop album since owes something to *Songs In the Key Of Life*. What they generally don't have is extremes of joy and anger, of deep blues and silly pop, and the grace to make those extremes talk to each other, and to us. That's livin' alright.

1977

HEART OF THE CONGOS

THE CONGOS

PRODUCED BY LEE PERRY
BLACK ARK/JANUARY 1977
UK CHART: DID NOT CHART
US CHART: DID NOT CHART
KEY TRACKS: 'Fisherman'; 'The Wrong Thing'; 'Can't Come In'; 'La La Bam-Bam'; 'Children Crying'

There's a perfectly reasonable argument that 'Fisherman' by The Congos is the most beautiful piece of popular music ever made. A slice of Jamaican dream music made from liquid sky and burning spices, it is sung by falsetto singer Cedric Myton in a girlish register on the edge of panic. The song's picture of fishermen toiling on the waves – the poor Jamaican worker twinned with Christ's disciples – is both joyous and doomed, a place where poverty, toil and the gospels meld, and where Myton, his fellow vocalists, and the best producer and musicians in Jamaica go to pay tribute, to never let us let it go. Perry's music glides and stings, voices and instruments suddenly flying out of the mix, yet housed in something so languid and pretty that the state of contemplative worship is never lost – it's simply a refusal to allow itself to become background music. 'Fisherman' is so immersive, spooked and Biblical and, somehow, sexy, it becomes a new kind of eroticised gospel music. It's a track so strong the Berlin producers Rhythm & Sound released a double album of 'Fisherman' versions. Being track one, side one of *Heart Of The Congos*, it's one tough act to follow. But follow it this album does.

The Congos were a Rastafarian vocal group in The Wailers' tradition, led by Myton, of The Royal Rasses, and tenor Roydel Johnson, school friend of production genius Lee Perry, and member of Afro-rasta innovators Ras Michael and the Sons Of Negus.

Elsewhere on this album, future crooning legend Gregory Isaacs is among the backing singers, '80s 'I Wanna

Wake Up With You'-hitmaker Boris Gardiner plays bass, Sly Dunbar is among the drummers, and lead guitar is from jazz-ska progenitor Ernest Ranglin. A supergroup, frankly, who allowed Perry to fashion the high artistic watermark of this thing we call roots reggae. Better than the best of Marley, you ask? Well . . . yeah. There's no insult in this. *Heart Of the Congos* is better than most things.

Much like the first Ramones album, *Heart Of The Congos* lays everything it's going to do on the line by opening with its best shot. But that's no problem, because, like Ramones, it immediately opens up an alien world you want to explore, knowing that you'll never quite unpeel its many layers. For example, what kind of noise is that, farting and mooing away at the back of 'Children Crying'? What makes it? What is it trying to say? Did they drag a baby elephant into the studio and ask it to sing harmonies, and then hit it with cymbals? Don't know, but I love it, and it provides welcome respite from the rasta high moral ground, almost as if Perry wasn't really buying this religious stuff and decided to blow raspberries at the singers.

The record is always disappearing, only to be released again by another smitten enthusiast. The original vinyl, on the Black Ark label named after Perry's fabled studio, featured these back cover shots of tough rasta guys preparing a net for fishing. Of course it did. When Two-Toners The Beat got given their own Go-Feet label to play with by Chrysalis in the late '70s, they went straight out and reissued *Heart Of The Congos*. Nevertheless, this vinyl lover has to give it up for the 1996 CD reissue on the Blood and Fire label, with veteran expert Steve Barrow's sleevenotes, a disc of spiffing bonus tracks, and a lovely booklet fronted by a montage involving Haile Selassie, and some fish. So, if you've never liked reggae or bought into the natty dread deal, all I can say is fair play, but this is music far too good to leave to dope heads, hippies and reggae obsessives. The Congos were fishers of men.

LOW

DAVID BOWIE
PRODUCED BY DAVID BOWIE AND TONY VISCONTI
RCA/JANUARY 1977
UK CHART: 2
US CHART: 11
KEY TRACKS: 'Be My Wife'; 'Breaking Glass'; 'Warszawa'; 'A New Career In A New Town'; 'Sound And Vision'

Low is an album about and made in sickness, addiction and depression. The reason that it was popular and accessible enough to change the course of music is that it is strangely optimistic, perhaps Bowie's most genuinely happy record, because it is his most honest and human. Its few lyrics refer directly to the things that had led Bowie to hit bottom in LA before escaping to Berlin in 1976; a flip-out in which he rammed a coke dealer's car and drove round and round a car park, wondering whether to let go of the wheel ('Always Crashing In The Same Car'); his acrimonious break-up with wife Angie ('Be My Wife'); his dalliance with the occult, which precipitated an obsession with Nazi mythology ('Breaking Glass'); his desire to sit in a darkened room, possibly forever ('Sound And Vision'). The instrumentals and near-instrumentals are tone-poem tributes to Eastern Europe, grounded by some of the bluesy funk of his *Young Americans/Station To Station* period. The loose, funky pianos, drums, guitars and horns are vital in an album generally seen as an ambient/electronic adventure inspired by Bowie's working friendship with Brian Eno. Without the soul-rock spontaneity, *Low* would be despairing and cold. But it is, in the end, about one of the oldest clichés in the book – when you hit bottom, the only way is up.

Playing *Low* and hearing opening instrumental 'Speed Of Life' reminds me what a shock it was that, among this face-off between catchy rock tune and claustrophobic, distorted soundscape, Bowie didn't start singing. Which reminds me that I didn't really like *Low* at the time. Not that I ever admitted it, because cockernee Dave had been a kind of God to me since hearing 'Starman' when I was nine, and whatever critical faculties I possessed at the ripe old age of fourteen did not stretch to dissing my alien-intellectual pin-up boy. But the hit 'Sound And Vision' just seemed like a pretty ditty on radio, and when I finally heard the album in the midst of punk, it just sounded boring. I'm increasingly convinced though, that *Low* doesn't make sense to anyone before they've experienced some sort of mental health crisis. I refer to mental illness in the wider sense, taking in everything from addiction to suicidal imaginings to that choking alienation we airily dismiss as 'being a teenager'. At fourteen, I had no idea where Bowie, Visconti, Eno and these extraordinary musicians were taking me to, or why it mattered. At forty-two, it seems as perfect a summing-up of surviving depression as Joy Division's *Closer* (see p.97) is of not surviving depression. Its battle between running away – to Poland, to a blue room, to cocaine – and facing up, is so purely expressed that the inevitable self-pity seems consumed by the pleasure of being an artist, the joy of jamming with friends, and the relief of not having to pretend you are Ziggy Stardust, or The Thin White Duke, or a guy who could chuck straight-arm salutes and Weimar imagery around without inspiring people to form Rock Against Racism. This was Bowie's hold over pop culture in the '70s, when even his worst moments produced something worthwhile in us.

Low instigated British alternative rock and the artier end of synth-pop. Everyone who loved Bowie, art-rock and/or punk heard *Low* as a way out of rama-lama thrash even before it had got going. It convinced people that Brian Eno was some sort of magician, and formed a 1977 quartet with 'Heroes' (see p.25), and Iggy Pop's *The Idiot* and *Lust For Life* (see p.12 and p.20) that introduced Berlin as a pop buzzword (even though it was largely recorded in Paris) and set a template for post-punk, indie-dance, and everything Radiohead-ish, including Radiohead. It thunks and shimmers and reverberates. Its maker got better, but only in the health, wealth and sanity sense.

DAVID BOWIE/LOW

MARQUEE MOON

TELEVISION
PRODUCED BY ANDY JOHNS AND TOM VERLAINE
ELEKTRA/FEBRUARY 1977
UK CHART: 28
US CHART: DID NOT CHART
KEY TRACKS: 'Marquee Moon'; 'Prove It'; 'See No Evil';
'Friction'; 'Venus'

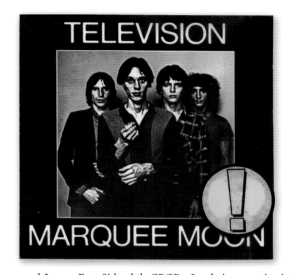

Now, this is a real Fear Of Music album. Canonised by rock crits but never sold a bean. Rarely meet a woman who's heard of it, let alone likes it. Ditto for anyone black, gay or, in fact, not a white middle-class male musician, journalist, DJ or trainspotter indie-rock nerd. It inspires the music press equivalent of hushed, reverential tones, which imply that this is not a record that can be grasped by the common herd, yet I've never read a decent explanation of what the record actually means. Man, I almost feel embarrassed about adding yet another layer of jazz-school-meets-bloke-rock snobbery to the whole affair. But I have to, simply because it is one of the finest albums ever made, and one that's become more of an emotional experience for me as time has passed.

In short, New York's Television introduced beauty to punk rock and in doing so invented The Bunnymen and The Smiths and R.E.M. and any unequivocally male rock band since who has rejected post-Hendrix penile dementia and attempted to communicate romance, mystery and emotional eloquence through the medium of the electric rock guitar. The reason it remains a cult snob item is because rock criticism has always insisted that *Marquee Moon* is about musical technique and intellectualism rather than raw emotion and pretty tunes. It's all so bloody South Bank Show, especially for a music baked in the same scuzzy oven as the Ramones.

Tom Verlaine, Richard Lloyd, Billy Ficca and Richard Hell formed Television in 1973, and led the scene based around Lower East Side club CBGBs. Lead singer, guitarist and songwriter Tom Verlaine went out for a while with Patti Smith and, once Hell left, set about concocting a garage band tone poetry, closely related to Patti Smith's rock-as-ultimate-freedom muse. *Marquee Moon* stands as one of rock's many Citizen Kane moments, perhaps because it caught Verlaine on the cusp of being a Great Musician, before the inevitable muso fascination with good taste and perfect technique dragged the childlike thrill from his music. Because, and despite Verlaine being 26 while recording *Marquee Moon* with former Led Zeppelin engineer Andy Johns, this feels like a record full of youth's concerns and immature wonder, summed up in a line from 'Friction': 'I don't wanna grow up/There's too much contradiction.'

What *Marquee Moon* is actually about is the tension between guitarists Lloyd (a player with a jazz mentality playing pop-rock rhythm) and Verlaine (a player with a punk mentality trying to play jazz). It's also about an explicit rejection of cock-rock and junkie glamour just exactly when that was needed, and a worshipful fascination for women and a critique of city life where, according to 'Guiding Light', there's 'Never the rose without a prick'. OK, that metaphor could be applied to anything, but I choose to take it as a Patti-inspired feminism because *Marquee Moon* is, very possibly, the least macho Classic Bloke Rock album in existence.

Most of all, *Marquee Moon* is guitars that sing without screaming, cry without whining and hit without bullying. If you like Razorlight and all those other twenty-first century new-new wave archaeologists, then *Marquee Moon* will make your heart fly. I really envy you that first listen.

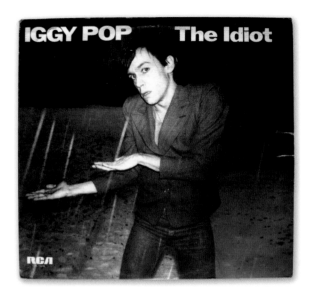

THE IDIOT

IGGY POP

PRODUCED BY DAVID BOWIE AND TONY VISCONTI
RCA/MARCH 1977
UK CHART: 30
US CHART: 72
KEY TRACKS: 'Nightclubbing'; 'China Girl'; 'Funtime'; 'Sister Midnight'; 'Dum Dum Boys'

If *Marquee Moon* was an explicit rejection of bad drugs and bad faith, an attempt to soar above Manhattan's claustrophobia, then Iggy Pop's first solo album is a wallow in urban decadence. Having retreated with Bowie to Europe, James Jewel Osterberg knew he had to clean up, and, like his English mentor, used his art as therapy, and found a music and a voice that could make that relevant to others. So much so that *The Idiot* has become an enduring cult classic to those of us who have no real idea how he could have felt. Iggy had not yet turned thirty, but sounded as ancient here as anyone might who'd spent their twenties in The Stooges, the most recklessly self-endangering rock 'n' roll band in history. *The Idiot* is what happens when you attach a newfound interest in Euro-pop and a love of funky soul to one fuck of an ugly hangover. But, 'cos Iggy is defiant punk rock-

er number one, it remains as much about shrugging and grinning and celebrating your worst instincts as it is about confession and self-pity. A comedy album, then. Albeit a black one.

And the laughs keep on a-coming, because the backing band here is, give or take a member or two, none other than . . . Tin Machine. Let us take a moment to ponder this. Has there ever been a worse thing in popular music than Tin Machine? How could the geniuses who backed Iggy at this point become, you know, Tin Machine? Have you ever heard the 'Tin Machine' song? It goes 'Tin machine, tin machine'. It's about cars. Dear, dear David. I love the guy.

Anyway, *The Idiot*. The future Tin Machine were, at this point, a twin-turbo, must-drive, Ferrari of a band, making music that was recognisably rock-pop, but rock-pop that had been left in a rusty box – a tin box, but of course – and left to decay through lack of oxygen and daylight. Iggy, meanwhile, had two themes (the decadence of the post-hippy, disco demi-monde and an addiction to corrupting young girls while feeling really fucking guilty about it) and two voices (Frank Sinatra impersonating Johnny Cash, and a needling, wheedling whine-howl thick with self-loathing). Together, people, they made unlikely magic and invented mutant disco without putting one song on the album you could dance to.

On the old vinyl LP, the first side is sort of pop, while side two is the sound of despairing repetition and 'Dum Dum Boys' and 'Tiny Girls' and promiscuity as 'Mass Production', and those titles say more than I could if I wrote all year. Side one's 'Nightclubbing' and 'Funtime' defined the art of hedonist sneering, while 'China Girl' is so vulnerable and diseased and wrong it damn near breaks your heart. Bowie later did 'China Girl' as a single. It wasn't very good, but he knew that. It was weird, though, hearing the line 'Visions of swastikas in my head' and knowing that – deep breath – Bowie was singing what Iggy had written about Bowie's coke-addled mid-'70s obsession with fascism.

It would be convenient to say that *The Idiot* got something rotten out of Iggy's system, but it didn't, and Bowie had to rescue him all over again in the late '80s. But, as a piece of sonic art that creates a mood of ambivalent darkness, this album is unbeatable. Iggy's iconic gift is that he's a true Dum Dum Boy who's so sharp he literally cuts himself. Must be a hard thing to live with, so others may live it vicariously.

LEAVE HOME

RAMONES

PRODUCED BY TONY BONGIOVI AND T. ERDELYI
SIRE/MARCH 1977
UK CHART: 45
US CHART: DID NOT CHART
KEY TRACKS: 'Pinhead'; 'Commando'; 'Suzy Is A Headbanger'; 'Now I Wanna Be A Good Boy'; 'I Remember You'

Now this is how to do it. Having changed the course of rock 'n' roll with your first album, don't hang about: get the next one out within eight months. Make it exactly the same as the first one, but with a few cuter tunes. For the front cover, try and look tough in a car park, instead of in front of a brick wall. Then just sit back and . . . wait for it to flop completely. Hang on, that can't be right . . .

So, why didn't the Ramones sell records? The recent Ramones documentary *End Of The Century* was suffused with defensiveness about this moot point, as are the sleevenotes for the 2001 CD reissue of *Leave Home*. The general defence seems to be that Da Brudders were too ahead of their time – too dangerous – for The Man to play on the radio, because if all the geeky kids (and, according to the chorus of 'Suzy Is A Headbanger', their geeky moms) of the late '70s had heard 'Swallow My Pride' they would've risen as one and smited The Man with tubes of acne cream and girly slapping, or something. This is the same US radio system that had played those really safe, bland records by Bob Dylan, Hendrix, the Stones, James Brown and all those other wet bands while everyone was fighting in the streets in the '60s. Censoring bastards or what?

The truth is that the Ramones' records were too odd to be radio rock in the late '70s. They were postmodern, slightly disturbing, and played by people who were deliberately subverting their own ugliness. But none of that makes the Ramones dangerous. Sure, they contrived a magnificent, high-concept template for any bunch of kids who had limited musical ability and no stud-muffin appeal but wanted to form a band. Sure, their greatest song 'Pinhead', a tribute to Tod Browning's extraordinary allegorical anti-fascist horror flick *Freaks*, threw a comforting arm around society's rejects, and reminded rock that it was invented by weirdos such as Elvis and Little Richard and Buddy Holly, rather than hippy narcissists. Live, the band created iconic imagery around the song, using just a banner bearing the legend, 'Gabba Gabba Hey', a chant pulled from *Freaks* that magnificently freaks out the end of the song.

But the Sex Pistols were preparing to release a song that did a little bit more than poke fun at teen boredom, and ended up facing the wrath of both the British establishment in the media and the working class in the streets.

If 'End Of The Century' is to be believed, the Ramones seemed kind of bitter about being the Ramones. All I can say is that, on *Leave Home*, they sound thrilled about it. That's the great thing about records. They never grow up.

TRANS-EUROPE EXPRESS

KRAFTWERK
PRODUCED BY RALF HÜTTER AND FLORIAN SCHNEIDER
CAPITOL/APRIL 1977
UK CHART: DID NOT CHART
US CHART: DID NOT CHART
KEY TRACKS: 'Trans-Europe Express'; 'Metal On Metal'; 'Europe Endless'; 'Hall Of Mirrors'; 'Showroom Dummies'

In the early 1990s, when computer-driven dance music had reached a peak of critical approval, Kraftwerk were often labelled 'The Techno Beatles'. Tempting to agree, what with all their visionary barrier-breaking and musical influence. But not true. Kraftwerk were The Techno Ramones. Or maybe the other way round, as Kraftwerk formed way back in 1971.

Like the Ramones, Kraftwerk designed a musical and visual package – a high concept – which was so perfectly formed they became trapped by it. Both bands' major influences were The Beach Boys. And, like the Ramones after *Rocket To Russia*, once Kraftwerk reached their recorded peak on this very album, they were doomed to sit back, consumed by creative inertia, as everyone took lazy facsimiles of

some of their easiest-to-grasp ideas, and made them loose, flexible, commercial. A Lester Bangs feature from 1975 revolves around Bangs and Kraftwerk's leaders Ralf Hütter and Florian Schneider having a faintly laughable discussion about the machines taking over the man through the then-relatively-new technology of the synthesiser. How could Kraftwerk know, while still in their twenties, that the machine set to control them was the music industry, and its endless ability to remake, re-model and reduce such big ideas to yet more showbiz product? It's become a quintessential pop star rule ... if in career doubt, make like a robot, as even Kylie and Robbie have recently reminded us.

In the same feature, Bangs described Kraftwerk's music as 'intricate balm'. Beautiful. The songs on this record define complexity made simple, and the less-is-more aesthetic. But they also ache. Maybe it's the loneliness within the sound, or the feeling conveyed that travelling the world is the best we can hope for, yet still not enough. Maybe it's just those graceful minor-key synth-riffs, like androids sighing. But what we can be sure of is that the title track invented electro-funk, and that the album, as a whole, is what any synthetic record has to live up to. It deconstructs disco, but with a love that defies intellectual exercise and gives disco back its soul. It defines the group's art, with the line about 'Elegance and decadence' within 'Europe Endless', and with the image of the star artist remixing himself in front of the looking-glass that makes 'Hall Of Mirrors' so haunting and wise. It has cornball humour, when the 'Showroom Dummies' break out of the shop window, and glass smashes, and the dummies go clubbing. And even has a little human failing, when they can't resist frothing (as much as Schneider's suave distance can possibly froth) about meeting Iggy Pop and David Bowie on 'Trans-Europe Express', just name-dropping Dum-Dum Boys when all is said and done.

And finally, there's the sleeve imagery, four men of wealth and taste, immaculate and charming and charmed, proudly but quietly basking in the afterglow of designing the

TRANS-EUROPE EXPRESS/KRAFTWERK

THE CLASH/THE CLASH

future. Yeah, maybe they do look like a technocratic Fab Four. Or Ralf and Florian's Balmy Army.

THE CLASH

THE CLASH
PRODUCED BY MICKY FOOTE
CBS/APRIL 1977
UK CHART: 12
US CHART: DID NOT CHART
KEY TRACKS: 'I'm So Bored With The USA'; 'White Riot'; 'Janie Jones'; 'What's My Name'; '48 Hours'

Where the hell do I start?

I guess the only way to start is by saying that The Clash was the most important album I ever bought. Not necessarily the best . . . I move around, on that point, depending on mood and whatever musical phase I happen to be going through when I'm asked. But definitely the most important, because, for better or worse, *The Clash,* twinned with the first four Sex Pistols singles, convinced me that music was much bigger than noise and entertainment, and that playing it or writing about was going to be my life. No other record takes me back so instantly and completely to a time when I felt everything was possible, and I felt I could change the world. When I play *The Clash* I believe, again, that rock 'n' roll music holds the key to making the world a better place. It's the antidote when I'm feeling jaded by twenty-eight years of not devoting myself to the revolution *The Clash* imagined. It packs powerful mojo, far more so than 1979's *London Calling,* which now picks up the critical kudos.

The rough, boxy sound conjures up a London based entirely around the facts of survival, boredom, compromise and refusal to compromise. The short, sharp songs find a kind of beauty, even while they suggest days of endless grey, and make England 1977 sound like a police state, which it sort of was. The cover of Junior Murvin's 'Police And Thieves' is too long and pretty clumsy, but it remains the punks' first stab at reggae, and is sung beautifully by Joe Strummer.

Strummer's death in December 2002 has lent an obvious sentimentality to any discussion of The Clash since. But the man did connect with so many boys in the late '70s, making us feel that, for all his dafter public statements and human flaws, he represented us. It's the narratives on this first album – the character studies of wage slaves and lost boys within 'Janie Jones', '48 Hours', 'What's My Name', 'London's Burning' and 'Career Opportunities' – that established that bond, not the later globally informed politics nor the love/hate relationship with America. But 'I'm So Bored With The USA' is still the greatest song about that arm-wrestle between fascination and resentment. And *The Clash* reflects the jagged rush of trying to live in London like nothing else. Hard and dirty and thrilled and disillusioned, a call-to-arms and a call of the wild.

Where the hell do I stop?

NEW BOOTS AND PANTIES!!

IAN DURY
PRODUCED BY PETER JENNER, LAURIE LATHAM AND RICK WALTON
STIFF/SEPTEMBER 1977
UK CHART: 5
US CHART: DID NOT CHART
KEY TRACKS: 'Clevor Trever'; 'Wake Up And Make Love With Me'; 'Billericay Dickie'; 'I'm Partial To Your Abracadabra'; 'If I Was With A Woman'

New Boots And Panties!! is The Clash's big brother, a family member whose desire for social change is submerged beneath a knowledge of just how low people can go. While The Clash could look at London from Notting Hill's bohemian squat-land, surrounded by Britain's liveliest counter-culture, Ian Dury was a thirty-five-year-old teacher, pub-rocker and street intellectual who'd seen a realer London, one that stretched from Bow to Southend and contained that unique cockney mixture of arrogance and stupidity, aspiration and ugliness, wisdom and ignorance. Yet the album's co-producer Peter Jenner was one of the pioneers of the Notting Hill counter-culture, and Dury was obviously well-versed in Carnival, early psychedelia and punk rock's first squalls too. Years before rap or punk-funk or chavs or Essex Man or Madness or Shaun Ryder, this record contained prophecies of all and the essence of what the 'new wave' of rock acts were trying to revive – a music that glamorised the everyday, that put the urchin loser at stage front, that refuted cock-rock while talking honestly about sex, that shortened the distance between performer and listener while letting you know, in no uncertain terms, that a figure such as Ian Dury was in no way 'ordinary' and, possibly, neither were you.

Unlike the albums I've written about so far, *New Boots* has dated. The music – a musicianly funk and hard rock, directly influenced by ancient cockney music hall and forged in the short-lived but important UK trend that was 'pub rock' – sounds quaint and, in the punkier numbers, old and sweaty. Dury himself is the reason that the album still stands up. Partially crippled from childhood polio and suffused with a self-deprecating beatnik intellectualism, carrying the memories of Britpop culture and fashion from trad jazz and skiffle through teds, mods and rockers to early punk's celebration of the reject, Dury's wordplay was dazzling and his voice a comfort, like a cheeky uncle who both frightened and delighted you with his stories and his razorblade wit. By kicking off the album with 'Wake Up And Make Love With Me' and its opening lines, 'I come awake/With the gift for womankind', he let you know that this was no castrated victim of circumstance. The album then proceeds to paint pictures of characters unleashing chaos in East End suburbs that were neither here nor there. 'Blockheads' pins down tribes of working-class men with 'blotched and lagered skin',

waiting for Thatcher to be their champion, making us all culpable. 'Plaistow Patricia' is a slut's story, which, notoriously, begins with Dury snarling 'Arseholes, bastards, fucking cunts and pricks!' And 'If I Was With A Woman' defines the album's heart, as Dury, reeling from being dumped, parades a kind of self-pitying misogyny so accurate that its hatred seems almost heroic, before the chorus sings back, 'Look at them laughing', Dury cutting his misogyny to ribbons, showing it up for what it is. The song's fade takes the word 'laughing' and flies with it, recognising the madness of men who want to control women. It's pretty stunning, and remains one of the reasons why the 'pimps' of millennial hip hop sound, to me, like total fucking dickweed mommy's boys. Dury laid himself bare here, and that sticks with a boy and, I hope, does him good.

New Boots was a big Brit hit without a hit single, a word-of-mouth album that charmed those older guys and girls suspicious of punk's basic thrashing, but as heartily sick of

poodle boys in spandex as their kid brothers and sisters. Plus, it had a hefty shot of disco, because that's where the working-class boys and girls were in 1977.

Still strange to think that both Ian Dury and Joe Strummer are dead now. But their best work is very much alive. I'll leave this there, before I get all sentimental.

SORROW TEARS AND BLOOD

FELA ANIKULAPO KUTI & THE AFRICA 70
PRODUCED BY FELA ANIKULAPO KUTI
KALAKUTA/SEPTEMBER 1977
UK CHART: DID NOT CHART
US CHART: DID NOT CHART
KEY TRACKS: 'Sorrow Tears And Blood'; 'Colonial Mentality'

Around twenty-four minutes long and consisting of just two very long songs, this is here because it makes a mighty funk noise. It's also here because, as it was being released in Europe, the band were having their homes burned down by the Nigerian military government, who figured, as an afterthought, that it would be a good idea to throw the bandleader's mother out of a window. In the wake of 'God Save The Queen' by the Sex Pistols, British punk rockers felt there was much at stake. But not even John Lydon was consigned to a life of beatings, harassment and imprisonment for the crime of expressing political opinion in popular song. Such was the life of singer, pianist, and horn player Fela Ransome Kuti, the son of a protestant minister father and a Nigerian nationalist mother, and the creator of Afro-beat.

Inspired by a late '60s spell in Los Angeles and the pro-black virtuoso funk of peak-period James Brown, Kuti blended Nigerian 'hi-life' music, jazz and funk into music for a thirty-piece band. His political activism led him to build his own commune, Kalakuta, with its own live venue, The Shrine, and a studio where he and his extraordinary musicians and singers recorded over fifty albums. I love his music

too much to leave him out of this book, and chose *Sorrow Tears And Blood* because the title track is my favourite Kuti tune. It bubbles and boils and swings and sings for just over ten minutes, as Kuti describes a scene familiar to Nigerians living under a corrupt military regime. Police and army come, 'Everybody run run run/Everybody scatter scatter'. Scant minutes pass before the goon squad leave. But it's long enough, because, 'Dem leave sorrow tears and blood/Dem regular trademark.' Kuti goes on to explain that the powers-that-be strike out because of fear, and align his people's struggle to the struggles of Rhodesia (now Zimbabwe) and South Africa. The subtle power and beauty of the music does the rest, balancing machismo and femininity in the choir of voices, easily accommodating the playful avant-garde sax of The Art Ensemble Of Chicago's Lester Bowie into a sumptuous sonic palette, black and blue and vivid and sexy and bursting with controlled fury and strength under duress.

Now, if you know more about Kuti than me – which wouldn't be hard – you'll know that Kuti was a polygamist with a reactionary attitude towards women. You may also have noticed that I'm a liberal pro-women, pro-queer, anti-hate kind of guy. You may also be a fan of Bob Marley or James Brown or any number of rappers or dancehall MCs who've peddled some form or other of anti-establishment politics, yet only define freedom as freedom for heterosexual men. I bring this up here because this book contains much music by people I'm not sure I'd like, and definitely don't agree with on fundamental points about gender and sexuality. But music is complex art. Its most humanistic noises are not always made by perfect humans. It's so comforting when an entertainer agrees with all your assumptions and reinforces all of your feelings about the world. But it isn't real. The therapy quacks call it 'denial'. Music is a dialectic, an argument, an unholy row, in more ways than one. I don't want to be the singer's girlfriend. And I want my own worldview to stand up without putting my fingers in my ears and going 'blah-blah-blah'.

Kuti died of AIDS-related illness in August 1997. Many who lived and worked with him say he just took too many physical beatings, which sounds suspiciously like yet another form of denial. There's much I don't understand about Nigerian culture. But I understand this music because it grips my heart and lightens my head. If music can't close the gap between reactionary Nigerian geniuses and mixed-race London liberals with a guilt complex, nothing can. This is what music's for.

LUST FOR LIFE

IGGY POP
PRODUCED BY THE BEWLAY BROTHERS (DAVID BOWIE)
RCA/SEPTEMBER 1977
UK CHART: 28

US CHART: DID NOT CHART
KEY TRACKS: 'Lust For Life'; 'The Passenger'; 'Some Weird Sin'; 'Tonight'; 'Sixteen'

While title, sleeve and the occasional light-hearted track tempt one to see *Lust For Life* as Good Cop to *The Idiot*'s Bad Cop, the better comparison is the hair of the dog after a really bad hangover. This dog, looking all-American and peachy keen and happy and still totally fucking sinister on the famous sleeve, is trying to make some light of his problems. But those problems – the typical rockpig recipe of heavy drugs and jailbait in leather – ain't going nowhere. The jokes are just a little more obvious here. Like the mutant Motown thunder of the title track assuring us that there'll be 'No more beating my brains/With the liquor and drugs' when, by the end of the old vinyl side one, Iggy's watching his baby turn blue and doing nothing about it except whispering sweet nothings.

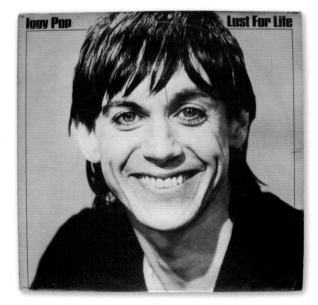

'Tonight', like *The Idiot*'s 'China Girl', was later covered by producer and co-writer Bowie in his mid-'80s blondo-blando period. Whether this was due to in-joke, lack of new Bowie material, or yet another attempt to help out his errant friend and inspiration with some unexpected royalties is a mystery lost to the rock dry-hump that was the 1980s. What is sure is that while made-in-France *The Idiot* sounded like Berlin, the made-in-Berlin *Lust For Life* sounds like New York. 'Lust For Life' is party chaos beneath skyscrapers, 'The Passenger' is a yellow cab through Manhattan's 'ripped backsides', 'Sixteen' is leering in the Lower East Side. In that sense, they still feel like vital glue for New York's coming meld of punk and disco, even though the one self-conscious disco track, the closing 'Fall In Love With Me', didn't quite work, while 'Lust For Life' and the hypnotic ska-punk of 'The Passenger' became keynotes in the growth of 'alternative' dance music.

'Some Weird Sin' still sounds like the sharpest lyric about the alienated outsider emotions – the deluded snobbery, perhaps – that leads to addiction, as Iggy looks at the mad parade . . . at a party? On TV? In the street? It can hit anywhere, and Jimmy should know . . . and the sight, 'Makes me sad and ill . . . Things get too straight . . . Oh, I know it's not for me.' And that's when he wants, 'Some dumb weird sin/Just to relax with.' It may not be the bleeding-heart confessional you want to hear, but it bears a clearer ring of truth than a cringing apology.

Lust For Life is truly a they-don't-make-'em-like-that-anymore record. Equal parts rock, pop and experiment, simultaneously instant yet packed with the kind of musical detail that keeps revealing new layers, able to incorporate big beats and plastic soul without getting all jive on yo' ass. But, mostly, it's infused with the bad-boy intellect of its author, while being easy to relate to for anyone who doesn't happen to be a donkey-dicked punk Godfather with bad habits. The jokes are friendly, but serious in their cautionary tales. My favourite is in the title track, in which Iggy barks that love is much like hypnotising chickens.

Joy Division's singer Ian Curtis hanged himself in May 1980 while Iggy's *The Idiot* spun on his stereo. I sometimes wonder whether, if he'd played *Lust For Life* instead, he might've just laughed death off.

LITTLE CRIMINALS

RANDY NEWMAN
PRODUCED BY LENNY WARONKER AND RUSS TITELMAN
WARNERS/SEPTEMBER 1977
UK CHART: DID NOT CHART
US CHART: 9
KEY TRACKS: 'In Germany Before The War'; 'Short People'; 'Baltimore'; 'Sigmund Freud's Impersonation Of Albert Einstein In America'; 'Jolly Coppers On Parade'

Randy Newman is a genius who attracts the very worst type of worship. Through no fault of his own, his career has been tainted by the admiration of that particular kind of music fan who delights in spreading Fear Of Music. In short, men – it's always men – who believe that 'getting' the satire in Newman's work makes them more intelligent and discerning than the proles. This is borne out by the accepted critical wisdom concerning this, the New Orleans-born and LA-based composer's only mainstream hit album. It must be the worst one because ordinary people bought it.

Well, you know, maybe it is. Lord knows, I don't have the long history of being absorbed by his music that makes me able to prove, conclusively, that this album isn't shallow compared to That One Only Me And My Mates Bought. Nevertheless, I have ears, and they tell me that getting material this incendiary and moral and subversive and heroically lacking in treating the listener like they're a moron into them good old pop charts is nothing short of a triumph, and something close to what I believe pop music exists to do. So, maybe the aforementioned hit, the US No.2 that is 'Short

People', is broad satire compared, for example, to the chilling slave-trader testimony that is Newman's 1972 classic, 'Sail Away'. But 'Short People' is more important because it must have been bought and loved by the very people it ripped the shit out of. Hell, maybe one or two of these poor pop-loving dopes even, you know, got the joke at their own expense.

Anyway, Randy Newman is the Jewish nephew of sound-track composer Alfred Newman. His parallel careers have seen him bag a string of Oscar nominations for movie scores and songs, including works as disparate as *Ragtime* and the two *Toy Story* pictures, while moving from Tin Pan Alley songsmith in the '60s to solo artist. His music is piano-led, often heavily orchestrated, utilises heavyweight LA session musicians, and is closer in spirit to traditional American music than rock. Aaron Copland, Fats Waller, Cole Porter and New Orleans jazz figure higher than, say, Bob Dylan or Brian Wilson, and Newman's music pretty much refuses to rock in a post-'60s-radio-pop way. His voice is a gruff, tobacco-chewing mumble, an exact midway point between country and blues, able to carry the very different characters who populate his songs without changing in tone at all. Almost every tune he writes sounds familiar, so familiar is he with the American idioms that formed the basis of pop as we know it. And almost every lyric he writes hurts.

Little Criminals stars two of his most well-known songs. 'Baltimore', as covered beautifully by Nina Simone and miserably by UB40, is a Newman rarity – a straightforward, hard-times protest song. The aforementioned 'Short People' smuggles its vicious anti-racist message undercover of a ridiculously catchy rinky-dink children's novelty song. He lists what is unpleasant about short people and concludes, in a wryly triumphant chorus, 'Don't want no short people 'round here!' Man, maybe that isn't subtle if you're well-versed in Proust and Swift, but if teachers and parents the western world over aren't using this song to show children the idiocy of prejudice, then that sure ain't Newman's doing.

Blessed with the airbrushed muso chops of Ry Cooder,

legendary session drummer Jim Keltner, and even a couple of Eagles in Glenn Frey and Joe Walsh, Newman pokes at the violent, greedy and bigoted colonial underbelly of the American dream on 'Jolly Coppers On Parade', 'Rider In The Rain' and 'Sigmund Freud's Impersonation Of Albert Einstein In America', which I really didn't make up. Newman's gift is to allegorise America in the form of dry jokes without punchlines. Newman finds a character and says what they say, and refuses to make the listeners' decision on the rights and wrongs of the character's worldview. He likes people, in other words, and believes we'll work it out because we are not the monsters depicted, unless we choose to be.

But I've left the song that brought me into this album until last, and this song is not about America. 'In Germany Before The War' is set like the tragic interlude in a musical, all mournful, lonely chords and tear-jerking orchestra, as Newman finds as sweet and vulnerable a singing voice as he can muster, and introduces a Dusseldorf shopkeeper in 1934, and brings us to a lovely chorus image of the shop-keeper taking his break by the Rhine, sitting by the river, but thinking of the sea. You prepare yourself for a tale of a victim – perhaps Jewish, perhaps not – of the coming Nazi storm, and feel pulled into wishing that the sweet old man would get out of landlocked Germany, and travel that sea, before it's too late. And so, as a subtly queasy harmony casts a shadow over the beginning of verse two, you get ready, and . . . the victim is someone entirely different. 'A little girl has lost her way,' he sees and notes, almost distractedly. The song flows like the river, but into gradually darker water, eerily reminiscent of the haunted, magical river that the children in Charles Laughton's film masterpiece *The Night Of The Hunter* traverse in order to escape Robert Mitchum's psychopathic preacher. At song's end, the shopkeeper seems almost content, as, 'We lie beneath the autumn sky/My little golden girl and I/And she lies very still/She lies very still.' Gulp.

Setting a story about the murder of a blond child in Nazi

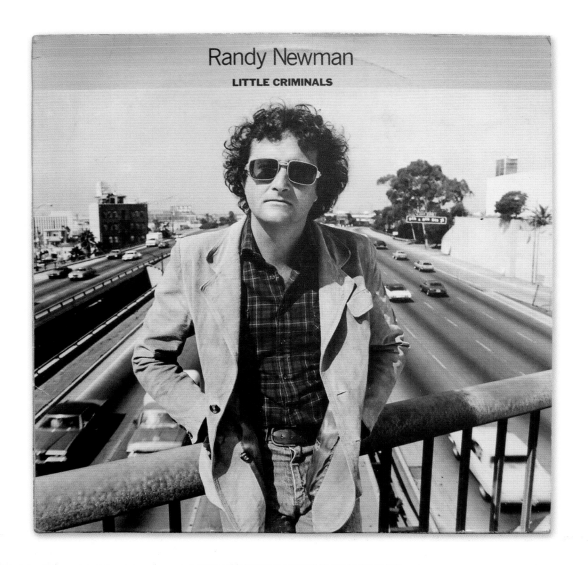

Randy Newman

LITTLE CRIMINALS

LITTLE CRIMINALS/RANDY NEWMAN

Germany is . . . I dunno . . . it just gives me goosebumps and carries layers of meaning and morality and horror beyond the scope of a normal pop song. It's just wrong somehow, and that's what makes it right. Play 'In Germany . . . ' after Iggy's 'Tiny Girls' or 'Sixteen' and that joke isn't funny anymore, but then again, both writers know that, which is why they try so hard to keep laughing. As for me, I'm looking forward to that inevitable moment in old age when a music journalist must retire to his study to write his memoirs, look back fondly at those happy times when Dizzie Rascal and G4 made proper music, and feel all smug and secure that, unlike short people, he got Randy Newman. At least, I hope that's what I feel. It's better than feeling implicated, isn't it?

TALKING HEADS '77

TALKING HEADS
PRODUCED BY TONY BONGIOVI, LANCE QUINN AND TALKING HEADS
SIRE/SEPTEMBER 1977
UK CHART: 60
US CHART: 97
KEY TRACKS: 'Psycho Killer'; 'No Compassion'; 'Don't Worry About The Government'; 'The Book I Read'; 'Happy Day'

In rock's official history, Talking Heads are not punk. Despite being incubated in the same CBGBs sweat pot as the Ramones, these New Yorkers are post-punk, or punk funk or new wave. Obviously, this debut album by David Byrne, Tina Weymouth, Jerry Harrison and Chris Frantz doesn't thrash, doesn't shout aggressively, and features a music drawn equally from folk, soul, funk, The Modern Lovers (see p.4), Captain Beefheart and what sometimes sounds like the old school marching anthem, in the collegiate American tradition. Furthermore, you'd be hard-pushed to find four more fresh-faced, sensibly coiffed and

modestly dressed young people than the ones staring winsomely at you from the back cover. But, Your Honour, I would contend that *Talking Heads '77* is punk rock to its bones, and that Talking Heads were a key punk band. You've got to separate Punk – The Brand – from what it truly was. And you have to understand what the whole notion of youth culture was at the time, in order to see the true nature of punk's rebellion.

Firstly, being clean-cut was an absolute statement in itself in 1977. Big Rock wasn't just long hair and a bare chest, but ran on the simplistic correlation that rebellion equalled dirt and scruffiness, and an excess of machismo or sluttiness, even though the lie of 'free love' and not being a 'suit' had long been exposed as just another showbiz trademark. David Byrne took a wide-eyed nerdiness from Harrison's former bandleader Jonathan Richman and understood that its time had come . . . that innocence now seemed eccentric, weird, even shocking. Byrne wasn't an innocent. The Scottish-born singer, songwriter and guitarist had spent far too long hanging with the tragically hip NY junkie crowd for that. But, like Television and the Ramones, he knew shocking Granny with your sub-Lou Reed/Keith Richards rockpig schtick was old.

So the first Heads shot unveils two beautifully drawn personas – the Richman-derived naïve geek singing about how fine a thing the modern world is and being sweet to everyone; and the same guy when alone . . . bitter, resentful, anxious, twitchy, cold and being driven slowly insane by his attempts to engage with city friends he can hardly bear to look at. Merge the two, and *Talking Heads '77* comes off as a manic depressive's diary, a mood-swing descent into the lonely madness of the 'Psycho Killer'. Sure, Byrne ends the album with being 'Pulled Up' by a loved one. But the gratitude is hysterical and, again, manic. Unlike Richman, Byrne refuses to seek solace in sex. This album is almost morbidly sexless, as if intimacy is a foreign land, and the clipped, jittery guitar that influenced everyone from XTC and Echo And The Bunnymen to Franz Ferdinand and The

Futureheads feels like shorthand for the pointless activity one undertakes when one is panicked by feelings of inadequacy. In short, Byrne's character needed a good shagging.

This, and the complex layers of positivity and loathing throughout the album, not to mention the preppy, thin poppiness of the sound, make it one of the most brave and rebellious records of the era, and an absolute template for every nervous nerd who ever became the unlikely, unsexy leader of a rock 'n' roll band in the ensuing years. Along with Costello, of course. But Elvis was, from the beginning, too sure of himself, too obviously ferocious and technically gifted, to make a record as subtle and unselfish as this. For Byrne, the showing-off came later.

It's also worth remembering that new wave was just a marketing term aimed at Americans who found the word 'punk' off-putting. And that punk as the 'aufentick voyss of wurkin'-class yoof' was just Brit music press propaganda put about by blokes who didn't want brilliant girls like Tina Weymouth, gays, weirdoes, or, indeed, bookish nerds taking over their macho rock action. In the real world, *Talking Heads '77* is true punk rock, as much as the Pistols, The Clash and the Ramones.

"HEROES"

DAVID BOWIE

PRODUCED BY DAVID BOWIE AND TONY VISCONTI
RCA/OCTOBER 1977
UK CHART: 3
US CHART: 35
KEY TRACKS: '"Heroes"'; 'Joe The Lion'; 'Blackout'; 'Beauty And The Beast'; 'V-2 Schneider'

As Iggy's *Lust For Life* is to *The Idiot*, Bowie's *"Heroes"* is to *Low* – the sound of someone emerging from a fog of misery. Recorded at Berlin's Hansa, once a pre-war Nazi social club straight out of the 'Cabaret' musical, this album is unavoid-

ably coloured by the legend of Bowie, Iggy and Brain (sic) Eno drying out, getting it together and inventing modern art-rock in the shadow of the Berlin Wall. It's dominated by the desperate romance of the much-loved title track, and has an odd construction consisting of rock songs on side one and instrumental mood pieces on side two, with the throwaway disco sketch 'The Secret Life Of Arabia' tacked on the end, like an upbeat afterthought. *"Heroes"* fans will look at my list of key tracks and note that I like my Bowie with tunes and Bowie singing. But if artful ambience is your bag, then 'Sense Of Doubt' and 'Moss Garden' will get you stroking your chin to your heart's content.

The mysteries of *"Heroes"* are really not that mysterious. How do you make an album sound so rounded and chunky, yet so rough and spontaneous? Hire talented musicians, make it up as you go along, print Take One. The title track turned out to be inspired by married producer Visconti and backing singer Antonia Maass stealing a kiss by the wall, rather than the original Bowie tall tale of watching two young strangers steal a moment every day, beneath the guards' turrets. The lie fitted, because it was more romantic, less seamy, and made the track feel even more universal, like Bowie had finally stopped thinking and started feeling. We probably should have been more wary of those quotation marks around the title.

The wailing power-boogie of 'Joe The Lion' – starring Bowie's sigh of 'It's Monday' on the middle-eight, not to mention a killer falsetto on the word 'dreams' – was a tribute to a performance artist called Chris Burden who did, apparently, get nailed to cars among other acts of prankish provocation. The odd, striking sleeve photo was, like the not dissimilar image for Iggy's *The Idiot*, inspired by 'Roquairol', a portrait by one Erich Heckel. The most thrilling bits of the album, the screeching gibbering guitar parts of Robert Fripp, were all recorded in one six-hour session, with Fripp plugged into one of Eno's briefcase synthesizers.

And, for posterity's sake, the cheesy evocations of Japan, Turkey and Arabia on 'Moss Garden', 'Neuköln' and 'The Secret Life . . . ' gave various provincial kids, including Siouxsie Sioux, Billy Mackenzie and David Sylvian, carte blanche to dream their own new romantic dreams of far-off places. Plus Duran Duran nicked the engineer, Colin Thurston, to reinvent their Brummie selves as toy town Bowies and Ferrys living the highlife as seen through the bottom of a glass of brandy and Babycham.

And . . . it's probably not quite as great as *Low*. But it'll do.

GREATEST HITS

ROXY MUSIC
PRODUCED BY ROXY MUSIC, CHRIS THOMAS, JOHN PUNTER, PETER SINFIELD AND JOHN ANTHONY
POLYDOR/NOVEMBER 1977
UK CHART: 20
US CHART: DID NOT CHART

KEY TRACKS: 'Mother Of Pearl'; 'Street Life'; 'Do The Strand'; 'Virginia Plain'; 'Love Is The Drug'

Bought on a whim from my local branch of Boots, the first *Best Of* by Roxy Music invaded my punk-obsessed world and gave me an essential alternative. Appropriately fake (only six of the eleven tracks were UK singles), with a dodgy 'that'll do' sleeve (a gold record hiding most of the perfect face of another perfect Roxy model), it was just a hasty cash-in for a band that had split, temporarily, in 1976. Oh, but what a cash-in! Whoever decided on the selection came up with a concept album on the vital subject of 'looking for love in a looking-glass world', as the sumptuous 'Mother Of Pearl' put it. The record exploded out of my speakers and, despite Ferry's age and sophistication and money and the fabulous life he satirised being superficially as far away from an awkward and angry fourteen-year-old's world as could be imagined, it pinned down my own romantic view of doomed love and desire for exotic thrill before it was even apparent to me.

The reason why the very technically accomplished, flash, insincere and elitist Roxy were embraced by Britpunks – unlike punk's chief villains the Stones, Rod Stewart and Pink Floyd – was because Ferry and his early partner Eno never pretended to be 'authentic'. There were no false promises to sell out, because Roxy were an art-school theory about rock and pop, unashamedly postmodern, and, as 'Do The Strand' suggests, 'A danceable solution/To teenage revolution.' While the hippy relics sold themselves as crusaders for a fairer world while snorting and hoarding enough money to bail out entire developing world economies, Ferry opened up the sheer truth of rock – that it was commerce that left you less capable of rebelling the more you exhausted yourself playing air guitar and wishing you were skinny. Ordinary boys join bands to get a fast track to la dolce vita ('Education is an important key, yes/But the good life's never won by degrees, no' – 'Street Life'), human beings in the modern world are seduced by spectacle and status, and those who achieve what

we all crave then have the cheek to moan about the lonely emptiness at the heart of it all. Chase that perfect girl, that perfect car, that perfect party, that perfect moment and – whether you're hanging out with Princess Grace in Monaco or Elsie Bucket at Anabelle's disco – you will snatch something like it from the air, and open your hand, and find . . . nothing at all. All glory is fleeting, all beauty is empty, all nightclubs close and leave you standing in the rain too fucked to find a cab. Oh, the thrill of it all.

But Ferry understood that resignation, ennui and solipsism were vital human impulses, and that art that pretended otherwise was lying, and that embracing them could be made thrilling, as long as you concocted a music that fizzed with restlessness and urgency, and reflected the bitter wit of the words. What's more – and I'm not sure how much I understood it then, but it belts me in the face now – there's not that great a distance between 'Love Is The Drug' and The Clash's '48 Hours'. Both capture the desperation for and the

pointlessness of the male search for sex at the weekend. Strummer travels on the tube but 'Can't get nothing at the places I've been', while Ferry parks some gleaming babe-magnet and gets his leg over at the end. But both are aimless and grubby, going nowhere fast. And was Johnny Rotten – a huge Ferry fan – sourcing 'Mother Of Pearl's 'Have you a future?/No, no, no, NO!!!' for 'God Save The Queen'? Ferry answers his own question with the most sinister 'yes' in pop history; whatever future he's seen, you suspect that it is heartless and cruel, and that his 'yes' is his own desire to join the landed gentry, which he did. This is, after all, the only UK rock star I can think of who's always admitted that he's a conservative.

Do I forgive him? Not the point! Thatcher and Reagan were real, my generation let them happen, Ferry just told it straight and refused to let his heart bleed. This record asks: can a music be so anti-rebellion, so insincere and inauthentic, that it breaks on through to the other side and becomes the very grain of life? Yep. Yes it can. And as evidence, I produce 'Virginia Plain' and its soundtracking of the greatest *Top Of The Pops* performance ever, a performance so perverse and wrong that I almost, at age nine, did a Dr Who and hid behind the sofa, and so sleazy that my Bowie and Jagger-worshipping Mum pronounced (with no compliment intended), 'They're just so . . . dirty.' And then there's the all-time great non-sequitur 'Rhododendron/Is a nice flower', from dance-craze satire 'Do The Strand'; and the bit in 'A Song For Europe' when Ferry as Charles Aznavour groans, 'Through silken waters my gondola glides/And the bridge . . . it sighs'; or the whole of the astonishing noise that is 'Street Life', which is a vivid pre-punk radio memory of being stunned by pop, and knowing I was being told something vital and forbidden about the adult world, and not knowing what it was, and that mystery making me wish they'd play it again and again and again, but also knowing that the agony of it ending meant I'd found in pop music a lifelong love.

I wouldn't trade this for another girl.

NEVER MIND THE BOLLOCKS, HERE'S THE SEX PISTOLS

SEX PISTOLS
PRODUCED BY CHRIS THOMAS
VIRGIN/NOVEMBER 1977
UK CHART: 1
US CHART: 106
KEY TRACKS: 'Bodies'; 'Holidays In The Sun'; 'Anarchy In The UK'; 'God Save The Queen'; 'Pretty Vacant'

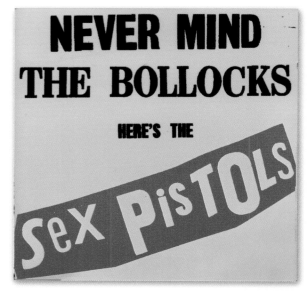

This album's opening salvo tells you something crucial about the Sex Pistols' impact and demise. The lyrical themes of 'Holidays In The Sun' and 'Bodies' – the Cold War and abortion, respectively – are complex, ambiguous, divisive. But the music charges straight through them, leaving room only for the pure fun of righteous anger. The marching feet and Hendrix-like guitar-as-artillery of 'Holidays . . .' may be ironic, the barrage of splenetic 'fuck's that literally splits 'Bodies' in two may well be the most horrified male response to a woman's right to choose ever recorded. But the noise is too much fun to allow for qualms or the juggling of subtext. This is still the purest air-guitar, sing-a-long pleasure a rock 'n' roll fan ever asked for, and therein lay the seeds of the band's destruction. No matter how heavy a metal fan claims Led Zeppelin or Black Sabbath – or The Stooges, for that matter – are, the towering wall of pure noise fashioned by guitarist Steve Jones and former Roxy Music producer Chris Thomas made, and still makes, every other rock album sound effete and muffled. It gave the band the true threat and everyman pop accessibility needed to be more than just another cult garage band in the tradition of The Stooges or The MC5, but also made most believe that John Rotten was a dum-dum bootboy when he was, in fact, arty, camp, sexually confused, anguished and full of a morally ambiguous insight and irony that the Pistols' macho power transformed into nihilism. That clash made for perfect rock 'n' roll, yet made the effect unrepeatable without the inevitable wander into the unforgivable dead-end that was Sid Vicious's 'Belsen Was A Gas'. So, when the truly vacant tried to take this white male power while being unable or unwilling to deal with Rotten's ambition and androgyny, the result was OI!, and inexorably, Nazi punk groups like Skrewdriver.

One of the oddest live music experiences I've ever had was at the 1996 Finsbury Park Sex Pistols reunion show. The show was predictably lousy, but the more striking aspect was the thousands of early-'80s-style, shaven-headed, cider-swilling and hideously ugly scum-punks who emerged from underneath some mammoth stone and turned the park and the surrounding area into a cross between *American History X* and the aftermath of World War One. Where did they come from? Where did they go back to? And what were they looking for, in these fat middle-aged Californian rock celebs, running their tired old 'Filthy Lucre' scam into the gob and vomit-encrusted ground?

The answer lies, surreally, in one of the greatest albums ever made, a tune-packed tirade that balanced fearlessness, when it came to the crumbling establishment of Olde England, and terror, when it came to women, sex and the masses, as Rotten waved goodbye to the monochrome squalor of 'No Irish, No Blacks, No Dogs' London, and accidentally welcomed the onset of Thatcherism, and its gleeful destruction of community and consensus, of our 'Submission' and their 'No Feelings'.

And even when you work all that out, *Bollocks* is still a raging joy. The danceable final solution to teenage revolution.

SUICIDE

SUICIDE
PRODUCED BY CRAIG LEON AND MARTY THAU
RED STAR/NOVEMBER 1977
UK CHART: DID NOT CHART
US CHART: DID NOT CHART
KEY TRACKS: 'Ghost Rider'; 'Frankie Teardrop'; 'Rocket USA'; 'Cheree'; 'Johnny'

The name was always a problem. If you've never heard Suicide, I imagine you're already thinking nihilism and numb punk rock. But New York's Alan Vega and Martin Rev were the twisted synth-pop duo who never got their pop due. What they achieved on this debut album was a unique mixture of base elements so perfect that they could neither follow it, nor turn it into pure pop.

Formed way back in 1971, but unsaleable until the mid-'70s CBGBs scene threw a spotlight on conceptual Manhattan sleaze, Suicide pitched Vega's nervy, echo-chamber rockabilly vocals against Rev's primitive electronics. While the music mixed up influences from '50s rock, early Velvets, girl-group and surf pop, and avant-garde minimalism, Vega (a sculptor by trade) carved spooked images of lost rock 'n' roll Johnnies, doomed working stiffs, teen dream girls; all haunted by the recent memory of Vietnam, the unhealed scars, the long murderous lie that uncovered an ugly truth. 'Ghost Rider' remains their keynote: a dead biker boy haunting the highways, a good-looking corpse in forever-leather, searching for some kind of redemption, unable to move on from a country where 'America, America is killing its youth'.

The sound fashioned by Rev and producers Leon and Thau is distilled essence of primal rock 'n' roll and Golden Age pop, retooled with swishing drum machine, droning analog synth and piping Farfisa organ to resemble nothing less than the pulse, the heartbeat, the womb. When Vega infects this extraordinary, genuinely beautiful noise with the hell-on-Earth scenario that is the epic 'Frankie Teardrop', it's like a waking dream that begins as a peaceful stroll through America's favourite comfort food – the nuclear family – and gradually becomes a living nightmare. Frankie's a hard worker, but he's poor and pressured and owes his soul to the company store. Isolated and abused beyond hope, he murders his wife and children. While the music undulates and calms, Vega slowly builds to panic and . . . screams. The greatest screams ever unleashed in music's name, screams that embody the strain and horror and violence at the heart of America's triumph, screams terrifying enough to uncover all the vilest creatures that lie beneath America's rock of ages. 'Let's hear it for Frankie,' Vega hiccups, the ironic master of ceremonies at the fakest show on Earth.

Every synth-pop duo – and especially Soft Cell (see p.125) – owes something to Suicide. Every band who drone, every rock singer who uses echo and reverb as spook effect, every group who immerse themselves in truth without the cheap and easy outlet of parent-baiting – they owe something, too. Even someone as superficially opposite as Bruce Springsteen admitted that Vega's vocal style and Rev's stark minimalism was a major influence on *Nebraska* (see p.144), an important tribute that illuminates the connection between Suicide's machine-modernism and the hobo testimonies of Woody Guthrie-era American folk music.

But the main thing about *Suicide* is . . . never listen to this record alone in the dark. It lays bare the fact that things that go bump in the night ain't ghosties and ghoulies. Our deepest fear is the black hole at the heart of our lives. The name was always a problem. Too close to the bone.

PINK FLAG

WIRE
PRODUCED BY MIKE THORNE
HARVEST/NOVEMBER 1977
UK CHART: DID NOT CHART
US CHART: DID NOT CHART
KEY TRACKS: 'Mannequin'; 'Ex-Lion Tamer'; '12XU'; 'Fragile'; 'Strange'

Trying to work out exactly when punk became something we now know as post-punk is tricky. Albums I've already covered by Television, Talking Heads and Suicide all have a claim, but, when it comes down to it, most of what these records tell you is that the arty American punk impulse was entirely different to the brutalist British one. In *This Is Uncool*, I credited 1978 singles by Public Image Ltd and Siouxsie And The Banshees. But what I was struggling to communicate was the emergence of post-punk as a short-lived commercially viable proposition. *Pink Flag* pretty much bombed. As Ramones and Suicide prove, new inventions usually do. Music lovers hear those bombs as Big Bangs, form bands, take their ideas and make them into enduring influences. And Wire have come to be as important in this respect as fellow ahead-of-their-time adventurers The Velvet Underground, Captain Beefheart and Iggy Pop.

Pink Flag is a twenty-one-track, forty-minute debut album by Colin Newman (guitar, vocals), Graham Lewis (bass, vocals), Bruce Gilbert (guitar) and Robert Gotobed (aka Mark Field, drums). Its shortest song, 'Field Day For

The Sundays', lasts twenty-eight seconds, yet doesn't seem remotely too short. Its influence stretches from Elastica, who based their entire short career on 'Three Girl Rhumba', to R.E.M., who covered 'Strange', to an American '80s band called The Ex-Lion Tamers, who formed to do nothing more than play *Pink Flag* in its entirety to eager American heartland kids who heard something so vital in UK post-punk that they were inspired to form the bands that invented twenty-first-century rock: Nirvana, Red Hot Chilli Peppers, Black Flag, Sonic Youth. It is a key example of the art school influence on rock's greatest waves, the four members meeting at north London art schools after being brought up in sleepy provincial towns. Indeed, Lewis was born and raised in Grantham, birthplace of one M. Thatcher.

Pink Flag takes punk's one-two-three-four thrash and cockney yap and makes it into irony and abstraction, youth club pop and prole art threat, fear and laughter, parody and purity, satire and insoluble aspirin for a headache called modern times. Named after the sleeve art (the band spotted a parade-ground flag on a deserted army base on their way to a gig) rather than any central concept, the album's spidery, dry, ridiculously confident opening shot of 'Reuters' and 'Field Day . . . ' creates a context of mistrust of media, and the album feels like an examination of the numbing manipulations of newsprint, glamour mags, porn and television. At one extreme, 'Lowdown' is a stalking metal breakdown of terror of sex, similar in dread to the Pistols' 'Submission'. At the other, 'Mr Suit' is a gloriously stoopid pastiche of anti-establishment thrash-rage. In-between, the five key tracks named above show pop a way forward, a deft balance of the brutal and the beautiful, melodies that charm, words that bemuse but never settle for pale angst, basics of a whole new way of playing and understanding rock 'n' roll. *Pink Flag* – how queer! – dismissed and destroyed OI!'s bonehead machismo before it even began, opened a door to a rock intellectualism without the usual snobbery or over-elaboration, and was as funny as it was biting. Thorne's itchy, scratchy production was extraordinary in its foresight, because although it's apparent that more conventional ear candy could've made the likes of 'Mannequin' and 'Ex-Lion Tamer' into chart hits, the holes the sound leaves – the unanswered questions and belief in our power to explore our own answers – is exactly why the record has endured and started so many smart talents on their road. A complete record leaves no room for doubt, no room to move, no space to scribble in its margins. *Pink Flag* is a template and an unfinished symphony that R.E.M. and Blur and Fugazi and LCD Soundsystem and Franz Ferdinand have wanted to complete. It's an act of generosity that will live on as long as art-rock does, and I dare say that that will be forever.

BEFORE AND AFTER SCIENCE

BRIAN ENO
PRODUCED BY BRIAN ENO AND RHETT DAVIES
POLYDOR (NOW VIRGIN)/DECEMBER 1977
UK CHART: DID NOT CHART
US CHART: DID NOT CHART
KEY TRACKS: 'King's Lead Hat'; 'Backwater'; 'No One Receiving'; 'Julie With . . .' ; 'Here He Comes'

Someone poking pop with a stick and smiling quizzically while it squirms should not make great pop music. But Brian Eno did and that's what makes him a unique figure in modern music. *Before And After Science* is his fourth solo album after quitting being the maverick element in Roxy Music and sounds, like the three earlier records, unfinished, pretty, jerky, jaunty and odd. Its opening track, 'No One Receiving', is a tribute to the entire plastic soul/funk phase of his friend and collaborator David Bowie, and the blueprint for all the globally-informed art-funk he would go on to explore with David Byrne. But Eno saw the possibilities of post-punk before punk even got going, and was so openly delighted he made the best song (and massively unsuccessful single) from this, 'King's Lead Hat', an anagram of Talking Heads. No, I didn't notice at the time either. How cool is that?

Pop's fave boffin was born in Suffolk and signed his art school application Brian Peter George St John Le Baptiste De La Salle Eno, which gives you some idea, class-wise, of why he couldn't be an actual punk rocker. But, in drag queen make-up and feather boa, and with synthetic fizzes and parps, he gave the sleaze and disease to early Roxy Music. Although his invention of ambient music and production of the likes of U2 and James joins with his Bowie and Byrne collaborations as the major source of his fame, there is something addictive and singular about his dalliances with singing pop songs. His voice is English, fruity and utterly unsuited to rock, and while the influence on the likes of XTC's Andy Partridge and Wire's Colin Newman becomes obvious in the saying, his singing voice was conspicuously bereft of the anger and frustration that the punks used to change rock's vocal boundaries. While I wouldn't go as far as to accuse any human of never having suffered, Eno's music sounded like the tunes and textures of a pretty nice life. He's a compelling argument for the idea that rock music had never had any connection with the blues whatsoever. Or at least, that it didn't have to, and probably shouldn't when made by clever, wealthy people from the English countryside. This music is the sworn enemy of fake authenticity.

But while his former partner Bryan Ferry built a career on playing with the ironies inherent within rock's past, Eno's muse feels free of the need to satirise. *Before And After Science* is roughly split into an uptempo pop half, and a half that points toward his 'Ambient' series of albums, *Music For Films*, *Music For Airports*, etc. The pop songs are itchy, funny and fun, the missing link between glam rock and post-punk. The ambient tunes are pretty, and evoke summer days in the country, and seem obsessed with sailing away, and don't get self-conscious about how Henley Regatta that may appear. It was made right after his Berlin sojourns with Bowie, sounds absolutely nothing like them, and was released at Christmas in a year when everyone wanted Santa to bring them punk, disco and Abba, as if he didn't want anyone to hear it. No one receiving, and he knew it, and if I'd just worked with Bowie and had Devo and Talking Heads to look forward to, I wouldn't give a hoot neither.

Or 'Cretin Hop' or 'Surfin' Bird' or 'Here Today, Gone Tomorrow' or almost any track from what is, in effect, The Very Best Of The Ramones. Trust me – buy the CD complete with single versions of 'Sheena . . . ' and 'I Don't Care' and top contextual sleevenotes from NY punk journo Legs McNeil that hopefully answer the essentially dumb question, 'But were the Ramones dum-dum, or really just plain dumb?' by pointing out all the secret ironies lyricists Joey and Dee Dee were making clear to anyone who came from nowhere and needed to feel it was really somewhere. When *Rocket To Russia* . . . erm . . . bombed, there was, of course, nowhere useful for the Ramones to go. But such concerns are *so* not the point. The point is a gangly freak with a very strange voice bawling 'LOBOTOMY!!!' through an echo chamber, and rhyming, 'LSD' with 'Golly gee!' over the best wall-of-guitar-sound ever built. It's the pop that rocked and the rock that popped and the cartoon you could touch and it gave voice to every kid who was and would be young, numb and full of dumb.

The Ramones were about the subversion inherent in convincing the old guard that you were fundamentally moronic, therefore creating a private joke that none of them were smart enough to understand. Now we had no need to tell 'em. That we had no cerebellum.

ROCKET TO RUSSIA

RAMONES
PRODUCED BY TONY BONGIOVI AND T. ERDELYI
SIRE/NOVEMBER 1977
UK CHART: 60
US CHART: 49
KEY TRACKS: 'Teenage Lobotomy'; 'Sheena Is A Punk Rocker'; 'I Don't Care'; 'I Wanna Be Well'; 'Rockaway Beach'

1978

WHITE MUSIC

XTC

PRODUCED BY JOHN LECKIE
VIRGIN/FEBRUARY 1978
UK CHART: 38
US CHART: DID NOT CHART
KEY TRACKS: 'Radios In Motion'; 'Statue Of Liberty'; 'I'm Bugged'; 'X Wires'; 'This Is Pop'

A key testimony in British new wave's need for restless urgency, *White Music* is a rattle and a poke, a provincial pop art classic, a vivid impression of a fairground whirling dervishly after you queasily disembark from the waltz. What's more, and despite all the geek-nerds we've already met in this book thus far, Andy Partridge, Colin Moulding, Terry Chambers and Barry Andrews out-geeked everyone, and made it work for them. Legendary punk/reggae photographer Dennis Morris does his best to lend the four some cool on the sleeve, but no amount of posing and pouting could obscure the fact that these were bookish middle-class boys from Swindon. The likes of David Byrne and Jonathan Richman were lent exoticism by being American, while punk's first wave was quintessentially urban. XTC were banging around in Wiltshire, 'Like a newtown animal in a furnished cage.'

'Newtown Animal's explanation of Partridge's itchy impatience summed up my teens in Peterborough in eight words, and was the new wave's first real acknowledgement that bored provincial kids, rather than Chelsea and Notting Hill hipsters living already bohemian lives, were the ones that actually needed new rock 'n' roll thrills and a reason to believe.

'Radios In Motion' is one of the all-time great album opener fanfares, a rush of Here We Are!!! Guitars, off-kilter verse that resolves into harmony power-pop bridge that flips into discord chorus, and Partridge's playful foghorn vocals. It's sound advice and advice on sound too, as Partridge urges 'the kids' to stop complaining about all those slow, boring songs and listen to global radio, which 'Gets you out of your red white and blues'. Top metaphor for freeing yo' mind so that yo' ass will follow, and I'm not sure he or anyone else could have predicted that, within twenty years, internet radio would let us make it real. But the song fizzes with memories of nights spent tuning tinny transistors to Radios Luxembourg and Caroline, trying to hear something other than the usual through the static. Actually, heroes like Luxembourg's Stuart Henry aside, they mostly played the usual anyway, but nostalgia for having nowt makes for much deluded romance.

'Radios In Motion' was a manifesto for the world musics XTC would craftily attach to their quintessentially English pop through the coming years, but also perhaps predicts Partridge's future agoraphobia, which provoked a refusal to tour from 1982 onwards. It's as if he already used music to travel without leaving his furnished cage.

Elsewhere, *White Music* takes the title's self-deprecating joke to extremes of joy, irritation, eccentricity and mania. 'X Wires' is insane speed-freak nagging. 'This Is Pop' almost writes a 'how to' manual for the new pop that would later be dubbed 'post-punk'. And 'Statue Of Liberty' is a robot ska paean to symbolic US freedom, as well as a smart spin on dirty pop innuendo that got it banned as a single for the obscene, revolting metaphor that is, 'I sail beneath your skirt.'

Can't help feeling sometimes – and forgive me if this sounds like the 'it were all fields 'round here' routine – that the Hays Code-style prudishness of pop radio and TV in the '70s made the art better. After all, if some talentless cunt can just say 'Fuck you, you Ho!' without anyone even considering that it's the misogyny, not the rude word, that offends, the tensions that create an atmosphere for great art are dissipated. There's nothing to kick against, because it seems that anything is allowed. It's a smart media con, convincing so many that graphic abuse is rebellion, when domestic violence stats suggest that 'Fuck you, you Ho!' is still pretty much the status quo in many furnished cages. Of course, there was always a far more efficient form of censorship available that doesn't turn scumbags into martyrs. Don't play the record, on the grounds that it isn't very good.

Not sure why XTC and *White Music* got me digressy there, except that XTC were one of those groups that felt like good, smart, uncynical people, and actually made exciting music, rather than dull and worthy music, out of that. There's still plenty of that around, but the difference was, in 1978–1982, that these nice people got in the charts, shifted units, defined the pop times. The only thing to add is that I always thought that 'I'm Bugged' – a barbed comment about all the cool little punks scuttling from under rocks that rode a lurching rhythm and atonal bassline that came to define post-punk's idea that when everything was out of tune, you got a different kind of tune – had a line that went, 'Dropped a little note/To a sympathetic stoat.' Do metaphorical stoats eat metaphorical insects? No matter, 'cos it's actually 'through a sympathetic's door'. Not as good, is it?

And finally . . . I don't really know what 'angular' guitar is, but if it exists, it's Andy Partridge's invention, an irritant, elastic, chopping, clanging, cattle-prod Wilko Johnson-on-acid style that beat PiL's Keith Levine, John McKay of the Banshees and the Gang Of Four's Andy Gill to the post-punk punch. The more one listens to *White Music*, the more one suspects that XTC directly influenced all the bands that came to be cooler than them. Sadly, The Great Rock 'n' Roll Swindon never came to pass.

ANOTHER MUSIC IN A DIFFERENT KITCHEN

BUZZCOCKS
PRODUCED BY MARTIN RUSHENT
UNITED ARTISTS/MARCH 1978
UK CHART: 15
US CHART: DID NOT CHART
KEY TRACKS: 'Love Battery'; 'Get On Our Own'; 'No Reply';
'I Don't Mind'; 'Moving Away From The Pulsebeat'

The Buzzcocks topped and tailed their debut album with the deliberately ham-fisted two-note guitar solo from 'Boredom'. 'Boredom' was the best-loved song from 1977's 'Spiral Scratch' EP, their first release and the first entirely self-financed record of the UK punk era. Their manager Richard Boon's New Hormones label essentially invented 'indie', and the record's success inspired Manchester to become Britain's pop city number one. But the Buzzcocks also lost their lead singer and lyricist Howard Devoto, who left amicably to form Magazine before they signed to EMI tributary United Artists. Guitarist Peter Shelley took over and became punk's very own Smokey Robinson-esque love poet.

Not that love had everything to do with it. Punk rock was about a loud raucous 'No!' and *Another Music . . .* revelled in that nay-saying. But, instead of no to government, parents, hippies or men in suits, Shelley echoed the Modern Lovers and said a very English no to the rules of rock 'n' roll and the symbols of modern consumerism. No to 'Fast Cars', no to empty sex, no to cheap thrills. 'Sooner or later/You're gonna listen to Ralph Nader,' Shelley wailed on 'Fast Cars', years before the US anti-corporate activist would run for President. While the buzzsaw wall of guitars evoked speed and indecent haste, Shelley sneered at his lover, 'All this slurping and sucking/You know it's putting me off my food,' in 'You Tear Me Up'. And, most memorably, Shelley brought 'Sixteen''s military grunge to a close by declaring, 'And I hate modern music/Disco boogie and pop/They go on and on and on and on and on/How I wish they would STOP!' *Another Music* drips with disgust and carries an aura of frantic, frustrated masturbation.

Shelley's camp asceticism left its mark on everyone from Morrissey to Neil Tennant, while his love songs were uniquely honest and witty dissections of need and disappointment. The single here, 'I Don't Mind' lays bare the paranoia that holds love back from true connection, pinpoints the pain and the shrugging involved in trying to keep your dignity, and twists the refusal to beg that hides a pride stripped bare. By the time you reach 'Fiction Romance', Shelley's cautious dip into the muddy puddle of hope is so hard-won that it illuminates all your romantic dreams, too.

It was definitely a wee Moment when boys fell in love with the gay Shelley's vulnerable love songs. Sure, the pace was bloke-rushing-to-climax fast and the guitars were full of fuzzy testosterone. But these elements couldn't drown the androgynous, anti-macho sensitivity of Shelley's worldview. Buzzcocks introduced more than a few punk blokes to their feminine side, and we found out we liked her company.

Album closer 'Moving Away From The Pulsebeat' even allowed punk rock its first drum solo. The first punks were already moving away from the 1-2-3-4! straitjacket they used as their first no.

THIS YEAR'S MODEL

ELVIS COSTELLO
PRODUCED BY NICK LOWE
F BEAT/MARCH 1978
UK CHART: 4
US CHART: 30
KEY TRACKS: 'Lipstick Vogue'; '(I Don't Want To Go To) Chelsea'; 'No Action'; 'The Beat'; 'This Year's Girl'

In a 1977 interview in the *NME*, Declan McManus famously told Nick Kent that the 'only motivation' behind the songs he'd written and performed as Elvis Costello were 'revenge and guilt'. Revealing the evil truth about your creative process became a whole new way of doing pop PR in the late '70s. Not that you'd be left in the dark about the artist's motivations after listening to *This Year's Model*. As 'Hand In Hand' exemplifies, Costello's early muse was based on saying out loud all the violent revenge fantasies that go through men's minds when they find themselves rejected, humiliated, impotent and powerless in any given situation. A world where one dreams of getting 'the bully boys out/To change

someone's facial design', and where, if love goes horribly wrong, 'If I'm gonna go down/You're gonna come with me.' The reason why so many women of that era love Costello is not because of the unconscious groupie masochism that inspired so many girls' love of The Stranglers, but because Costello explained what men felt in terms women believed and understood.

This Year's Model introduced Costello's long-term backing band The Attractions, although drummer Pete Thomas, bassist Bruce Thomas and keyboardist Steve Naïve weren't yet considered permanent enough to co-credit on the sleeve. And, while Naïve's wheezing and piping ivories gave a rich, cinematic mystery missing from Costello's *My Aim Is True* debut, the former computer programmer and twenty-two-year-old family man who became the punk era's most celebrated geek pinned down his favourite subject: the torturing Ex who was now sleeping with someone else; a someone else who was always better-looking, more macho, bigger of dick and (you told yourself) smaller of brain than you. *This Year's Model* laced that very male inner torture with caustic soda-pop art about soft porn, emotional (and actual, on the eerie flaming torch song that is 'Night Rally') fascism, sex as commodity, numb emotions, fake feelings, and a suspicion that, as the brutally, beautifully powerful 'Lipstick Vogue' accuses, 'love is just a tumour – you've got to cut it out.'

It's tempting here to just go through lyrical barb after lyrical barb – oh, what the hell, here's my favourite, from 'The Beat': 'I keep thinking about your mother/Oh, I don't wanna lick them/I don't wanna be your lover/I just wanna be your victim' – but those painfully accurate lights shone upon male neurosis do tend to overshadow the sticky sickness of Costello's voice, the ability to meld Beatles, Stones, Dylan, reggae, soul and country in his early songs, and a sound shaped by The Attractions and Nick Lowe that found some ideal balance between live energy and studio detail. *This Year's Model* is a masterpiece, and perhaps Costello's greatest album, made before he got self-conscious about gaining distance from punk and the scope of his talent, before a desire for highbrow approval started to overwhelm his desire for revenge and guilt. The cover shot nails it; the cool jerk, pointing his camera at us, capturing too much, snapping everyone who's fucked him over, an eerie reminder of the photographer/serial killer of Michael Powell's *Peeping Tom* movie. Somewhere off-camera, a beautiful girl reclines, mascara eyes absent, lipstick mouth silent. She holds very still for the shot. She's not moving at all.

SATURDAY NIGHT FEVER – THE ORIGINAL SOUNDTRACK

VARIOUS ARTISTS
COMPILATION SUPERVISED BY BILL OAKES
RSO/MARCH 1978
UK CHART: 1
US CHART: 1

KEY TRACKS: 'Jive Talkin', 'Night Fever' and 'Stayin' Alive' by Bee Gees; 'Disco Inferno' by Trammps; 'More Than A Woman' by Tavares

I know. You were wondering when that last word in this book's subtitle was actually going to kick in. Hey. Better late than never.

Obviously, when a record and a movie become as much of a commercial phenomenon as *Saturday Night Fever*, it always marks the beginning of the end of the trend. Although there were plenty of mighty disco tunes to come, the scene that the movie dramatised – with its tribal rituals and secret understandings, with its world-changing and underground connection between black, gay and female dance and dress codes – was inevitably diluted by mainstream acceptance. Everyone wanted a piece of disco as either producer or consumer, and when that happens the inevitable dialectic between exploitation and elitism resolves

itself in what we know as that good old pop bandwagon. Before too long, disco's ubiquity resulted in an anti-homo 'disco sucks' backlash and the blame was laid squarely at the door of Travolta's trousers and the hair, medallions, teeth and falsettos of the Brothers Gibb.

After all these years, there's still an accepted theory that 'fake' disco destroyed 'authentic' soul. None of these theorists seem too interested in why, if soul was so strong, their salt-of-the-earth soul singers were so willing to ditch it for disco money, or how vitally important disco was to our all-too-slow acceptance of open homosexuality. You can't help wondering what's truly being said when the only authentic reality is always a heterosexual one, particularly in a world where Afro-American entertainers quite obviously lie about their ghetto experiences (and sexual preferences, obviously) in order to fit in with post-gangsta hip hop's one-dimensional version of black reality.

Whatever, whatever. Because if you can't respond to the grace of 'Night Fever', the ferocity of 'Disco Inferno', or the yearning worship of 'More Than A Woman', then, yep, you probably are somebody who thinks dancing is embarrassing and is too stone deaf to hear anything in these songs except the thump-thump of the kick and snare. The rest of us could hear the thrill of sex, the anticipation and letdown of all our Saturdays, the wah-wah guitars and subtle percussive swings of master musicians, the sexual panic in the Bee Gees' voices, the ecstasy of dancing and dancing together, the community of the weekday loser and the weekend winner, the dazzle of pop, and the distant drums of house music. And if all that rings a bell with you, if you're feeling infused by memories of physical release and human connection and sexual desire under lights that flutter like love at first sight, then, hey, I'm with you, put down this book. You shouldn't be reading. You should be dancing.

THE MODERN DANCE

PERE UBU
PRODUCED BY PERE UBU AND KEN HAMANN
BLANK-MERCURY/APRIL 1978
UK CHART: DID NOT CHART
US CHART: DID NOT CHART
KEY TRACKS: 'Non-Alignment Pact'; 'The Modern Dance'; 'Street Waves'; 'Humor Me'; 'Life Stinks'

Slick segue, eh? Who says frustrated DJs can't mix?

Back to boys on girls, lyrically speaking. Track one, side one of the debut album by Ohio's pre-punk avant-garage inventors Pere Ubu. It's called 'Non-Alignment Pact' and it should be a rock standard like 'Stairway To Heaven' and it packs a metaphorical punch on the subject of 'Women are a foreign land' that even Costello might envy. There's a precipitous bass harmonic, and an idiot Chuck Berry geetar rip, and then a headlong charge down an alleyway that still smells of Iggy And The Stooges. Then a voice . . . huh . . . a voice. The wail of a big baby trying to be Ray Charles. And it demands, with comic futility, 'I wanna make a deal with you girl and get it signed by the heads of state . . . It's my non-alignment pact . . . Sign it!' The big baby's running out of time, so he tries emotional blackmail: 'I can see the world in flames/And it's all because of you/or your thousand other names.' He lists a few of those thousand other names, ending, of course, with that all-American beach babe Barbara-Ann. And just in case she doesn't yet understand that his desire for her is gonna fry the whole wide world, he thrusts that pen at her like it's a red hot poker. 'It's all because of you girl! Sign my non-alignment pact,' and you know she's just standing there grinning, shaking her head, reaching for the box of matches in the pocket of her hip-hugger jeans.

You have a right to wonder where the girls' voices are in all this male accusation and panic. Be patient. They're on their way. You have to cast your mind back to a world long before all the biggest, sassiest pop stars were all female, and

THE MODERN DANCE/PERE UBU

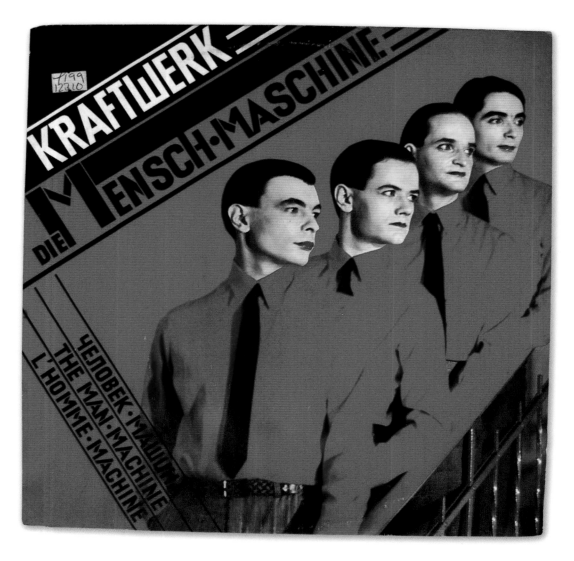

THE MAN MACHINE/KRAFTWERK

when a woman's rock 'n' role involved the application of loose lips in a tour bus, or, if she'd really gone up in the world, a hotel room. Most of the first punks couldn't quite bring themselves to put a chick in the band. But their honesty about their utter terror of womankind opened a space for a new kind of woman to wonder what they were so scared of. Until then, you had weird and wonderful guys like plump-punk pioneer David Thomas to guide you through the highways and byways of Fear Of Lust with post-Beefheart and Roxy art-synth-sax-guitar-pop imagination, breaking glass and urban static and cod-reggae and reckless glee.

Of course, Thomas's questing for truth, surreal warbling, and wobbling girth meant that Pere Ubu were doomed to marginal acclaim and zilch sales for the next twenty-seven years and counting, despite concocting an art guitar pop that contained every trace element that has sustained US college rock since the mid-'80s, and has ended up the blueprint for post-punk's current commercial ascendancy. And while *The Modern Dance* is a warm and wise quasi-concept album about the eternal dance between girl and boy, it's also haunted by a lost boy called Peter Laughner, a former member of Pere Ubu and mid-'70s US punk poster-boy who died of the predictable drug overdose in June 1977. His 'Life Stinks' ('I need a drink/I can't think/I like the Kinks/Life stinks') is included here, a sad goodbye, a defiant epitaph, a smart-dumb explanation for his absence. All part of an album that dares to stride naked into the conference chamber.

THE MAN MACHINE

KRAFTWERK
PRODUCED BY RALF HUTTER AND FLORIAN SCHNEIDER
CAPITOL/MAY 1978
UK CHART: 9
US CHART: DID NOT CHART
KEY TRACKS: 'The Model'; 'The Man Machine'; 'Spacelab'; 'Neon Lights'; 'The Robots'

The record that connects the coldness of circuitry and the warmth of the soul, reminding us, with melodies that seem as ancient as twinkling stars, that machines are, after all, the product of the dreams of humans.

SOME GIRLS

THE ROLLING STONES
PRODUCED BY THE GLIMMER TWINS
ROLLING STONES/JUNE 1978
UK CHART: 2
US CHART: 1
KEY TRACKS: 'Shattered'; 'Respectable'; 'Before They Make Me Run'; 'Miss You'; 'Beast Of Burden'

The Rolling Stones' response to punk. Sure, as far as the PR went, the increasingly irrelevant old misanthropes were disinterested in anything other than moolah and their own lofty disdain for, well, everyone. But *Some Girls* showed that punk stung. That somewhere beneath the endless layers of self-defence and a career that increasingly resembled a botched military campaign, the simple fact that someone had not just usurped their rebel chic, but pinpointed them as the enemy, gave The Glimmer Twins (the production sobriquet for Jagger and Richards) one tiny glimmer of a creative reason to exist. The result was ten short, sharp tracks, including a disco exploitation that didn't suck, a comedy song, a Temptations cover, and five messy and inspired rock 'n' roll songs that represent the last time that a group of human beings called The Rolling Stones got together and played some songs and convinced themselves that that, in itself, might have benefits other than fiscal.

Still, punk couldn't change Jagger's attitude to women.

The title track is a litany of poor-little-rich-fuck misogyny with a side order of racial stereotyping. Less wholly predictable was 'Faraway Eyes', a country pastiche with a panto redneck vocal and a 'satirical' lyric at the expense of the Bible belt that's about as funny as David Baddiel. The weird thing about this is that Richards had famously hung out with Gram Parsons, and his love of country and more enlightened view of America's southern states had provoked much of the Stones' best early-'70s music. What was even weirder is that Richards responded to Jagger's moronic piss-taking by giving 'Faraway Eyes' some of the loveliest pedal-steel playing this side of Nashville. Perhaps the last spurt of energy that *Some Girls* represents was spurred by the Statler and Waldorf of white boy blues indulging in some kind of musical handbags-at-dawn.

Keith's own 'Before They Make Me Run' is, therefore, a highlight for all of us Stones fans who are on Keith's side . . . which is everyone. One of those hard rockers which just seems to flow out of the band's fingers without thinking, its defiance about Keith's riskier lifestyle choices comes down to the choice line, 'I wasn't looking too good but I was feeling real well.'

But to be fair to Lip Boy, it's hard to connect the author of 'Some Girls' and 'Faraway Eyes' with the author of 'Respectable' (a rollicking twelve-bar sprint which puts the bitch-dissing in a wittily self-deprecating context), 'Beast Of Burden' (a bruised soul ballad that's become a Stones standard) and 'When The Whip Comes Down', where Jagger roars and drowns in pure StonesSound, and gives a rent-boy testimony that's utterly convincing and truly compassionate. Jagger's pre-'80s ability to observe life and inhabit other people reaches extraordinary heights in closing track 'Shattered', as Lord Lippy Lipfield surveys a trashed-out chaotic New York over a two-chord art-rock thrash, fashions a stream-of-consciousness rap out of – my God! – actually questioning himself, and brings on the heat of 'Surviving in the street' so artfully that you really don't care that the grammar school boy from Dartford in Kent has had less contact with 'the

street' than his third cousin, the Earl Of Lippington. Attached to pop innocence by liberal use of the vocal chant 'shadoobie', 'Shattered' gives us 'People dressed in plastic bags' who could be bums but could also be punks, and teases us with the shock-horror enquiry, 'Success – does it matter?', before concluding that, yes, don't be silly, got you going there, because, 'Pride and joy and greed and sex/That's what makes our town the best – Now look at me!' Funny, vivid, brilliant, and one of the greatest ever rock band's (yeah, I know, I can't help it, blame my mother) greatest ever songs, its avant-savant savoir-faire promised a whole new direction for The Rolling Stones. Sadly, as we all recall, The Rolling Stones died in a freak inbreeding accident and were replaced by puppets made from the leathery bits of dead debutantes, held together by old rope and knotted donkey hair. Still, who would have wanted to watch the original members shambling around the world's arenas, shot full of sheep glands or something and farting away at a tawdry pastiche of bum notes and 'will this do?' while people young enough to know better shelled out £60 a ticket when any fool could hear that the Strolling Bones tribute band round at The Blimey & Begorrah had far more of the Stones in 'em for a pint of wallop and a packet of pork scratchings? Thank goodness the fates intervened to make sure that never happened.

CAN'T STAND THE REZILLOS

THE REZILLOS
PRODUCED BY BOB CLEARMOUNTAIN, TONY
BONGIOVI AND THE REZILLOS
SIRE/JULY 1978
UK CHART: 16
US CHART: DID NOT CHART
KEY TRACKS: 'Can't Stand My Baby'; 'No'; 'Somebody's
Gonna Get Their Head Kicked In Tonight'; '(My Baby Does)
Good Sculptures'; 'Flying Saucer Attack'

CAN'T STAND THE REZILLOS/THE REZILLOS

PARALLEL LINES/BLONDIE

All the punk must seem terribly worthy so far. Ramones, Pistols and Buzzcocks undoubtedly had jokes, but they had subtext and irony and a subversive intention. But it's important to know that, at the time, there were a whole bunch of punk affiliates who were just silly. Not stupid, with all the dumb insolence that implies. Nope, just plain silly. Generally, this made for decent singles, the kind you liked at the time and then felt a little embarrassed about. But Edinburgh's Rezillos made a great album. Again, this isn't because there are dimensions that are not immediately apparent, or musical layers that only emerge after careful study. Indeed, the major irony of the wonderfully titled *Can't Stand The Rezillos* is that the band got signed to Madonna's future label, were assigned two heavyweight US producers including Ramones veteran Bongiovi, and got to record in the legendary Power Station studio in New York ... all to make a record that sounds like a jelly fight in a Dundee scout hut. The Rezillos were just fast, loud, camp, trashy, and had a great guitarist and two great singers, one of whom remains one of the most underrated pop singers and female presences of her generation. Or to put it another way ... I can't help it, I've still got a hopeless crush on one Fay Fife, who was/is what you get if you mix a Shangri-La, a couple of years at art school, and the kind of tomboy who looks and sings as if the major part of her make-up ritual involves finding her knuckle-duster. Man, of course your Siouxsies and Debbies and Chrissies (Fay's real name was Sheilagh Hynde!) were exotic and untouchably charismatic. But Ms Fife seemed like one of my scary youth club urchin girlfriends who just happened to be touched by vocal genius and an intrinsic understanding of the finer points of the pop art trash aesthetic. Who wouldn't fall in love?

What else you need to know is that guitarist Jo Callis, who occasionally called himself Luke Warm, wrote most of the melodies and comic-book sci-fi B-movie and kid-angst lyrics, and later became head tunesmith for The Human League. The only thing wrong with The League circa Dare is that Big Phil didn't make Fay Fife join the band, and perhaps change the name to Fay Fife and her Human League. Eugene Reynolds had Kramer hair and bug shades and sang like a frog. The B-52's pretty much copied the aesthetic, but made a cool conceptual art noise instead of something that sounds like being spanked in the mush by a dayglo dustbin lid while cartoon birds fly round your face. Did I mention that Fay Fife sang words like 'radge' (Scots slang for mental), 'feeling' and 'OI!OI!OI!' with a unique interpretive subtlety that calls to mind Dinah Washington, or possibly the St Trinians school choir? Oh ... and the bass player on this record was called William Mysterious.

Did I mention Fay Fife?

PARALLEL LINES

BLONDIE
PRODUCED BY MIKE CHAPMAN
CHRYSALIS/SEPTEMBER 1978
UK CHART: 1
US CHART: 6
KEY TRACKS: 'Heart Of Glass'; 'Picture This'; 'Fade Away And Radiate'; 'One Way Or Another'; 'Hanging On The Telephone'

Mod suits with baseball boots. Ultra-modern disco and postmodern Buddy Holly. Clem Burke's drumming. A smile that doesn't smile, a heart-of-stone leer that made Debbie Harry's hands-on-hips glare seem positively cuddly. There are so many reasons to dislike Blondie but they made them all reasons to love 'em, and *Parallel Lines* is the one album proper where their contrivances, their template for *Blonde Ambition*, added up to *Pop Deluxe*. Harry's watch-me-can't-touch-me oozed out of the songs, as swoonsome as it was icy, and brought us the first mainstream female pop star who cut right through the virgin-or-whore straitjacket which is still the required dress for femme pop's padded cell. Women wanted Debbie more than men, because they needed to see a woman who could have sex and still own her own. *Parallel Lines* was the soundtrack to this year's role model, full of sly allusion to impossibly sexually slippery New York, yet homely enough with its cheap organs and mulleted musicians and girl-group singalongs to make you feel you could share in this adventure, that even rejection and heartbreak could be danced away because, as 'Picture This' dared to dream, the next offered telephone number might be akin to 'A sky full of thunder'. All this, and more surprises, from this year's girl.

Q: ARE WE NOT MEN? A: WE ARE DEVO!

DEVO
PRODUCED BY BRIAN ENO
CHRYSALIS/SEPTEMBER 1978
UK CHART: 12
US CHART: 78
KEY TRACKS: 'Satisfaction (I Can't Get Me No)'; 'Come Back Jonee'; 'Sloppy (I Saw My Baby Gettin')'; 'Shrivel Up'; 'Mongoloid'

Sometimes happy coincidence plays a big part in writing. The day I was writing this entry, for example, my wife was at home getting bewildered and angry about one of our society's many secret abuses. She was working for a charity/pressure group called Values Into Action, which works on behalf of people with learning difficulties. Today, she was ploughing through a report on human rights regarding those we used to call the mentally handicapped, stopping occasionally to read out another casual confession from a doctor or a nurse that, without the consent of the 'client', they kept people with no history of violence or crime doped up and incarcerated, because it keeps their 'challenging behaviour' away from us, because it's cheaper than aiding them to live a free and functional life. Then I walked back

into my study, and Devo were singing a song called 'Mongoloid'.

'Mongoloid' is a robotic, off-kilter nursery rhyme about a man who has what we now call Down's syndrome and who is 'Happier than you and me'. 'He wore a hat/And he had a job,' and while he conformed to expectation, 'nobody even cared'. But the key line is that his condition 'determined what he could see'. This mongoloid was left alone because he was invisible. Because what we identify him as and call him determines what we can see, and we'll see nothing but discomfort, guilt, embarrassment, inconvenience. The song's implicit threat is that, once someone notices his difference, once he attracts attention to himself, then he will lose his freedom, his human rights. The other meaning of the song, particularly in the light of the band's view that humans are 'de-evolving', reverting back to 'monkey men' and 'pinheads' as the next track 'Jocko Homo' calls it, is that he really is no different to anyone, because even 'His friends were unaware'. What truly terrifies us about the mongoloid is our suspicion that we're mongoloids too . . . we just learned to fit in.

The debut album by the strange, boiler-suited, outwardly zany post-punks from Akron, Ohio, is an album about rules, of conformity, of cool, of rock, of pop, of romance, of sex, of consumerism . . . and how badly they fit us. Eno's glam-in-a-cage production, Jerry Casale's David Byrne-meets-Andy Partridge yelp, and Bob and Mark Mothersbaugh's nagging, jagged, seasick tunes merge to form yet more avant-garage, disorientating the listener while injecting neurosis and anxiety into the Stones' 'Satisfaction' and the Chuck Berry-subverting 'Come Back Jonee'. Regarding the perennial rock dream personified by cars and girls, cars were death or some cheap motor that didn't get you far, and, like the later Gang Of Four, Devo didn't ignore sex but recognised it as part of the problem, worrying away (or laughing hard?) about missed holes and wandering hands. Their extraordinary, absolutely goddam classic version of 'Satisfaction' takes Jagger's triumphant definition of what it was to be young, willing and able to see through the lies of the '60s and go on to fuck the girl (period willing) and take the world, and made it into an orgy of sexual failure, and trying to buy success, and losing all over again. For the Stones, the world was a dumb girl, there for the taking. For Devo, you were the one who got fucked, and the pleasure was only in understanding the rules of engagement.

Devo were one of those key post-punk acts who were killed by their own cleverness and desperation to – oh yes – fit in during the 1980s, making formula ironic student disco hits for college noo-wave fans until realising that being the punchline of your own joke still made you a laughing stock. Mark Mothersbaugh now makes soundtracks for films that exploit the popularity of The Rugrats. He brings home the bacon. Nobody even cared.

BEST DRESSED CHICKEN IN TOWN

DR. ALIMANTADO
PRODUCED BY WINSTON THOMPSON
GREENSLEEVES/SEPTEMBER 1978
UK CHART: DID NOT CHART
US CHART: DID NOT CHART
KEY TRACKS: 'Poison Flour'; 'I Killed The Barber'; 'Best Dressed Chicken In Town'; 'Gimme Mi Gun'; 'Just the Other Day'

As much a punk rock artefact as anything boasting thrashing guitars and a London accent, *Best Dressed Chicken In Town* showed British rock kids just how thrilling reggae could be. The two most influential Englishmen of the time – John Peel and Johnny Rotten – bigged up this record until we succumbed, and we found a music of ebullient groove, anger, humour and surrealism courtesy of the quirky, proto-rap art that was Jamaican toasting or DJ. It spoke in strange tongues and introduced realities from a land both far away and, due to Britain's increasingly influential West Indian presence, the man who lives next door.

Best Dressed Chicken is actually a compilation of singles recorded in Kingston between 1973–76 by Winston Thompson, aka Dr. Alimantado. Self-produced with the likes of dub originators Lee Perry and King Tubby as engineers, the tracks are in the style originated by U-Roy. A popular vocal tune is taken, twisted, stretched, vandalised and vaporised, and the 'toaster' puts a new vocal on top, blending song, rap, chant, scream and mumbled aside into something that generally comments on a hot topic of the day among ordinary Jamaicans. The end result, when the DJ is fully committed and everything falls into place, is a collage music that exposes the roots of hip hop, the dance remix, and the entire ethos of sampling. *Best Dressed Chicken* held cult crossover appeal because the backing tracks were as urgent as rock 'n' roll and as experimental as psychedelia, and because Thompson's vocals were outrageous and relatively simple to get for those who didn't understand Jamaican patois. Hugely influenced by James Brown, Thompson can do things with the word 'say' that close all gaps between preacher, seducer, stand-up comic and street-corner ranter.

The subjects of the best songs were deadly serious, but performed without the bullying machismo that now characterises the dancehall DJ. On 'Poison Flour' and 'Just The Other Day', Tado makes incisive links between JA agriculture – the closing of farms, the raising of prices, a shipment of contaminated flour – and the exploitation of the working class with rapier wit. 'I Killed The Barber' and 'Gimme Mi Gun' expose ghetto violence and the state's attacks on Rastafarians, somehow conjuring heroic defiance without descending into empty bravado. The voices of great reggae singers such as Gregory Isaacs and Horace Andy call-and-respond softly to Thompson's ribald testimonies, while the music rages and kids and gets cosmic. 'Poison Flour', in particular, is simply one of the most thrilling, frightening, stunning pieces of music ever conceived, a ragged army of minor-key scales and vocal jousts that reveals the oft-posited contention that political songs are clichéd for exactly what it is – cowardice and solipsism.

This is one of the major reasons why we were so sentimental about the passing of John Peel. I would never have heard this record if it wasn't for him, and this record made my life better. We can safely assume that no one will ever say this about Chris Moyles.

CHAIRS MISSING

WIRE
PRODUCED BY MIKE THORNE
HARVEST/SEPTEMBER 1978
UK CHART: 48
US CHART: DID NOT CHART
KEY TRACKS: 'Outdoor Miner'; 'I Am The Fly'; 'Mercy'; 'I Feel Mysterious Today'; 'Practice Makes Perfect'

One of the greatest guitar-rock albums of all time, the second Wire album is the perfect cross between the intimate minimalism of punk rock, and the enigmatic complexity of art-rock. It faces off constantly between beauty and ugliness, the creepy and the grungy, and makes a connection between the unsettling psychedelia of early Pink Floyd and the boisterous pop-metal of the Sex Pistols. We've already mentioned, in the entry for Pink Flag (see p.30), the long list of bands Wire influenced, but Chairs Missing forces you to mention The Beta Band, The Cure, Fugazi and maybe anyone since who made guitar music feel free to go anywhere it chooses without becoming bombastic or remote from the listener. The key track list above could easily read 'Used To'; 'Marooned'; 'Heartbeat'; 'Being Sucked In'; 'French Film (Blurred)' and would still be right, and wrong, and both.

As to why this band were so great, I find myself going back to the final line of 'I Feel Mysterious Today', when Colin Newman sings 'Did you ever conceive that you too can leave exactly when you like?', with his unique mix of raised-eyebrow tease and cockney friendliness. More and more you feel that Wire were obtuse and surreal because they could be, because that was the freedom that they were grateful for, and that they knew enough to know that the majority on this planet didn't have it, unless it was fought tooth and nail for. Perhaps this is why, although they have all the period charms and sonic quirks of a punk rock band, they sound so different . . . because they weren't angry, and wouldn't fake it, and were, in fact, delighted with their lot in life, and decided that punk, rather than say, disco or soft-rock, was the way they wanted to express that.

On the other hand, Chairs Missing could be one big obvious call for bloody revolution. I'm just guessing. Guessing, making you do the brain work, never taking one easy option, is what keeps you coming back to a music that never sounds quite the same as the last time you heard it. Few records make that kind of magic. It's a game of musical chairs where you always get to sit, but you're never sure what you're sitting on.

CANNIBALISM

CAN
PRODUCED BY CAN
UDM/OCTOBER 1978
UK CHART: DID NOT CHART
US CHART: DID NOT CHART
KEY TRACKS: 'Mother Sky'; 'Mushroom'; 'Halleluwah'; 'Yoo Doo Right'; 'Father Cannot Yell'

For years the only thing I'd heard of Cologne's Can was their one pop hit. 'I Want More' was this big catchy disco-meets-prog rock thing that went Top 30 in 1976, and I loved it. Lots of people said that Can's earlier stuff was a direct influence on my heroes Public Image Ltd, but still I didn't go investigate, largely because Can were pre-punk and had beards. But no problem, because it's great to discover things in your thirties, just as you're heading towards 'I know everything' territory.

Can were a ludicrously ahead-of-their-time collection of German squat-hippies who, from 1969 onwards, played a music that sought to give intellectually driven, avant-garde rock a funk pulse. *Cannibalism* is a compilation of Can's greatest moments from 1969 to 1974, where you can hear PiL, Talking Heads, Killing Joke, Blur, hip hop, trip hop, drum 'n' bass and Keane. I know, cheap shot. But why do cheap shots feel so good?

Playing from improvisations rather than formal song writing, they fashioned hypnotic drum and bass grooves – courtesy of the funkiest white rhythm section ever Jaki Liebezeit (drums) and Holger Czukay (bass) – over which vaguely demented, but entirely logical and often beautiful things would be done. Irmin Schmidt used keyboards as texture, Michael Karoli put traditional guitar licks in bizarre places with a wit and skill that makes him one of the great unsung guitar heroes, and some men yelped. And sang and screamed and mumbled and wailed and pleaded and cajoled. The first was Malcolm Mooney, who managed one album before succumbing to a nervous breakdown. His woman-worshipping howls for mercy could, perhaps, be summed up by the line from the disco-in-space masterpiece that is 'Father Cannot Yell', 'Woman screams "I am fertile!" And father can't yell.' He was replaced by Japanese ranter Damo Suzuki – tributed later by Mark E. Smith on The Fall's 'I Am Damo Suzuki' – who lasted four whole albums before running away to join the Jehovah's Witnesses. This band was not Coldplay. Suzuki's English-as-third-language, lyrical cut-up approach could, perhaps, be summed up by the line from ecstatic drone-poem 'Mother Sky', 'I say mothers ain't too cool like Mother Sky . . . Shalalooooooo!' Now that's one hell of a conversation on gender.

Another great thing about *Cannibalism* – apart from the fact that no matter how 'out there' a tune heads, it always sounds like the band are going to suddenly start giggling and launch into 'Woolly Bully' – is that the short sleevenotes are by none other than Pete Shelley of the Buzzcocks. He writes, 'I would never have played guitar had it not been for the late Marc Bolan and Michael Karoli of Can,' which perfectly sums up the unique mix of arty bedroom cult music and vivid surreal pop mania that begat British punk and everything that it led to for the next five years. Indeed, the best argument I can make to you about why Can aren't the apotheosis of boy-snob, no-tunes, Fear Of Music-creating music, of why you'll love this band without having to work to 'get it', is that you can play *Cannibalism* right next to T.Rex's *Electric Warrior* and they yell at each other like patriarchs of pop picking the kids up from music's eternal playground of possibilities.

Can – if they'd had a shave they would have been huge.

GERMFREE ADOLESCENTS

X-RAY SPEX

PRODUCED BY X-RAY SPEX
EMI/NOVEMBER 1978
UK CHART: 30
US CHART: DID NOT CHART
KEY TRACKS: 'The Day The World Turned Dayglo'; 'Identity'; 'I Am A Poseur'; 'Germfree Adolescents'; 'Let's Submerge'

Let's stick with thoughts about hippies and shaving for a moment. It's taken a few years to be accepted, but a truth about punk it that its most powerful presences were lapsed hippies. Malcom McLaren, John Lydon, Joe Strummer . . . all had been counter-culture longhairs at one time or another. The reason they despised hippy so much – apart from the obvious fact that setting yourself against the Last Big Thing is always a good commercial idea – was because it was originally a politically motivated youth tribe, yet had become a bunch of stoned fools hiding behind big hair and bad clothes, mithering about their failure to change the world,

GERMFREE ADOLESCENTS/X-RAY SPEX

and allowing the last subconscious vestiges of a radical thought to be removed by the pretty lasers and flying pigs at Pink Floyd concerts. So you cut your hair and buy some good clothes and make your music sharp and to the point and replace spectacular light shows with spectacular human interaction. But your basic ideas are still the same. Society is based upon the lie that you are what you buy. You see through this and attempt to act naturally and bond with others and create your alternative vision of society, or you live your life like the zombies staggering around the shopping mall in George Romero's *Dawn Of The Dead*. *Germfree Adolescents* is one of the most pungent and cogent critiques of what consumerism is, what it would become, and how it destroys our best attempts to be what we truly are. And the singer, lyricist and star of this most punk of punk records, Poly Styrene, was a hippy.

Before becoming Poly Styrene and forming X-Ray Spex in London, Brixton's Marion Elliott had been an itinerant traveller, an alternative fashion designer and a failed pop-reggae singer. She was 19. Mixed-race (her dad was Somali), feminist and possessed of an astonishing instinctive intellect and a paint-stripping avant-soul roar of a voice, she wrote a set of songs that betrayed the horror of having been smart enough to understand exactly what was going on. We were controlled by advertising and alienated by the built-in obsolescence of the plastics that surrounded us. Inundated by images of 'perfection' we could not hope to match, we shaved and cleaned and sprayed and took our flaws and smells and flesh away and replaced it with gooey stuff made of plastic and dead animals and walked out of our door and hoped to God we were acceptable and that someone wanted to fuck us and wondered why none of us could see or taste or smell each other, under all that Listerine and toothpaste and paint.

Whenever I watch an American teen comedy, and a character – always a girl – sees or hears or smells something basically human and exclaims, 'Eeyooh', with that prissy disgust that the American mainstream sees as a little spoilt but essentially correct, I think of Poly's huge teeth and braces on *Top Of The Pops*, and wonder how someone so young got our future so right.

The music is a sort of Pistols-derived metal with kazoo-like saxophones, which works spectacularly well on hit single 'Identity', which I pick out here because it's terrifying. Poly looks in a mirror and sees . . . the woman Marion Elliott? The punk rock star Poly Styrene? All of us? All three, specifically, because what she sees of herself is filtered through everything the media wants her to see, and once she sees what's really there she is so traumatised she wants to break the glass and slit her wrists. But she's no fool. She's already doing what we all do and imagining the post-death interview, because none of us exist outside the reality show we're all starring in on our own private twenty-four-hour channels. 'Did you do it for fame?/Did you do it in a fit?', the interviewer asks breathlessly, before asking the real question: 'Did you do it before you read about it?' Even suicide is inauthentic in Poly's nightmare world.

No surprise, then, that Poly went nuts, got better, quit music and retreated into the Hare Krishna cult. She makes a record every now and again, but not with any hype or careerism involved, presumably because she couldn't cope with the postmodern irony of being a plastic punk pop star, everything she despised, even if the wider point was satirical. What she left was a voice that epitomised punk's real aim, which was the attaining of freedom. Every time you hear a female rock singer who cuts through all the soft-porn subterfuge that corporate pop has used to repress and package female performers and consumers, the voice always sounds like Patti Smith, or Ari Up of The Slits, or the wonderful, courageous Poly. They could just be copying them. But I suspect it's because those three women found the source of something true about women, and if you find it too, you can't help be part of the same choir.

THE SCREAM

SIOUXSIE AND THE BANSHEES
PRODUCED BY STEVE LILLYWHITE AND SIOUXSIE AND
THE BANSHEES
POLYDOR/NOVEMBER 1978
UK CHART: 12
US CHART: DID NOT CHART
KEY TRACKS: 'Mirage'; 'Jigsaw Feeling'; 'Metal Postcard';
'Nicotine Stain'; 'Carcass'

The first thing you have to understand about Siouxsie and Steve Severin is the ambition and success of their imaginings. Susan Dallion and Steven Bailey of suburban Bromley imagined themselves as part of Bob Fosse's *Cabaret*, innocent decadents in a fascist nightmare. By the time Susan was nineteen, she was a suitably perverse version of Liza Minnelli as Sally Bowles and the female punk face of London. They imagined themselves as part of Andy Warhol's Factory and, although they were so far from subterranean New York in the 1960s, they became the centre of the 'Bromley Contingent' of kids who coalesced around the Sex Pistols, forming a sexually ambiguous family of hip urchin outsiders. Susan imagined herself as Siouxsie, and she and Steven imagined themselves playing an art-rock version of The Lord's Prayer at the 100 Club punk festival with Sid Vicious on drums and future Ant Marco Pirroni on guitar, and then Siouxsie imagined herself subverting the entire notion of the 'groupie' by using her sexuality to goad Bill Grundy into goading Steve Jones into swearing on peaktime TV, and launching punk as a mainstream obsession. Then Sioux and Severin became fans of '30s anti-Nazi Dadaist photo-montage artist John Heartfield, and imagined that they could use rock 'n' roll as a satirical exposé of the fascism that threatened to become a mass movement in the late '70s. Their use of swastikas, the word 'Jew' in early song 'Love In A Void', and a fantasy of industrial megalomania in 'Metal Postcard', from their debut album *The Scream*,

were, of course, misunderstood. But it wasn't being accused of flirting with fascism by a few self-righteous critics that caused any great problem. It was us, seeing Siouxsie as the untouchably beautiful, utterly formidable result of all these imaginings, and hearing Kenny Morris and John McKay reimagine the possibilities of rock drums and guitars, and being stunned by a sound so inky black, so clanging with disturbance and private neurosis, and deciding that the thing to do with this was buy black clothes and lots of mascara and invent 'goth'. When pop reaches a mass of people, irony dissipates utterly. The Clash and the 2-Tone bands became the anti-fascist standard-bearers because their opposition was obvious. The Banshees were grabbed onto as the punk band you could love without having to engage with anything other than private disgruntlement and a bland view of anti-parent perversity.

Still, maybe it doesn't matter. *The Scream* is still with us and still a darkly comic storm of musical innovation and youthful dread. I can't believe that four people pulled off something so brave and complete when barely out of nappies. But that's the power of imagination and politics, the two strongest things a young artist can make into smart bombs.

ALL MOD CONS

THE JAM
PRODUCED BY VIC COPPERSMITH-HEAVEN AND
CHRIS PARRY
POLYDOR/NOVEMBER 1978
UK CHART: 6
US CHART: DID NOT CHART
KEY TRACKS: 'Down In The Tube Station At Midnight'; 'In
The Crowd'; 'The Place I Love'; 'To Be Someone (Didn't We
Have A Nice Time)'; 'Billy Hunt'

The third Jam album still amazes. First album *In The City* is tough retro fun, second album *The Modern World* is an embarrassing train wreck, and neither give any clue of what an overworked and undervalued twenty-year-old from Woking would uncover while writing songs under deadline stress in the Summer of 1978. Paul Weller's rejection of punk's preachy demand – and of a punk scene that had dismissed him as a conservative country bumpkin even while stealing his riffs – took him from gruff mod revivalist and spent force to THE voice of the young British everyman in the four minutes that 'Down In The Tube Station . . . ' took to articulate our worst nightmares. Taking his cue from the storytelling skills of The Kinks' Ray Davies and the pop power-trio virtuosity of the early Who, Weller wrote a great concept album about male self-pity. This might sound like backhanded praise, but self-pity is a perfectly reasonable subject for art, and the self-pity of men is the perennial main ingredient for male violence. *All Mod Cons* – and what a great set of puns that title is – cast The Jam as victims of the music business (the title track, 'To Be Someone'), tribal street violence ('Tube Station', 'A' Bomb In Wardour Street'), consumer conformity ('In The Crowd'), and jealousy of men who seem, from beneath, to have everything under control ('Mr Clean', The Kinks' 'David Watts'). So Weller pens his own sequel to 'David Watts', embodying the loser male dreaming of a superhero alter-ego who'll sort out every insult with pure violence. 'Billy Hunt' rhymes with what Weller's character wants to be and is a scream, a tirade against the testosterone fantasies of bullies beaten by the reality of capitalism. *All Mod Cons*, more than any other rock album, provides a brilliantly written set of insights into the strain of British manhood that becomes football hooligan, right-wing skinhead, or just bloke-in-mob-who-wants-a-scrap-come-closing-time. Why was Weller so sharp on this subject? Because it was a part of him. *All Mod Cons* zings and stings with self-laceration.

But Weller wasn't just another suburban thug because he had his art, and the other part of that art *All Mod Cons* established was Weller's twin dream of deliverance – a quiet green place, and a perfect woman who loves you. 'English Rose' and 'Fly' were the conventional, plaintive love ballads of a man desperately in love at the time, and putting an ocean between himself and punk rock. Somewhere in that vast sea was an island Weller named 'The Place I Love', which he told us, with odd linguistic clumsiness, was 'Not within a yard of the trendy do's'. A private pastoral paradise, it was the place where Weller could declare, 'I'm making a stand against the world,' one of the most heroically futile lines in pop history, a line I still adore and see as the key to this record. Like X-Ray Spex and the Banshees, the age of the writer of such complex insights astounds, and the music makes this intelligence so soulful and subtle and real that you feel as if a stand against the world is not just possible, but compulsory.

THE BEST OF EARTH WIND & FIRE VOL. 1

EARTH WIND & FIRE
PRODUCED BY EARTH WIND & FIRE, SIG SHORE
CBS/NOVEMBER 1978
UK CHART: 6
US CHART: 6
KEY TRACKS: 'September'; 'Fantasy'; 'Shining Star'; 'Love Music'; 'Can't Hide Love'

Yow. How much do I adore Maurice White sneering the word 'Yow'? Much. Whenever an Earth Wind & Fire song is in severe danger of tripping over its own quasi-mystical pomposity, the great Maurice would just throw out a chewy, screwy, 'Yow' to let you know he knew. It's one of the great musical winks in pop history.

Chicago eleven-piece EW&F were one of the great commercial phenomena of the 1970s. Formed by Memphis-born singer/arranger/producer/composer Maurice White, who played drums in the 1960s on Chess and Motown soul, with the Ramsey Lewis trio, even with John Coltrane, they were the jazz-funk band that took cosmic black consciousness ideas from George Clinton, Sun Ra and avant-garde jazz, and made them into everyman pop. Though our knowledge of them is now dominated by the disco perennial that is 'Boogie Wonderland' (see p.61), EW&F were a far more ambitious rarity than any one dance classic could convey: a group adored by almost everyone who loved black music in the '70s, from mainstream soul and pop fans, to the ecstatic audiences at their legendary mother-shipping live shows, to soul connoisseurs who voted them the best band in the world year-upon-year in British black music mags *Echoes* and *Blues & Soul*. This collection of 1975–78 hits contains the reasons why they ruled, and yet have fallen off the critics' choice radar in the twenty-first century.

We critics like things obvious. If the singer sings, 'I am in existential torment,' then we can safely say he is in existential torment, and praise him for being deep, emotionally honest and authentic. If the singer sings, 'I love you and I'm happy,' we can safely say that he is a bland person who is just trying to ingratiate himself with a mass audience. Your average listener, being a little smarter, is not so easily fooled by the surface of things. When they looked at and listened to Earth Wind & Fire, they saw and heard a group working and thinking and striving and struggling to make a profound and complex musical vision into something that anyone could understand and feel lifted by. So, while the songs might say, 'Love will conquer all,' the dark and tough African rhythms, the charging and expansive horns, the tear-stained and holy ghostly falsetto harmonies of Philip Bailey, and the communal strength and glorious restlessness of the music made the subtext constant and insistent. The music said, 'We know life isn't this easy. We know bliss is hard to find. But before we can change anything, we have to overcome. And how can we find that will unless we believe there's a Utopia worth fighting for, and singing about?' A message that big only works if the music is accessible and generous enough to dwell on the connections between black and white and male and female and conformist and rebel, and make us sing the same song, dance to the same beat, dream the same dream, in order to understand that we are more similar than the world allows us to know. In the joy of, say, 'September', lies a vision of a promised land, a spiritual connection between listening, dancing, worship, sexual love and a communal spirit that only music, at its very best, allows us to experience in an era dominated by the lie of competition.

And if all that's a bit idealistic for you, then just wait for the bits where Maurice goes 'Yow'. They sting.

1979

LIVE AT THE WITCH TRIALS

THE FALL
PRODUCED BY THE FALL AND BOB SARGEANT
STEP FORWARD/JANUARY 1979
UK CHART: DID NOT CHART
US CHART: DID NOT CHART
KEY TRACKS: 'Frightened'; 'No Xmas For John Quays';
'Bingo-Master's Break-Out!'; 'Industrial Estate'; 'Underground
Medicin'

The Fall's debut album is perhaps their best, if only because
Mark E. Smith's bitterness is leavened by the thrill of being
here. The production is surprisingly clean, the plastic piano
a maddening USP, the Smith themes easier to pinpoint than
on later, artier or rockier Fall albums. It feels like the work of
someone too clued up for this world, doomed to crawl the
streets of Salford, Manchester, appalled by what passes for
fun, hoovering drugs and feeling the fear, getting back to
some poky room surrounded by piles of books and ultra-
cool psychedelic, soul, rockabilly and art-rock records,
knowing he's better than everyone, finding no solace at all in
that knowledge.

Fans of the album will spot that 'Bingo-Master's Break-
out!' was not on the original album. The 2002 reissue (on
Smith's own Cog Sinister label) added the three tracks that
make up the first Fall single, and 'Bingo-Master's Peter Kay
and *League Of Gentlemen*-predicting playground twist
makes *Witch Trials* even more complete. *Like Never Mind the
Bollocks* and *The Clash*, it feels like old scripts ripped
up and scores settled. Unlike them, it's under no illusions
that rock will change to meet it. It suspects that there's no
community out there to accept it. Listen to it and you can't
imagine how this turned into a thirty-album, twenty-seven-
years-and-counting career. But, as an example of intellectu-
alised working-class anger, it's nigh on unbeatable.

ARMED FORCES

ELVIS COSTELLO AND THE ATTRACTIONS
PRODUCED BY NICK LOWE
RADAR/JANUARY 1979
UK CHART: 2
US CHART: 10
KEY TRACKS: 'Chemistry Class'; 'Two Little Hitlers'; 'Green
Shirt'; '(What's So Funny 'Bout) Peace, Love And
Understanding'; 'Accidents Will Happen'

Proof that this book is written live, no overdubs. What I said
a couple of pages back about *This Year's Model* probably
being Elvis Costello's best album . . . really, I thought it was.
And now I've just played *Armed Forces* and . . . well . . .
blimey! What a record. Not just Costello's best, but one of
the best albums ever made. The toughest and best thing anyone can do when making an album is identify a theme that
bears a complex but unavoidable truth about the world, and
write a bunch of songs that illuminate that theme, and then
perform and produce them in such a way that anyone can
immerse themselves in the music and hear it as aural pleasure and worry about the theme itself only if they really want
to. It's where an artist and a listener commit to each other
and connect to each other in a way that has an almost supernatural significance – a conversation between two people
who have never met, which makes both parties' lives better.
Armed Forces is such a perfect example of this magic that it
leaves me in tears, even before you get to the Big Idea. And
the Big Idea is pretty enormous: the cruelty of the world in
geo-political terms is explicitly connected to the cruelty we
display in our personal relationships. The fascist regime and
the military massacre exist because they mirror the way we
treat our loved ones, particularly our lovers. There is no
other record that has thought this and made it stick. And to
write, play and produce this in the style of John Lennon
singing with Abba is both as audacious and generous as pop
music gets.

Also, and at the risk of sounding like the Johnny Mathis-loving talking gorilla from *Not the Nine O' Clock News*, the production on this album is amazing. So much musicianly power made so pretty, so much ornate loveliness that somehow suggests malignant ill-will and sticky fear. 'Are you ready for the final solution?' Costello asks over an agonising suspension of song in 'Chemistry Class', his voice a romantic threat in which disbelief at the chaotic psychological violence of our love affairs dissolves into a nightmare of the Holocaust. The nightmare rises from 'the damage that we do we'll never know', because 'Accidents Will Happen', and the accidents of love and lust destroy lives. Meanwhile, one set of (English) cannon fodder blow away another (Irish) set of cannon fodder on 'Oliver's Army', nice boys are recruited into the 'Goon Squad', names are taken through the TV on the bewildering but blistering 'Green Shirt', and, as we pretend that none of this is happening, we're addicted to the distraction of couplings where 'Two little Hitlers will fight it out until/One little Hitler does the other one's will'.

On the US version of *Armed Forces* that I love the best, Costello's strange declaration in 'Two Little Hitlers' – 'I will return/I will not burn' – segues into a final shot at redemption, a shot of hope, a stronger ending. '(What's So Funny 'Bout) Peace, Love And Understanding' is a refutation of both punk and Costello's own paranoid pessimism, singing out a demand for humanity's finest qualities in the deepest, most macho and soulful voice he ever sang in, implying that Costello has the strength to carry you there, refusing to accept the worst or plead for the best. It breaks my heart. It makes one of rock's greatest long-players even better.

SECONDHAND DAYLIGHT

MAGAZINE
PRODUCED BY COLIN THURSTON
VIRGIN/MARCH 1979
UK CHART: 38

US CHART: DID NOT CHART
KEY TRACKS: 'Permafrost'; 'I Wanted Your Heart'; 'Back To Nature'; 'Feed The Enemy'; 'Believe That I Understand'

Let's talk bass. One of the most fundamental things about the period of rock that we're now dealing with is the plethora of astonishing bass-players. The art-punks' fascination with reggae, funk, disco and Can persuaded them to place bass at the centre of their noise, a deep, physical and black way out from under the thrash of the Ramones and the metal wall of the Sex Pistols. The list is long but worth making: Paul Simonon of The Clash; Peter Hook of Joy Division; Tina Weymouth of Talking Heads; Steve Severin of the Banshees; Dave Allen of Gang Of Four; Jah Wobble of PiL; Bruce Foxton of The Jam and, yes, even Sting and, perhaps especially, Jean-Jacques Burnel of The Stranglers, who single-handedly made his morbid, misogynist and cynical little band listenable. All gave post-punk a sensuality, swing

THE UNDERTONES/THE UNDERTONES

and depth that rock usually can't be arsed with, and all were so distinct that they overtook the singer and guitarist as the key element of their bands' sounds.

The Fall, The Attractions and Magazine all had bass heroes. Marc Riley (now better known as radio presenter Lard), Bruce Thomas and Barry Adamson are all key to the first three classic albums of 1979. They offer intimacy and humanity when their genius singers become remote and superior, and they really had to do that, because Mark E. Smith, Elvis Costello and Howard Devoto could be as remote and superior as anyone has a right to be when making popular art. *Live At The Witch Trials*, *Armed Forces* and *Secondhand Daylight* all often sound like conversations between the sex and sinew and pulsing humanity of the basslines, and the body-revulsion and bookishness of the singer and songwords, dramatising that eternal tension between intellect and instinct, articulating the envy and inadequacy we analytical, thinking boys feel in the face of athletic, macho boys who get straight to . . . ahem . . . the meat of the matter. Without their bass-players, all these smart geeks would've just been irritatingly smug and off-puttingly sexless.

Of course, Smith, Costello and Devoto had other things in common. They came from the north-west of England, and balanced surreal articulacy with northern plain-speaking. They were undernourished and weird of face and wore bad clothes until they became great clothes. And their favourite subjects were fear, paranoia and an overwhelming suspicion that people were more stupid than they could possibly imagine. For Smith, that was about bourgeois values, hellish environments and woolly thinking. For Costello and Devoto, it was largely about love and sex. So, while Costello suggested that love was a tumour, and pairing-off was a war between two little Hitlers annexing the Poland of each other's free will, Devoto began from that premise and dived into its murky depths, alternating between howling in fear and laughing his head off.

Secondhand Daylight is the second album by Devoto, Adamson, keyboardist Dave Formula, guitarist (the late) John McGeoch and drummer John Doyle. It explains why Devoto left the Buzzcocks, because Magazine's music was more closely related to the despised progressive rock than it is to punk. The sharp, anti-hippy elements lie in Devoto's deliberately slimy-creep vocals, and the ahead-of-its-time fascination with film music, particularly the spy thriller mood-jazz of the great John Barry. Devoto used these frosty, suspenseful backdrops as fuel for lines coloured by half-remembered B-movie dialogue. 'This is as close as I get,' Devoto tells another enemy lover on the hysterical epic that is 'I Wanted Your Heart', and it conjures weasels in trench coats, pointing guns, always backing out.

The album ends with Magazine's greatest song, one of the best rock songs by anyone, in fact. 'Permafrost' is a threat set to a sullen, shimmering throb, where a simple but spectacular McGeoch guitar solo is another pistol poked into your spine, and where Devoto finally steps over the line, lets his fear of love control him, tries to play the sexual heavy. 'I will drug you and fuck you', he seethes, in a voice never matched in its nastiness, its madness, 'On the permafrost.' Its implication – that men can only resolve their own weaknesses in violence, or, at least, a sexual imitation of violence – is as final and horrible as any conclusion to any album ever made. But its horror was not the conservative's hatred of people, but the radical's challenge to transcend. For this listener at that time, having your worst potential instincts explained to you at sixteen was education at its best. Devoto, like Costello, set down the terms for trying to become a better man. Thank fuck I was listening to them, and not The Stranglers.

THE UNDERTONES

THE UNDERTONES
PRODUCED BY ROGER BECHIRAN
SIRE/MAY 1979

UK CHART: 13
US CHART: DID NOT CHART
KEY TRACKS: 'Teenage Kicks'; 'Male Model'; 'Get Over You';
'Girls Don't Like It'; 'Billy's Third'

Like so many best things, the best album ever made about being a teenage boy covers a multitude of complexities with the deception of simplicity. Feargal Sharkey, Mickey Bradley, Billy Doherty, and brothers John and Damian O'Neill came from Londonderry in northern Ireland, and their songs ignored 'the troubles' so obsessively that they provided the most profound information about growing up under occupation. All teenage rock 'n' roll is about escape, to some extent. But The Undertones had more to escape from than most. By writing a set of classic songs about girls, hormones and teenage chaos they not only set up their own escape from a grim reality, but humanised a nation of people we saw as nothing but one-dimensional murderers and victims. All those '70s news images of poor boys born to kill, die or suffer were suddenly illuminated; of course, they were just like us. They wanted girls, fun, male-bonding, girls, orgasms, clothes and girls. The Northern Irish 'reality' of soldiers, terrorists, bombs and bigotry added up to nothing when compared to your feelings for the perfect girl, the perfect record, the special thrill of partying in a place where you had to create your own culture. *The Undertones* is suffused with the agony and ecstasy of being young, and is one of the few records that truly understands that the pain and the pleasure are roughly the same beautiful thing, and that we are more alive between the ages of sixteen and twenty than we will ever be again, for better or for worse.

But *The Undertones* is even slyer than that. Behind the high-impact pleasures of Sex Pistols guitars, Ramones urgency, catchy melodies, Bechiran's sparkling production and the extraordinary, androgynous white soul voice of Feargal Sharkey, is the depiction of an underground milieu almost as culturally and sexually slippery as Lou Reed's New York. The opening glam-thump fanfare that is 'Family Entertainment' is surely about incest . . . possibly parental abuse. The album's great anthem, the immortal 'Teenage Kicks' is a paean to masturbation, the only song to make wanking sound romantic and a source of masochistic joy rather than dirty shame. The girls celebrated in the likes of 'She's A Runaround', 'Get Over You' and 'I Know A Girl' are outcasts, rebels and Miss Understoods . . . the blueprints for all those bullied but adorable Goths, geeks, lesbians and mavericks that spark great American teen movies and TV serials. The extent of their admiration for these feminist firebrands, particularly within the lyrics of John O'Neill and the adoring quiver of Sharkey's voice, is because these girls come from a place where 'rebel' has an entirely different connotation to the rock norm, and where any woman not willing to conform to either of the most extreme ends of the protestant-catholic divide was risking something far more violent than being labelled a slut or a witch. For The Undertones, these girls are role models for their own liberation and are duly treated with an earthy awe.

And then, of course, there was 'Jimmy Jimmy', where a small 'silly' boy who 'did what he was told' disappears in an ambulance that no one sees. At the time, the band denied all suggestions that it was about a victim of the Irish conflict, but, let's face it, they had to, not so much for their own safety, but for the subversive resonance of the song. After all, post-Undertones, The O'Neill brothers formed That Petrol Emotion, a band devoted almost entirely to Irish republican agitprop. They were modern, committed, smart and worthy. Yet the entire TPE catalogue didn't come close to the power and poetry of the opening line of 'Get Over You': 'Dressed like that you must be living in a different world.' It's that ability of the brave, imaginative, working-class young – to create a different, better world in their own backyard using nothing but art, fashion and defiant self-belief – that The Undertones captures so spectacularly. It's a youth club where the pop always pops, the times are always good, and the traumas of home can't compete with the thrill of a better future.

I AM

EARTH WIND & FIRE
PRODUCED BY MAURICE WHITE
CBS/JUNE 1979
UK CHART: 5
US CHART: 3
KEY TRACKS: 'Star'; 'In The Stone'; 'Boogie Wonderland';
'Can't Let Go'; 'Let Your Feelings Show'

It was tempting to just stick this in with the December 1978 EW&F best-of (see p.53) and have done with it. The music is pretty much identical to the naked ear, and the themes of universal love even more so. But *I Am* has to stand alone, simply because it is the high watermark of an extraordinary group, and a hugely popular attempt to present a complicated truth. The album's title may appear to be promoting that great American value, the primacy of the individual, but the songs themselves argue that the only way to understand one's self is to embrace community, and that these two apparently contradictory aims are absolutely and irrevocably connected. When placed in the context of Afro-American music and life, and the legacy of the (unfinished) struggle to escape from slavery, *I Am* is revealed as an argument against the aggressive materialism of both the 1980s, and of a new generation of black American attitude which found its expression in commercial hip hop. In Maurice White's worldview, cleverly submerged beneath all those crossover-friendly platitudes about love and dancing, is a discourse about his community's denial of the horrors and humiliations of the past, and how those who ignore their own history are condemned to believe their salvation lies in Rolex and Rolls-Royce . . . Or whichever brand name is elected God this week, made holy by the very fact that none of its worshippers can attain it. And what is God if not The Great Unattainable?

So status-anxiety begats competition begats greed begats crime begats black-on-black violence. And what makes Maurice and Co. so amazing is that they say that without ever saying that. Earth Wind & Fire were survivors of an era where the most visionary soul and jazz performers gave their audience enormous credit for picking up subtext and subtle layers of meaning without allowing self-righteousness to interfere. They trusted us. It's a moot point whether it's rappers or their audience who've done most damage to that bond of trust over the last twenty years. But it perhaps explains why Earth Wind & Fire sound cheesy and irrelevant to rap-educated ears. The true genius of a group like this is written in the stone. But who's got the time or desire to go mining anymore?

THE B-52'S

THE B-52'S
PRODUCED BY CHRIS BLACKWELL

DRUMS AND WIRES/XTC

ISLAND/JULY 1979
UK CHART: 22
US CHART: 59
KEY TRACKS: 'Rock Lobster'; 'Dance This Mess Around'; '52
Girls'; 'Planet Claire'; 'There's A Moon In The Sky (Called The
Moon)'

The B-52's' world is close to perfection. It's a place where you can be under the sea, or directly under a volcano, or on the moon, or on a planet called Claire where no one has a head, and yet there's no danger at all, as long as you keep dancing and imagining. In this world those two things go hand-in-hand, and challenge the very idea that rock 'n' roll ever had to mean anything real at all.

Originally a five-piece-band from Athens, Georgia, The B-52's were led by a fairground barker called Fred Schneider and a human Theremin called Kate Pierson. Their twin lead vocals were the friendliest gender war around, as Pierson's extraordinary girl-group trills and hollers gave the band all their sex and colour, while Fred just shouted non sequiturs in a cracked nasal tone that suggested a kind of benevolent madness. Their great achievement was concocting a dance music that owed nothing to funk, disco or reggae . . . particularly ironic as their producer Blackwell was the white guy who brought reggae to the wider world through his promotion and rocking-up of Bob Marley. What Blackwell understood was rhythm sections and the importance of space – hooray! – in a sound. The drums and bass swing and punch through everything. The guitar is punk-tough but chugs nuttily rather than thrashes. And Pierson's peerless organ comes in and laughs and points, sneers and wiggles and giggles, and then sods off before it can become an irritating gimmick. It all works out best on their debut album – as it so often does – because it's too new to sound anything but innocent. And when you're throwing a party like 'Rock Lobster', where catfish chase dogfish and the boys wear the bikinis, any hint that this inspired silliness is an actual job of work kills the whole thing stone dead.

Switch off the album before the 'ironic' version of Petula Clark's 'Downtown', though. It gives away The B-52's' game in advance.

DRUMS AND WIRES

XTC
PRODUCED BY STEVE LILLYWHITE
VIRGIN/AUGUST 1979
UK CHART: 34
US CHART: DID NOT CHART
KEY TRACKS: 'Making Plans For Nigel'; 'Complicated Game';
'Ten Feet Tall'; 'Scissor Man'; 'Helicopter'

When I hear XTC's third album I'm immediately back in Peterborough in 1979. I'm sixteen and queuing for tickets to see them at the Wirrina stadium. 'Rock Lobster' is playing in my head and I'm completely obsessed with pop and still at school and every record in 1979 just seems like the new Meaning Of Life. Post-punk and punk-funk and disco and 2-Tone and early indie-pop. All of them have so much character and inspiration and groove. And now bands have started coming to Peterborough and XTC are perhaps the best. And one of the loudest, too. XTC weren't no quirky pastoral wimps . . . at least, not yet.

The reason why *Drums And Wires* is the best XTC album is because it's the XTC album that best represents the band as equals. Drummer Terry Chambers does a star turn, flitting from tribal rumbles to reggae to disco to rock with power and purpose. Guitarist Dave Gregory replaces Barry Andrews's kitschy keyboards and becomes Andy Partridge's six-string twin. But bassist Colin Moulding is the key man here. It's almost as if, having absorbed Partridge's entire unique style of songwriting, he sets out to be better at it, and largely succeeds. The album submerges XTC's clever-clever archness beneath the tension of a friendly(?) rivalry, and it's the quiet, unassuming Moulding who ends up writing and singing XTC's two best angry songs.

There are levels of personal resentment within 'Making Plans For Nigel' that one can only guess at. The hit single uses a monumental groove – a sort of industrial reggae, with all reggae's usual gaps filled with concrete – to tell the tale of middle-class boys whose lives are mapped out by their doting parents. In Moulding's moulding hands, the line, 'He has his future inna British Steel' is both the slyest of jokes and the bleakest of white-collar nightmares. Not least because, within a few years of Thatcherism, no one would have a future in British Steel.

And while Partridge responds with quirk-rage classics – the thinly disguised revenge-of-the-nerd evil nursery rhyme that is 'Scissor Man', the fear-of-women punk-disco fun of 'Helicopter' – Moulding provides the shattering end to the album. 'Complicated Game' is simple satire made into fierce rage by the dubwise storm of the band's performance. Moulding begins in a whisper, asking if he should put his finger on the left or right. Then a girl asks which way she should part her hair. Then a boy asks where he should put his vote. It's such a puzzling decision to make that God Himself finally asks Moulding where he should put the whole wide world. But Moulding's been trying to explain the reality of things, should God have cared to listen. 'I said God it really doesn't matter where you put your world/Because someone else will come along and move it/And it's always been the same/It's just a complicated game.' The final shrug is not a shrug at all. It's the reason the world gives for fucking with the most inarguable facts of right and wrong. And Moulding's howling now and the band boil up a tightly leashed hysteria at the thought of how easily so few convince so many that the world is too complicated to change for the better.

Maybe it was all a sort of therapy for Moulding. Because he never wrote anything so incendiary again, and seemed content to settle for a long stretch as Partridge's quiet sidekick. Still, never mind. For a few months in 1979, he was the best songwriter in the smartest, most original pop group in existence. And if he says he's happy, he must be happy in his work.

UNKNOWN PLEASURES

JOY DIVISION
PRODUCED BY MARTIN HANNETT
FACTORY/AUGUST 1979
UK CHART: DID NOT CHART
US CHART: DID NOT CHART
KEY TRACKS: 'Disorder'; 'New Dawn Fades'; 'She's Lost Control'; 'Shadowplay'; 'Interzone'

Joy Division, lest we forget, began as just another Manchester punk band, inspired to thrash by seeing the Sex Pistols. Then their manager Rob Gretton decided not to sign his band to a major and stuck with local label Factory, despite the fact that Factory owner Tony Wilson had no money to throw at them, and Wilson put them in a studio with a mad junkie producer called Martin Hannett who wanted to be the Phil Spector of The Grim North. Hannett fucked endlessly with the sound and the band members' heads and, it seems, only lead singer Ian Curtis approved of what he was doing. But Hannett was right and created a sound that reflected the dark edges of the city, a rock that rejected all known forms of rocking, that transformed Peter Hook's bass into lead instrument, that moved with the clunks and clanks of mechanised industry, that smashed glass and suggested the swish of cars on night's rainy streets, that made you believe that it was the desolate, echoey noise of the thoughts inside Ian Curtis's head. It was a dry, spacey, dirty, elegant, inky thing, and, more than all the other innovators of the era, it sounded like nothing that anyone had ever done before.

And then there's the words and the voice.

The voice was granite and sex and pain and brutal honesty. On 'Insight' it sings, 'I remember when we were young' at the age of just twenty-three and sounds like the oldest of all voices, like a rock of ages. Within the rolling, blessed, bereft beauty of 'New Dawn Fades' it croons, 'A loaded gun won't set you free, so you say,' with so much horrible yearning for relief, and then howls the word 'Me' with such self-loathing that you almost want the loaded gun to end this nightmare for the owner of the voice, who didn't ask for this . . . none of us did.

But, at this point, on this record, relief comes from mystery and thrill. 'Shadowplay' brings Manchester to life as the setting for a northern film noir, where meeting a girl for a city centre night out becomes a drama of waiting, of assassins on the dance floor, of Barney Sumner's guitar laughing and weeping as it pulls the trigger, of the unbearable betrayal as the voice sings, 'I let them use you . . . for their own ends!' Nights out at Annabelle's in Peterborough were never like this.

And 'Interzone' is great because it's the strangest heavy metal, like someone sucked all the air out of Motorhead. It's a dirty job . . .

Joy Division is why I can't listen to Nirvana, or Nine Inch Nails, or any of those other hate-myself-and-want-to-die pornographers of misery. The insights are too shallow and vain, the music too plain, the hope too absent. Maybe it's because I'm an Englander, that Curtis's view of depression – and Hannett's exquisite framing of it – is something that I do relate to. You want to scream 'Rape me!' or somesuch tantrum, but you don't because it's showy and undignified and rape is something done to you, not craved. And if the British working class don't have a stiff upper lip and an ability to front it out, we have nothing. Curtis's deep, rich, impossible voice is the very essence of stoicism and strength under pressure, and the fact of his suicide doesn't negate that. Perhaps his voice was not the real him, but what he wanted to be. *Unknown Pleasures* sounds like a man trying to cure himself, not wallowing in the pleasurable self-pity of his goodbye to this cruel world.

Not that I'd play this to someone who felt suicidal. It's too precise, too much of a kill or cure. Which, in its way, explains why we've ended up with Coldplay. Empty misery is soothing to those who don't want to look too closely at the facts. Some of us, though, would rather take it, and take it straight. And, yep, obvious, but, yep . . . *Unknown Pleasures* puts my problems into perspective, because I've never hurt like this. Nowhere near.

OFF THE WALL

MICHAEL JACKSON
PRODUCED BY QUINCY JONES ('DON'T STOP 'TIL YOU GET ENOUGH' CO-PRODUCED BY MICHAEL JACKSON)
EPIC/AUGUST 1979
UK CHART: 5
US CHART: 3
KEY TRACKS: 'Don't Stop 'Til You Get Enough'; 'I Can't Help It'; 'It's The Falling In Love'; 'Get On The Floor'; 'Off the Wall'

My sixth-form common room had a stereo and precisely three albums. *Zenyatta Mondatta* by The Police, *Bat Out Of Hell* by Meatloaf and *Off The Wall* by Michael Jackson were the only three records all of us could listen to without wanting to kill each other. Ever since then, the mere mention of either Bat or Zenyat is like some brainwashing trigger mechanism, whereby I revert to a miserable wretch in an ill-fitting hoodie, wondering how I ended up in a school where the college-bound seventeen-year-olds found Blondie too extreme. Yet I never stopped loving *Off The Wall*, and it still triggers teen romance in discos and discovering black pop and everything exciting and hopeful about being young and, well, up for it. But, there's a sadness too, and it's nothing to do with wishing I was young again. It's all to do with Michael. Because once upon a time – and I realise this will sound somewhat bizarre – once upon a time, Michael Jackson was a symbol of all that was great and good about humanity.

This wasn't to do with his work for charity or something, or anything, in fact, to do with Michael Jackson – The Real Person. He was something to admire and feel good about because he was a beautiful young black man who sang and – especially – danced better than anyone else. When this man strutted his elegant stuff, he could make an atheist believe in God. And then . . . we figured Elvis had the ultimate fall-from-grace story, but Michael – give the boy his due – set about making that gross decline look like small beer.

Ah, but look at the *Off The Wall* cover shot! Michael standing in front of a brown brick wall – like an uptown black Ramone! – with thumbs in pockets of tuxedo trousers, giving it a bit of Jazz Hands. He is confidence, taste and charm, and the smile is the essence of pleasure and hope and how-do-you-do?, and the nose is broad and the skin is deep brown and, best of all, the hair is an Afro. A big black African Afro which carries no hint of its future as a set of wet strands plastered over what's left of this face, in some surreal parody of what someone might believe is the ultimate racially unspecific do. I'm looking at this picture now, and the innocent beauty of it, a classic pop style that represents, utterly, the mix of black soul and gay disco and the jazz virtuosity of the great Quincy Jones that is the music I'm listening to now, and it breaks my fucking heart, and that's well before I get to wondering just who and how and how many people this Perfect Boy has . . . well, you get it.

But *Off The Wall* is still the greatest black pop deluxe album ever made. And, to paraphrase another similarly disgraced pop star who gave me innocent pleasures as a boy, I'd rather remember Michael Jackson this way.

FEAR OF MUSIC

TALKING HEADS
PRODUCED BY BRIAN ENO AND TALKING HEADS
SIRE/AUGUST 1979
UK CHART: 33

US CHART: 21
KEY TRACKS: 'Cities'; 'Air'; 'Mind'; 'Animals'; 'Life During Wartime'

Why do particular songs mean so much to you?

Sure, I know. There are the songs that provide a life soundtrack, the ones you associate with school, first kiss, first disco, falling in love, a holiday moment. No puzzlement there. No, I mean the ones that you associate with nothing except themselves, and which don't even bear some direct lyrical reference to your own life or worldview. Yet, when you hear them, they make time stop. They fascinate and inspire and set off hours of contemplation of the meaning of meaning. They lift you up where you belong, where the eagles fly, on a mountainside. Bet you're thanking me for putting that in your head for the rest of the day. I am cruel and unusual, occasionally.

Anyway, 'Cities' by Talking Heads doesn't feature Joe Cocker or give me disturbing feelings about Richard Gere. I don't even remember first hearing it. Yet I'm kind of obsessed with it. It's one of their fast and flailing funky ones, where all the instruments bicker and laugh at themselves. It's about cities. David Byrne sings about looking for a city in which to live, and what might attract you to it. He suggests that Birmingham (I surmise Birmingham, Alabama, but maybe not) might be good because it has a 'dry ice factory', which would be 'A good place to get some thinking done'. He observes that London is 'A small city' where people sleep all day, 'If they want to! If they want to!' Man, even typing that fills me with joy and I haven't the faintest bleedin' clue what he's on about. I guess, before any other subconscious reason for the grip 'Cities' has upon me, it has the funniest vocal performance, a stew of hysteria about almost nothing at all . . . except, of course, that the place you choose to live in is one of the most important decisions you ever make.

Fear Of Music is an album that reflects the way we think. Not what we think, but the way our minds flit from one subject to another, and alight on something, and obsess about it

FEAR OF MUSIC/TALKING HEADS

until we've excavated all its humours and horrors and realised we're driving ourselves recognisably insane. At least, I assume that's how we all think, otherwise it's just me and David Byrne, which scares me. It's the best record by pop's leading student of paranoia and psychological turmoil, whose gift is understanding that the fear of insanity is closely related to – inseparable from – how funny and stimulating dallying with it can be. So *Fear Of Music* gets darker and darker as you sink into its world and unpeel its layers, but can be listened to while washing-up and thinking about the Spurs midfield without casting you into a world of pain. For those of us who live with the mental health issue best encompassed by the word 'PANIC!!!', I think this record, and early Talking Heads generally, sums up what it feels like, and why it isn't always that bad, can be quite creative, and is, sometimes, a living hell. This is why 'Animals' takes the thought that non-humans must have an easier life without an intellect to a conclusion which is mainly hilarious, but kind of not. Why 'Life During Wartime' could actually just be called 'Life' and would still carry the same post-holocaust imagery. Why 'Drugs' is the only description of being on drugs which sounds both thrilling and terrifying, while also being comically mundane.

I've said why this book's called *Fear Of Music*. Maybe this record's called *Fear Of Music* because the paranoid's greatest wish is for peace of mind (as 'Heaven' puts it, 'Heaven is a place where nothing ever happens'), and David Byrne thought that making music would be his psychological salvation, and, after four years in the biz, it had become the opposite: the trigger for all fears of responsibility and money and power and approval and broken friendship and just royally fucking up. Like they say, you can't run away from yourself, not to art, not to a better city. For some, I suspect London or wherever they are is always dark, dark in the daytime.

ENTERTAINMENT!

GANG OF FOUR

PRODUCED BY ANDY GILL, JON KING AND ROB WARR
EMI/SEPTEMBER 1979
UK CHART: 45
US CHART: DID NOT CHART
KEY TRACKS: 'I Found That Essence Rare'; 'At Home He's A Tourist'; 'Anthrax'; 'Not Great Men'; 'Damaged Goods'

'Just keep quiet/No room for doubt' – 'Guns Before Butter', Gang Of Four. 'No room to move/No room for doubt' – 'Feed the Enemy', Magazine

Post-punk was about doubt, whereas disco and black pop were about aspiration, affirmation and comfort, and punk and reggae were about the high moral ground and the surety that provides, the bands that tried to meld punk with all those more musical musics were suspicious of absolutes. They were curious, well-read, counter-cultural boys and girls, and the more you know about history, sociology, politics and the world outside your own, the less sure about anything you become. This is why many of us choose not to. It makes every move harder when you become someone who constantly questions why you're making it and, more disturbingly, who's making you make it. There is no pop album that looks at doubt and where it stems from more surgically than *Entertainment!* by Leeds-based students Gang Of Four.

Andy Gill, Jon King, Dave Allen and Hugo Burnham wrote songs derived from a Marxist analysis of the world, and determined to find a new kind of rock 'n' roll that would make that idea something other than the most boring thing a pop kid could contemplate. To this end, they used punk's lo-fi urgency as a base on which to add funk, African rhythms, dub and – quite uniquely and with extraordinary vision – old-fashioned, white rhythm 'n' blues, with liberal doses of the Stones and the amphetamine cattle-prod guitar of Wilko Johnson, from Canvey Island's legendary Dr Feelgood.

As their career progressed, it became obvious that no one could make Marxist analysis into Big Chart Pop, and disillusion and compromise seeped out of their later records. But the Sex Pistols had made many young people believe that anything was possible, and the Gang Of Four's first album therefore makes life-altering magic out of blending a bleak, anti-pop worldview with the thrill of being allowed to do this by, of all people, EMI. Its brilliant tensions come from utter faith in their quest to inform and excite and the inevitability of revolution, battling with a view of the world that implied – by its dreadful doubt of the realness of everything – that we had been conned and brainwashed so thoroughly that revolution was impossible. It's an album by young men who know too much and are still foolish enough to think that that's a good thing.

So, although Gang Of Four never became huge, they attracted fanaticism among those who could bear the message, or simply found the complete re-wiring of groove irresistible. The main place that this happened, with an irony that the four must have appreciated, was the Evil Empire of The USA, whose attitudes to human interaction and popular entertainment were lampooned on *Entertainment!*'s blood-red sleeve art, where a cowboy offers the hand of brotherhood to a native American, because, 'Now he can exploit him.' American outsiders such as Kurt Cobain, Michael Stipe, Flea and Anthony Kiedis related, and formed some bands. And then, after being pretty much wiped from history for fifteen years, the millennium ended and began and Gang Of Four were rediscovered by a whole new set of young college boys and girls. They continue to be something close to The Coolest Band In The World, as everyone cops their rhythms, guitar style and deliberately blank, human voices. It's nice to hear, and it's woken up the Brit alternative rock scene a little, and I'm glad the GO4 get to reform and sell some back catalogue.

But none of these new bands are actually anything like Gang Of Four, and, despite hacks like me flagging up the post-punk revival, yer KillerKaiserFerdinands have nowt,

really, to do with post-punk. These smart kids are sure that they want to be rock stars and are sure that contriving a way to do that is surely absolutely fine. Politics is a bummer. There is no room for doubt, because doubt doesn't sell for long. The post-punk bands proved that. As interviewees, they don't want to take responsibility for anything other than being consumed. Gang Of Four and the art-music scene they were central to was explicitly about the fact of being consumed.

Entertainment! sees the world as a Matrix-like product of false consciousness. Even our most personal choices – love, sex and leisure – are hallucinations, products to be bought and used in specific ways, otherwise the ingredients won't work and the manufacturer will take no responsibility for your breakdown. The twist is, we asked for it, and renew that plea every day. 'I knew I'd get what I asked for,' Gill and King sing on ' . . . Essence Rare', knowing but helpless, their irony

their only succour. The whole record hurts, but with such a charge of freshness and fury that, even though it makes you feel guilty for not making this false construct stop, it delights with how right it is, even about things that hadn't truly formed in 1979, and surround us now.

One of the very, very greatest records ever made. But not everyone will like. Some lives are so full they leave no room for doubt.

LIVE AT THE COUNTER EUROVISION 79

MISTY IN ROOTS
PRODUCED BY CHRIS BOLTON WITH DANIEL LÉON AND PHILIPPE OHSÉ
PEOPLE UNITE/SEPTEMBER 1979
UK CHART: DID NOT CHART
US CHART: DID NOT CHART
KEY TRACKS: 'Ghetto Of The City'; 'How Long Jah!'; 'Judas Iscariote'; 'Sodome And Gomorra'; 'Man Kind'

You may be thinking, if you've been reading right up to this point, that this chap takes his 1979 albums really, really seriously. And you'd be right. But it wasn't all dark-night-of-the-soul and revolutionary tracts and black American virtuosity. Some records, just occasionally, made me laugh, and still do.

I don't want to be too backhanded to British roots reggae band Misty In Roots, particularly as they're still recording and performing (they have a website at www.mistyinroots.ws), which is kind of heroic. They were one of the key bands of the Rock Against Racism movement, and John Peel played this album to death, which is where I heard it, and why I loved it. But there are very few musical genres that take themselves as seriously your Rastafarian 'roots and culture' types, and even fewer that have been allowed to by their diehard fans and we music journalists. Now, there's reggae I take very seriously indeed (see The Congos, p.8), but isn't there anyone else that has an affection for this stuff because it's, you know, kinda silly? And pretty camp?

So this here live album begins with a bloke called William Simon Smokes (I know, I know) making a speech about the deep meaning behind the music. I think he's supposed to sound simultaneously spiritual, authoritative and stoned. He just sounds gay. It's brilliant, I'm really not complaining. He implies that the good people of Brussels – where this socialist festival affair is taking place – are cabbages. Anyway, he finishes his speech, a sudden cut, and we have one of the eight members of Misty In Roots making another introduction. Slightly less gay, slightly more stoned. 'I'd like to say good evenin'. Or good mornin'. This one called "Man Kind" . . . you . . . a sinner.' Cheers! Let the bacchanal commence!

From here on in, it's seven tracks of truly great live reggae, all rousing harmonies and doubled-up 'steppers' rhythms (no, I steadfastly bloody refuse to call them 'riddims'), churchy organ swells providing the prettiness, chopping guitar and militant bass providing the skankiness. 'Ghetto Of The City' is an all-time reggae classic, full of guys shouting 'Killah!', making frog noises, and doing the funny high popping noise from the back of the throat, like Althia & Donna on 'Uptown Top Ranking'. But the laughs just keep on coming. Another spoken intro for 'How Long Jah!' consists of a guy intoning 'How long must we feel the pain?' in the manner of a granny with backache. Each song treats what I think we can safely assume is a largely white middle-class audience to yet more damning judgements upon their entire existence. Someone switches the echo button on during the jolly 'Judas Iscariote' (obviously Slade fans) and a bloke actually says, 'Rub-a-dub fashion!' I mean, this really wouldn't be here unless I loved it to bits. But did we ever really take this Old Testament tosh and Marley-robbing seriously?

Best of all, though, is the Ramones-ish art statement of it all. A member of the band makes his 'listen up, you unworthy lefty nerds! This one's even more vengeful and misanthropic than the last one' intro speech, and the drums roll portentously and . . . the song is exactly the same as the last one! Like, identical! Maybe it really is a sly concept album about rock fans who insist all reggae sounds the same. What better way to take the piss than make a whole album that does?

What can I say. We take our pleasures where we can, and this record makes me giggle, and do comedy skanking round the lounge, and these are pleasures indeed. I hope the band aren't too offended if they see this. But, considering most of their lyrics were informing me that God was going to consume my part of the planet in eternal hellfire and the dreads would skank upon our graves, I think we're roughly quits.

CUT

THE SLITS

PRODUCED BY DENNIS BOVELL
ISLAND/SEPTEMBER 1979
UK CHART: 30
US CHART: DID NOT CHART
KEY TRACKS: 'I Heard It Through The Grapevine'; 'Ping Pong Affair'; 'Shoplifting'; 'FM'; 'Typical Girls'

> 'We consciously thought about getting girl rhythms into music and concluded that female rhythms were probably not as steady, structured or as contained as male rhythms. We wanted to keep the rhythms skippy and light.' – Viv Albertine, The Slits

The quote above, taken from the sleevenotes for the 2000 reissue of *Cut* written by Mark Paytress, is a wonderful thing. Partly 'cos it's always comforting to have what you thought about a piece of art confirmed by one of the artists. But mainly because ... it's just such an inspiring leap of imagination, and a key hint to others about how you make a piece of art that stands the test of time, and truly matters. In short, you work out what you're doing and why. And if your what and why have no objective reality – like, for example, there is no scientifically provable reason why male and female rhythms are any different at all – it's irrelevant, because your execution of the idea makes it real.

The debut album by The Slits also carries that idea as a contradiction. London girls Arianne 'Ari Up' Foster, Tessa Pollitt and Viv Albertine found their female rhythm in conjunction with two men – drummer Peter 'Budgie' Clark and reggae producer Dennis Bovell. But this makes perfect sense. Punk was chock-a-bloc with men who actually liked women, and believed in feminism. Admittedly, they weren't always great at putting this over in public (I'm just remembering John Lydon's repulsively misogynist outburst about Jordan in *I'm A Celebrity*. Old age or verbal diarrhoea? Dunno. But he's still married to Ari Up's mother Nora. Weird, unfathomable, Johnny), but they weren't terrified of a feminine side, particularly in the warp and weft of the work. Budgie and Bovell were the technically accomplished craftsmen generous enough to allow the inspired amateurism of The Slits to take flight. Makes your heart glad, don't it?

What all this means is that *Cut*, on first listen, is bewildering. On second, third and fourth you can still feel completely unmoored by it. Rock, pop, punk, soul . . . all depend on making the listener feel comfortable with where they are. This is usually done by having an intro that sees one or two instruments set the scene with the basic theme, and then a pause to give suspense, and then . . . Diddley Diddley CRUNCH! CRUNCH! That would be the drums telling you, 'suspense over . . . and you knew what was coming, and isn't the ground nice and familiar?' It's that satisfying simplicity that saw rock-based pop supplant classical and jazz as what people mean when they say 'music'.

Cut, however, rejects this utterly. It slides and insinuates its way into every song. It picks up themes and then discards them, bored. Ari Up sings each word as if it can only be sung this way once, or else it's cheating. Every time it threatens to become self-indulgent and tediously experimental, The Slits throw in a beautiful harmony, or a piano spreads the prettiest pleasure, or the drums and bass step forward and run their fingers down your spine. And one day, you're listening, and you're not lost at all, you're travelling with every twist and turn, tingling with pleasure, stunned and realising that you're listening to one of those very few records that will never get old or boring because you'll never be able to gather all of its information. And you realise why you didn't get it at first, and why you're so filled by it now. It's because . . . it's the sound of freedom. Complete, uncompromised, defiant, at all costs, freedom. No wonder it was unfamiliar.

The songs, therefore, are all about the familiar enemies of the post-punk world. Marriage, sexism, possessive love, heroin, consumerism, TV and radio, suburbia. All traps, and all traps sprung by the freedom of SlitSound. *Cut* is the culmination of post-punk's refutation of everything, notwithstanding *Metal Box* (see p.72), because, while the rest of those artists sounded like they'd seen too much, and implied that freedom wasn't possible by the very nature of how trapped they felt they and we were, The Slits made liberation into musical flesh. Their songs about their friends Keith Levine of PiL ('Instant Hit') and Johnny Rotten and Sid Vicious ('So Tough') brought home that refusal to believe in 'the real world', too, as they make it clear, with a quizzical compassion, that they simply don't understand the boys' addictions and complaints. They laughed at the details, skipped right over them, and suggested a world of infinite possibilities, just as the '80s hammer was coming down. They opened a door, which was immediately snapped shut.

Cut is the most wonderful denial of an oppressive and repressive world ever committed to tape. When people say The Slits were ahead of their time, they understate. They were imagining a future that we've not even come close to.

REGGATTA DE BLANC

THE POLICE
PRODUCED BY THE POLICE AND NIGEL GRAY
A&M/OCTOBER 1979
UK CHART: 1
US CHART: 25
KEY TRACKS: 'Message In A Bottle'; 'The Bed's Too Big Without You'; 'Walking On The Moon'; 'Reggatta De Blanc'; 'Bring On The Night'

So, that door snapped shut, that '80s hammer . . .

Stewart Copeland's drums hammer out the first churning charge of 'Message In A Bottle', and twenty-five years of hating Sting are punched out of my brain. It's the guiltiest of pleasures for me. After all, The Police are the end of everything The Slits suggested was possible, and the beginning of the big empty din that we needed in the '80s to drown out the big empty din of ourselves selling out. Everything about the band was despicable and predicted all that was most despicable about the coming cultural clean-up. The horribly naff, contrived image, what with peroxide and tight things with stripes being the only way that they could convince us that they weren't session musos on the make, but cool new-wavey types. The blatant appropriation and bleaching of black musical innovation, performed with an utter lack of guilt that a white middle-class git should honestly get away with being Marley's ghost. Their invention of an adult-pop-rock aesthetic, copped by everyone from Dire Straits and Phil Collins to Keane and Coldplay, that aims itself at those whose resentment at not being young anymore requires something that faintly resembles what the young are doing, but with the spine extracted, and nothing but unspecific, shrugging misery left where its soul should be. When one has consigned oneself to a life of meaningless toil yet can't accept it, one wants one's culture to resemble meaningless toil given heroic resonance. It's no coincidence that the most successful Police rip-off band were called Men At Work.

Then there's the meaningless band name. The album titles that thought they were sly plays on words, but just meant that you'd called your album *White Boat Race*, and didn't know everyone was laughing about it. And any man that obsessed with his own cheekbones should be getting therapy, not fucking global stardom.

Still . . . love this record. Ha! People, pop is a broad church and its charms are manifold. For example, though it may be true that kitsch is merely Polish for shite, there really are occasional moments in popular culture when somebody makes something so bad it becomes genius. Behold the title track of *White Boat Race* (or, by strict French translation, White a Kind of Necktie), where Copeland plays reggae backwards as if bombing a small country with drumsticks, and Andy Summers does his pre-U2, chiming guitar octaves thing, and an army of Stings hook up to Copeland's nuclear snare drum and start shouting . . . wait for it . . . 'JAH!' Jah. Bloody Jah! Then, having established theme, the chorus of Stings change tack and plump for, 'Eey-oh! Eey-yay! Ee-yay-oh!' Sting is soooo Jamaican at this point that he is showing black people all over the world what blackness truly is, if you have de reggae in yo' soul, Mon.

It's fab. Really. I get this huge surge of adrenalin every time I hear this evil thing. I suspect there's a part of me that

admires someone who is completely useless . . . and really, really doesn't care. The trio's self-belief tramples all over the crassness, turns into an inspiring statement of intent, because they know that what they're doing will make them massively rich and adored, and is there anything more worth believing in than that, if you are a person bereft of either shame or integrity?

Nope. Guess not.

SPECIALS

THE SPECIALS
PRODUCED BY ELVIS COSTELLO
2-TONE/OCTOBER 1979
UK CHART: 4
US CHART: 84
KEY TRACKS: 'Blank Expression'; 'Stupid Marriage'; 'A Message To You Rudy'; 'Nite Klub'; 'Too Much Too Young'

'Just because you're nobody/Doesn't mean that you're no good.' What a line. Admittedly, at first glance, even first listen, it doesn't have the rapier wit of Lydon, nor the bravura word skill of Costello, nor the psycho-dramatic power of Ian Curtis. But this line from The Specials' 'Doesn't Make It Alright', sung by Terry Hall with a strength that reveals all the compassion behind it, is absolutely key to the extraordinary impact of what was, when you come right down to it, a ska revival band. The Specials made music about many things, but it always came down to one. The working class spent much of their time fighting each other. This is convenient for the ruling elite. So . . . stop. Divide and rule, racial difference, sexual distrust, bad environment and that good old 'no future' excuse were no excuse whatsoever. Wise up. See that our similarities are far deeper than our differences. Look at the real problem. Unite. Simple.

And, although I have no intention of dismissing the Friday-night pissed-bloke punch-up, nor the fact that peo-

A MESSAGE TO YOU
RUDY

DO THE DOG

IT'S UP TO YOU

NITE KLUB

DOESN'T MAKE IT
ALRIGHT

CONCRETE JUNGLE

TOO HOT

MONKEY MAN

(DAWNING OF A)
NEW ERA

BLANK EXPRESSION

STUPID MARRIAGE

TOO MUCH TOO
YOUNG

LITTLE BITCH

YOU'RE WONDERING
NOW

2
TONE

SPECIALS/THE SPECIALS

ple are still attacked on our streets for reasons racial or sexual, nor the fact that there will always be plain old bad violent people around ... Britain has become safer for the young and 'other' in the last twenty-five years. The Specials were effectively split up by the tribal violence that affected almost every show they played. Going to a gig or a club in 1979 meant running a gauntlet of hate and violence, afterwards, usually, but often during your choice of entertainment. The Specials absorbed the punches and kicks on our behalf and played a major role in changing things for the better. They proved, at great personal risk, that a few people can change the world with an unwavering moral stance, and, lest I forget, some of the best fucking pop music anyone in this country has ever made. They're heroes, and this first album was their most heroic and persuasive statement.

Of course, there's more to 'Just because you're nobody . . .' than anti-racism and breaking up gang-fights. 'Blank Expression', 'Stupid Marriage', 'Too Much Too Young' and 'Little Bitch' formed a mini-opera towards the album's end, a discourse on the young working-class male's fear of women. Rejection, girl-as-property, marriage, teen pregnancy, parenthood and the middle class inspire comedy, compassion, anger, revulsion and a brutally honest questioning of where boy-meets-girl goes from here, prefaced by the date-in-dystopia nightmare that is '(Dawning Of A) New Era'. And guitarist Roddy Radiation's 'Concrete Jungle' took the band's courage a step further, owning up to being personally scared of violence, of not being hard, despite how sharp and hard they all looked on that generation-defining monochrome sleeve.

Elvis Costello's production was superb and vital, balancing reggae space, punk power, and pop accessibility in such a way that this very male band became girl-friendly in a way that The Clash or the post-punkers couldn't dream of. The album was everywhere at the end of 1979, marking a moment – which seems so distant in a twenty-first century where the phenomenon of the ubiquitous album has become inextricably linked with music that stands for nothing and kneels to everything – when the biggest pop was allied to the clearest message.

Most of us feel like nobodies. The Specials understood that and convinced a generation that they were good. We still live in a world that this record helped to shape.

LES PLUS GRANDS SUCCES DE CHIC: CHIC'S GREATEST HITS

CHIC
PRODUCED BY NILE RODGERS AND BERNARD EDWARDS
ATLANTIC/DECEMBER 1979
UK CHART: 30
US CHART: 88
KEY TRACKS: 'Le Freak'; 'Good Times'; 'My Feet Keep Dancing'; 'Chic Cheer'; 'I Want Your Love'

Awww . . . FUCK OFF!!! No, come back, not you! I'm merely singing the original hookline of what the world came to know as 'Le Freak'. See, it was New Year's Eve in New York City, the end of the year of Our disco/punk Lord 1977, and Nile Rodgers and Bernard Edwards went to party at the ultimate discotheque, the legendary Studio 54. They'd been personally invited by the androgynous fashionista Queen of NY nightlife, Ms Grace Jones (see p.75), and their global disco hits, 'Dance Dance Dance (Yowsah, Yowsah, Yowsah)' and 'Everybody Dance', were the key 54 floor-fillers. And they were mates with the manager. So a night of Masters Of The Universe glory was assured, except . . . the bouncers wouldn't let them in. You're not on the list, yeah, everyone knows the manager, yeah, you're Chic . . . right. Rodgers and Edwards gave up, got drugs, went home and threw their own New Year's Eve party.

Two key elements made the party a little different, though. Firstly, they were 24/7 musicians, so they plugged in their instruments and jammed on da fonk. Secondly, they were royally pissed off that making the music that made Studio 54 didn't stop them from being, in the final reckoning, just two more black men who were too uncool to be allowed into a poxy bleedin' disco. So, as they played, they swore. Loudly, repeatedly, therapeutically. Suddenly . . . they were in a place they recognised, playing a groove that had legs, that had Hit written all over it. As the beats locked in, the chorus and the cursing locked in with them. And . . .awwwww . . . FUCK OFF!!! Being hitmakers who wanted their dancefloor wonders to get on daytime radio, they figured they should change the words. And there it was, amidst much hilarity and vindication: 'Awwwww . . . FREAK OUT!!!'

That true tale of pop alchemy is recounted by Daryl Easlea in his definitive Chic biography, *Everybody Dance: Chic and the Politics Of Disco* (Helter Skelter Publishing). It's a proper pop story, that one, suffused with untold levels of irony encompassing class, race, fashion, drugs, New York, the most famous disco of all time, and the mysterious alchemy of pop genius. It also neatly sums up the unique nature of the hit singles collected on the band's *Best Of*. Because Chic were masters of black music's key component: the coded message. Ever since the days of slavery, Afro-Americans had used hymns, work songs and field hollers to exchange information that couldn't be spoken straight . . . about escape, about migration to the north, about how to stay strong and survive the horror and injustice of human bondage. And those white gang bosses were far too stupid to understand. Some things don't change.

Chic honed a perfect, exquisitely crafted dance-soul music, presented with a veneer of faux-European sophistication (shortcut; speak French. Everyone thinks that's sophisticated) and boy-girl, smiley showbiz glitz. All the words said, on the surface, was . . . Dance. Have fun. It's on us. But the lyrics of 'Good Times', 'Le Freak', 'My Feet Keep Dancing' and hits like 'Lost In Music' and 'I'm Coming Out' (written by Chic for Sister Sledge and Diana Ross respectively) bore secret messages, sly jokes and, most risky of all, a sneaky critique of the entire notion of black people dancing away their

blues, instead of using them as triggers for political change. They used references to old dances ('Let's jive and jitterbug') and old dance fantasies ('Stompin' at the Savoy', Fred Astaire and Ginger Rogers) to imply that nothing was moving forward, that the hot new thing was just the cold old thing given a fresh lick of paint and a higher price to pay. You're not on the list. You're not coming in.

The reason why something suffused with satire and cynicism will be causing uninhibited dancefloor joy long after you and me are dead and gone is . . . they did all this out of love, not moral superiority. The love is in the melodies and harmonies, the lush orchestral arrangements, the rhythmic heat generated by Rodgers, Edwards and drummer Tony Thompson, all push and pull, fire and skill, sadness and joy, sex and momentum. They were, for a short time, the best dance band on the planet, which is just another way of saying the best singles band on the planet.

As for why we dance, and what it means, and why the boogie never stops, and whether that's good or bad, I'll leave it to 'Good Times', possessor of the most famous, copied and sampled bassline of all time, to explain, in a way that suggests that the song and the band were never about dancing, but about slavery and its many levels: 'Young and old are doing it, I'm told/Just one try, and you too will be sold.'

METAL BOX/SECOND EDITION

PUBLIC IMAGE LTD
PRODUCED BY PUBLIC IMAGE LTD
VIRGIN/DECEMBER 1979
UK CHART: 18
US CHART: DID NOT CHART
KEY TRACKS: 'Poptones'; 'Careering'; 'Memories'; 'Swan Lake'; 'Graveyard'

Writing about this record is tough. Not least because it's my strongest musical memory of 1979, and, as you've probably

LES PLUS GRANDS SUCCES DE CHIC:CHIC'S GREATEST HITS/CHIC

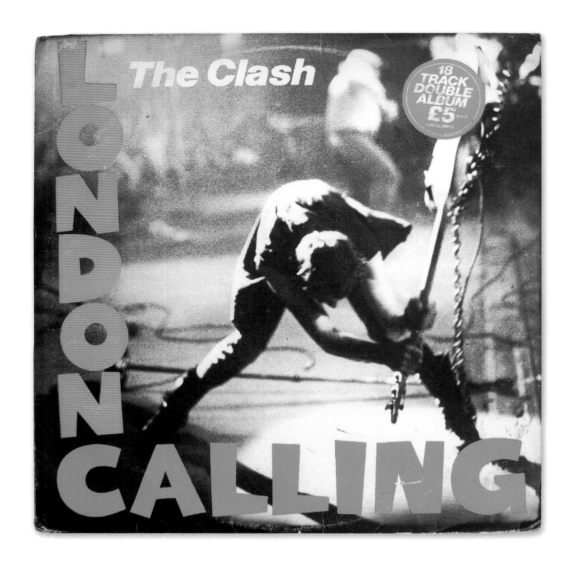

LONDON CALLING/THE CLASH

worked out, 1979 is my favourite musical year, and, in many ways, the creative and moral centre of this book. The records of this year took big ideas inspired by punk and black music to their logical conclusions; ideas about music, art, image, politics, race, gender, sexuality and morality that I still believe in, absolutely. And Johnny Rotten was largely responsible for much of this.

So the greatest album he made takes on a monolithic significance. In *Metal Box* you get the biggest clues to who John Lydon is, and what made him, and why he would give up and sell out. You get disco and funk and dub and punk and ska and Can-inspired art-psych and Indian music and middle-eastern music and pretty much every edgy sonic texture except rock, which PiL rejected more determinedly and successfully than any other rock band. You get an overload of information about late-'70s London, its rich and its poor, its monsters and victims, its decay and its grandeur, its centre and its suburbs, its whiteness and its blackness, its drugs and its traps. You get the dread of someone who's seen the future, the Cold War, the right-wing backlash, Thatcherism, the end of consensus, and what this will mean to youth and free expression and anyone who doesn't want to sign up to greed and 'there is no such thing as society'. Mostly, you get fear and grief, because guitarist Keith Levine was a junkie, and Lydon and bassist Jah Wobble had already watched one junkie friend die in public, and were frightened by the thought that they were partly responsible, and that it was happening all over again. They were frightened by the death of John's mother, by endless hassles with an establishment still punishing Lydon for exposing its hypocrisies, of fans like me who had elected John to be our Jesus, and refused to accept that he was a young bloke who wanted something approaching a normal life. Instead of taking his advice, and wising up, and sorting ourselves out, we just replaced Jagger or Bowie or whoever with him, and then added some bizarre expectation that he would change the world for our benefit, or die trying. This man was twenty-three-years-old and got his day job by miming to an Alice Cooper record in a clothes shop. What were we on about?

Yet *Metal Box* is, sonically, a beautiful record, the very essence of the 'flowers in the dustbin' Lydon had called us on 'God Save The Queen'. Even the depression and exhaustion of 'Albatross', the rape victim's testimony of 'Poptones', the last throwaway joke of 'Radio 4', are made with love and fascination. The exquisite less-is-more production, the attempts to change the rules of presentation with the spectacular (and spectacularly user-unfriendly) film canister packaging, the plethora of different voices Lydon uses to method-act each song, the improvisational splendour of Levine's guitar, the undulating eroticism of Wobble's bass, even the Spinal Tap-esque drummer problem whereby no one seems to know who played which fabulously funky drum part . . . everything about it feels complete, and like a gift to an audience who didn't really deserve such immersion in ideas, and such effort in making them happen. But this gift is like something you're scared to open, especially at night, especially when alone. It's a masterpiece made from sheer agony, and time – and many rip-offs – hasn't made it any easier for the faint of heart.

LONDON CALLING

THE CLASH
PRODUCED BY GUY STEVENS
CBS/DECEMBER 1979
UK CHART: 9
US CHART: 27
KEY TRACKS: 'Guns Of Brixton'; 'London Calling'; 'Brand New Cadillac'; 'Spanish Bombs'; 'Rudie Can't Fail'

But even though the best record of the best year is drenched in despair, no one would really want to end 1979 on that note. No, it's gotta end with good, old-fashioned, idealist, Utopian, hopelessly romantic . . . hope. What else? And who else?

London Calling has become punk's keynote long-player because, unlike Ramones or *Never Mind The Bollocks* or *Metal Box*, it doesn't imply a dead-end. It carries no baggage, even though the members of the band had seen exactly the same nightmares as their friends/rivals in Sex Pistols/PiL. It behaves as if all traumas past and present can be easily dismissed by . . . rocking. Righteously. Man, the naivety! But that's what The Clash brought to the table unlike any other band: an absolutely unshakeable faith in the redemptive powers of rock 'n' roll. And the roll part of that is vital, because rock is as solid and ugly as the word implies, and rock 'n' roll is as groovy and flash as the phrase implies, and the reasons are: blackness, roots and dancing. Incorporate rhythm 'n' blues, country, rockabilly, ska, jazz and soul into what you do, and you tap into instant optimism, because those musics were born from the working class's need to sing out truths to each other, and feel the weight of those truths, and to keep on dancing, fucking and living anyway. Add punk, reggae, funk and disco and you keep away from the dead-end of nostalgia, but attach yourself and your audience to history, the real social history, the one not made by 'great men'. The end result, when recorded with the commitment of crusaders and the skill of artisans, is the last great party before the lights go dim . . . one that also lets you know that, no matter what They do, they won't stop the eventual, inevitable throwing of the next one.

London Calling uses London as the starting point for a journey around the world, and back to the past, and into the future. Its macho power is always leavened by warmth and compassion and the androgyny that Mick Jones brought to the party. It makes connections between the Spanish Civil War ('Spanish Bombs'), doomed '50s method idol Montgomery Clift ('The Right Profile'), the Afro-American Stagger Lee or Stack-o-Lee myth ('Wrong 'Em Boyo'), the Jamaican/British rude boy myth ('Rudie Can't Fail'), suburban ennui ('Lost In The Supermarket'), insane early British rocker Vince Taylor (the blistering cover of his 'Brand New Cadillac'), and the imminent Brixton riots ('Guns Of Brixton') that were invisible until The Clash made them, as if they were making a great documentary about the secret counter-culture, and decided to make a musical instead.

Therefore, its greatest triumph, the reason why kids continue to seek it out, hear it and love it, is that it's one of the few 'classic rock' albums that says repeatedly, proudly, loudly and clearly . . . this music is not about the band. Our problems, issues, moans, and private dramas are irrelevant here. This is about us. All of us. And, if you've gone far enough to acknowledge that all is not right with the world, and to believe it can be changed for the better, then . . . here's our small contribution. And if you haven't – no problem. We love you, too, and we hope one or two of these tunes make you dance. *London Calling* is the biggest argument against the myth that show business is about the ego of the performer. Bad show business is about that. Great, life-affirming show business is about humility. Now that's entertainment.

1980

THE PRETENDERS

THE PRETENDERS

PRODUCED BY CHRIS THOMAS (EXCEPT 'STOP YOUR
SOBBING', PRODUCED BY NICK LOWE)
REAL/WEA/JANUARY 1980
UK CHART: 1
US CHART: 9
KEY TRACKS: 'Brass In Pocket'; 'Kid'; 'Lovers Of Today';
'Mystery Achievement'; 'Up The Neck'

A classic album about having a weakness for male junkies. Well, OK, I can't actually prove that that is what the first Pretenders album is primarily concerned with, and I definitely don't want to make the gargantuan talents of Akron, Ohio's Chrissie Hynde seem smaller than they should be. But when you listen to these songs of maternal strength, romantic/sexual longing for 'Tattooed Love Boys', and occasional exasperated bitching; and then you see the company she kept as part of the London rock scene – Sid Vicious, Johnny Thunders, Nick Kent, junkies all – and then recall that Pretenders guitarist James Honeyman-Scott and bassist Pete Farndon were both dead of heroin ODs by mid-1983 . . . well, I think we're in perfectly justified educated-guess territory. Men who become addicted to heroin are generally high maintenance and become dependent, if they weren't in the first place. But Hynde was and had been surrounded by them, as she bounced between the States, London and Paris. And the songs on this record treat vulnerable men as if they were irresistible children.

Of course, there was music too, and it was instant No. 1 material. Sex Pistols producer Chris Thomas took the Pistols' wall-of-guitars and made it chime, and float, and trade off between the macho riff and a very feminine pop eroticism. Guitarist Honeyman-Scott is spectacular throughout, and I still don't know how Farndon and drummer Martin Chambers made the stiff, oompah rhythm of 'Kid' glide and sigh so. But . . . it's Chrissie's voice in the end,

ain't it? The ultimate in tender toughness, able to plead and kiss and seduce and weep without ever shedding its strength, or tipping into self-indulgence. The best pure voice of its era, surely, and one that made, say, Debbie Harry or Siouxsie seem harsh and soul-less in comparison.

Which is why the album's one false note is the bitchy, new-man-dissing of 'Private Life', and why I'm sticking to my theory about this album. 'Private Life' is a fine song and the band play white reggae better than most. But it needed Grace Jones – who covered it later in 1980 – to give it the right note of imperious icy contempt. Hynde sings it as if embarrassed, rushing through lines in a guilty blur. She just likes useless men too much to play dominatrix. One always got the feeling that she believed, if she just loved the hapless git enough, she'd make him whole. It's a mug's game, of course. But it gives The Pretenders a coded, savage sadness Chrissie Hynde never quite located again.

COLOSSAL YOUTH

YOUNG MARBLE GIANTS

PRODUCED BY YOUNG MARBLE GIANTS AND DAVE
ANDERSON
ROUGH TRADE/FEBRUARY 1980
UK CHART: DID NOT CHART
US CHART: UNRELEASED
KEY TRACKS: 'Brand-New-Life'; 'Credit In The Straight
World'; 'Wind In The Rigging'; 'N.I.T.A.'; 'Choci Loni'

WANNA BUY A BRIDGE?

VARIOUS ARTISTS

PRODUCED BY VARIOUS
ROUGH TRADE/APRIL 1980
UK CHART: DID NOT CHART
US CHART: DID NOT CHART

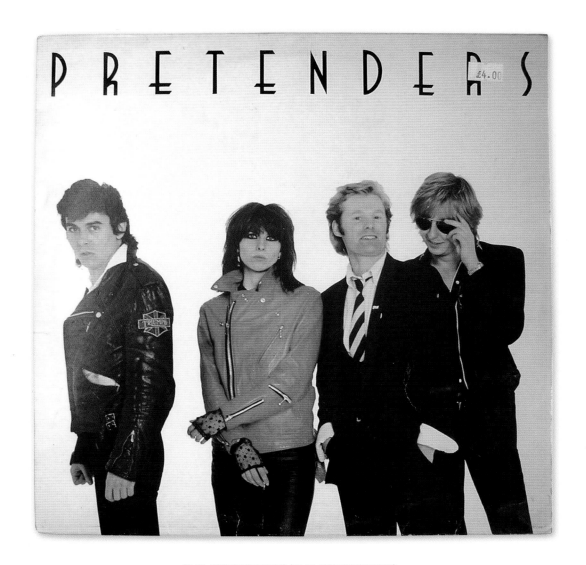

THE PRETENDERS/THE PRETENDERS

In January 1978, a record shop in Notting Hill, west London, named after violent gay sex with the lower orders decided to become a record label. It put out a single by a French punk band called Metal Urbain. Over the next six years it released cutting-edge classics by, among many others, Scritti Politti, The Slits, Pere Ubu and Aztec Camera, before discovering The Smiths, the jewel in British indie's crown. Twenty-seven-and-a-bit years later – and despite going belly-up in the early 1990s – Rough Trade is still here, and still putting out great and important albums by The Strokes (see p.350), The Libertines (see p.355), The Fiery Furnaces (see p.362) and Antony And The Johnsons. Rough Trade's leader Geoff

Travis occupies a role in British musical culture every bit as crucial as John Peel's – perhaps more so, as Travis has always put his money where his principles are.

The aesthetic that inspired and sustained Rough Trade is best summed up by these two relatively obscure cult gems from the turn of the 1980s. *Colossal Youth* is the one and only album by Welsh trio Young Marble Giants, a record that still defines the idea of stripping punk down to its minimalist basics and finding the beauty, androgyny and quiet revolution beneath the din. *Wanna Buy A Bridge?* is a fourteen-track compilation of Rough Trade singles designed to woo those post-punk curious Yanks – hence the wry title alluding to American entrepreneur Robert P. McCulloch buying London Bridge in 1968 when, allegedly, he'd thought he was buying Tower Bridge.

No other long-player captures the vivid colour, smart-dumb humour and counter cultural thrill of post-punk, early indie or peak-era Rough Trade quite as well as *Wanna Buy ...* It makes merry with the eclecticism of Rough Trade's stable, leaving the politics, vocal eccentricity, and musical experiment to forge genuine links between veteran jazz/pop interpreter Robert Wyatt, the boy-punk shouts of Stiff Little Fingers, Spizz Energi and Swell Maps, the feminist sex-pop of The Slits, Essential Logic, Kleenex, The Raincoats and Delta 5, the splenetic punk-funk of The Pop Group, and the faux-naïve piss-taking of Television Personalities. The virtuoso pop hearts of Wyatt (with a heartbreaking rendition of a Chic ballad that murders the original in its bed) and Scritti Politti's Green illuminate the righteous fury of The Pop Group and Kleenex and the scabrous electro-punk of Cabaret Voltaire, making every track a gem and a blueprint for future punks of an adventurous, anti-sexist nature. It's also bathed in the atmosphere of '70s/'80s Notting Hill, London's counter-cultural centre until it became a sort of bohemian theme park in the '90s, and the place where many of Rough Trade's motley crew lived and squatted in order to be nearer the Jamaicans they worshipped and the old hippy radicals they purported to despise, but who actually bequeathed them all their best ideas.

In *Colossal Youth*, however, variety is eschewed for one of the most defined pop sounds ever made, where brothers Stuart and Philip Moxham strip rock of its drums, wires and shouting, and replace with a chunky rhythm guitar, a cheap keyboard and drum machine, and the extraordinary voice of twenty-one-year-old Alison Stratton, who explores life, dread and loneliness with a blank, superficially passionless croon that somehow exposes everything – love, war, nostalgia, friendship – to question. It's like a Robert Bresson movie on wax, possibly that one about the donkey. The YMGs' greatest moment – 'Final Day', an 80-second B-side that features on *Wanna Buy A Bridge?* – nukes the world but dwells on the calm and the peace of the aftermath, pausing only to point out that the rich will live longer in their bunkers, while the poor are 'the people who never had a say' in the world's inevitable fate. The song is so powerful that you have to remind yourself that the nuclear apocalypse – the favoured subject of many an early-'80s artist and writer – never actually happened. Everything defiantly anti-cock-rock since that has put up with being labelled twee by boys afraid of its rejection of machismo – the C86 bands, the Sarah record label, America's Beat Happening and K label, riot grrl, Belle & Sebastian – started here, with Colossal Youth's colossal small-is-beautiful achievement.

All of which proves that Rough Trade was the best and bravest record label in Britpop history, and is still pretty great, and that Geoff Travis deserves some kind of medal for visionary services above and beyond. In lieu of that, track down these albums and award the guy your own private gong.

THE CORRECT USE OF SOAP

MAGAZINE
PRODUCED BY MARTIN HANNETT
VIRGIN/MAY 1980

UK CHART: 28
US CHART: DID NOT CHART
KEY TRACKS: 'A Song From Under The Floorboards'; 'I Want To Burn Again'; 'Because You're Frightened'; 'You Never Knew Me'; 'Sweetheart Contract'

The third Magazine album is a key transition point in British pop. The albums in this book are moving from the domination of punk and post-punk – 'alternative' guitar musics – to records full of chart ambition, catchy tunes, dancefloor beats and colourful textures. There was now a generation of musicians who'd been excited by the Pistols but also by disco, reggae and the pop of their childhoods. Bands began to question whether rock and the electric guitar were really the cutting-edge, or just another form of codified conformity. Hit LPs such as *The Specials* and *Reggatta De Blanc* had, in their very different ways, broadened the range of what you could do while still retaining some

I JUST CAN'T STOP IT/THE BEAT

relationship with punk and its audience. So it was entirely natural that a band from a punk background, but with prog-rock-standard musicians, attempted, on *The Correct Use Of Soap*, to make a radio-friendly pop, complete with funk, soul and disco rhythms, horn solos, keyboards-to-the-fore, girly backing vox, even tender ballads. Joy Division's producer Martin Hannett was brought in to give his fellow Mancunians a clearer, less dense and aggressive sound, while keeping the mystery and edge intact and not letting it get all Boomtown Rats. Everybody involved got it dead right. And then . . . no one bought it.

The problem was that, no matter how hard he might try, there was no way that Howard Devoto could be a pop singer. *The Correct Use Of Soap* is almost a concept album about love, with moments as sincere and vulnerable as they are satirical and intellectual. But the more Howard sang the word, the less like a lover did he sound. No matter how much he would try to croon in the increasingly fashionable post-Bowie mode, his voice would always drift back to slimy needling or haughty sarcasm. And not by accident . . . but because he was trying to say something honest and uncomfortable about what men needed from women, and, in order to do that, he had to let his voice be him at his worst as well as his best.

So the title combines with the songs and becomes something about washing away teenage nerd cynicism about, and fear of, sex, love and women, and trying to admit vulnerabilities and commit; becoming, as one song puts it, a 'Model Worker' at life and relationships. Not exactly a traditionally successful pop theme either, particularly when the singer still insists on rhyming 'Philadelphia' with 'healthier', and, in the same song, telling jokes about Dostoyevsky's *Crime And Punishment*: 'I could've been Raskolnikov/But Mother Nature ripped me off.'

Nevertheless, there are few more convincing moments in alt-pop than when Devoto sings, 'I still turn to love/I want to burn again,' in a song for anyone whose ever tried to reason their way out of an abusive, damaging relationship, but can't

because they believe that the choking fumes and peeling skin are where love's passion and power resides. Elsewhere, 'A Song From Under the Floorboards' remains the Great Lost Punk Soul Hit, bassist Barry Adamson illuminates a version of Sly Stone's 'Thank You', and Dave Formula's dramatic synths and witty, elegant pianos expertly balance old and future pop. Indeed, the more you listen to *The Correct Use Of Soap*, the more you wonder if Duran Duran (and their former Magazine producer Colin Thurston) just copped the sound wholesale to define their new romanticism – pausing, crucially, to extract anything that sounded like doubt, discomfort or intellect.

In fact, you can't help listening to Magazine without wondering if they were just too many clever men in one group, at least for times when punk, pop and disco were all about pulling the audience close and assuring us that the artists were 'just like us'. Magazine just couldn't help sounding lofty and superior. The best compliment I can pay them is that, for the substantial few of us that adored them, they were the only band good and true enough to get away with looking down their noses at us.

I JUST CAN'T STOP IT

THE BEAT
PRODUCED BY BOB SARGEANT
GO-FEET/MAY 1980
UK CHART: 3
US CHART: DID NOT CHART
KEY TRACKS: 'Mirror In The Bathroom'; 'Hands Off . . . She's Mine'; 'Twist And Crawl'; 'Big Shot'; 'Tears Of A Clown'

Back in the day, when discos were discos and women were grateful, each no-jeans-no-trainers-tie-compulsory small-town dance night had a 'bit for the boys'. This would comprise perhaps four to six tracks that had some sort of bloke-rock element, so yer pissed lads could bond and lose some stand-and-leer inhibitions without dancing to a disco or girly chart-pop song, and therefore running the risk of being labelled homosexual. Motown, northern soul, glam, silly metal and new wavey punk all had their day in the bit-for-the-boys sun, before even the Peterboroughs of this world slowly got wise to the idea of 'alternative' clubs where you might be allowed to dance to a broadish spread of non-disco, non-pop stuff, and not have to wear Mr Byrite's finest, and boys and girls might find musical common ground. But before that there was 2-Tone, which, upon its sudden and spectacular arrival on pop's radar, defined the bit for the boys, and finally banished 'Smoke On The Water' from the Malibu and slingbacks world it and its spotty, spoddy cousins were never meant to be part of. The obvious thing about 2-Tone is that its mix of ska, punk, reggae and pure pop had enough blokeiness for the boys, and enough melody and rhythm for the girls. The stranger thing is that we found ourselves dancing manically in glitzy cattle markets to lines like: 'Mirror in the bathroom recompense/For all my crimes of self-defence/Cures you whisper make no sense/Drift gently into mental illness.' Yowsah yowsah yowsah!

'Mirror In The Bathroom', from which the above lines are pulled, is one of the prime examples of how the new '80s pop wave was, for a couple of splendid years, strongly informed by the dread and questioning of post-punk. Indeed, the debut album by Birmingham's Beat is full of ebullient reggae-punk-pop anthems masking a heart of darkness and confusion. Unlike The Specials' Jerry Dammers, The Beat's lead singer and lyricist Dave Wakeling was no conviction politician, and also had no Madness-style character comedies in his repertoire. 'Hands Off . . . She's Mine' satirised male possessiveness as fear of emasculation. 'Click Click' toyed with suicide as a viable option. 'Twist And Crawl' funked up insanity and self-disgust. The extraordinary 'Two Swords' even questioned 2-Tone's anti-Nazi *raison d'etre*, suggesting that we were only fighting to, 'Always attack those things in someone else/Reflections that you

can't face in yourself.' No wonder The Beat wandered into slow death, once their music began to reflect Wakeling's resigned pessimism.

But for one album this band was the ultimate in danceable depression. Veteran saxophonist Saxa brought a vital shot of Carnival rum 'n' sun to every benevolent solo; future Fine Young Cannibals Andy Cox (guitar) and David Steele (bass) proved you really could play reggae and soul rhythms with punk urgency and not lose the swing of the thing: and toaster Ranking Roger replaced guitar solos with inspired rhymes and soprano hiccups, persuading nice white people to suddenly exclaim, 'I was walking down de road with a heavy, heavy load' and 'Hands off me daughter!!!' in hokey Jamaican accents, preparing the ground for hip hop to make wiggers of us all.

This led to fourteen tracks that, like many of the albums we'll be bigging up between here and 1982, sounded like a Greatest Hits album . . . no flab, no filler, no boring experimental bits. For a couple of years the best young musicians and writers on the planet decided that making proper pop music was the very biggest and cleverest thing you could do. It didn't last and from 1983 onwards, chart pop seemed content to drift gently away from mental illness. Unless, of course, you figure greed and desperation are suitable cases for treatment. If so, you'll really like The Beat.

TRAVELOGUE

THE HUMAN LEAGUE
PRODUCED BY THE HUMAN LEAGUE, RICHARD MANWARING AND JOHN LECKIE
VIRGIN/MAY 1980
UK CHART: 16
US CHART: NOT RELEASED IN USA
KEY TRACKS: 'Crow And A Baby'; 'The Black Hit Of Space'; 'Dreams Of Leaving'; 'W.X.J.L. Tonight'; 'Being Boiled'

Before they split into two quintessential '80s hit bands, The Human League were post-punk pop experiment personified. Entirely electronic, eschewing songs of love and rebellion for dryly comic preoccupations with sci-fi, religion and political literature, and featuring one member, Adrian Wright, who appeared to do nothing except make slides for their live show – a proto-Bez with a projector – they were lampooned in The Undertones' 'My Perfect Cousin' as 'art school boys' advising rich kids on how to play with synthesizers. More than any other band, the early League symbolised punk's split between those who saw it as a working-class male guitar music that should be discouraged from change, and those who saw it as a springboard for sexually ambiguous, anything-goes adventure. Of course, the adventurers were right and proper and sexier and made the better music. Of course, they all lost it eventually by allowing the music business to divide them from audience and roots, thereby reflecting the breakdown in community deliberately caused by free market economics. Hey ho.

Travelogue is the second album by Sheffield's Wright, Phil Oakey, Ian Craig-Marsh and Martyn Ware, and one of the most purely entertaining musical artefacts of the post-punk era. Its opening shot, 'The Black Hit Of Space', takes the idea of the ubiquitous hit seven-inch single on a trip into *Astounding Tales* territory, imagining a record of such bland universality that it literally sucks the whole of humanity into the void. Yeah, I know, where do you want to start . . . Celine Dion or Coldplay? Whichever way, the triumph of shite always throws up one unanswerable question: 'How can it stay at the top/When it's swallowed all the shops?'

From there, the League take us on a space safari that balances the blackest humour and the saddest human tragedy, presenting the nightmare of the refugee as a paranoia thriller for 'Dreams Of Leaving'; telling child-catcher horror stories to errant children on 'Crow And A Baby'; presenting the encroaching redundancy of the radio DJ as a tragic plea for survival on 'W.X.J.L. Tonight'. The music blends Kraftwerk, Giorgio Moroder and the BBC Radiophonic Workshop with the gnarly, geeky enthusiasm that only boys obsessed with *Dr Who* can muster. The synths undulate and conjure dreams of rockets and solar systems while Phil Oakey's extraordinary voice attaches everything to the ground, the blunt Yorkshireman reinvented as comic-book astronaut, solving intergalactic problems with nuggets from James Burke science programs and a clip round the ear.

Travelogue's characters are old; ancient, probably, immortal, perhaps. Yet this is a record preoccupied with death, although not in a goth, nihilistic-metaphor-for-stunted-alienation kind of way. This is death as inevitability and adventure. So, despite making the UK Top 20, it simply wasn't going to make hits, and everyone knew that by 1980. Oakey threw Marsh and Ware out of the band they'd formed, hired two fab girls, and went for brash synths and wry optimism. Marsh and Ware formed Heaven 17 and went onto a successful career making black-music-lite for the likes of Tina Turner and Terence Trent D'Arby. Both came close to making a black hit of space, and eventually got sucked into their own void.

DIANA

DIANA ROSS
PRODUCED BY BERNARD EDWARDS AND NILE RODGERS
MOTOWN/MAY 1980
UK CHART: 12
US CHART: 2
KEY TRACKS: 'My Old Piano'; 'Upside Down'; 'Tenderness'; 'I'm Coming Out'; 'Have Fun (Again)'

Diana Ross was made to be a Chic vocalist. I know that's a backhanded compliment to pay the most successful female vocalist of all time, but it's true. The brilliance of her work with The Supremes lay in the child-like vacuity of her voice. Whereas everyone else on the label was bringing the screams of the gospel church and the scar of slavery to mainstream pop, Ms Ross was bringing an empty longing, upon which both producers and audience could project their own emotions. The blank vocal canvas was exactly where Chic worked – the female vocals provided hooks while the power and elegance of the grooves gave you the information and the passion. That's the template male dance producers have used ever since, hiring largely female singers to play an agreeable but essentially characterless Trojan horse role for their formula beats. The fact that no one ever pulls off this sexist cynicism like Chic is because Nile Rodgers and Bernard Edwards knew exactly what they were doing, while their legion of copyists are just doing it because that's how you get in the charts. Having the best formula, musically, might have had something to do with it, too.

Ms Ross obviously suspected all this. Once recording had finished, she heard the finished tracks, freaked at just how much she'd been relegated to a musical effect on her own album, and implored her career mentor and Motown founder Berry Gordy to order a remix. This largely consisted of turning Diana up and the music down. Good move. *Diana* remains her biggest solo album and Chic's major production success, and it worked out artistically, too. *Diana* is unique: a solo artist's biggest commercial and musical triumph which reveals how bereft of soul and passion the singer is, even as the record works its magic. It tells you everything you need to know about Diana Ross, the decline of Chic, their coming success as hack producers, the death of disco, Diva Syndrome, the coming of modern R&B, the rabbit-in-headlights desperation and banality of mainstream '80s pop and the increasing struggle of hit producers to shift the required amount of units while still making music of quality, with love.

As for Chic's habitual juggle of thematic ironies, 'I'm Coming Out' is obvious, and no one will ever convince me that Ross didn't understand the value of acknowledging her gay following. But among the sublime grooves and insidious hooks lies Chic's usual sneer . . . somewhere between wearily imploring us to 'Have Fun (Again)', getting Diana Ross to imply a sexual relationship with 'My Old Piano', and ending the album with a stalker's anthem called 'Give Up'.

Gotta love 'em.

CRISTINA

CRISTINA
PRODUCED BY AUGUST DARNELL
ZE/JUNE 1980
UK CHART: DID NOT CHART
US CHART: DID NOT CHART
KEY TRACKS: 'Is That All There Is?'; 'Don't Be Greedy'; 'La Poupée Qui Fait Non'; 'Disco Clone'; 'Jungle Love'

Cristina Monet was – and still is – a lingerie model, a writer, a Harvard graduate in History and English Literature, a theatre critic, a satirist, a beauty, an agent provocateur, and a motor-mouthed intellectual. Everything, in fact, except a pop singer. But that was the early '80s, when punk had convinced a great many that lack of musical technique was no barrier to the implementation of a Great Pop Idea. It's also, come to think of it, very now, when anyone can become a star and pop producers have sinister machines which can make Foghorn Leghorn sound like Aretha Franklin, as long as Foghorn's willing to sell his arse to the tabs and have his feathery chest butchered into torpedo tits, preferably on peak-time Channel 4. Like many things in this book, Cristina and her extraordinary record label Ze were a prophecy, an insight into a future where the shit things we sang about would become standards of success, sell-outs to be worshipped and aspired to.

The Ze label was formed by Monet's partner Michael Zilkha, heir to the Mothercare millions and a future oil magnate who fell in love with New York punk and disco while working at the Village Voice, and decided to take a break from the family business and make records with the likes of John Cale, Suicide (see p.29), Was (Not Was) (see p.119), James White, Lydia Lunch and, most lucratively, Kid Creole And The Coconuts. Kid Creole's alter-ego August Darnell, his arranger Andy 'Coati Mundi' Hernandez, Zilkha and Ms Monet kicked off this multi-coloured funk-punk project by conspiring to make a brilliant, ridiculous concept album based around the idiot joys of New York's disco demi-monde. Cristina, of course, did not sell a bean. But Monet's cruel, transgressive ironies and sugar-coated big band arrangements did, by Darnell's own admission, provide the template for the future success of Kid Creole. Think camp Latin-tinged, Broadway musical tunes with a disco beat and snotty songs about the whole of New York going all *Boogie Nights*, which were talk-sung by a squeakier Marlene Dietrich suffering from terminal ennui interrupted only by handfuls of downers and masochistic sex. As Ms Monet herself told me in interview in 2003, 'I have fan clubs at the homosexual theatre departments of Swiss boarding schools. This is not chartbusting stuff.'

Nevertheless, Zilkha's French partner Michel Esteban began to reissue Ze's catalogue in 2003, and Cristina's timeless sneer at the inevitable dumbing down of everything was made even better by the addition of bonus tracks which should always have been on the album first-time around (despite being annoyingly re-named *Doll In The Box*, a prime example of just how stupid people from record companies think we are, now that irony has been re-defined as 'embracing our inner uselessness'). The first ever Ze single, 'Disco Clone', sees Ms Monet duetting kitschily with a young Kevin Kline. But the big bonus for all those who I so want to be seduced by Cristina comes in the inclusion of 'Is That All There Is?', her bad-taste cover of Peggy Lee's Grammy-winning 1969 hit. This bizarrely hypnotic version repaints the already sublimely cynical song in tacky, nagging post-punk hues, and vandalises the original with smashing glass party-

in-hell effects, lines about Quaaludes, and a reference to our heroine and her imaginary boyfriend which goes: 'We'd take long walks down by the river and he'd beat me black and blue . . . and I loved it.' It was all set to be a hit in late 1980, when the song's composers Jerry Leiber and Mike Stoller – the rock Golden Age heavyweights who wrote 'Hound Dog' and signed The Shangri-La's, among many other world-changing things – objected and threw an injunction at the song. More than a shame, considering how deftly Cristina's version updates the worldview of Lee's version. But, hey, it's in your shops now and it is one of the greatest singles ever made. No, really, ever.

As for the rest of the album, it's difficult to imagine a record that would annoy the meat and potatoes, now that's what I call music, smugly conservative fan of 'real rock' more than Cristina. All those happy orchestras! All that waspish kitsch! All that uncompromised femininity! All that unashamed bad singing! By a girl!

Who just whispered Madonna?

SEARCHING FOR THE YOUNG SOUL REBELS

DEXYS MIDNIGHT RUNNERS
PRODUCED BY PETE WINGFIELD
PARLOPHONE/JULY 1980
UK CHART: 6
US CHART: NOT RELEASED IN USA
KEY TRACKS: 'There, There, My Dear'; 'Burn It Down';
'Thankfully Living In Yorkshire It Doesn't Apply'; 'Tell Me When My Light Turns Green'; 'I'm Just Looking'

Blimey blimey trousers – this one's a toughie. OK . . . let's go with facts that sound like myths, and maybe are.

The first Dexys album begins with a radio dial being tuned. It lands on Deep Purple's 'Smoke On The Water', then 'Holidays In The Sun' by the Sex Pistols, and finally 'Rat

searching for the young soul rebels

dexys midnight runners

SEARCHING FOR THE YOUNG SOUL REBELS/DEXYS MIDNIGHT RUNNERS

Race' by The Specials, who Kevin Rowland and Co. had enjoyed their first public profile by supporting. Then the radio is snapped off, and Rowland shouts 'Jimmy!' He is shouting at trombonist Big Jim Patterson, but the whole band shout back, 'Yeah!' Then Kev hollers, 'Now!' The band repeat their 'Yeah!' with military precision. And then Rowland sneers, voice dripping with disgust, 'For God's sake burn it down!'

Now, Deep Purple, you know, so far, so predictable in 1980. But if you think the Sex Pistols and Specials are admired and credible now, then you've got to realise that slagging either off in 1980 was plain old heresy. They were the avatars of doing-it-for-the-kids, working-class-worshipping, tribal fashion male pop cool. To make it the first statement of your first album was . . . bewildering, frankly. Whose side were Dexys on? But then, Rowland and partner Kevin 'Al' Archer had made a punk record called 'Johnny Won't Get To Heaven', about what a wanker Johnny Rotten was, as The Killjoys way back in 1977. It stands to reason, if you think about it, that if punk was about rejecting the cultural status quo, then the first target of that rejection must always be the hippest thing at the time, not the longhairs whose time had passed anyway. Kevin Rowland was not just the only pop star, but one of the few humans who understood that and saw it through.

Before the album was released, the band stole the tapes and held them to ransom in order to get a better royalty rate from EMI. They hid them under their parents' beds. It worked, but, unsurprisingly, various members quit the mayhem and Dexys parted company from EMI before the whole 'Too-Ry-Ay'/'Come On Eileen' comedy dungarees and wedding hit jiggery-pokery made serious raggle-taggle moolah.

The sleeve shot is an all-time classic. A green-tinted photo of Catholic families being evicted during The Troubles in Northern Ireland, the buzz of activity, atmosphere, pain and fear frames a boy whose dapper defiance hits the same note of conscience-pricking strength under pressure as the famous last shot of Francois Truffaut's borstal drama *Les Quatre Cents Coups* (The 400 Blows). The boy's crombie and overnight bag gave the band the perfect excuse for their donkey-jacketed longshoreman image, which, they insist now, was an accident caused by their original proto-new-romantic image being too gay for the fans of the 2-Tone bands they supported. All the key members of the various Dexys incarnations have such a wry, wind-up sense of humour that I'm still not sure whether their insistence that they really wanted to look like Spandau Ballet is yet another inspired, myth-making pisstake. Legend has it that the cover star himself once turned up at a Dexys gig waving a giant cardboard cut-out of himself as a boy.

On 'Love Part One', a prose-poem backdropped by Lisa Simpson-style beatnik sax, Kev delivers a refutation of romantic love driven by all the inappropriate, sweary resentment that only a bitter and sex-starved young man could muster. But on the back cover, the accompanying note to the song says, 'These words could be incorrect – I hope you are less confused.' Aw. Bless.

Kevin Rowland's wonderfully intense use of the word 'fuck' throughout this album reminds you that 'fuck' used to mean something, before hip hop and Joe Pesci killed it.

The best way to appreciate Dexys is to notice all the jokes – in the songs, on the cover – and understand that this much anger and commitment has to be leavened by droll humour or else you'd just go mental.

On 'Keep It', Rowland pinpoints with tragic accuracy the catch-22 of making pop-rock which sees you appointed as a spokesman for difference and leader of a rebel tribe. 'You give credit for might, inspiration and sight/But you miss the point . . . you won't join in the fight.' We elect our rebel rock icons as a replacement for revolution, while convincing ourselves that they are an inspiration. It's safer, really. Rowland knew this absolutely, which is why he couldn't bring himself to be Strummer or Weller. Which makes it all the more extraordinary that the lyric was written, not by The Kevmeister, but by saxophonist Jeff Blythe.

Rowland's singing on this album pulls off the impossible – a way for a white Englishman to sing American soul without ever trying to fake being black or American. The torrent of hiccups, yells, twisted croons, strained falsettos and tearful wails embodies that great British pop rule – you know the one, it goes 'Ridicule is nothing to be scared of' – better, even, than dear old Adam Ant ever could.

Brass. Lots and lots of brass.

And finally . . . *Searching For The Young Soul Rebels* is one of the very best albums ever made. If you already agree with that statement, don't let the tedious, chin-stroking, it's-all-been-downhill-since-The-Beatles, mellow good taste or heroin in the eyeball brigade convince you otherwise. They just don't like it up 'em.

CROCODILES

ECHO AND THE BUNNYMEN
PRODUCED BY DAVID BALFE, BILL DRUMMOND AND IAN BROUDIE
KOROVA/WEA/JULY 1980
UK CHART: 17
US CHART: DID NOT CHART
KEY TRACKS: 'Villiers Terrace'; 'Rescue'; 'Crocodiles'; 'Pride'; 'Stars Are Stars'

So – post-punk and doubt and dread. The first Bunnymen album may be a clue to how rock would head away from the unlikely celebration of harsh truths to something more general and ornate. But there is still enough fear in *Crocodiles* – even before you clock the dubby bass or the scratchy guitars – to make it a key post-punk record. All Liverpool's Ian McCulloch, Will Sergeant, Pete DeFreitas and Will Pattinson did was add a re-embracing of Classic Rock to the post-punk mix. They were The Beatles, The Doors and Lou Reed filtered through the sensibility of Television and Gang Of Four. And you don't need to be Delia Smith to know that

recipe's gonna taste just fine, as long as you don't overcook it.

But what makes *Crocodiles* special is doubt and dread. Ian McCulloch came to define – invent, virtually – the lippy northern rock star, telling everyone who'd listen that his band were the greatest in the world, and that he, personally, was the coolest man alive. Liam Gallagher gets constantly compared to Lennon and Lydon, but it's Mac that his entire schtick is based upon, albeit with a few monkey-man thug elements pinched from Ian Brown. But Mac was bluffing, which is why the early Bunnymen truly were one of the greatest British rock bands ever. The tension that ignited the freaked sensuality of their rock lay in the gap between what a northern working-class boy has to be to survive – hard, witty, invulnerable – and what Mac revealed in his voice and lyrics, which was fear of failure, the burden of responsibility, the vulnerability of the smart, beautiful boy who worshipped at the altar of Bowie, and who'd probably been accused of being a poof plenty of times, and had had to learn how to front it. The early Bunnymen were uniquely able to craft a rock that sounded both panic-stricken yet sexy, that was suffused with fear of war, drugs, death and their own inevitable failure, yet was strong enough to face down that fear without denying its existence.

I fell in love with the band immediately because that was exactly how I felt at seventeen . . . scared, but beginning to suspect that smart, strong people embraced their fear, and used it as fuel to move on, and move up. On 'Pride', Mac sang brilliantly and honestly and accurately about having made the decision to do something different with your life, and how the people who love you beat you up with both their expectations and their derision. On 'Villiers Terrace', Mac played the innocent at the grown-up party, watching the hard drugs and the madness, equally repulsed and fascinated, and knowing that, in the world he was choosing to live in, he would have no choice but to become one of the monsters.

And Will Sergeant played guitar like a warning and a

ECHO AND THE BUNNYMEN   CROCODILES

CROCODILES/ECHO AND THE BUNNYMEN

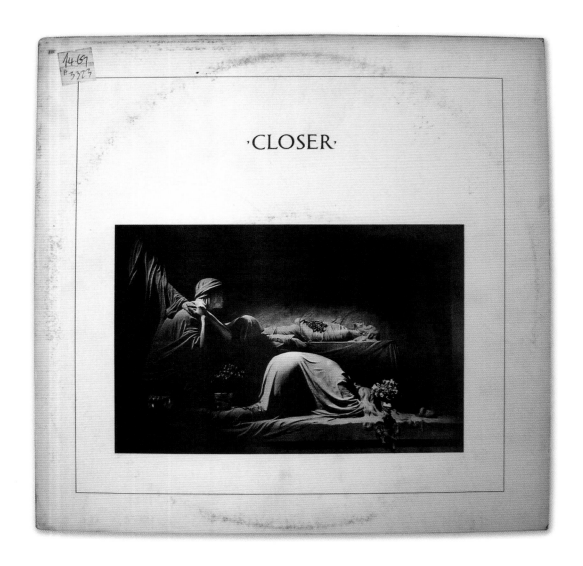

CLOSER/JOY DIVISION

siren and a caress and a convulsion, and never did more than he must do, because De Freitas and Pattinson were a world-class rhythm section, effortlessly funky without ever copying disco. And Mac's voice was so American it didn't sound American anymore, and it re-connected alternative rock to the pleasures of the flesh, without ever stooping to a leer. All this jazz made *Crocodiles* an iconic album of its times, and made it snappy.

CLOSER

JOY DIVISION
PRODUCED BY MARTIN HANNETT
FACTORY/JULY 1980
UK CHART: 6
US CHART: NOT RELEASED IN US
KEY TRACKS: 'Twenty Four Hours'; 'Decades'; 'Isolation'; 'A Means To An End'; 'Passover'

Because when you don't have Ian McCulloch's wit and bluff, you end up here.

The problem with *Closer* is that it's impossible to sepa-rate from the fact of the lead singer's suicide in May 1980. Impossible. Believe me, I've just spent hours – and twenty-five years – trying. I could try and blame melodramatic music critics and death cult-obsessed fans for that, and take the high moral ground, but I'd just be lying through my endearingly crooked teeth. The reason that *Unknown Pleasures* is now hailed as their classic album is that you can listen to it for pleasures known or unknown without feeling disturbed and distressed for hours afterwards. *Closer* will always sound like a suicide note, because it was. Smack. Brick wall.

Musically, *Closer*'s best moments are far more beautiful and profound than anything else rock has to offer. Its worst moments are just ugly and emotionally exhausting, because they are hopeless. But the most painful thing about *Closer* is

not about sifting the likes of 'Twenty Four Hours', 'Atrocity Exhibition' or 'Isolation' for clues to what Curtis was about to do. It's the negation of something we all want to believe. Because the writing and singing of Ian Curtis are as accom-plished and deeply soulful as art gets. Yet it made no differ-ence to him. It wasn't catharsis or therapy. Which means that the psychological truism of personal freedom of expression making life worth living . . . is not true.

Closer is far beyond the reach of ninety-nine per cent of popular music. I don't listen to it much.

THE AFFECTIONATE PUNCH

THE ASSOCIATES
PRODUCED BY THE ASSOCIATES, MIKE HEDGES AND CHRIS PARRY
FICTION/AUGUST 1980
UK CHART: DID NOT CHART
US CHART: NOT RELEASED IN US
KEY TRACKS: 'Paper House'; 'Amused As Always'; 'A Matter Of Gender'; 'Even Dogs In The Wild'; 'Deeply Concerned'

I do listen to this, though, even though the lead singer also committed suicide. But then, Billy Mackenzie waited until January 1997 to take his own life, after the death of his mother. The first Associates album isn't just removed in time from this tragedy . . . it suggests both a solid sanity and a lust for a polymorphous life. Two songs in and you forget the rock-death baggage.

Billy and his musical partner Alan Rankine came out of Dundee, Scotland, with a degree in left-field glam (Sparks, Bowie, Roxy Music), a penchant for hedonism, a surreal sense of humour and a taste for musical adventure. They would later become out-of-place pop stars circa *Sulk* (see p.135), but this first album belies their later reliance on brit-tle hysteria and echoey electronics. It relies on bass, guitar and piano, and Billy's legendary voice. It's produced dry and simple, so you can hear exactly how elegant and gifted a musician Rankine was. And, for the one and only time, Billy Mac sounds as solid, weary and strong as he does wild and eccentric. I seem to be rare among Associates fans in feeling that this first cut was their deepest.

If you've never heard this record, I figure that, if you like '70s Bowie, torchy Scott Walker, early Bunnymen and early Cure (Robert Smith guests, unrecognisably, on 'A'), then you'll probably like *The Affectionate Punch*. Thematically, the title neatly sums up Billy's blend of compassion and cruelty, passion and sarcasm. Despite being just twenty-three, Mackenzie was disinterested in typical male youth angst. 'Logan Time' has its roots in sci-fi movie and TV series *Logan's Run*, about a future where everyone is killed at thirty. Over a ballad backing with military undertones, Billy admits his fear of reaching thirty, but from the perspective of someone looking forward to not being alone. 'My Generation' it ain't.

Elsewhere, the organically funky 'Amused As Always' appears to critique the shallow preoccupations of the new romantics months before their impact on the mainstream. 'Transport To Central' features a sinister narrator manufacturing . . . a pop star? The Messiah? Possibly both or neither, but the line, 'His jawline's not perfect/But this can be altered' still chills. 'Paper House' shreds bourgeois ambitions with an outrageous trade-off between stuttering rhythm and operatic swoon. 'Even Dogs In The Wild' comes off as a camp post-punk take on finger-clicking cabaret, until you suss that the words express a shocked loathing of parental abuse. It was this refusal to frame lyrics with obvious backings that made The Associates an instant thinking-alternative-pop-kid's obsession, but made them impossible to fit into the mainstream for any length of time.

'A Matter Of Gender' is, more than the later hits, I suspect, the keynote Billy Mac track. A dynamic but dry rock-pop song which seems conventional without sounding like anyone else, it updates Bowie and Marc Bolan's take on British male sexuality and narcisscism, as Billy admits to a married woman (there's a deliciously overwrought mention of 'the seventh commandment') called 'Marguaritte' (sic) that, despite her many appealing qualities, she's not getting any, not from him. 'I don't know whether to over or under-estimate you . . . For when I come over/You then put me under . . . Personal taste is a matter of gender.' When set against the deadpan drama of the tune, you end up laughing over your own puzzlement. Is he coming out? Is all this over and under as dirty as it sounds? Is 'Marguaritte' a woman, or a man, or something else much more interesting? 'Gender-bending' would soon become a pop trend, but the Georges and Marilyns were never as intriguing – nor sexy – as this.

SCARY MONSTERS

DAVID BOWIE
PRODUCED BY DAVID BOWIE AND TONY VISCONTI
RCA/SEPTEMBER 1980
UK CHART: 1
US CHART: 12
KEY TRACKS: 'Fashion'; 'Ashes To Ashes'; 'It's No Game (No. 1)'; 'Teenage Wildlife'; 'Scary Monsters (And Super-Creeps)'

The last David Bowie album. Well, the last great Bowie album, the last of what is surely the greatest run of uninterrupted great albums, from 1971's *The Man Who Sold The World* to this one, eleven in total . . . and the last Bowie LP in this book. And what makes *Scary Monsters* especially great is that this isn't down to hindsight. *Scary Monsters* is about not striving to be the greatest anything anymore. It's Bowie's valedictory goodbye, and fuck you very much.

Now, obviously, such statements don't come without a smidgeon of self-pity and petty narkiness. Having been the only major artist to run a parallel career to punk without either being either dinosaur villain or patronising cheerleader, he finally acknowledges its existence on 'Teenage Wildlife', barking with melodramatic vulnerability at 'One of

SCARY MONSTERS/DAVID BOWIE

the new wave boys . . . Same old thing in brand new drag'. Which all seems a little uncharitable, until you realise the harsh truth of the following lines: 'Corner sweeping into view/As ugly as a teenage millionaire.' This album is about the inevitable sell-out of the counter-cultural rocker, as he/she realises their passion is a fashion, just like everything else, and the kids will not make the world a better place, so accept the conventional pop career, or drive yourself insane, make your choice. There's no self-referential No. 1 hit that makes that point, and makes that choice, more elegantly and blatantly, than 'Ashes To Ashes', where Major Tom, Bowie's ancient astronaut from his first hit, 'Space Oddity', begs to come down to Earth. The key point of the song and the album is Bowie's self-preservation: for reasons only he knows, his ability to make cutting-edge rock-pop and image to match, and make a different kind with every new record, was linked to driving himself towards yet another rock death. Drink, drugs, depression, damaging relationships, weird obsessions with the occult and fascism; all of those artrock-boy vices were the very stuff his best work came from. That probably isn't that rare . . . what is, is that someone as big as Bowie should announce so publicly that he's choosing life, so, sorry if the next twenty-five years of celebrity bonhomie and banality and money-making are a disappointment, but . . . what did any of you do with my life-changing iconic impact anyway? What do you ever do with anybody's? You change your clothes for a while, use us to establish your hip credentials around town . . . and then buy the boxed set and whinge about how much more radical it was in your day! Well, Buddy, I ain't living on the edge just so's you can live vicariously for the risks I take. Go bother someone else for answers, and while you're at it . . . uh, sorry . . . got rather too into character, then. I was just one step from writing in stage-school mockney guv gawd luvaduck.

So anyway, *Scary Monsters*, with its sarcastic and stomping and funky and sneering take on the Berlin sound of *Low* (see p.9), "*Heroes*" (see p.25) and Lodger, with its bookend track 'It's No Game' – which opens the album with throat-shredding mania and therefore hope out of chaos, but closes the album with calm resignation, and therefore despair out of repression – is one fuck of a brilliant record to make out of misanthropy and betrayal. The fact that it was No. 1 and invented the '80s is just the ironic cherry on top.

MORE SPECIALS

THE SPECIALS
PRODUCED BY JERRY DAMMERS AND DAVE JORDAN
2-TONE/SEPTEMBER 1980
UK CHART: 5
US CHART: 98
KEY TRACKS: 'Stereotypes'; 'Do Nothing'; 'International Jetset'; 'Pearl's Café'; 'I Can't Stand It'

Well, that really was a whole bunch of sensitive white boys in a row, now wasn't it? Particularly at the kick-off of a decade that we still associate with jolly white versions of black music, garish hair and clothing choices, and right-wing politics pretending to be apolitical. But then, the early '80s, mid-'80s and late '80s bear little or no relation to each other, in a pop cultural sense, which is why '80s nostalgia is such a matter of subjectivity. The Specials, for example, are rarely described as an '80s band, attached as they are visually and thematically to punk. But, in truth, they defined the early part of the decade more than any other group. They represented a steadily improving working-class attitude to racial tolerance, even while a right-wing government and press were doing everything in their power to turn back the clock. They were more image-conscious than any new romantic group or MTV-friendly corporate megastar. They blended black and white musics from around the world without ever sounding like a bleaching of reggae, soul or disco. And, although they were working-class lads from Coventry in one sense, they were, like all great pop groups, as arty, literate and articulate – both lyrically and musically – as anyone from Bowie/Eno World. Their second album, *More Specials*, is one of the riskiest albums ever set before a large, loyal fanbase. And, along with their final 'Ghost Town' single, it represents both their greatest work, and pop music's most fundamental truths about being an ordinary British citizen in the early 1980s and, through timeless resonance, in the early-twenty-first-century Now.

Firstly, Jerry Dammers subverts the band's ebullient ska-punk sound by filling it with mud and blood, and bouncing it all off one of those cheap and nasty keyboards with beats like the quickstep and the cha-cha programmed onto a primitive tinny drum machine. It's the instrument of seaside entertainers and cheaply-produced muzak for downmarket shopping centres, yet, by forcing this sound to incorporate reggae, Latin, '60s girl-pop and middle-eastern roots music, he makes a piece of junk into something beautiful and evocative. Elvis Costello's sparse, splashing production for *The Specials* is eschewed for a ragged polyphony plucked

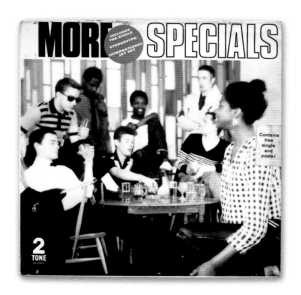

from the jazz-carnival mutation that was early ska – the world-changing Jamaican virtuosity of the likes of The Skatalites, Don Drummond and Roland Alphonso. The racial mix and update comes from the voice of Terry Hall, the last word in sardonic blank-generation insolence.

Like *Scary Monsters*, the album is bookended by different versions of the same song. 'Enjoy Yourself', a 1950 hit for dance band leader Guy Lombardo, is squeezed for every ounce of sarcasm on the subject of 'live for the moment'. The opening version is ragged and manic and camp. The closer is sweet, exhausted and resigned. The subject is, of course, the inevitable coming of our old favourite, The Atom Bomb That Never Actually Dropped. These ironic calls to party hearty frame tales of drunk blokes wrapping themselves around lamp-posts while a rude boy bigs up his hi-fi ('Stereotypes'), girls getting dumped for not empathising with lonely old slappers ('Pearl's Café'), aimless fashion victims being beaten up by coppers and accepting that as normal ('Do Nothing'), losing oneself in the vacuum-packed consumer paradise of an airport lounge ('International Jetset') and an overall suggestion that all those sensitive white-boy feelings of alienation are not down to being misunderstood, but due to capitalism stealing our souls and replacing them with robot parts that march us through life fulfilling a function that suits no one but the obscenely rich and powerful.

So The Bomb didn't drop. Listening to *More Specials* makes you realise that we still behave with the terror and apathy of people waiting to be vaporised. Plus the tunes are really, really catchy.

KILIMANJARO

THE TEARDROP EXPLODES
PRODUCED BY DAVID BALFE, BILL DRUMMOND AND MIKE HOWLETT
MERCURY/OCTOBER 1980

UK CHART: 24
US CHART: DID NOT CHART
KEY TRACKS: 'Treason'; 'Bouncing Babies'; 'Ha Ha I'm
Drowning'; 'Sleeping Gas'; 'When I Dream'

Less a rock classic than an odd pop nugget. Like Magazine's *The Correct Use Of Soap* (see p.85), the first Teardrop Explodes album was about arty, punky types from the damp north-west of England predicting how big '80s pop was going to sound. More keyboards, less guitars. Funky disco rhythm sections. Strong musicianship. Catchy choruses and clean production. Baffling lyrics sung with a vaguely heroic pretentiousness. The difference between Magazine's commercial flop and the Teardrop Explodes' short-lived period as an early Smash Hits pin-up was simple: that would be Cope, first name Julian.

Julian Cope now is one of Britain's few remaining eccentric intellectuals, re-politicising the whole hippy-druid-pagan history thing in his book *The Modern Antiquarian: A Pre-Millennial Odyssey Through Megalithic Britain*, and on his eco-warrior website, Head Heritage (www.headheritage.co.uk). He still makes records too, and they're usually self-consciously but enthusiastically nuts with the occasional moment of psych-pop genius. But, back at the turn of those crazy '80s, Julian was a beautiful boy with a bushy blonde bob and a disquietingly perfect English voice, who was also one of The Crucial Three, a mythical band who never played a gig but did provide a song – 'Books' – that turned up on both *Kilimanjaro* and *Crocodiles* (see p.94), as well as some kind of creative springboard for Cope, Echo And The Bunnymen's Ian McCulloch, and Wah!'s Pete Wylie. The three were music-press gold, as they bickered at each other Scousily about who was the most Godlike, and promoted a scene that had sprung from Eric's, a semi-legendary Liverpool punk rock venue. Apart from these three gob-shites, Eric's gave British pop Bill Drummond (The KLF), David Balfe (Blur's mentor and subject of their 'Country House'), Pete Burns (Dead Or Alive), Ian Broudie (The Lightning Seeds) and Holly Johnson (Frankie Goes To Hollywood). *Kilimanjaro* remains the most enduring early '80s Liverpool-pop long-player, despite the fact that Cope was actually Welsh, with a family home in Tamworth, Staffs.

The main gimmick of *Kilimanjaro* is the trumpets, played by session veterans Ray Martinez and Hurricane Smith. Resisting both the horniness of Earth Wind & Fire and the brassiness of Dexys, Teardrop trumpets sounded like the ancient battle fanfares of mythical kings, and gave these strange little monkey puzzle grooves an almost comic air of Importance. This was Important, because punk's aftershocks were fading into grumpy murmurs and we were fast approaching the 'Go For It!!!' years, where no one had a clue what 'it' was, but understood that it better be gone for before those nice men at the record label consigned you to a life of supporting the Angelic Upstarts in Finland. So, while the trumpets Went For It!, Copey and Co. could concentrate on blending jazz-funk, Scott Walker, quaint English psychedelia in a Syd-Barrett-lost-intellectual-stud-muffin-on-acid vein, long-lost pop-hippy genius Kevin Ayers, and vocals that sounded like Little Lord Fauntleroy on steroids. The thrust of the lyrics can be neatly summed up in one line from the haunting and lovely 'Poppies In The Field': 'The poppies are in the field/But don't ask me what that means.'

So we didn't. But we thought it was, you know, kind of deep. From tiny acorns such as this, entire 'Vienna's are grown.

REMAIN IN LIGHT

TALKING HEADS
PRODUCED BY BRIAN ENO
SIRE/OCTOBER 1980
UK CHART: 21
US CHART: 19
KEY TRACKS: 'Once In A Lifetime'; 'Born Under Punches'; 'Seen And Not Seen'; 'Houses In Motion'; 'Listening Wind'

There was this period in 1980 when everybody went a bit African. Sure, we all know the obvious ones – Bow Wow Wow and Adam Ant inspired by Malcolm McLaren to get some Burundi drums in the mix, and make some dirty jokes based on being all naked and stuff. But from Teardrop Explodes's album title to the tribal rumble of Killing Joke, it all goes a bit dark continent for the next few pages. Admittedly, much of this is down to the white middle-class belief that black people – and especially Africans – are, you know, closer to the earth. More . . . instinctive. You know . . . unspoiled. And they dance well, have large penises, and are really good at middle-distance running. But all this slightly dodgy exotica and primitivism did make for some fine pop, so I'll just leave this high moral ground; look, coming down, nothing to see, move it along.

Anyway, the artists who committed most completely to trying to evoke Africa without resorting to cliché were David Byrne and Brian Eno. *My Life In The Bush Of Ghosts* is on its way (see p.110). But before that, there was this.

Remain In Light is outrageously fucking fine. It even contains the kind of transgression which, although done very subtly here, would still probably cause some kind of controversy if written now. 'Listening Wind' is a song about a man from an unnamed African nation. His name is Mojique. He 'sees his village from a nearby hill' and 'thinks of days before Americans came'. He decides that the foreigners and their 'free-trade zones' are simply invaders, here to destroy his people's lives, this time through western free-market values rather than guns and slave ships. He plants a 'device' in the free-trade zone. The wind he listens for is the sound of the blast, 'Come to drive them away.' The politics and emotions that underpin terrorism explained in just under five minutes, with what can only be described as sympathy, if not empathy. The music is a dreamy sway. This is so far away from either punk or agit-pop it may as well have been beamed down from a distant planet. It wants to explain, rather than berate, and it does so with unlikely sweetness.

But Chris Frantz and Tina Weymouth are the heroes of this album. That would be the drummer and the bass player. Nothing in music is harder – and more a labour of pure love – than playing funk quietly. It means bringing the rhythm inside of you, making it a part of your body, rejecting utterly the desire to show your virtuosity, to roll and thump and plunk, because such vulgarities are an interruption of – an argument against – the purity of pure groove. On 'Houses In Motion', Frantz and Weymouth reach a state of sultry, spiritual grace, pulling every audible beat back while pushing the inaudible – the beat of the body and the breath, the Great Connection between all humans, no matter what differences culture and history have forced upon us – constantly forward. Embedded within the undulating pulse of 'Houses In Motion' is the reason why late-'80s house forged a connection between dancers that made the hippy and punk tribes seem shallow and contrived and doomed to fail in comparison. Feel, and feel together, and feel free at last.

And it gets even better. 'Born Under Punches' is the funkiest groove ever played by a white group. Drums so understated, like a preppy Funkadelic. Polyphonous guitars, bass and synth-bass trading lines, thrusting and parrying, music as utter end in itself. The paranoia of 'Fear Of Music' (see p.66) is still in Byrne's narrative, but this time with a music which seems to take something from every continent and jams it into joyful release. Here's a chance to dance your way, out of your constrictions. An animal yelp throws away Byrne's last vestige of the uptight anonymous New York-psycho-nerd. Now you can see him grinning and dancing and throwing off clothes and neuroses. Enduring image, I know. Still, I'll make up for that by mentioning 'The Great Curve', which is not about a coastline or a wave or a mountain, but the fact that 'The world moves on a woman's hips'. 'Course it does. What else could move us more deeply?

But the song that really pulled me inside *Remain In Light* all those years ago was not one of the big funk epics, not even the hit single and world-changing masterpiece that is 'Once In A Lifetime', which I've decided to leave be here because I gushed so gushily about it in *This Is Uncool* that I honestly have nothing left to add. The song that initially stunned me was 'Seen And Not Seen', a Byrne spoken-word piece set against a fluid and sensual evocation of some dream jungle, like a travelogue of Africa without any noises that we usually associate with Africa. In a deep, calm whisper, Byrne tells us of a man who sees faces in magazines or on TV that he likes more than his. He believes that, if he concentrates hard enough, his face will morph into something better, something resembling his ideal . . . our ideal.

I found myself lost in this short story because it made me realise just how often a person's face tells you correctly about their basic character. The dead-eyed sneering guy who really is violent and aggressive. The chubby-cheeked woman with the laughing eyes and wide mouth who really is the earth mother type. And so on. So maybe we do make our face into the shape we want it to be. Or maybe it makes itself, despite ourselves.

But what I liked most was the subtle psychological horror Byrne introduced at the end:

'Although some people might have made mistakes . . .
They may have arrived at an appearance that bears no relationship to them . . .
They may have picked an ideal appearance based on some childish whim, or momentary impulse . . .
Some may have gotten halfway there, and then changed their minds.
He wonders if he too might have made a similar mistake.'

This enthralled the teen me in the same way as those *Astounding Tales* comics, full of horror stories with twist endings, had enthralled me as a pre-pubescent. And it led me into the rest of *Remain In Light*'s kaleidoscopic web of sound, a music as big and physical, in its white arty way, as Earth Wind & Fire's. There's a world in this album, one that mourns the coming death of instinct and rails against the coldness of bourgeois homogeneity. It's a world hotter and scarier and more magical than the one we live in. That's what the best music makes. That's what makes the best music.

KILLING JOKE

KILLING JOKE
PRODUCED BY KILLING JOKE
MALICIOUS DAMAGE/OCTOBER 1980
UK CHART: 39
US CHART: UNRELEASED IN USA
KEY TRACKS: 'Change'; Requiem'; 'Complications';
'Wardance'; 'Bloodsport'

Things wrong with British rock, part 282: British rock bands in 2006 are too obsessed with a career to have any real belief in anything, except their own success. For Coldplay, Keane, Athlete, etc, read the New Labourisation of rock, where substance and principle is replaced by an empty populism, and winning – getting enough votes to win an election, shifting units – is the end in itself. Many people seem to adore this approach to making music, presumably because the banal emotions, the lyrical platitudes, the lack of any actual point, perfectly reflects the white liberal middle-classes' penchant for selling out and feeling mildly guilty about it, and needing everything they consume to reassure them that the mild guilt is more than enough to justify their submission to consumerism and their terror of being judged a failure in terms of status. This feeling of needy, enervating ennui is easy to exploit in terms of songwriting. If you hit particular notes on a piano, move through particular changes in chord or key, then that music will say, 'Oh dear'. This is not emotional music. This is maths.

So the rest of us who think music might serve a more useful function than an emollient bath oil with soothing aloe vera continue to search for musicians who believe in things so strongly that their music is suffused with that belief – even if the set of beliefs in question are stupid, muddle-headed, Utopian, apocalyptic, obscure, scary or just plain challenging. Musicians such as Notting Hill's punk-metal-funk fusioneers and accidental inventors of industrial music, Killing Joke.

In 1982, the band's leader, keyboardist and shamanistic shouter Jaz Coleman, for example, believed so strongly that the world was going to end that he fled to Iceland. Yeah, I know, Iceland is actually in the world, but the line between genius and madness is a thin one, don't you know. Anyway, he was so convincing that Killing Joke's bass player Martin Glover, better known as soon-to-be successful dance/pop/rock producer Youth, went with him. And they stayed there a bit, presumably checking out their occult prophecy tomes and eating puffin, until one day, after a couple of months, they realised that the world was still, you know, there. And they came home and got on with making records and Youth left and so on and so forth. But, and here's the not altogether shocking twist . . . once they'd got this out of their systems, the band weren't very good. They started to make rousing, stadium-friendly goth-U2 anthems. They settled.

And actually they reformed recently and made a really good album called, oddly, *Killing Joke*, just like this, their first album. In the meantime Coleman had become a respected classical composer. But that's all by the by. While I realise that wishing complete mental meltdown on anyone who strums a guitar is somewhat brutal, the truth is that the first three Killing Joke albums are works of crunching, doomy funk-metal genius because the people who made them were utterly fucking nuts, and they were utterly fucking nuts because the state of the planet in the year that added Reagan to Thatcher sent them into an apoplectic rage that forced them to make art that they believed mattered and screw it if no one ever plays this on the radio and Macca and Elton never want to hang out with them. And doing that – engaging absolutely with what you absolutely believe to be crucial to human existence, even if no one else agrees – is a risk to your own mental health AND THE ENTIRE FUCKING POINT OF MAKING ART. Sorry to shout, but . . . people, we should be demanding more from our white and white minstrels than being Enya for post-grads.

And on a mundane but necessary note, the Joke's extraordinary 'Change' – the best disco-metal tune ever – was not on the original first album, but now is courtesy of the 2005 reissue, so therefore takes its rightful place as the keyest of key Killing Joke tracks. If you cop a listen to it and you do not wiggle your butt and feel completely mentally empowered and physically re-energised, then The Best Whinging Mewling Lickspittle Lighters-Aloft Corporate Festival Fake Indie Power(less) Ballads . . . Ever! is available at Tesco Express for a price your poor addled resigned mind is paying with your every waking breath. Have fun.

KINGS OF THE WILD FRONTIER

ADAM AND THE ANTS
PRODUCED BY CHRIS HUGHES
CBS/NOVEMBER 1980
UK CHART: 1
US CHART: 44
KEY TRACKS: 'Dog Eat Dog'; 'Kings of The Wild Frontier'; 'Antmusic'; 'Feed Me To The Lions'; 'The Human Beings'

And speaking of nutters . . .

Stuart 'Adam Ant' Goddard's recent mental health problems provide a timely reminder that chucking around variations on a theme of mad/nuts/bonkers and so forth can come off glib and flippant when confronted with the real thing. But if ever a pop album rode to glory on a sort of madness, then this is it. So you're a native American and a cowboy and a pirate and an ant. You're going to sing about ant invasions and warrior braves and shiver-me-timbers and shagging and how rubbish any pop is that isn't about ant invasions and warrior braves and shiver-me-timbers and

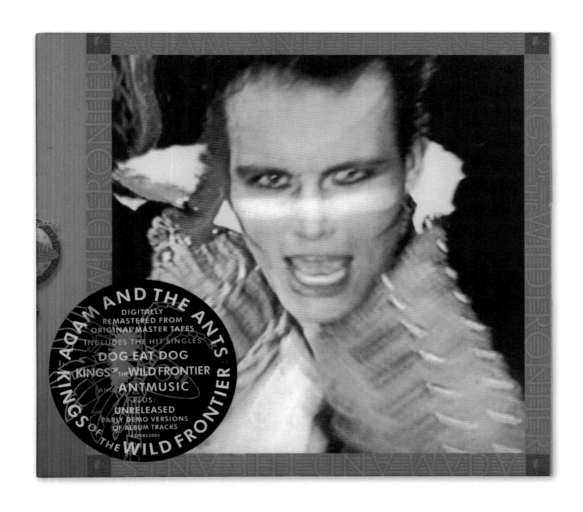

KINGS OF THE WILD FRONTIER/ADAM AND THE ANTS

shagging in a voice pitched somewhere between Anthony Newley and a strangled yelp and a matinee idol croon. This will all be backed by twin African drums, Duane Eddy guitars and the odd metal power chord, and funk bass, and will be punctuated by men chanting 'AWWWWW' in what can only be described as a gay spaghetti western style. You've actually pinched most of the look from The Village People, for Christ's sake, but you'll go with the thing that it was given to you by Malcolm McLaren before he stole all the former Ants to form Bow Wow Wow, because it's a neat revenge on all the west London punk elitists who've laughed at you for the last four years. Oh . . . and the album will be produced by one of the drummers. Sure, go ahead, Kid. Can we write this off against tax?

But this ludicrous venture went on to change British pop overnight. In the four months it took to get to No. 1, the joy it brought to we pop kids ensured that the pop zeitgeist moved from angry guys in modish suits telling us what a bunch of apolitical saps we were and how it probably didn't matter because we were all going to be nuked, to pretty peacocks in make-up and curtain material being really, really serious about being really, really silly. The Adam sound closely resembled the Gary Glitter sound, and the Ant/Numan-inspired new romantic/futurist/daft haircut wave was re-tooled glam rock, aspiring to be Bowie, Bolan and Ferry while largely being Alvin Stardust and Mud with a crucial smidgeon of panto existentialism. It was awful and thrilling in roughly equal measure and, in hindsight, it feels like a generation agreeing that it probably was doomed so, sod it, let's cake the make-up, and dance. *Kings Of The Wild Frontier* did this, whether Adam truly meant it or not, and the thing that makes this a better album than most of what followed in its wake, apart from risk and the aforementioned insanity, is its vindicative anger. This was one of those rare records which is so sure that it will make the singer a star that it's largely about its own inevitable triumph. As one of the very first musicians to see the Sex Pistols and understand entirely that the old order was dead, Adam's subsequent

rejection by the punk cogniscenti and ridicule from the music press for his early bondage-goth-cabaret schtick had hurt. But, as he summed up beautifully a little further down the pop line, 'Ridicule is nothing to be scared of.'

The album convinced us because it was utterly triumphant, and that triumphalism was borne out of sheer agony and a reckless determination to be bigger, prettier and more important than any of his tormentors could dream of becoming. He pulled it off, for a short while. But you pay for that kind of obsession with stardom as the only self-justification, to the point, one imagines, where you end up waving a gun around outside a Camden pub twenty years later, and getting sectioned in the Royal Free Hospital. I still love the bloke, though, and really hope he's over it. Why tread on that ant? He's done nothing to you. There may come a time when he's treading on you.

SOUND AFFECTS

THE JAM
PRODUCED BY VIC COPPERSMITH-HEAVEN AND THE JAM
POLYDOR/NOVEMBER 1980
UK CHART: 2
US CHART: 72
KEY TRACKS: 'That's Entertainment'; 'Pretty Green'; 'Start!'; 'Man In The Corner Shop'; 'But I'm Different Now'

There are plenty of valid reasons why *Sound Affects* is my fave Jam LP – the cute pop-art sleeve, the Gang Of Four influence, the memory of seeing them play at Skegness around this time, the Lennon-style granny shades Weller wore on the 'Start!' video. But the main reason is because it contains the four best songs Paul Weller ever wrote. Which means four of the best British guitar pop songs anyone ever wrote. They go a little like this.

'Man In The Corner Shop' is the sweetest and cleverest

lyric Weller penned from a socialist perspective, and a nastier take on the wistful slice-of-life vignettes that McCartney often wrote for The Beatles. In an English anytown there is a corner shop, and the man who owns it is envied by one of his customers, a man who works in a factory. Not that the corner shop owner derives any real satisfaction from this, because in order to remain his own boss he works long hours just to make ends meet. Besides, he sells cigars to the man who owns the factory. Now there's a man to be jealous of . . .

And Weller doesn't over-egg the British-class-system pudding as he could, because the song is really all about the last verse: 'Go to church do the people from the area/All shapes and classes sit and pray together/For here they are all one . . . For God created all men equal/They know/That God created all men equal.' And this is sung – spat – with an irony bitter enough to swallow *Das Kapital* whole.

'Start!' is, of course, the album's big hit, and, yes, it cops so completely from George Harrison's 'Taxman' that it was sampling before anyone knew what sampling was. But I always figured that Harrison didn't sue because he knew that, for once, The Beatles had been improved upon.

'Pretty Green' is where Weller's very brief interest in post-punk hits a home run. Like 'Start!', it strips down The Jam until you realise just how funky they could have been, and hooks up the Gang Of Four's spare punch to a melody that only a true pop kid could write. What 'Pretty Green' says about money isn't startling in itself. But, like The Wu-Tang Clan's 1994 anthem 'C.R.E.A.M (Cash Rules Everything Around Me)', it freshens old news by making it feel like the back of your own mind talking, and like a reinvention of the blues.

But the best-ever Weller song is 'That's Entertainment', an alternative national anthem for all those of us who would rather face up to what Britain is, in all its beauty and horror, than sign up to several generations-worth of 'You've never had it so good' denial. It's an acoustic guitar, and subtle swinging percussion, and two chords and a change for the chorus, and six verses of caustic, poetic imagery that fits This Place 2006 just as well as That Place 1980. Every lover of the song probably has a favourite verse. This one's mine:

A smash of glass and the rumble of boots
An electric train and a ripped up phone booth
Paint-splattered walls and the cry of a tom cat
Lights going out and a kick in the balls

Weller's voice is just beautiful, too; bruised yet strong enough to carry all our fears and fight all our battles. The best compliment I can pay *Sound Affects* is to say that most of it is good enough to live with this masterpiece.

1981

MY LIFE IN THE BUSH OF GHOSTS

BRIAN ENO–DAVID BYRNE

PRODUCED BY BRIAN ENO AND DAVID BYRNE
EG/FEBRUARY 1981
UK CHART: 29
US CHART: 44
KEY TRACKS: 'Regiment'; 'America Is Waiting'; 'The Jezebel
Spirit'; 'Help Me Somebody'; 'Moonlight In Glory'

Having succeeded in blending New York art-punk with Afro-funk on Talking Heads' *Remain In Light*, Brian Eno and David Byrne decided to delve further into the idea and dispense with pop song altogether. Instead of traditional lead vocal and melody, the dome-headed duo decorated their dense, atmospheric rhythms with found voices, taped from radio talk-ins and devotional records. The result became a touchstone for future dance producers who wanted to produce grooves that worked the dancefloor without a conventional pop focus. *My Life In The Bush Of Ghosts* pretty much invented the cut 'n' paste production methods that later touched techno, hip hop, trip hop and the whole jazzy phat chill-out beatz thang.

The title is pinched from a 1954 novel by Nigerian author Amos Tutuola, a story of an eight-year-old's adventures in the bush after his abandonment during a white slaver raid. Tutuola, who died in 1997, was a controversial figure in Nigerian literary circles, often accused of playing up to African 'primitive' stereotypes by writing in pidgin English, and even of plagiarism. Nevertheless, Tutuola set off something precious in the imaginations of Eno and Byrne, whose own *Bush Of Ghosts* subtly examines the tension between stressed-out modern America and its fear of black (skinned) magic. While the title evokes chilling African Yoruba folk-tales, and various singers evoke their pleas to their Gods, other voices explore exorcism, fundamentalism and good old-fashioned American panic. 'America is waiting for a message of some sort or another,' an exasperated San Francisco radio talk-show host ponders on the opening track. 'No will whatsoever . . . absolutely no integrity!' It's never made clear exactly who he's accusing but, with his crackling indignation forced into the warp and weft of this artified Africana, suddenly locking into the monstrous stomping groove, suddenly finding some kind of chorus hook before being cast adrift again, the anonymous ranter comes off like the announcer at the end of the world.

The album's finest and most influential moment is 'Regiment', where Lebanese mountain singer Dunya Yusin is plucked from an album called *The Human Voice In Islam* and pleads to Allah over the funkiest, plunkiest bassline this side of Sly And The Family Stone. The endlessly detailed but essentially discreet layers of drums, percussion, Arabic-flavoured synth, and glistening, droning guitars form a mesmerising backdrop that hits just the right key in order to transform Yusin into a blues singer, making so many links between cultures that you almost feel like you're being immersed in a global day of yearning.

Eno and Byrne may be striving to evoke ghosts of slaves, of victims of Christian-Islamic conflict, of poor Americans lost in their own bush of spooks. But God – a non-denominational one – is the album's star, getting raised by an anonymous, terrifying exorcist for 'The Jezebel Spirit', by a southern Baptist preacher on the rousing 'Help Me Somebody', by Algerians on 'Qu'ran', by an Appalachian Christian choir on 'Moonlight In Glory'. The only ghost to fear, the album seems to suggest, is that big old Holy Ghost, the one that takes possession of so many souls, the one that seems to spread more fear than solace. The Reverend Paul Morton, for example, who stirs up the New Orleans faithful in true blues fashion on 'Help Me Somebody', just makes you think of Hurricane Katrina, and the lines of abandoned Afro-Americans queuing for aid, and what someone like Morton might have to wail and preach to keep their hopes alive. Like many of the best albums released at the turn of the '80s, *My Life In The Bush Of Ghosts* feels more chillingly accurate about the twenty-first century than tomorrow's news headlines. Except that the Bush we have to worry about ain't nowhere near Nigeria.

SOLID GOLD

GANG OF FOUR
PRODUCED BY JIMMY DOUGLASS AND GANG OF FOUR
EMI/MARCH 1981
UK CHART: 52
US CHART: DID NOT CHART
KEY TRACKS: 'Paralysed'; 'A Hole In The Wallet'; 'What We All Want'; 'Outside The Trains Don't Run On Time'; 'He'd Send In The Army'

The best completely tuneless record ever made. The Gang Of Four, hung up on booze, drugs, deep funk and the imminent collapse of the human soul under the onslaught of '80s free market economics, bury melody under the clammy silt of Afro-funk rhythm in a way that even the inventor of the beat-is-the-tune idea, James Brown, might consider a tad extreme. Considered a career-suicide album by some, the absolute essence of the band by others, *Solid Gold* is unflinching in its despair, relentless in its rhythms, bleakly appropriate in its fit of medium to message, and horrifyingly right about everything, from Andy Gill's spoken-word testimony from the perspective of a redundant worker (three years before the miners' strike) in 'Paralysed', to the sex/money equation worked out most funkily on 'A Hole In The Wallet', to the domestic militarism and fascism explored in 'Outside The Trains Don't Run On Time' and 'He'd Send In The Army'. There is nowhere left to duck and cover here, no ear candy to sweeten the bitter truths . . . and no tunes to help you breathe more easily. Or, as 'In The Ditch' sings so I don't have to; 'Get down. Down to the floor.'

PLAYING WITH A DIFFERENT SEX

AU PAIRS
PRODUCED BY AU PAIRS
HUMAN/APRIL 1981
UK CHART: 33
US CHART: UNRELEASED IN USA
KEY TRACKS: 'It's Obvious'; 'Diet'; 'Come Again'; 'We're So Cool'; 'Repetition'

Back in the pre-politically-correct '70s, one of the running jokes of British TV and blue film comedy was the au pair. An au pair was a woman – always a woman – who came to England to study and took a live-in job as a home help in return for accommodation and some pocket money. I would imagine that this still exists. But we don't talk about au pairs anymore, largely because the joke insisted that all au pairs were Swedish, blonde, pneumatic, over-sexed and compliant enough to shag the man of the house while the missus was out shopping. Yep, TV viewers really were that easily amused back in the day.

So a bunch of students from Birmingham, inspired by punk counter-culture, Patti Smith and Gang Of Four, decided to subvert the joke by calling their feminist band the Au Pairs. The two girls in the group, singer/guitarist Lesley Woods and bassist Jane Munro, were not blonde, compliant or given to domestic servitude. The two boys in the band, guitarist/vocalist Paul Foad and drummer Pete Hammond, weren't too keen on going 'PHWOOAR!' or slapping short bald men on the head while a wacky sax instrumental played in the background. Benny Hill might be more famous – and bizarrely popular in America among rappers like Snoop Dogg – than the Au Pairs. But the feminism of bands like this is a major reason why the fat twat got chucked off telly and British comedy writers were forced to grow up. That and sheer embarrassment, one suspects.

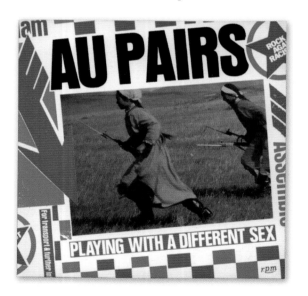

The Au Pairs need to be re-discovered like their creative uncles in the Gang Of Four because, like Patti Smith and The Slits, they proved that womens' liberation was sexy. The now-defunct *Sounds* magazine once described Lesley Woods as 'The Eartha Kitt of rock 'n' roll' and that was spot-on; her voice was an erotic purr, a come-on, a mellifluous flirtation even as she was singing about wife-beaters (their cover of Bowie's 'Repetition'), British crimes in Northern Ireland ('Armagh'), how crap 'new men' are in bed ('Come Again'), domestic drudgery ('Diet'), state sponsoring of the heroin trade ('Headache'), dumping her boyfriend to shag women ('Dear John'), the inevitable failure and underlying possessive-ness of open relationships ('We're So Cool') and conventional romance as a con conceived to tie women to the home ('Love Song'). Their sinuous, itchy dub-pop was actually far more accessible than Gang Of Four's, hence the healthy sales of this, their one great album. They remain the perfect example of the glory of the original indie movement – funny, danceable, intelligent, politically committed believers in a better world, impossible to satisfy in as many ways as you can imagine . . . and actually independent. No wonder they've been swept under the Britpop carpet, in a world where indie has come to mean 'careerist rock by men who can't play metal'.

The RPM label reissued this wonderful record on CD in 2002 with the addition of the best early Au Pairs singles so, if you are one of those who've noticed that ferocious and entirely accessible female artists like Peaches, Sleater-Kinney and Le Tigre still don't get any radio or TV play, and under-stand that misogyny in rock is not a guilty secret but a fuck-ing requirement, and are not fooled into believing that, because bloke-rock isn't as honest as hip hop about its fear of women who won't be sold as cheesecake, it must mean that white men are more enlightened than black men . . . if you're not fooled by that lie nor satisfied with the largely dire, sexless music that this whitewash habitually chucks at you, then you are going to love this record, and I'm going to love you, you enlightened bastard, you.

HEAVEN UP HERE

ECHO AND THE BUNNYMEN
PRODUCED BY HUGH JONES
KOROVA/WEA/MAY 1981
UK CHART: 10
US CHART: DID NOT CHART
KEY TRACKS: 'Heaven Up Here'; 'No Dark Things'; 'It Was A Pleasure'; 'A Promise'; 'With A Hip'

A funny thing happened on the way to this entry. I'd written this long, somewhat accusatory and guilt-ridden sermon on why U2 beat Echo And The Bunnymen in the early '80s battle-of-the-big-rock-bands, and how the Bunnymen's second album was the truest musical prophecy of the rapidly developing uselessness of My Generation, and, just as I was typing in the last word, I got one of those Microsoft, 'Your computer has just royally fucked up. Sorry for the inconvenience' messages . . . and lost every word I'd just written. What can I say, except that the divine intervention of flawed technology sometimes saves your bacon, sizzle-wise, because I probably would've gone with my mid-life crisis moan and . . . really . . . who needs it?

What I'd really like to say about *Heaven Up Here* is that it's one of the keynote albums of my life. Its itchy, gushing, imperious yet intimate blend of post-punk funk and classic rock pomp backdrops a set of great, funny lyrics about wallowing in misery, getting pissed and drugged to the eyeballs, and knowing that all this is just a distraction from Important Stuff Like Fighting The Man, but seizing each moment of hedonist chaos like a lifeline, and maybe forgiving yourself. Its big, heroic, lighters-aloft moments are . . . not ironic, exactly. But knowing, and deliberately overwrought, and subtly satirical at the expense of the stadium melancholy they knew was coming, and became a part of inventing. Ian McCulloch's voice is in love with itself, and therefore knows exactly when to howl off-key, bark like a dog, and steal from Jim Morrison, Lou Reed and Del Shannon's 'Runaway'. The beats are elastic and strong, and Will Sergeant's guitar shimmers and skips and stabs in all the right places, the places where there is a thrilling incompleteness that your soul gets to fill.

And yes, there's definitely a narrative about literally falling over yourself to escape the prospect of life becoming hell on Earth, hence the 'Heaven Up Here', where the booze and drugs take you. And a sly sub-plot about the idiot joys of convincing yourself that you're cool, even as you're vomiting snakebite over that grey trenchcoat you bought from Oxfam after seeing Jean-Paul Belmondo in *A Bout De Souffle*. 'We're all groovy, groovy people,' Mac hiccoughs spectacularly on the title track, before the party turns to chaos and everybody falls over. But Mac's found a friend, a solid presence for the night. 'Me and the wall . . . we're OK, we're OK!' The room spins, the coke spills, the drummer kills himself on a motorbike (RIP Mr de Freitas), Bono becomes a world statesman. This is one hangover that never goes away.

NIGHTCLUBBING/GRACE JONES

NIGHTCLUBBING

GRACE JONES

PRODUCED BY CHRIS BLACKWELL AND ALEX SADKIN
ISLAND/MAY 1981
UK CHART: 35
US CHART: 32
KEY TRACKS: 'Pull Up To The Bumper'; 'Walking In The Rain'; 'I've Seen That Face Before (Libertango)'; 'Use Me'; 'Nightclubbing'

Grace Jones was right with Ian BunnyMac when he cribbed from Del Shannon on 'Over The Wall' and sang, 'I'm a-walking in the rain/To celebrate this misery.' For her 'Walking In The Rain', she's strolling through Manhattan's dirty night, and celebrating its own misery and her own defiant gesture. 'Feeling like a woman/Looking like a man/Sounding like a no-no/Mating when I can,' she glowers, braving the showers to go to – where else? – the disco.

But she also knew that there is only one thing better on dance-pop records than handclaps: synthetic handclaps. The handclaps on this, the fifth album by the gender-bending Jamaican model and ultimate symbol of New York '70s/'80s punk-disco club culture, sound like sex, God and electricity. They are triggered, of course, by drummer Sly Dunbar, who, with his bass-playing partner Robbie Shakespeare, defined the shape of this stupendous record and the terms of the thrilling, short-lived, but incredibly influential early-'80s crossover between Jamaican reggae, American funk and global pop.

Ms Jones was what can only be described as an alternative diva. That is, she made records aimed at the disco, wrote few of her own songs, and looked like a cross between a black cyborg and a designer hat-stand . . . which is to say, so strikingly, androgynously beautiful and intimidating and alien that her core audience was of course made up almost exclusively of gay men. After three camp but uninteresting albums of hi-energy fare, visionary Island label founder Blackwell came up with a better idea for her Warm Leatherette fourth album: hook the woman up with Sly & Robbie's Compass Point studio houseband in the Bahamas, cover a more arty selection of songs including post-punk classics such as Joy Division's 'She's Lost Control' and The Normal's 'Warm Leatherette', make her into ironic pan-African S&M transgender gold-dust. In point of fact, she never became that big. But, in *Nightclubbing*, she did make an album that stands as one of the touchstones of '80s dance-pop, and which always sells, because it never dates.

Defining herself here as the ultimate blankly perfect post-Warhol product on 'Art Groupie' – 'Dont ask me any questions/My personal life is a bore/Admire me in glory/An art groupie . . . that's all' – Jones covered Sting's 'Demolition Man', Iggy Pop's 'Nightclubbing' and Bill Withers's 'Use Me' in the style of the imaginary star of Attack Of The 50ft Transexual Dominatrix, and embodied Lloyd Cole's heroine with 'Cheekbones like geometry and eyes like sin' three years before he sang about her on *Rattlesnakes* (see p.171) on a Jean Paul Goude-designed album sleeve that seemed to become more unlikely and stunning the more you stared at it. I'm staring at it now. It's unlikely and stunning.

Sly & Robbie backed it all with a funk-reggae hybrid that felt like the inside of a taxi that knows a secret thirty-minute route from Kingston to Studio 54 via Paris and Brixton, but only for the beautiful and damned. And those synthetic handclaps? If the way they shoot electro-shocks into your spine on 'Use Me' isn't quite enough, then their application to the dirtiest set of car/sex double-entendres ever dreamed up by someone other than Chuck Berry or Prince on 'Pull Up To The Bumper' is like being slapped in the kisser by a lorry-load of forbidden fruit. Chris Blackwell was one smart geezer; he distributed and funded the Ze label, worked with the Talking Heads rhythm section in the shape of Tom Tom Club, had an inside grip on the whole Manhattan hip hop/disco/Afro-reggae/art-punk/lowlife/high fashion satirical pop schtick. And here, he, Jones and her Jamaican musicians compressed all that scene's best ideas into thirty-eight minutes of sparkling pop sleaze.

Now, when you hear someone banging on about manu-factured pop in that 'I feel really old so let me celebrate who-ever turns up in *Heat* in a way that suggests that if you don't like Girls Aloud you must be a musty old librarian with no sexual organs because then no one will notice that I'm more terrified of The Kids and old age than I ever thought possi-ble' kind of way, the thing to do is point out that great man-ufactured pop is intellectually charged, dangerous, challeng-ing and fucking weird. Elvis. Motown. Ms Grace Jones. Why accept anything less?

DURAN DURAN

DURAN DURAN
PRODUCED BY COLIN THURSTON
EMI/JUNE 1981
UK CHART: 3
US CHART: 10
KEY TRACKS: 'Planet Earth'; 'Girls On Film'; 'Careless Memories'; 'Anyone Out There'; 'Tel Aviv'

No other pop album of the early '80s so crystallised the end of punk's protest, nor made emptiness sound so energised. The first Duran Duran album took all the most synthetic bits of Bowie, Roxy Music, Magazine, Giorgio Moroder, Gary Numan and new romantic inventors Japan, trans-formed any doubt and pain into a gauche excuse to suck in their cheeks and pout, and guiltlessly seethed with a desper-ate desire for fame, money, sex and cheap thrills. They brought a very British male clumsiness and sweat to Grace Jones's nightclub full of mannequins, and in so doing made the impossibly glamorous VIP room feel accessible to any young Brit blokes and birds who could afford mascara and hair gel. Plus I barely knew a single girl who didn't want to fuck John Taylor, and, in hindsight, it's easier to see the . . . ahem . . . relief of being able to fantasise about either being or shagging a member of a band who simply didn't care about anything other than winning pretty.

Duran Duran has dated so little because, no matter how much some of us want pop to be essentially counter-culture, more of us want pop to symbolise an achievable dream of sex and glory and provide a mindless submission to hor-mones and adrenalin. From a lad's perspective, being John Taylor or Nick Rhodes was definitely a stretch. But being Andy, Roger or Simon was a piece of piss. Le Bon's nasal foghorn whine is still funny and awful but so right for a funk-rock music that is almost falling over itself in the race for cash, coke and pussy, and which never even considered beating 'em in its desire to join 'em – 'em, of course, being the transatlantic rock elite. Duran Duran didn't care for their Birmingham hometown or politics or shame or art and didn't care who knew it. In 2006, they wouldn't be noticed among the scramble of dullards and cunts. In 1981, they were a blast of glee among the guilt-ridden rebels. They became ludicrous, but kept a straight face because they could afford to be ludicrous, and because, in Nick Rhodes, they had one true art groupie whose entire existence was a Warholian wink.

More than any other album – even *Thriller* (see p.151) – *Duran Duran* destroyed the inspiration of rebellion in early-'80s pop and implicitly embraced Thatcher, Reagan and the innate understanding that there were winners and losers and that the thrill of knowing you were bound to win could be concentrated into three-minute rushes to the finishing line, no prisoners taken, no doubts about the point of winning entertained. It could have sounded evil, but Duran Duran made it sound tough and delicious and like a tank crashing through a barricade. But then, not all good things say good things, and nowhere is that dichotomy more apparent and constant than pop in general, and Duran Duran in particu-lar.

JUJU

SIOUXSIE AND THE BANSHEES

PRODUCED BY NIGEL GRAY AND SIOUXSIE AND THE
BANSHEES
POLYDOR/JUNE 1981
UK CHART: 7
US CHART: UNRELEASED IN USA
KEY TRACKS: 'Monitor'; 'Arabian Knights'; 'Into The Light';
'Head Cut'; 'Spellbound'

By 1981, punk had firmly established the idea of 'alternative' pop and rock. So, while Duran Duran presented sex and sin in a non-threatening manner for straight pop kids, Siouxsie And The Banshees survived the punk culling by injecting a Velvet Underground-derived fascination for dark eroticism and pounding rhythms into post-punk rock. Bassist and co-founder Steven Bailey had, after all, named himself Severin after the sex-slave in the Velvets' 'Venus In Furs'. Severin and Sioux found a drummer (Budgie, formerly of The Slits) and guitarist (John McGeoch, formerly of Magazine) capable of mixing thundering power with inky and ornate subtlety, and got on with writing an album that painted Sioux as a vampiric dominatrix, angst-ridden yet imperious, distant yet earthy, spooky and spooked. And, on *Juju*, the Banshees became Duran-pop-in-negative and invented and defined goth.

Now obviously, as British youth tribes go, goth was just about the most useless, pointless and joyless. But all that was down to lots of lousy bands who cynically exploited the white middle-class-teen's guilty need for a pantomime of alienation. *Juju* remains one of the great sonic adventures – a lush, rumbling and intense concentrate of drum-bass-guitar virtuosity and a quite breathtaking understanding of the teenage connection between sex and fear. On the tracks that make up the vinyl side two – 'Night Shift', 'Sin In My Heart', 'Head Cut' and 'Voodoo Dolly' – Sioux beckons you into her bedroom of occult ephemera and patchouli vapours and just as you're anticipating the greatest night of perverse tantric sex ever, the door slams shut and you realise that the room is a dungeon and that Siouxsie is actually fifteen feet tall and has snakes for hair and is holding a terrifying implement and you want to make a bolt for it but . . . actually, you know, no pain, no gain, right? Except that sex with Siouxsie is as impossible as sex with Grace Jones, and in that desire for the impossible and the humiliation that may lie in achieving it, lies the impossible thrill of *Juju* at full volume.

The Banshees negotiated an awful second album (1979's *Join Hands*) and the hasty dash for freedom of original drummer Kenny Morris and guitarist John McKay because they were as ambitious and eager for an elitist stardom as the Durannies. But *Juju* is not empty; witness both the startling anti-elite Arab male rant that is 'Arabian Knights' – 'Veiled behind screens/Kept as your baby machine/Whilst you conquer more orifices/Of boys, goats and things' – and, at the other extreme, the horny lather Sioux gets into over buying a primitive wood carving on 'Head Cut'. Elsewhere, the astonishing 'Monitor' makes the Big Brother nightmare into a deeply funky churn of emotion and release, the perennial horror motifs of cursed childhood and dolls and toys smothers you in black and blue, and McGeoch, who later wasted his time and talent on the banal stadium new wave version of PiL and tragically and mysteriously died in his sleep in March 2004, conjures light from strings and pedals. His spidery climbs and chimes and graceful yet shocking changes of mood bind spells and tingle spines. *Juju* is simply one of the most beautiful and inspired guitar recordings ever conceived, and it's matched by the rumble and tumble of Budgie and Severin's murderous rhythms.

Juju evokes terror and madness and barbarism and death . . . and strives to make each invocation of the dark into an aesthetic, erotic dream. Their friend Robert Smith of the Cure – among many others – watered down this album's majestic edge and made millions. But the true dark action is here, where the sin in your heart never hides behind shame.

WAS (NOT WAS)/WAS (NOT WAS)

WAS (NOT WAS)

WAS (NOT WAS)
PRODUCED BY DON AND DAVID WAS AND JACK TANN
ZE/AUGUST 1981 (ALBUM RETITLED *OUT COME THE
FREAKS* IN *2003*)
UK CHART: DID NOT CHART
US CHART: DID NOT CHART
KEY TRACKS: 'The Sky's Ablaze'; 'Wheel Me Out'; 'Carry Me
Back To Old Morocco'; 'Tell Me That I'm Dreaming'; 'Where Did
Your Heart Go?'

MUTANT DISCO

VARIOUS ARTISTS
PRODUCED BY VARIOUS PRODUCERS
ZE/OCTOBER 1981
UK CHART: DID NOT CHART
US CHART: DID NOT CHART
KEY TRACKS: James White And The Blacks – 'Contort
Yourself'; Coati Mundi – 'Que Pasa/Me No Pop I'; Kid Creole
And The Coconuts – 'Annie I'm Not Your Daddy'; The
Waitresses – 'I Know What Boys Like'; Material & Nona Hendrix
– 'Bustin' Out'

On some busy street in some American city, a man tells a story and doesn't care if we're listening. A brass band provides a stately New Orleans-style soundtrack. He is recalling his life as a boy, and being with his father. His father was an alcoholic. His father would grab the boy and share his hallucinations.

'The sky's ablaze with ladies' legs, he used to say/They're kicking from the clouds/Shoes fall through the morning haze/And splat like eggs among the crowds/Can you see 'em, Boy?' The boy could not respond, as he watched his father's eyes spin wildly. All he could do is wonder how his father could bear life like this. The man he has become has no answers even now. And we who listen know that the point of the story is not how the alcoholic father copes or even what he sees. The point is that his child was scared and scarred for life. And the other point is that so is all America, in the year of Our Lord 1981.

So few heard the first album by Was (Not Was) that the perception of this big band led by Detroit's David and Don Was (originally David Weiss and Don Fagerson) is forever fixed by 'Walk the Dinosaur', a godawful pub-soul hit from 1987. But before the Was brothers became slick corporate hacks, they made a debut album that remains pop's only surrealist anti-Reagan, post-Vietnam big-band jazz-rock masterpiece. 'The Sky's Ablaze' was simply the strangest and saddest song housed within a uniquely bleak and industrial cover shot of rows and rows of cheap housing, blown up until distorted, and slanted beneath a red and orange and black-spotted sky that looked like nuclear fallout and creeping death.

'The woodwork squeaks and out come the freaks,' laughed the opening track, and out they came, casualties and madmen and hobos and hecklers, all housed within huge slabs of muso-disco which were occasionally ripped apart by metal guitar from Wayne Kramer of legendary '60s Detroit political punks The MC5. The musicians were (unfairly) uncredited, sacrificed for the sleeve's eerie mystery, but the vocalists were many, some white, some black, some male, some female and some not human at all, as Ronald Reagan himself interrupted the disco apocalypse that was 'Tell Me That I'm Dreaming' to ask, 'Can we who man the ship of state deny that it is somewhat out of control?' Well, no, obviously, and in response Was (Not Was) sent out waves of panic-induced irony and weirdness about tea in Morocco, former scientists, toupees, rusty cans of corn and choking on fish in order to illuminate the chaos of urban America under attack from mad admirals.

Was (Not Was) presumably wanted mutiny in 1981. By 1987 they were saluting the flag and jerking off the captain for fun and profit. In 1983 they paused to kick off the re-evaluation of both metal and easy listening by employing Ozzy Osbourne and Mel Torme as guest vocalists on the bizarre *Born To Laugh At Tornadoes* album. Man, what a decade the '80s was. Nevertheless, the 2003 reissue of this stunningly perverse and inspired album now features the single 'Wheel Me Out', which invented dance-rock and is absolutely fucking deadly, and you should buy this album and be amazed that pop was ever this ambitious and satirical and danceable.

As if to prove that New York's irony-drenched art-pop label Ze was surfing a creative tidal wave just as the punks were jumping ship, they released a label showcase compilation that pulled in everything extraordinary about arty punk and disco, and gave it a name. *Mutant Disco* was also re-released (and expanded) in 2003, and tells you all you need to know about the kaleidoscopic, intellectual, sarcastic and prophetic world of Ze, where the artists tried to have their cake and eat it by making disco-pop that laughed at disco-pop. You could say they failed. But the idea that dance music and pop can contain ironies that illuminate the worst of us, and therefore politicise the quintessentially ephemeral, persists, even if it doesn't shift units. And who cares who shifts units? I'll stick with the romance of the implausible, and I hope you will too.

THE BEST OF BLONDIE

BLONDIE
PRODUCED BY MIKE CHAPMAN, RICHARD GOTTEHRER AND GIORGIO MORODER
CHRYSALIS/OCTOBER 1981
UK CHART: 4
US CHART: 30
KEY TRACKS: 'Atomic'; 'Rapture'; 'Dreaming'; 'Union City Blue'; '(I'm Always Touched By Your) Presence Dear'

It's *The Best of Blondie*. Think The Everest Of Mountains, or The Pacificest Of Oceans, or The Johnniest Of Depps. Got it? Good. Next!

SEE JUNGLE! SEE JUNGLE! GO JOIN YOUR GANG, YEAH. CITY ALL OVER! GO APE CRAZY

BOW WOW WOW
PRODUCED BY COLIN THURSTON, BRIAN TENCH AND ALAN TARNEY
RCA/OCTOBER 1981
UK CHART: 26
US CHART: DID NOT CHART
KEY TRACKS: 'Chihuahua'; 'Sinner, Sinner, Sinner'; 'Go Wild In The Country'; '(I'm A) TV Savage'; 'Jungle Boy'

The story goes that in 1979, the pre-success Adam Ant paid Malcolm McLaren £1,000 to tell him where he was going wrong. McLaren gave him some ideas involving native chic and African rhythms while actually busying himself with stealing Adam's band. He teamed guitarist Matthew Ashman, bassist Leigh Gorman and drummer Dave Barbarossa with a fourteen-year-old Burmese beauty called Myant Myant Aye, who he had renamed Annabella Lwin, and apparently met in a launderette. He then schooled his quartet in the ways of said native chic and African rhythms, and made Annabella sing surreal, soundbite lyrics about sex, primitivism, home taping and fantasy jungles while taking her clothes off. After the kind of middling success that can only be dispiriting to a man who had shocked the world with the Sex Pistols and was attempting an ongoing satire of the society of spectacle, he lost interest and Bow Wow Wow became just another '80s new wave pop group, lost in obscurity.

And all this is true, but not quite the whole truth. Because although McLaren did see musicians as annoying necessities in his grand schemes, and did gleefully wind up

SEE JUNGLE! SEE JUNGLE! GO JOIN YOUR GANG, YEAH CITY ALL OVER!
GO APE CRAZY!/BOW WOW WOW

the music press and the US establishment (and Ms Lwin's parents, who threatened to sue over their daughter's state of undress on this album's sleeve parody of Manet's 1863 masterpiece *Dejeuner Sur L'Herbe*) with Lwin's budding sexuality, the forgotten truth about Bow Wow Wow is that their music was genuinely extraordinary. Again, manufactured pop doesn't have to be bland, or played by studio hacks, or bereft of any point other than exploitation. In fact, much of the best formula genius is a comment on exploitation, and nowhere is that more apparent than on the first, ludicrously-titled album proper by McLaren's second best music project (and no, I haven't forgotten 'Buffalo Gals').

See Jungle! is an attack on western bourgeois values – including our obsession with youth sex and dishonest hiding of it (see the early career of Britney Spears) – against a backdrop of tumbling African highlife rhythms, popping funk bass, surf/spaghetti western guitar twang, hilariously rabid vocal chants, and joyful pure pop choruses. McLaren's lyrics are full of prescient prophecies and killing jokes, including quite extraordinary coded predictions of the west's increasing desire to downsize and eat natural (the hit 'Go Wild In The Country' and 'Jungle Boy'); Diana never becoming Queen ('(I'm A) TV Savage'); the macho punk violence of moshing ('Elimination Dancing'); the increasing unsexiness of the electric guitar ('Mickey Put It Down') and the growing rejection of fathers as necessary parents ('Hello, Hello Daddy (I'll Sacrifice You)'). The music's vivid tumble – a kaleidoscope of globally informed ideas and unique imagination – is so technically accomplished that it can't help but put a salutary spin on how far rock's musical standards have fallen, in a world where we believe that what Radiohead play is as muso as it gets. While the things that hip hop and R&B producers can do with machines has become the real equivalent of Hendrix and The Beatles, rock has become a music where no one successful now could actually play the hits of Bow Wow Wow. Yes, I realise that no one wants to. But it really is just as well for the twenty-first-century rock plodder that trends have not re-embraced Bow

Wow Wow or The Ants, because current rock musicians simply aren't good enough to play this stuff. And this band could do it all live, too, at one point with another McLaren discovery, one 'Boy' George O'Dowd, on backing vocals. The point is proved by the three producers on *See Jungle!*, whose tracks all sound exactly the same, suggesting that all even Duran Duran's Thurston could do with such incredible players is press the Record button and stand well back.

It was around this period of the early '80s that music fans lost interest in who their favourite musicians were. This seemed liberating at the time – an escape from all those hippy relics banging on about Eric Clapton, an embrace of fabulous, stylish Idea!!! over dull old technique – but, in hindsight, it just meant that musicians were under no pressure anymore to find their own distinct way of playing. And why bother, when samplers, pro tools and ear candy machines can easily replace that proverbial nine-tenths of perspiration, and shift more units than one-tenth of inspiration? So if I come off like a Grumpy Old Man sometimes, well, tough, frankly. Because, in the case of Bow Wow Wow's misunderstood and visionary call of the wild, it really did used to be all fields 'round here.

DARE

THE HUMAN LEAGUE
PRODUCED BY MARTIN RUSHENT
VIRGIN/OCTOBER 1981
UK CHART: 1
US CHART: 3
KEY TRACKS: 'Love Action'; 'The Things That Dreams Are Made Of'; 'The Sound Of The Crowd'; 'Do Or Die'; 'Don't You Want Me'

Yep, Pop with a capital P was on a roll in 1981. Records of vivid colour and rare wit, which ran with punk's rejection of virtuosity for virtuosity's sake, and twinned thematic ambi-

THE HUMAN
LEAGUE
DARE

21st Anniversary Edition featuring Love And Dancing

tion with the desire to make hits, and found new ways to make music sound new, and made it catchy and danceable and nothing more or less than pure pop. When I hear CD:UK-era pop and believe that today's pop lover is being treated with utter contempt by performer, producer and the idiot media that backs up the whole sorry charade, it's *Dare* by The Human League – the best pop album of my lifetime – that is playing in my head.

Dare is the reason why readers' polls in music papers dropped all the best musician categories. The sound fashioned by Phil Oakey, producer Martin Rushent, and musicians Ian Burden and (former Rezillo) Jo Callis was so complete and perfect that it sounded like it was simply thought into existence. The brash brilliance and shock-white optimism of the layers of synthesiser twinned with the words of opening track 'The Things That Dreams Are Made Of' (written, rather amazingly, by Oakey's onstage projections partner Adrian Wright) and made teens everywhere believe that life was more thrilling than any previous generation could ever have thought possible. When Phil sang, in the

bluff, blank baritone that felt like it carried all the moral authority that our leaders would never possess: 'Everybody needs love and adventure/Everybody needs cash to spend/Everybody needs love and affection/Everybody needs two or three friends/These are the things . . . the things that dreams are made of,' man, it's impossible to describe how grateful and lifted we felt, because we knew that pop was almost always about the endless self-regard and ego of the performer, but the League understood that pop exists to make us feel that our lives are worthy, and its best practitioners are capable of transforming the mundane into the magical. Indeed, Oakey's entire gamble of dumping the band's musicianly founders Martyn Ware and Ian Craig-Marsh (they formed Heaven 17) and replacing them with two girls – the wonderful Joanne Catherall and Susan Sulley – who couldn't play, sing or dance, but were better than all that because they represented the working-class pop audience, being glamorous on the cheap, being cheeky and tough and indefatigable, making the best of what they had and deserving to strike gold – the entire gamble was about demystifying showbiz and stating that prole beauty and prole art were actually better than stage-school fools and pampered brats employing battalions of posh stylists to make them appear . . . better than us. Pop stars are not better than us. No one is better than us.

It's for that exact reason that Beyonce Knowles's entire public life will never produce anything that has one ounce of the sexiness or soul of Joanne and Susan dancing clumsily on *Top Of The Pops*, or Phil's iconic lopsided haircut. And the great thing about *Dare* is that you don't need to have seen it or felt it back then because it's right here, captured for eternal posterity, in every thunking drum and blaring synth and loving word of this album. No matter what pop puts me through I still believe in *Dare*.

SINGLES GOING STEADY

BUZZCOCKS
PRODUCED BY MARTIN RUSHENT AND MARTIN HANNETT
UNITED ARTISTS/EMI/NOVEMBER 1981
UK CHART: DID NOT CHART
US CHART: DID NOT CHART
KEY TRACKS: 'What Do I Get?'; 'Why Can't I Touch It?'; 'Ever Fallen In Love?'; 'You Say You Don't Love Me'; 'Love You More'

While the production skills of Martin Rushent – an unsung genius of the punk/post-punk period – encapsulated a new pop era with *Dare*, a collection of sounds he helped shape signalled the end of an old one. This compilation of the first eight United Artists Buzzcocks singles and their accompanying B-sides didn't just let you know that the band no longer shifted units and were about to be dropped, but it has the unique distinction of being a truly great Greatest Hits that never charted. Not anywhere, at any time. Rock 'n' roll as a pop singles genre was over, and arguably stayed over until the Britpop trend of the mid-'90s. What's more, the idea that guitar rock could be androgynous, queer, witty, intelligent, and painfully articulate in its sad laughter at love and sex, was all set to be something that The Smiths had to carry alone throughout the rest of the '80s.

Still, to stress the positive, the *Singles Going Steady* that you'll find on CD in your local stockist is a better, more complete album than the original US-only set released in the UK as a failed 1981 stocking-filler. Like so many of the albums in the previous pages, the commercial imperatives of exploiting back-catalogue and the compact disc's longer playing time have enabled those much-maligned major labels to put tracks on albums that always should have been there. In this case, this means that the 2001 version of *Singles . . .* has the grossly underrated A- and B-sides of Pete Shelley and Co.'s last four (flop) UA/EMI singles. Awkwardly caught between the thrash-pop they invented and a pop market that

demanded sweeter noises, hastily tacked-on brass sections and slower tempos, the likes of 'You Say You Don't Love Me', 'Are Everything' (produced in trademark Manc Phil Spector style by Joy Division producer Martin Hannett) and 'What Do You Know' are drenched in a resigned sadness. Times had moved on like scorned lovers move on, and the Buzzcocks, being a truly heart-on-their-sleeve band, couldn't help but convey the feelings of being dumped by fashion in music about being dumped by boys and girls. Pop's tough, we know. But Pete Shelley was vital to the best traditions of British pop, his slyly gay love songs and defiantly camp demeanour helping to make a space for the provincial queerosity of Messrs Almond, O'Dowd, Morrissey and Tennant. This album will always be the Buzzcocks at their best – a crunchy, rude, heroic losers' blend of street-punk art and pure pop heart.

TIN DRUM

JAPAN
PRODUCED BY STEVE NYE AND JAPAN
VIRGIN/NOVEMBER 1981
UK CHART: 12
US CHART: RELEASED IN 1991. DID NOT CHART
KEY TRACKS: 'The Art Of Parties'; 'Visions Of China'; 'Still Life In Mobile Homes'; 'Cantonese Boy'; 'Talking Drum'

And talking about lovely reissue jobs, in 2003 Virgin re-released this, the fifth, best, biggest and last Japan album, in a sumptuous box packed full of sultry shots of David Sylvian's improbable cheekbones and enigmatic lips, not to mention single mixes and what have you. Oooh, you want to just hug and kiss it, you do, it being so touchy and feely and faux-oriental, in an upmarket Chinese takeaway sort of way. One thing it doesn't have, though, in the booklet full of sexy snaps, is one bloody word from Sylvian or anyone else about what the fucking hell the goddamn album was about! I mean, they were called Japan. And they made an album about China. Except that it didn't tell you anything about China. It just told you that this band were elegantly miserable, and that they seemed to think that all the clothes and chopsticks and bowls of rice that denote The Idiot's Guide To Being Chinese were . . . interesting. You know . . . aesthetically. The original cover shot – where a sepia-tinted, immaculately coiffed and intellectually bespectacled Sylvian sits eating rice underneath a bare light bulb and a portrait of Chairman Mao – implies that millions died in the Cultural Revolution to ensure that Catford's leading Bowie/Ferry clone had the ideal setting to showcase his new haircut. Which, when you think about it, is exactly the sort of western decadence those Commies despised in us.

But in the end, I suspect that there are no sleevenotes about the inspiration behind this astonishing music because none of them want to reveal that they're all a bit thick and pretentious. Or maybe none of them want to talk about a time when they were on the verge of becoming the biggest art-pop sensation in Britain since Bowie first Ziggified us, and ended up splitting, not because of a vicious argument over the respective merits of the Chinese and Japanese economic systems, but because the really hot lead singer nicked the bass-player's bird. But hey . . . Mick Karn may have been unlucky in love, but, even though Sylvian wrote the theme tune, sang the theme tune, it's Karn's fretless bass that does most to make the other-worldly music contained within *Tin Drum* one of the most beautiful and artful noises ever to grace mainstream pop.

'Ghosts' was the big hit single and remains the Japan song most likely to turn up on an oldies station, but . . . oh, it sucks, frankly, with its proto-Coldplay self-pity and dumb sixth-form angst masquerading as deep sensitivity. Skip it, and go back to opening track, 'The Art Of Parties' (and if that isn't THE quintessential new romantic song title, then I'm a member of The Lotus Eaters), and the album's first line: 'Once I was young/Once I was smart/Now I'm living on the edge of my nerves.' Oh, the delicious vanity! Oh, the 'Bryan Ferry with a migraine' vocals! But, oh, especially, the

music; an outrageous tumble of beats and tones and brass and notes that just didn't seem to bear any resemblance whatsoever to anything Western pop could do, or would do again. The album just flows from there, incorporating glam, funk and Afro-beat without ever compromising the natural fluidity of it all, and Nye makes it all sound ridiculously warm and huge. I know saying that your life is incomplete until you've experienced Steve Jansen's drum break on 'Visions Of China' seems really sad and anal, but . . . Your life is incomplete until you've experienced Steve Jansen's drum break on 'Visions Of China'.

There are many contenders in this book for The Best Purely Musical Noise . . . Ever! But Japan are right up there for what they achieve on *Tin Drum*, which is an entirely believable idea of what the Far East sounds, looks and smells like for people who have no intention of ever going there. With added staring into the distance, enigmatically. And noodles.

NON-STOP EROTIC CABARET

SOFT CELL
PRODUCED BY MIKE THORNE
SOME BIZARRE/PHONOGRAM/DECEMBER 1981
UK CHART: 5
US CHART: 22
KEY TRACKS: 'Say Hello, Wave Goodbye'; 'Tainted Love'; 'Bedsitter'; 'Sex Dwarf'; 'Chips On My Shoulder'

Apart from being the album that invented the Pet Shop Boys, the debut Soft Cell LP is the only record I can think of that decides that making like Suicide (see p.29) playing northern soul is the best soundbed for a dance-pop album about being a twenty-something sex-obsessed gay man with a dirty mind, living alone in London, and living the high and low life around Old Compton Street, Soho. It's as timeless and of its time as *Dare*, and makes up with lyrical wit and

and naughty innuendoes, constantly teetering on the edge of entering a doorway into somebody else's hell. Almond and Ball make such potentially disturbing material into teeny pop by the generous application of nagging hooks and winking nudges, performed with such naïve gusto that some accused Almond of being afraid to come out, even though he and this record were so blatantly out that Soft Cell almost obliterated the idea that anyone, anywhere was ever truly in. In Non-Stop Erotic Cabaret's streets, everyone has something to hide, and especially you and your monkey.

This record also contains 'Seedy Films', which may well be the worst song and the very worst vocal performance on any album in this book, but is part of a long-playing musical experience so funny, endearing and true – with particular regard to the punk generation's terror of getting old – that it remains vital to the beauty of the enterprise. If Almond and Ball were never as good again, it's probably because it takes a certain amount of youthful naivety to get something so potentially nasty so upliftingly right. Can you really write a couplet as great as Marc does for 'Bedsitter' – 'Watch the mirror, count the lines/The battle-scars of all the good times' – and Garland it with just the right amount of 'Je Ne Regrette Rien', once it inevitably becomes just another depressing truth? That would be a 'non'.

camp perversity for its occasional lapse into musical 'will that do?' Twenty-two-year-old Southport escapee Marc Almond and fellow Leeds Poly student Dave Ball capture absolutely the tacky thrill of Soho's sleaze when you're too young and horny to worry about the politics and exploitation of its peep shows, porn shops and brothels. Like many an out-of-town boy before them, they watch in fascination as family men in suits sneak into Soho's cramped doorways, turned on by the guilt and shame of exploring their repressed desires, doomed to never get what they want. And despite his youth, Almond already understood that this wasn't just about dirty old men paying for skin mags or rough trade, but that this was where people from wildly different places, sexualities and generations had furtive affairs, masochistically left themselves open to blackmail, found themselves as sex workers through loneliness and vulnerability, or simply walked the streets giggling at the titillating sights, covering their fascination with embarrassed laughter

1982

YOU CAN'T HIDE YOUR LOVE FOREVER/ORANGE JUICE

YOU CAN'T HIDE YOUR LOVE FOREVER

ORANGE JUICE
PRODUCED BY ADAM KIDRON AND ORANGE JUICE
POLYDOR/FEBRUARY 1982
UK CHART: 21
US CHART: DID NOT CHART
KEY TRACKS: 'Felicity'; 'In A Nutshell'; 'L.O.V.E. Love';
'Consolation Prize'; 'Falling And Laughing'

The first Orange Juice album came out at least a year too late. By Feb 1982, silly old Haircut 100 had already taken a cutesy-wutesy version of Postcard pop's jangle-funk and faux-collegiate dress sense into the charts. So, while music nerds like myself knew that Edwyn Collins and Co. had already made an album (now available as *The Glasgow School* on Domino) but decided not to release it, plumping for the bigger production budget of major label Polydor, your more casual pop kid just saw another pop-funk band who didn't sound as polished as what was already available. But those who loved this truly loved this, and still do.

You Can't Hide . . . contains many of the elements of bad beigeness that would come to characterise the 'second British invasion' of the mid-'80s – cheesy horn sections, loud disco drums, female fake-soul backing vocals. But the difference here was that OJ had a modest charm, a ready wit and the loveliest twin guitars – courtesy of Collins and the enterprising James Kirk – this side of The Byrds. This album navigates a unique path between ambitious musicality and endearing clumsiness, which makes it, more than anything, the template for the uncommercial side of indie-pop.

Blending elements from the third and fourth Velvet Underground albums, funky soul, country-rock and Television's ringing twin guitars, Orange Juice were also one of the first groups who weren't just open about their influences, but laughed at themselves and with their fans about their precious faves and pored-over record collections. 'I wore my fringe like Roger McGuinn's', Collins croons self-deprecatingly on 'Consolation Prize', 'I was hoping to impress.' But beneath the jaunty, winking veneer lay a theme of broken trust, as Collins and Kirk accuse various lovers and friends of brutal selfishness. The courtly language and belief that everyone is an insensitive clod except themselves may have caused a certain Mr Morrissey to prick up his ears.

Nevertheless, the album's potential preciousness is overwhelmed by faith in the listener, and a happy rejection of cool. Nowhere is this more apparent and bizarrely lovely than on their cover of Al Green's 'L.O.V.E. Love', where Edwyn, knowing full well that his vocal technique is bound to fail to match that of the greatest singer who ever hit a freaked falsetto, goes right ahead and gives it everything anyway. The end product is so sincere, loveable, lovestruck and true that it re-defines what we might think of as soul. Sadly, in Pop World, awkwardness and truth rarely win out over cold professionalism. But the commercially unsuccessful Orange Juice are rightly worshipped and copied now. And who gives a flying one for Paul Young?

YOUTH OF AMERICA

WIPERS
PRODUCED BY GREG SAGE
GIFT OF LIFE/FEBRUARY 1982
UK CHART: DID NOT CHART
US CHART: DID NOT CHART
KEY TRACKS: 'When It's Over'; 'Youth Of America'; 'Taking Too Long'; 'No Fair'; 'Pushing The Extreme'

One of the most exciting moments in the writing of this book was hearing this record for the first time. I borrowed a whole bunch of records from friends, wanting to hear as much as possible before making my final list. This was one I borrowed from a very fine rock journalist called Manish Agarwal. I was curious about Wipers because their main man, Greg Sage, had been one of the underground punks that Kurt Cobain was so vocal about when Nirvana hit big. I'm not a Nirvana fan, but I still admire the way that Cobain flagged up his every influence at every possible opportunity. So I put Manish's vinyl copy of *Youth Of America* on my deck, and spent the rest of the day scraping myself off the floor. Blown away doesn't come close.

Guitarist/songwriter/singer/pianist/producer Sage is one of those awkward bastards who believes in stupid, naïve ideas like integrity and art. Forming Wipers in 1977 in Portland, Oregon, his punk rock impulse was to make fifteen albums in ten years, rarely touring, refusing to promote himself as a 'rock star', producing everything himself, looking only to break even. He has a website at www.zenorecords.com where he explains, with as little bitterness and self-pity as he can muster, that the music business has done everything it can for the last twenty-eight years to stop him. It all rings true.

Youth Of America, the second Wipers album, consists of just six songs and lasts for less than thirty minutes. It is a strong contender for the best guitar-rock album of all motherfucking time. It sounds like someone put all the best things about The Saints, The Stooges, Kraftwerk, PiL and movie theme master John Barry into one burst of frantic creativity. It sounds like driving at 200mph through a swamp searching for crocodiles and the meaning of life. It has so many tunes played with both taut economy and extravagant flamboyance that you feel afterwards like you've just heard fifteen albums condensed into one shot of critical mass. It defies physics, chemistry, semantics, sudoku and every bad rock song's right to exist. It's available with 2001's Wipers Box Set along with the first and third Wipers albums for the price of one CD, because Sage means it, Man, with no irony, and it must be bought by everyone who suspects that modern civilisation is being drained of blood and soul by the fatuous shite we are sold and told to admire.

This album is the very essence of rock 'n' roll.

THERMONUCLEAR SWEAT

DEFUNKT
PRODUCED BY JOE BOYD AND JOSEPH BOWIE
HANNIBAL/MARCH 1982
UK CHART: DID NOT CHART
US CHART: DID NOT CHART
KEY TRACKS: 'Illusion'; 'I Tried To Live Alone'; 'Avoid The Funk'; 'Ooh Baby'; 'For The Love Of Money'

Almost forgotten and never a seller, Defunkt were a multiracial New York five-piece band that represented the ultimate punk-funk experience for those of us lucky enough to see and hear them. Led by trombonist Joe Bowie, younger brother of free-jazz legend Lester Bowie, Defunkt melded the hard funk of James Brown, jazz both left-field and straight-ahead, the cosmic metal of Hendrix and the speed and pessimism of punk rock. The current revival of all things post-punk has seen the 2005 reissue of this album with their equally brilliant eponymous debut, and their one other completely essential record, the double A-side single 'The Razor's Edge/Strangling Me With Your Love' – another stunning double CD for single-album price, and no, no one's paying me a bonus for this unashamed plugging.

Thermonuclear Sweat wins out over Defunkt because, among the terrifying intensity of their keynote tracks, it includes the light straight-jazz relief of versions of Kenny Burrell's 'Cocktail Hour (Blue Bossa)' and Charlie Parker's 'Big Bird (Au Private)'.

It also includes a rampaging cover of The O'Jays' awesome 'For The Love Of Money' which, very strangely, simplifies the original's monumental opening guitar riff by way of shamelessly ripping off Spandau Ballet's 'Chant No. 1', a hit the previous summer.

Defunkt's musicians were, and I'm sure still are, stupidly good. Drummer Kenny Martin played funk beats like an entire Boys' Brigade marching band animated by Tex Avery. The guitars of Kelvyn Bell and future Living Colour leader

Vernon Reid held a raging conversation about the nature of electricity and fire. Female bass player Kim Clarke was the most intimidating and supercool presence in '80s music, and played bass like she had twenty fingers, ten thumbs and the history of funk in her bones. Bowie himself was a suave black junkie muscle-boy whose laconic vocals and slapstick trombone interjections and chants negotiated a thin, thrilling line between brutal misanthropy and wild laughter. The sadness, self-loathing and pessimism of most of their lyrics (mostly written by a Budapest playwright called Janos Gat) is leavened by the cartoon nature of Defunkt funk, the very definition of great musicians pushing themselves to the limit of tempo and intensity until you feel like everything's bound to collapse. The album reaches its highest peaks when it feels like the music has started to play the musicians.

What Defunkt are truly about is the collapse of black community politics under the assault of Reaganism. Like Gang Of Four, the band rejected agit-prop and went for the truth jugular, making their audience – and themselves – more culpable than The Man. Onstage, they were like a sub-terranean shadow version of British 2-Tone, a show of multi-cultural solidarity that suggested strength and opti-mism through the band's very existence. So you could baulk at final track 'Believing In Love', a Gat lyric that insists 'Believing in love is just a fallacy/Some nigger's fantasy.' But the song has to be taken in context with the astounding 'I Tried To Live Alone', a disgusted critique of male inadequacy where Bowie's love is revealed only as desperate need, and inevitably as a complete loss of identity: 'When we are together/We can't see/Which one of us is you/And which one is me.' It's the same character's shame in 'Believing In Love', where Bowie sings of a decaying relationship where, 'The hand that used to stroke you/Is now the fist that hits you hard.' Defunkt's minimalist lyrics suggested that self-loathing, violence, sex and drugs are all nothing but escape from the challenge of making things better, as Bowie fanta-sises about fleeing a burning Earth by spaceship in the defin-itive 'Illusion'. This is tough, unflinching stuff, an album and

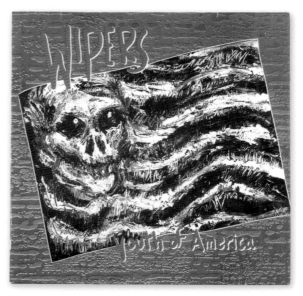

a band saying a huge, fuck off 'No!' to the escapist fantasies that sustained the black music of the period.

What Bowie and Gat think of hip hop's development, and the commercial success of putting a contemptuous materialist twist on the exact things that Defunkt dwelled on, is anyone's guess. But I hope Joe, Kim and Co. are still playing and living, because their art is the secret missing link between the doped-up agit-funk of Sly Stone and George Clinton and the politicised fury of Public Enemy. If I was a rich man, I'd start my very own Punk And Funk Hall Of Fame, just so's I could inaugurate the mighty Defunkt.

COMBAT ROCK

THE CLASH
PRODUCED BY THE CLASH (MIXED BY GLYN JOHNS)
CBS/MAY 1982

COMBAT ROCK/THE CLASH

UK CHART: 2
US CHART: 7
KEY TRACKS: 'Straight To Hell'; 'Death Is A Star'; 'Sean Flynn'; 'Atom Tan'; 'Car Jamming'

So there was this rock 'n' roll band who became the standard-bearers of an entire genre. And these 'punks' did something that had become discredited in their industry – they worked. Constantly and obsessively for over five years. By the end of 1980, they'd made seven long-playing vinyl sides of recorded music, and an accompanying pile of non-album singles and B-sides, and played so many shows that everyone who could possibly have an interest in their rebel rock had seen them play and agreed they were the best live band in the world. And then, because it had taken America a while to understand this punk rock stuff, all that work paid off, and paid off all their debt. Because in 1982, America was feeling nostalgic about more optimistic times, and wanted a new Rolling Stones, or, at least, the kind of all-purpose stadium rock superstar group that the Stones had been and U2 were soon to become. Problem was, the band had spent so much time together that they couldn't stand the sight of each other, and the drummer, of all people, was killing himself with smack. For the first time since they began, recording was a nightmare of writers' block, formless jamming and outright personal hostility bordering on violence.

But the record company hired a rescuer of distressed albums called Glyn Johns to make this album work, because they knew that everything had come down to this moment, when America would hand this band the keys to the Kingdom. And he made it work, having had experience of doing the same thing for The Beatles, the Stones and Led Zeppelin. Even then, what the record company was presented with was a set of melancholy and surreal funk, blues and reggae-influenced dirges which dwelled unhealthily on the Vietnam war and the evils of American multi-nationals. Except . . . except, the drummer had written a perfect dance-rock hit called 'Rock The Casbah', which not only had a catchy chorus, but poked obvious fun at Middle-Eastern tyranny, which would make a western kid feel good that his country allowed him to listen to rock 'n' roll without bothering him with the messy details. And the guitarist had written a big, dumb, Stones song called 'Should I Stay Or Should I Go?' which might actually be about how much his band hated him, but just came off like a love song for air guitar. Perfect.

So the album made the band huge in a country that fascinated them to the point where they had become its most committed fans and its most savage critics. Just like in those old '60s days when protest rock made everyone money that they never expected rock music to ever make. The band supported The Who in humungous stadiums.

Then everyone heard how depressing the album was, even though its eerie meditations on war and cities and the defeat of the global working classes were also very beautiful. And the band sacked the guys who had written the hits and ran from what they could've been, what they'd worked tirelessly for, because by shooting themselves in the foot, they acknowledged that punk rock couldn't be stadium rock. It had been about change, not co-option. They would never be able to smile as the lighters were raised and the fans yelled songs about overturning the status quo while the band became Status Quo. Or maybe they just ran out of tunes, having made so many, and just couldn't face hiring old rockers to make them make sense.

Many years later, a Jeans company would make the guitarist's Stones' song into an advert and a No. 1 hit. And the US soldiers whose exploitation the band had sung about with such eloquent sadness and plaintive wisdom played the drummer's hit while they bombed Iraq. And a bloke writing a wee book about great albums figured that all this had something to do with the death of dreams, and rock 'n' roll's final sighing acceptance that it couldn't change the world, but that the world could always change rock 'n' roll.

SONGS OF THE FREE

GANG OF FOUR
PRODUCED BY MIKE HOWLETT, JON KING AND ANDY GILL
EMI/MAY 1982
UK CHART: 61
US CHART: DID NOT CHART
KEY TRACKS: 'We Live As We Dream Alone'; 'Call Me Up'; 'I Will Be A Good Boy'; 'Life! It's A Shame'; 'I Love A Man In Uniform'

The third Gang Of Four album, like Combat Rock, looks at America with what could usefully be described as shock and awe. Although the music on *Songs Of The Free* is more accessible through production ear candy and an attempt to write some conventional pop hooks, the previous two albums believed, somewhere among the truth and bleakness, in positive change. Here, the pressure on the band to write hits to keep their record deal begins to colour their sound, and embodies their analysis of our surrender to consumerism and wage-slavery, with particular emphasis on American economic and military power. They replaced original bassist Dave Allen with a good-looking (and talented, to be fair) American female bassist Sara Lee. And, having already shown a gift for ironic album titles, they went on to top themselves – pun intended – in 1983 by making a horribly compromised sub-Heaven 17 dance-pop album called, wait for it, *Hard*. It bombed completely and finished the group.

Gang Of Four saw all that coming, if *Songs Of The Free* is anything to go by. The lyrics, mainly written by the brilliant Jon King, lay bare the inevitable triumph of Thatcher and Reagan's redrawing of our psychology with a mordant humour summed up by the opening lines of 'The History Of The World': 'When I was in my mother's womb/Social structure seemed a simple thing.' Sex, love, work, money, home – The Human League's things that dreams are made of – are here the stuff of nightmares . . . a Matrix-like world where none of our 'natural' desires can be trusted, so defined are we by the triumphant history of capitalism. Musically, their sound is transformed into Big Rock by crashing drums and reverb-with-everything, as their music acts out 'The space between our work and its product' examined so brutally and fearfully in 'We Live As We Dream Alone'. Despite the superiority of their first two albums as a whole, this funk-rock anthem now feels like their definitive statement; a graphic howl of agony at the ease with which capitalism convinces us that 'there is no such thing as society', where a flirt with fascism is, in the end, no different from our impulse to 'lie in the arms of lovers' – with a side-order of double-edge on the word 'lie'.

Songs Of The Free and *Combat Rock* mark the final nail in the coffin of punk's challenge to the musical and social order. Although the following few albums feature sparkling pop by young Brits who were inspired by punk's surge of new values, the last real albums by The Clash and Gang Of Four wave anti-establishment punk's white flag – but succeed in making great, multi-layered art out of resignation and exhaustion. Play *Songs Of The Free* next to *The Lexicon Of Love* (see p.136) and you can feel the end of an era and the true beginning of the 1980s.

SONGS TO REMEMBER

SCRITTI POLITTI
PRODUCED BY ADAM KIDRON AND SCRITTI POLITTI
ROUGH TRADE/AUGUST 1982
UK CHART: 11
US CHART: UNRELEASED IN USA
KEY TRACKS: 'The Sweetest Girl'; 'Faithless'; 'Asylums In Jerusalem'; 'Jacques Derrida'; 'Gettin', Havin' and Holdin'

Now this is where I get my own, very particular, fear of music. It stems from memories of interviews with Scritti Politti's Green Gartside in music papers in the early 1980s, whereby the gangly Welsh former art student and Young Communist would cross conversational swords with a similarly intellectual journo like Ian Penman or Paul Morley and . . . I wouldn't understand a single fucking word they were talking about. There are many key revelations about yourself and the world inherent in being a teenager: reading a Green interview provided the revelation that there were people of roughly my generation that were much, much cleverer than me. I'm not sure I ever got over it.

So I approach a critique of the debut Scritti Politti album – a unique and modestly epic fusion of pop, reggae, funk, soul, jazz and lyrics submerged in the deep end of political philosophy – with a very teenage trepidation. Like, I know that Jacques Derrida, who died in 2004, was an French-Algerian literary critic and philosopher famous for inventing 'deconstruction', a way of reading and interpreting text which went on to profoundly influence post-structualism and postmodernism. But I don't know what any of that means. Green's lyrics give you that creepy feeling that a joke is being told that would be hilarious only to, maybe, Stephen Fry and Gore Vidal – and that somehow you're the butt of it. My love of this record isn't based on masochism, though. It's because, for me, music, like books and smart friends, should be cleverer than me. That can come out in a particularly boneheaded guitar riff that I know I would never have thought of, even if I played guitar. Or it can be Green, talking way over my head, making music out of a desire to make economic and sexual revolution sound creamily romantic. If you want a theory about what shapes a person's taste in popular music, here's one: most people prefer music that tells them that they're just about as clever as they ought to be. In short, almost nobody likes a smartarse.

Green Gartside had a smart arse, a 6'6" frame, the face of a matinee idol, the hair of Princess Diana, and a voice of buttery, unforced androgyny. If anything, his later major-label albums with American musos proved the point that he was just too perfect . . . with every early '80s credible pop box ticked. But Songs To Remember, made after recovering from a heart attack (at twenty-three!) brought on by stage fright, is one of the few albums covered in this book that bears no resemblance to any record before or after it was made. Like I say, fear of being revealed as a big dummy precludes me from . . . ahem . . . deconstructing Green's lyrics. So I'll simply recommend it by saying that Green and collaborators, including beanpole white rasta Tom Morley and left-wing jazz-pop legend Robert Wyatt, pull off the coup of making a music that makes the uniting of the working classes and the sexual coupling of man and woman as passionate, revolutionary, dreamy, optimistic and – crucially – inextricably intertwined as they obviously are, because he believed that the harsh divisions and fractured humanity excavated by the Gang Of Four could still be healed by soul music and radical thinking. What a wonderful thing to have faith in, and to base a body of music upon! And if that doesn't seduce you, then here's a joke, from 'Jacques Derrida', of course: 'To err is to be human, to forgive is too divine/I was like an industry . . . depressed and in decline'. See? Too funny to be scared of, I realise now.

SULK

THE ASSOCIATES
PRODUCED BY MIKE HEDGES AND THE ASSOCIATES
ASSOCIATES/WEA/JUNE 1982
UK CHART: 10
US CHART: UNRELEASED IN USA
KEY TRACKS: 'Party Fears Two'; 'Gloomy Sunday'; 'Skipping'; 'Club Country'; 'No'

June 1982 saw the release of two albums that defined the British pop year. Representing the last kicks of the post-punk/new pop impulse, *The Lexicon Of Love* (see p.136) and *Sulk* were both albums that flew toward grandiosity on the shift away from rock electric guitar, and were both about losing at love. But where ABC's famous debut played it for laughs, and submerged any real pain by presenting lost pop love as little more than a vehicle for ideas, the third Associates album flitted between flippant joy and black agony, making an unlikely commercial success out of the mood swings of manic depression.

Bookended by two oddly banal instrumentals, *Sulk* begins with hysterical sadness and moves gradually toward some kind of celebration. Billy Mackenzie's voice – an instrument as deliciously seductive and technically accomplished as that of Jeff Buckley (see p.268) – careens through words that play with a Lennonesque surrealism and, like Lennon's best, suddenly slam into focus with an unforgettable, vivid phrase. The album's first vocal track, the crackling, stately, windswept 'No' provides an image whereby a bereft Billy is forced to 'Tear a strip from her dress/Wrap my arms in it'. His melodrama reaches its peak on a version of 'Gloomy Sunday', a suicide ballad made famous by Billie Holiday which, according to legend, curses everyone who sings it. The facts of Billy's suicide in 1997 can't help but make his lovely, reverent version a spooky, disturbing pleasure.

It would be handy to blame those pesky kids for Billy and partner Alan Rankine's lack of success post-*Sulk*. But the pair split soon after its making, unable to cope with pop success and the drugs that came with it. The Associates' albums that followed didn't feature Rankine, and were, therefore, not The Associates. They also didn't feature drummer John Murphy and bassist Michael Dempsey, who bedrocked Mackenzie and Rankine's flights of fancy with torrid virtuosity, nor the production of Mike Hedges, whose wall of brittle, reverberating sound carried the Associates' eccentric mix of mischief and misery with exquisite poise. So much so that a daft, vulnerable Scot screaming about the euphoria of 'Nude Spoons' still makes a funny kind of pop sense.

THE LEXICON OF LOVE

ABC

PRODUCED BY TREVOR HORN

NEUTRON/MERCURY/JUNE 1982
UK CHART: 1
US CHART: 24
KEY TRACKS: 'The Look Of Love'; 'Date Stamp'; 'Poison Arrow'; 'All Of My Heart'; 'Tears Are Not Enough'

'It was like disco, but in a Bob Dylan way.' So says producer Trevor Horn of *The Lexicon Of Love*, in the sleevenotes of the 2004 Deluxe Edition. There goes my space-saving one-line review. But more has to be said of a record which pulled off The Big Rare One; that is, being the best record in Britain and being the No. 1 record in Britain, at one and the same time.

The debut album by Sheffield's Martin Fry, David Palmer, Stephen Singleton and Mark White is a British pop landmark – a joyfully synthetic, danceable, girl-friendly, anti-rock orchestral pop album that still gets into all the Best Album Ever polls – a beacon of stoical insouciance among all the tortured strummers and bummers. Singer Fry's wry Bryan Ferry-meets-Smokey Robinson wordplay was, like so many of those agonised rock classics, inspired by being dumped by a girl. Unlike your dressed-down whiner, Fry did what every broken-hearted soul would like to do, and usually does, in their own way – he laughed at it, and danced through it, and made it into an open 'fuck-you' letter that the world opened, read and cheered.

The Lexicon Of Love also opened up a door for pop that was abruptly slammed shut by Michael Jackson's *Thriller* (see p.151) six months later. ABC's ambitions were artistic rather than material. They were gawky and ordinary and made an album that exemplified the democracy of pop by proving that gawky, ordinary boys could make enormous, virtuoso pop, and prove that music, itself, is the true pop star, as The Beatles had proved over and over again. They believed that the best pop was the most overtly intelligent pop, and that intellect was something to be proud of. The aforementioned 2004 sleevenotes talk of *The Lexicon Of Love* as if it was influential, but this is nonsense – once

is as familiar as Wham! yet as multi-layered and deep as, well, Dylan. *The Lexicon Of Love* is the *Citizen Kane* of British pop albums, and the anonymous girl who broke Martin's heart is its Rosebud.

IMPERIAL BEDROOM

ELVIS COSTELLO AND THE ATTRACTIONS
PRODUCED BY GEOFF EMERICK
F BEAT/JULY 1982
UK CHART: 6
US CHART: 30
KEY TRACKS: 'Man Out Of Time'; 'Beyond Belief'; 'You Little Fool'; 'Town Crier'; 'Pidgin English'

'What are words worth?' trilled Tom Tom Club in their 1981 hit 'Wordy Rappinghood'. And a year later you could but wonder, as the albums we've just looked at from The Clash, Scritti Politti and ABC talked at us nine-to-the-dozen, all puns and similes and manic chatter, as if fitting in as many as possible before words were forever banned. Elvis Costello's seventh album in just five years out-blathered them all as if handing over pop's bragging rights to the following month's 'The Message', the Grandmaster Flash And The Furious Five single that established hip hop as pop's new talking shop. Costello, as almost always, talked about lovers, and how easily revenge and guilt could transform them into haters. On *Imperial Bedroom* his voice reaches its peak in both storytelling and smart-aleckery, over songs and music that harked back to Sgt Pepper Beatles, right down to being shaped in the studio by the Fab Four's engineer Geoff Emerick.

Beginning with 'Beyond Belief', the most admired album opener of Costello's career, we're given an inky blue context in which to put some of the sweeter sounds that come later. Costello's deep, tired voice is housed in a bass-heavy, almost dub version of a pop-rock style that Costello had made

Thriller became the biggest-selling record of all time by replacing lyrical excellence with marketing excellence, there was no opportunity for guys like Fry and Co. to make pop as literate and creatively ambitious as this, and aim it squarely at the mainstream. Trevor Horn might have recycled many of this album's sounds and techniques for Frankie Goes To Hollywood, but it was Fry's journalist chum Paul Morley's marketing ideas, along with Horn's subtlety-rejecting, crashing din that made Frankie a phenomenon, not the completely empty songs and performances. The debut ABC album remains a complete one-off – a brief shining moment when arch high-concept mingled with genuine passion, and inspired amateurism squeezed sparks from technical perfection, and where you can hear a band working hard beneath the gloss, because that old cliché about inspiration and perspiration is true. Punk, post-punk, disco, Motown, glam and all the possibilities suggested by all the best pop since the Ramones found a home somewhere among the gleeful pretensions and intense integrity housed inside the swelling strings and swaggering swings of this album, a record which

ELVIS COSTELLO and the ATTRACTIONS

IbMePdErRoIoAmL

IMPERIAL BEDROOM/ELVIS COSTELLO AND THE ATTRACTIONS

uniquely his over the previous five years. 'I'm just the oily slick on the wind-up world of the nervous tick,' he mumbles, somewhat playfully, and we may struggle for the literal sense of that, but we know that Elvis's slimeball persona is going to be given full-rein, and that that is where he finds his toughest, truest line on the human heart. From there, a lonely housewife suspects her husband and best friend are sleeping together ('The Long Honeymoon'), important men lie with cheap hookers ('Man Out Of Time'), lost men stumble around women, ('What's the use of saying I love you when I'm drinking to distraction?' – 'Little Savage'), become impotent ('Boy With A Problem', co-written with Squeeze's Chris Difford), dally cruelly with Lolitas ('You Little Fool'). The music ranges from mellow chanson, through ornate chamber-pop to the Bunnymen-ish freak-outs that bookend the stunning 'Man Out Of Time'. At album's end, Costello gives us a full-on orchestral ballad, a song to take him closer to the Burt Bacharach he was aching to become and would later work with. 'Town Crier' smiles sadly about trying to pull down the walls of cool that men erect to protect themselves from surrender to love, and aches with the knowledge that the unashamed cleverness of his words and music, was, in a pop era about to be transformed by *Thriller* (see p.151), erecting a similar barrier between himself and his audience. 'If you don't believe my heart is in the right place/Why don't you take a good look at my face?' he pleads, at one point, undercutting his own sincerity with a lovable Presley impression.

Costello waved goodbye to any ideas of being a pop star on *Imperial Bedroom*, heading for the classic singer-songwriter high ground, the punk allowed into pop's golf 'n' Grammy set. 'Man Out Of Time' lacerates yet another facet of Costello's self-image with the line, 'The high heel he used to be has been ground down.' The joke hovers on the ceiling of Elvis's Imperial Bedroom, both amused and appalled at man's inhumanity to woman, and woman's power over men, and at the arrogance with which Costello had barged his way onto punk's bandwagon, before shrug- ging, and winking, and walking on water all the way to America.

UPSTAIRS AT ERIC'S

YAZOO
PRODUCED BY E.C. RADCLIFFE AND YAZOO
MUTE/AUGUST 1982
UK CHART: 2
US CHART: 92
KEY TRACKS: 'Don't Go'; 'Bring Your Love Down (Didn't I)'; 'In My Room'; 'Tuesday'; 'I Before E Except After C'

Upstairs at Eric Radcliffe's Blackwing Studios in grimy old London Town, one Vince Clarke set about phase two of an ingenious musical career. Having led Depeche Mode to record deal and charts by writing all their songs, he shock-ingly departed, and decided to swap his pretty Basildon-boy bandmates for a big-boned female pub-blues singer called Alf. Would this signal a change of direction for our King of cute synth minimalism? Uh-uh. He simply understood that the pretty bleepings that he wanted to make would soon drive everyone nuts without some soulful contrast. Alison 'Alf' Moyet's throaty belt of a white soul voice would be ideal – particularly if you wanted to get a little arty on everyone's arse and needed the vocals to cut through your new found fascination in cut-up voices and the kind of extraneous chatter that was de rigueur in 1982.

The debut album by Yazoo (shortened to Yaz in America to avoid confusion with the Yazoo US folk-roots label) pro-vided the template for every nerdy male boffin-meets-gutsy-diva duo from Eurythmics to Portishead and beyond. Clarke's adherence to melodic minimalism enabled him to make an album that worked on a gut radio pop level for its singles, but where the aesthetic gap between Clarke's futur-ism and Moyet's traditional vocal virtues made for a disem-bodied, dysfunctional long-player that worked on a haunt-

down to recording it. But Upstairs At Eric's is dominated by good stuff, yet has become a forgotten album. It deserves better for making chart-topping art out of an Odd Couple chemistry, for its sense of adventure and accessible experiment, and for its ability to find optimism within a set of lonely, late-night scenarios. Neither Clarke (with Erasure) nor Moyet (solo) came close to matching it again, and it sounds, in hindsight, like one of the last great post-punk art-pop statements, smuggled into a bright shiny pop era by its modest mood, and the underlying mystery of the relationship between the fey Clarke and the intimidating Alf.

NEW GOLD DREAM (81-82-83-84)

SIMPLE MINDS
PRODUCED BY PETER WALSH
VIRGIN/SEPTEMBER 1982
UK CHART: 3
US CHART: 69
KEY TRACKS: 'Someone Somewhere In Summertime'; 'Big Sleep'; 'Colours Fly And Catherine Wheel'; 'Promised You A Miracle'; 'Hunter And The Hunted'

I started looking up the lyrics for this, the sixth and best Simple Minds album. I got to the fifteenth mention of 'day', the twenty-eighth mention of 'gold', the 145th mention of 'dream' and the 884,322nd mention of 'love', and figured I should stop wasting valuable writing time. The soundscape of *New Gold Dream . . .* does the very un-1982 job of dissolving words anyway, with producer/arranger/man of exquisite taste Peter Walsh casting singer Jim Kerr adrift, low in the mix, bathed in echo, his trademark 'Bryan Ferry does Vic Reeves' pub singer bellows, belches and dives reduced to sound effects amidst the golden (sorry) glow of drones, washes and burbles. Or, to put it another way, the words probably aren't that important.

Except that 'Belief is a beauty thing' seems quite impor-

ing, intimate level. Beginning with the era-defining synthfunk of 'Don't Go', the album inhabits a terrain of lonely bedsits lit by bare electric bulbs that smash right on cue ('In My Room'), where thirty-year-old mothers flee their families, only to be dragged back to the domestic trap by the pull of maternal nature and the thought of her child's 'helpless voice' ('Tuesday'), and where a Suicide-lite electro-rockabilly song revolving entirely around a broken phone line ('Bad Connection') is followed by an avant-garde cut-up of talking voices, including that of producer Radcliffe's Mum, whose laugh of delight is allowed to break free at the end of 'I Before E Except After C', and never fails to make you smile at the wonderful absurdity of pop pretension.

Sure, the big hit 'Only You' still hasn't recovered from the horror of the following year's hit cover by lefty a cappella berks The Flying Pickets; and the attempt by the song 'Goodbye '70s' to boot the previous decade into touch and be MODERN!!! sounds like no one cared when it came tant. The key line from 'Promised You A Miracle', the hit single that changed Glasgow's Minds from struggling art-disco cult to fully-fledged stadium-rockers-in-waiting, sums up this album's stunningly lovely exercise in bliss. Like *Dare*, *The Lexicon Of Love* and *Sulk*, *New Gold Dream* . . . was an album by one of NME's New Pop Golden Boys which, for one dazzling 1982 moment, made you believe that New Pop's ideals had won; that you could make hit records out of the other side of punk's doubt and endless questioning, by insisting that pop's great escape could be made more deep and true by reading and travelling and thinking and searching. In this context, pop optimism comes with a balancing tone of disquiet, of anxiety, of an understanding of the world's cruelty . . . but, in the end, the music could trample through all that with the glittering prizes of dancing and celebration of life, no matter how hard the little matter of living it might become.

Then *Thriller* (see p.151) came and sold more than any record had any right to, and business concluded that pop was simple escape into icon worship and songs about nothing except their own triumph as money-spinners. Good ideas were old showbiz moves given a postmodern twist by better technology and the amount of money spent on making the singer into a dancing werewolf for the video. Pop and rock were separated again into girl/boy, gay/straight, teen/twenties, working-class/middle-class audience targets, and a group like Simple Minds didn't have any qualms about turning up the drums and guitars, mixing the singer louder, and making all their subtle breathless implications of a better world into sub-U2 liberal symbols of self-serving apolitical piety. Simple Minds became, of course, the most laughable group of their era, but their sell-out was no more egregious than the majority of 1976–82 artists covered in this book. They were just noisier and more persistent.

But before that, they made this: an album that blended Roxy Music, Japan, Brian Eno and David Byrne and a large unfashionable dollop of pre-Phil Collins Genesis, and hooked it all up to Derek Forbes's rugged and startlingly fine funk basslines, and set out down a beatific sonic river in a boat marked Hope, Rapture and Ain't Life Grand?

Doomed forever to bargain-bin status due to the lead singer's future penchant for Che Guevara berets, white doves and songs that contrived to make Nelson Mandela and Belfast as boring as plywood and as empty as my wallet, I can only advise that you sneak a copy up to the shop counter hidden between, say, a Nick Drake album and the latest issue of *Asian Big Ones*, run home before anyone sees you . . . and be charmed, balmed and becalmed (by *New Gold Dream*, not *Asian Big Ones*). It's one of the most purely beautiful sonic tapestries British pop hath woven, and anyone who says different is a Big Country member.

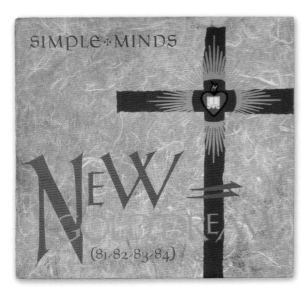

THE DREAMING

KATE BUSH
PRODUCED BY KATE BUSH

VIRGIN/SEPTEMBER 1982
UK CHART: 3
US CHART: DID NOT CHART
KEY TRACKS: 'The Dreaming'; 'There Goes A Tenner'; 'Sat In
Your Lap'; 'Get Out Of My House'; 'Suspended In Gaffa'

So Kate, love, you've established yourself as the one mastur-batory fantasy that nice collegiate New Men can admit to without shame, and, oh, yeah, you can sing a bit, too. But it's fourth album time, and we're well into the greed-is-good decade, and we need hits 'n' tits 'n' Big Wobbly Hits! So . . . what you got for us, kid? What's that? An album dominated by tales of war, terrorism, crime and pain, often sung in fake Aussie or cockney accents, with a single and title track fea-turing children's entertainer Percy Edwards making animal noises and Rolf Harris on the didgeridoo, and which appears to show zilch interest in pop, punk, disco or any of the life concerns of your largely British white middle-class audi-ence? Yeah, very funny. I like a chick with a sense of humour. You slay me. Now . . . what have you really got for us?

Well, she wasn't joking. *The Dreaming* was the Kate Bush album that let those of us who figured she was just an out-of-place prog rocker novelty act with the odd good single know that she was, in truth, one of the few British artists capable of transcending the '80s triumph of the bland through creating entirely on her own terms, and giving the audience the trust that they would happily travel with her, even to the Outback. It begins with 'Sat In Your Lap', a typi-cal '60s/'80s gimme everything! song, except that the twist – and with the Bushmeister there's always a twist – is that she's not after money or fame, but knowledge and intellect. One problem: 'I want to be a lawyer/I want to be a scholar/But I really can't be bothered.' The album's mood is set by the drums of Preston Hayman, which are thumping in a post-Adam tribal manner, but are mixed to sound removed, dis-tant, like your subconscious banging away somewhere under layers of chaotic inner dialogue, the guilty conscience that won't let you be.

The album follows this ironic hard-luck story with another – 'There Goes A Tenner', the testimony of a failed safe-cracker, complete with bizarre mockernee accent. And it's all vaudeville pianos and short-story cuteness, until Bush's old-lag-under-questioning begins to reminisce about his childhood. His father's 'pockets floating in the breeze', and the image of money scattering, from the blown safe, from his father's pockets, and Kate sings, 'There's a ten shilling note/Remember them?/That's when we used to vote for him,' and she climbs softly to those last few words, and the song suddenly seems to be about any trapped regretful adult, recalling the comforts of helplessness, mourning times passed. Breaks my heart every time, and I still can't imagine how she travels, in three-and-a-half minutes, from awkward comic short story to imagery and basic old-fash-ioned notes and chords that feel like an excavation of human folly, regret, economics and failure, looked at not with a mis-anthropic contempt, but with an all-embracing affection and empathy.

And on it travels. 'Pull Out The Pin' looks through the eyes of an anti-American guerilla, echoing the understand-ing of terrorism displayed in Brian Eno and David Byrne's *My Life In The Bush Of Ghosts* (see p.110). It's brave and uncomfortable, and reminds you that pop doesn't do this sort of thing any more, largely because the American Right have made it clear, since the '80s, that free speech is not allowed in music, and that there are plenty of efficient ways to ensure that music doesn't question Western power and values, other than government censorship. They'll just ensure that the conglomerates who control the promotion and distribution of pop destroy your career and that the media leave you open to physical threat from extremists and patriots. It simply isn't worth writing a 'Pull Out The Pin' anymore, even when it's obvious that your song is not encouraging terrorism.

The title track is so extraordinary that it shatters the album into two halves. Rolf and Percy provide nutty noises for one of the strangest singles in pop history (it stalled at

THE DREAMING/KATE BUSH

No. 48 in Bush-loving Britain), a bizarro world of dirge-Afro-reggae rhythm, Kate's Aussie accent, kangaroos bouncing off the roofs of vans, aborigines being mown down and 'mistaken for a tree', cartoon laughing in 'I Am The Walrus' mode, and a call-and-response hook that goes 'See the light ram through the gaps in the land' 'cos the girl really could have been a poet, but what a waste that would've been. The album ends with more animal-human fusion madness in 'Get Out Of My House', as Ms Bush turns your basic 'I Will Survive' women's kiss-off lyric into something stunning and scary, by reasoning that locking the door on departing bloke and never letting him back in needs a high degree of being stubborn, and what animal symbolises stubborn? Yep, you got it. That would be a mule. So the album's studio engineer Paul Hardiman is instructed to honk 'EEY-ORE!!!' over and over again. It's hilarious and horrifying and how Bush's melody and arrangement enables it to be music, to be wonderful music, involves the application of music's greatest attribute – magic. Pure, indescribable, mysterious magic.

And with one forty-three-minute leap into madness and magic, Kate Bush was free to make *Hounds Of Love* (see p.182).

NEBRASKA

BRUCE SPRINGSTEEN
PRODUCED BY BRUCE SPRINGSTEEN AND MIKE BATLIN
CBS/SEPTEMBER 1982
UK CHART: 3
US CHART: 3
KEY TRACKS: 'State Trooper'; 'Highway Patrolman'; 'Atlantic City'; 'Johnny 99'; 'Open All Night'

'There's just a meanness in this world.'

The final line from the opener and title track of Bruce Springsteen's sixth album serves as its central theme. Recorded solo, without Springsteen's legendary E Street Band, on a four-track cassette recorder, the rawness of popping mikes and vocal distortion included, just acoustic guitar, voice, and occasional harmonica, *Nebraska* saw the man they made The Boss undercut his audience's expectations for the first time, and, like Ms Bush, emerge bigger and better for it.

Nebraska was where Springsteen established the idea that each of his albums would subvert the musical and thematic preoccupations of the previous one. Until *Nebraska*, Springsteen was seen by many as a cheesy macho romantic, establishing blue-collar rock as a heroic concern, profiting from baby-boomer nostalgia for simpler times. But *Nebraska* ran from the messy mixture of pub-rock anthems and maudlin ballads that was 1980's *The River*, and presented us with the dark side of the characters in his most famous song, 'Born To Run' – pointing out that once you make that impetuously youthful, blithely rock 'n' roll, legendary American escape from small-town conventions into the vastness of America, you still have to survive and live with the consequences of your actions. Here, the optimistic teens on a motorbike have been hardened by poverty, alienation, and 'the meanness in this world' into killers, itinerants dragged into crime, poverty-stricken losers, and the ordinary folk who have to deal the reality of those who want to live in the quintessential American road movie. It could be the soundtrack to *Thelma And Louise*, so deftly does it question the entire notion of machismo. It's a temptation to call it his best album, but *Born to Run* and *Born In The USA* are so different to *Nebraska*, yet such a connected part of the same long story, that comparison is specious. They're sections of a body of work, and one of the most integral in recent American history, in any artform you can mention.

Being a record that consists of ten short stories, eight of them delivered in the first person from the viewpoint of very different characters, the lyrics demand to be described in detail, but make it impossible for each without making this entry a book in itself. But if any song captures the spirit of *Nebraska*, it's 'Mansion On The Hill'. Is there another millionaire rock star who could make you feel the sincerity of a song like this? Here, the architectural embodiment of the American Dream is seen only as a cruel taunt to the poor who live below. Springsteen can buy a dozen of those mansions, but sings this song from the perspective of a man who has lived his entire life in its shadow, growing up travelling to the rich man's home, just to hear the sounds of joy and laughter that echo from behind its steel gates, gates forged by the factories that divide the mansion from the people below. His vision and purpose are so strong and true that he cuts straight through our notions of liberal rock stars who want their cake and eat it too, as he forces us to see the mansion as a literal bringer of darkness to the edge of Anytown, USA. Who cares that he's rich and you're not? This song and this singing are worth more than petty envy or hipster cynicism, and he knows it.

Other elements that sum up the mood:

1) Everything that happens here seems to happen in a car, the ultimate economic driver of America's way of life, the mode of escape, the steel trap that cuts the protagonists off from their fellow sufferers, the reason for the roads that provide scenes of crimes and crashes and chases and yet another long day's journey into night.

2) The album always reminds me of my favourite author, the cult US pulp fiction writer Jim Thompson, whose ripping yarns of guns and girls would always descend into an existential hell, an American Gothic landscape where insanity and horrific violence fills the characters' psychological void, just as Springsteen ends two of *Nebraska*'s songs with the protagonist asking, hysterically, to be delivered 'from nowhere'.

3) Springsteen admitted the influence of New Yorker Alan Vega, whose reinvention of the echoed rockabilly howl led *Suicide* (see p.30) and his own, more guitar-led solo albums. Like Springsteen, Vega also sings of doomed, alienated American vets and ghosts and victims and escapees and prisoners of economics, and his influence is particularly strong here in 'Johnny 99' and 'State Trooper', an astonishing thing that boils down the history of rock 'n' roll to base elements, and lets loose one of the spookiest screams in existence.

4) *Nebraska* is also an album about the relationship between cars, rock and the radio, a glimpse of deliverance before another state trooper interrupts your favourite Roy Orbison tune to tell you, through crackling static, that he's gonna shoot you down like a broke-dick dog before you reach the Canadian border. Even though he's your brother. There's just a meanness in this world.

THE NIGHTFLY

DONALD FAGEN
PRODUCED BY GARY KATZ
WARNERS/OCTOBER 1982
UK CHART: 44
US CHART: 11
KEY TRACKS: 'New Frontier'; 'The Nightfly'; 'I.G.Y.'; 'The Goodbye Look'; 'Green Flower Street'

Springsteen's *Nebraska* comes to a typical American conclusion. Its final song is 'Reason To Believe', which is not the Tim Hardin standard, but is a song about finding hope amidst the despair, an attempt at an upbeat ending after nine previous songs about deprivation, death and eternal loserdom. Which leads us nicely to the first solo album by Bruce's fellow New Jersey product Donald Fagen, who, with his partner Walter Becker, had spent the previous decade establishing Steely Dan as the most cynical, satirical and downright smart-arse jazz-funk-influenced rock band in America. Just like Springsteen, Fagen decided to make his solo debut into an exercise in contrariness, and based the whole thing around – heh – baby-boomer nostalgia for simpler times. Played by the cream of California's smooth jazz set – Marcus Miller, Larry Carlton, Randy Brecker, etc – *The Nightfly* comes on like the jazz remix of Lawrence Kasdan's

THE NIGHTFLY/DONALD FAGEN

Motown-obsessed yuppies in *The Big Chill*, except that the generally downbeat Fagen fucks with the '70s/'80s-come-down part of the script. The optimism of being part of JFK's generation of fresh-faced students, poised on the frontline of the 'New Frontier', is allowed to stand – no sneers, no sell-outs, no Vietnam or Nixon gatecrashing the freedom party. The result is one of the most musically lovely albums of any era, and a sonic masterclass in how to produce high-tech prime-time adult radio pop without becoming banal.

At least . . . that's how it appears. But when I say no sneers, what I mean is no obvious ones. *The Nightfly* is one of those truly subversive pop artworks, in that the clean, bright sumptuousness of the music, and the clean, bright positivity of the chorus hooks, allow the listener the luxury of taking it all on face value, while the true theme of the record is how easily the post-war generation's facile, self-satisfied, patriotic vision of the future was corrupted by falsehood, compromise and betrayal. Beneath the *American Graffiti*-style '50s imagery of Dave Brubeck, beautiful well-read and well-bred girls, all-night jazz DJs and dreams of being 'Eternally free and eternally young', lies . . . well . . . lies. The middle-class collegiate know-all in denial of the race war, sexual betrayal, US military bullying and ultra-violence that lies in wait for those high on being selected as the brightest and best. The lyrics of 'I.G.Y. (International Geographical Year)', 'Green Flower Street', 'New Frontier', 'The Nightfly' and 'The Goodbye Look' contain a winking tirade of killing jokes at the expense of American middle-class folly, and the luscious lope of Fagen and Katz's Latin and blues-tinged jazz-pop just makes the jokes all the more cruel and unusual.

An easy-listening album suffused with a casually expressed horror that implicates its own audience, *The Nightfly* is one of pop's greatest hidden masterpieces, and one that unveils a fresh, unpalatable truth every time you're able to wrench yourself away from its perfect surface, and dive into its murky satirical depths.

MIDNIGHT LOVE

MARVIN GAYE

PRODUCED BY MARVIN GAYE
CBS/OCTOBER 1982
UK CHART: 10
US CHART: 7
KEY TRACKS: 'Sexual Healing'; 'Midnight Lady'; 'Rockin' After Midnight'; 'Joy'; 'My Love Is Waiting'

The facts of Marvin Gaye's death weigh heavy upon his final album. Gunned down by his apostolic minister father on 1 April 1984, the former Marvin Pentz Gay Jr died as he lived – troubled, unfulfilled, and in violent conflict with his dad. But the truth is – and this pops up time and again in this book – that *Midnight Love* would be every bit as great if Gaye was still alive and selling Tupperware from a stone-clad semi in Epsom. Sure, it can't help but touch you when, for example, that golden voice sings 'You know I love to live' in the self-explanatory 'Joy'. But it's not the spooked genius who made 'I Heard It Through The Grapevine', *What's Going On* and *Let's Get It On* foretelling his own sudden demise. It's the cry of a man trying to convince himself it's true. And that feeling is not the sole province of tragic Motown legends.

After splitting from Motown, not making a UK hit since 1973, and spending time going nuts and escaping the tax-man in, of all places, Belgium, Gaye's return was an unlikely triumph. *Midnight Love*'s impact on soul – or R&B, if you must – was immediate and dramatic. Its sonic palette of softly pattering drum machines, itchy, trebly guitars, discreet horns and shuffling, anti-disco rhythms became the dominant soul template right through until swingbeat fused hip hop, pop and soul in the early '90s. *Midnight Love* reinvented the '70s soul-funk era's blend of good taste, syncopated rhythm and lyrically overt, but vocally understated sexuality. It was a Great Pop Moment when opener 'Midnight Lady' established its undulating groove and Gaye, for whom

tries one last desperate gambit to get his bay-bee to come on over and give him the cure to what ails: 'Please don't procrastinate/It's no good to masturbate.' Not sure I agree, mind you, but anyone who can get 'procrastinate' into a song about begging for a shag wins the argument, hands . . . um . . . down.

SINGLES 45'S AND UNDER

SQUEEZE
PRODUCED BY SQUEEZE, JOHN WOOD, ROGER BECHIRAN, ELVIS COSTELLO, PHIL MCDONALD AND ALAN TARNEY
A&M/NOVEMBER 1982
UK CHART: 3
US CHART: 47
KEY TRACKS: 'Pulling Mussels (From The Shell)'; 'Take Me I'm Yours'; 'Cool For Cats'; 'Is That Love'; 'Another Nail In My Heart'

cocaine had become just one of many demons, gleefully moaned 'Something's goin on in the men's room', with just the right amount of lascivious fuck-you-osity. The edge that hit the album home came in Gaye's allusions to his mental problems – the haunted 'Baby! I got sick this morning/A sea was storming/Inside of me' from the timeless 'Sexual Healing' was especially heart-rending – and his commitment to the worship of sex, music, love and Jesus as his salvation.

Two other things of note: the man who contributed the rousing closer 'My Love Is Waiting' and the multi-tracked guitar duelling that lights up 'Rockin' After Midnight' is called Gordon Banks, and how I wanted the former England World Cup-winning goalkeeper to have retired and become a brilliant soul session man. But, you know, it's not the same Banks. The other thing is that the album's most startling couplet is conspicuous by its absence from the original lyric sheet. As 'Sexual Healing' fades on Marvin's pleadings, he

They were ordinary guys, were Squeeze. From Deptford, south London, the kind of blokes who always seemed like they'd stand their round. Diamond geezers. Pub rockers who somehow progressed way beyond the pub. But they occupy a unique position in their late '70s/early '80s time and place. They were loved for no other reason than that they wrote really great songs, and sang them with humour when appropriate, and sincerity when regretful, which, in most of their songs, they were. *Singles 45's And Under* compiles their peak period singles, and became one of those 'every home should have one' Best Ofs.

The vinyl album splits their hits neatly – with Jools and without. Jools Holland, that is, who, before becoming the most obsequious music TV presenter of all time, played keyboards for Squeeze. Surprisingly, in light of that whole boogie-woogie-joanna thing he's got going on, Holland's tunes use abrasive disco synths melded adventurously and cleverly

SINGLES 45'S AND UNDER/SQUEEZE

with Glenn Tilbrook and Chris Difford's traditional song craft, while the post-Holland hits are more rootsy, all soul pastiche pianos and organs.

These much-loved singles are pitched somewhere between Paul McCartney, whom Tilbrook resembles vocally, and one-time producer/mentor Elvis Costello, with whom Difford shared a losers' view of boy meets girl. There was a bit of Ian Dury too, particularly in Difford's cockney-rapping 'Cool For Cats'. It's very 1982, in the sense that it unleashes a deluge of words, and that most of them are smart, precise, occasionally obtuse, but full of character and ribaldry. It's one of the very few albums in this book that I have no qualms about describing as sensible and solid, and honestly mean it as a compliment. I listen to it when wanting something direct and rootsy, but much more musically subtle and experimental than it seems on the surface. And the extraordinary 'Pulling Mussels (From The Shell)' is a better, weirder working-class holiday song than either Blur's 'Girls And Boys' or The Streets' 'Fit But You Know It', and I hope that compliment makes up for the 'sensible and solid' bit, which I'm finding it hard to make more exciting than it is.

A KISS IN THE DREAMHOUSE

SIOUXSIE AND THE BANSHEES
PRODUCED BY SIOUXSIE AND THE BANSHEES
POLYDOR/NOVEMBER 1982
UK CHART: 11
US CHART: UNRELEASED IN USA
KEY TRACKS: 'Slowdive'; 'Green Fingers'; 'Painted Bird';
'Obsession'; 'Melt!'

A gothic psychedelic sex-pop album, with jazz bits. If you're thinking that that description really suits The Cure – and especially their breakthrough hit 'The Lovecats' – then note that Robert Smith temporarily replaced Banshees guitarist John McGeoch after this record, then made a side project album as The Glove with Banshees co-founder Steve

Severin, then released 'The Lovecats' in October 1983, just three months after Siouxsie and Banshees drummer Budgie had teamed up as The Creatures and scored a Top 20 hit with a big band jazz cover called 'Right Now'. I'm just saying.

On ... *Dreamhouse*, the last unimpeachably great Banshees album, Sioux and Co. defined their worldview that humanity is an endless series of creepy horrors hiding beneath what you're assured is normal. Solution? Remain a child at heart, ignore all parental mores and impulses, and have lots of pervy, obsessive, fetishist sex that smells of that whole orgasm-as-le-petit-mort thing that the French have got going on. Severin's 'Melt!', for example, is a dreamy shagadelic ballad featuring suicide, burning throats, choking, decapitation, handcuffs, blood, sperm, poison, discipline and someone being fingered at a funeral. I think that nice bit of rhyming slang James Blunt should cover it.

The production is credited to the Banshees, but they should probably get a slap for that, because the sound is very much the same wall-of-brittle-sound-in-a-wind-tunnel that engineer Mike Hedges gave to The Associates for *Sulk* (see p.135). This works especially well for closer 'Slowdive', a deliciously sensual one-chord drone in which Sioux invents her very own '50s-style dance craze: 'Get your head down to the ground/Shake it all around . . . Put your knees into your face/See if you can race . . . Jump back like a hound/Emit a howling sound' . . . you get the idea. It's very funny, in its painful death-dance way, but the thing is – much like when Severin gets Sioux to wail 'My chest is full of eels!' on 'Cascade' – you can never tell whether the Banshees are joking or not. That's why we loved them, and the entire class of '76–'79 of which this album represents pretty much the last dying gurgle of inspiration. They trusted us to work it out. That trust between artist and fan is the basis of great pop art, and was almost fatally broken, in mainstream pop terms, by the next behemoth in our list.

THRILLER

MICHAEL JACKSON
PRODUCED BY QUINCY JONES
EPIC/DECEMBER 1982
UK CHART: 1
US CHART: 1
KEY TRACKS: 'Billie Jean'; 'Human Nature'; 'The Lady In My Life'; 'Wanna Be Startin' Somethin'; 'Thriller'

Not since The Beatles' *Sgt Pepper* in 1967 had anyone made the world feel like we were all singing the same song. And, just as Live Aid became an '80s, pro-status quo version of Woodstock's dissolute chaos, *Thriller* turned The Beatles' era's dreams of peaceful revolution and a world run by Utopian youth, into our acquiescence to a Higher Power – the perfect pop star, more talented and beautiful than we could ever be allowed to dream of, waving his commercial triumph in our faces and getting us to love him for it. That's been the template for the superstar pop album ever since,

particularly from the urban side of the tracks . . . and how useful and committed Jacko was to getting the word 'black' out of the equation.

Thriller proved that doing anything first is an irrelevance – making the suckers believe you did it first is the whole of the law. People still believe that the simultaneous global first showing of the John Landis-directed video for 'Thriller' was a landmark . . . The Beatles and Elvis already did it, way back. People still believe that nobody had fused disco with rock until 'Beat It' – see almost every album in this book thus far, and let's not even start on Stevie Wonder, Sly Stone, George Clinton, Curtis Mayfield . . .

But what the marketing men behind *Thriller* taught the producers of art and entertainment product is that being The Biggest Selling Album Of All Time sweeps aside doubt. If the post-punk albums we've looked at thus far are about morally sure artists casting doubt on the consumer capitalism that had replaced God as the West's *raison d'etre*, then

Thriller was about an artist with a defective moral compass embracing the modern world and celebrating his triumph over it. Doubt is all over songs like 'Billie Jean', 'Wanna Be Startin' Somethin', 'Beat It' and the sublime, AIDS-aware anthem to promiscuity that is 'Human Nature'. But no one cared that the singer seemed obsessed with paternity suits and horrified by women because the singer had elected himself the King Of Pop, and we wanted to be at the coronation, because saying 'No!' becomes tiring when you think you're the only one saying it. Everyone from toddlers to grannies to Goths said 'Yes!' to Michael, and we felt like we belonged to the '80s, and that maybe going along with the greed and violence would be OK.

What *Thriller* also did was make the pop album bigger than the rock album. If you got the right classy producer, the cleanest, most technically accomplished sound and musicians, songs of great harmonic deftness, and marketed the artist as rich and immaculate, you could do what no one had pulled off before Jacko and make people feel good about choosing a mainstream pop record, rather than a cool art-rock album in the *Sgt Pepper* or *Dark Side Of The Moon* mould. The session musicians on *Thriller* were better musicians than, say, Eric Clapton, and more modern too, with their funky new synths that made everything sound punchy yet controlled and . . . antiseptic. The prophecies of dehumanisation by extreme cleanliness found on X-Ray Spex's profound *Germ-Free Adolescents* (see p.49) came to pass here, on Thriller, an album that replaces the sweat of soul with the great smell of soap. It's no surprise that its maker attempted to remove his skin, and every other outward sign of being One Of Us.

So – why's it here, then? Man, I didn't say I didn't love it. Evil things are appealing . . . that's what makes them evil. You don't change the entire course of pop if all you have is obscenely expensive marketing. Between Michael growling 'You're a vegetable' like a drooling nut job on the Manu Dibango-plagiarising 'Wanna Be Startin' Somethin', to the final old-school soul vocal ad lib of British soul composer Rod Temperton's 'The Lady Of My Life', I still luxuriate in the high watermark of US Urban Contemporary muzak, staring at the sleeve and admiring the boy's tiger cub, white suit, and big, flat, beautiful African nose. Michael Jackson may have ruined pop. But compared to his face, pop got off lightly.

1983

ONE FROM THE HEART – MUSIC FROM THE MOTION PICTURE

TOM WAITS AND CRYSTAL GAYLE
PRODUCED BY BONES HOWE
COLUMBIA/FEBRUARY 1983
UK CHART: DID NOT CHART
US CHART: DID NOT CHART
KEY TRACKS: 'This One's From The Heart'; 'Old Boyfriends';
'I Beg Your Pardon'; 'Picking Up After You'; 'Broken Bicycles'

In 1982, Francis Ford Coppola decided to convalesce from the fraught, wildly over-budget making of *Apocalypse Now* by making a light love story. Set in a highly stylised (and entirely fake) Las Vegas, ageing partners Frederic Forrest and Teri Garr fall out, cheat on each other, and reunite while the music of Tom Waits serenades us with the characters' inner feelings. Despite Coppola's generous attempt to make two ordinary people into romantic leads, therefore assuring us that we're all stars in our own personal romances, the movie bombed. Thankfully, it left us with a magical soundtrack album.

One From The Heart is Tom Waits's final goodbye to pop-jazz songwriting before his spectacular reinvention as music's foremost junkyard hobo. Much of its magic lies in the delicious contrast between Waits's broken rasp and the clean, clear perfection of Crystal Gayle's country-politan croon. The rest lies in the songs; a beautifully performed set of jazz ballads tributing – but never merely pastiching – Cole Porter, Hoagy Carmichael and their fellow sophisticats of the pre-rock pop era. The true object of desire is neither of the two lovers, but the Great American Songbook, and its composers' ability to romanticise human foible with graceful and quietly savage wit.

Coppola approached Waits after his son played him 'I Never Talk To Strangers', a Waits duet with Bette Midler from his *Foreign Affairs* album. Coppola admits, in his sleevenotes for the 2004 CD reissue, that he based the film upon Waits's songs. And what a script our gruff Californian raconteur came up with, where, for example, a song like 'Picking Up After You' makes warm romantic comedy out of mutual domestic loathing, and where Waits sums up a very male, single-life fantasy – 'I'll be livin' on chicken and wine/After we're through' – and then twists the knife by finding the title's other meaning – 'With someone I'll pick up after you.'

Crystal Gayle's showcase song, 'Old Boyfriends', perhaps explains why neither movie nor soundtrack were hits. Because, in the end, it's all just too sad, despite the film's happy ending. Gayle's voice is bereft and exposed in its clarity, as she sings of old flames who 'look you up when they're in town/To see if they can still burn you down'. As Waits puts it on track nine, 'You Can't Unring A Bell', and the quiet, stately, near-classical settings of 'Old Boyfriends', 'Broken Bicycles' and 'I Beg Your Pardon' do nothing to obscure the truth and pain at their core. Unlike Donald Fagen's *The Nightfly*, with which it shares a love of cool jazz and classic American song, *One From The Heart* is not a smuggling of ugly themes under cover of sweet muzak. It gives it to you straight on the subject of love and ageing, even when it's joking.

If you've ever wasted your time on, say, Jamie Cullum or Harry Connick Jr because you love vocal jazz, then treat yourself to this beautifully conceived heartbreaker, and hear the real thing without the soft soap.

OFF THE BONE

THE CRAMPS
PRODUCED BY ALEX CHILTON AND THE CRAMPS
ILLEGAL/MAY 1983
UK CHART: 44
US CHART: DID NOT CHART
KEY TRACKS: 'Garbageman'; 'Human Fly'; 'The Crusher';
'Goo Goo Muck'; 'I Can't Hardly Stand It'

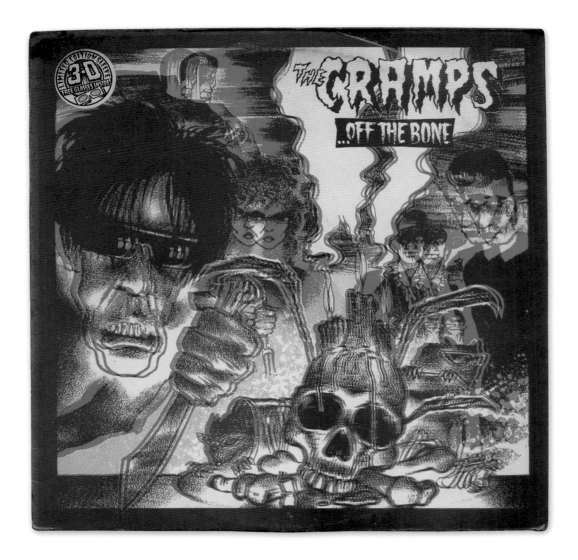

OFF THE BONE/THE CRAMPS

POWER, CORRUPTION AND LIES/NEW ORDER

On the surface, the muso jazz and classic songwriting of *One From The Heart* belongs on an altogether cleaner and classier planet from a minimalist trash 'n' roll band who hover defiantly on the edge of bumbling musical ineptitude. But maybe not. Because *One From The Heart* is about the highs and lows of marriage, and New York's Cramps are led by Lux Interior and Poison Ivy, rock's happiest husband and wife team. Not only do you suspect that Lux and Ivy would love to spend the rest of their lives in a stylised film set based on Vegas, but their perennial togetherness seems to be based on mutual bad taste, perversity, and drug-fuelled sexual ghoulishness.

Off The Bone collects The Cramps' finest moments from their first five years. Playing rockabilly and garage-punk, including lots of gonzo cover versions, without a bass guitar but with the ambience of a pneumatic drill, they take their manic cue from a 1950s maverick called Hazil Adkins. Adkins was a crazed West Virginian one-man rockabilly band who wrote songs about red meat, outer space and imaginary dance crazes and recorded them on primitive reel-to-reel tape, thereby inventing punk, Captain Beefheart, and DIY lo-fi before The Beatles had oohed their first ooh. The Cramps responded to his inspiration by inspiring a perennial rock 'n' roll subculture made of hair grease, girl groups, Betty Page, sci-fi B-movies, second-hand lounge suits and frilly shirts, fishnet tights, *The Addams Family* and *The Munsters*, John Waters and Russ Meyer films, and a complete rejection of both 'intelligent' rock and every music-related fashion since the teddy boy. For example, my home town of Brighton has a long-running club called Born Bad. Advertised by a pic of a '50s bad-girl pin-up, the club plays rockabilly, garage and girl groups. The club is named after a superb set of compilation albums showcasing minimalist rock obscurities from the '50s and '60s. What they had in common? All covered by The Cramps. One suspects this modern-world-rejecting sub-species will continue to exist long after Lux and Ivy have departed to that great alien B-movie in the sky.

The music on this record strips away all frippery and mainlines all of rock 'n' roll's secret dirt and dumbest impulses. Made of mania, hysteria, diphtheria and leopard-skin underwear, it believes that the whole world wants to be Elvis, and therefore is. It's music like flies on turds and like Bo Diddley and Screaming Jay Hawkins being buzzed by stray electric waves from Uranus. It sounds like this because it needs to, and it's funny because it's deadly serious about how funny rock 'n' roll is. And it's all led by a howling, whooping walking echo machine called Lux Interior, who used to be Erick Lee Purkhiser from Ohio, but made himself into a living cartoon because, as he sings on his wife's Iggy-Pop's-entire-life-and-career-in-three-and-a-half-minutes composition 'New Kind Of Kick', 'Life is short/And filled with . . . stuff.' Oh yes, it is. Some of life's best stuff is on this record.

POWER, CORRUPTION AND LIES

NEW ORDER
PRODUCED BY NEW ORDER
FACTORY/MAY 1983
UK CHART: 4
US CHART: DID NOT CHART
KEY TRACKS: 'Age Of Consent'; 'Leave Me Alone'; 'The Village'; '5-8-6'; 'Your Silent Face'

New Order gave a great many introspective student types permission to get happy and dance. Their second album arrived just two months after 'Blue Monday' had made every other contemporary dance record sound clumsy and antique, and *Power, Corruption And Lies* essentially stretched 'Blue Monday' into forty minutes of sparkling electro, kept intimate and fragile by Barney Sumner's unapologetically weak voice. It was an album of surprises – the portentous title, keyboardist Gillian Gilbert's move to centre-stage, the almost complete surrender to gay scene electro-disco and hi-NRG, and a couple of musical jokes that lifted the veil of misery involved in being the former Joy Division.

'5-8-6' begins as a stumbling exercise in synthetic minimalism before yet another priceless hi-NRG riff wanders slowly forward. The band's delight in new technology is summed up when the chorus refrain 'I heard you calling' is sequenced into a stuck-record stutter. 'I heard you-heard-you-heard-you', Barney trills in his sweetest girlie voice, and you can still hear the childlike delight in the sonic trick, even after almost twenty years of techno introducing the 'glitch' – the deliberate mistake – into mainstream music. The best way to delight a listener is to surprise them, with a profane lyric, a key change or an emotionally satisfying chord sequence . . . or a sound like a stuck record . . . that makes the spine tingle. '5-8-6's magic moment is still one of the all-time great communications of sheer dance joy from artist to listener.

But it wasn't all pioneering machine glitch. 'Your Silent Face' pulls off a moment that throws the entire New Order myth – Ian Curtis's suicide, the enigmatic sleeve art, the European high art references, the entire mise-en-scene of bleak, industrial doom – into humorous doubt. The song's stately Kraftwerkian melody wends its lovely way through Sumner's habitual fey-yet-lofty lovelorn lyrical accusation, spinning a miserable yarn around the sadness of silence, and all the things 'we' can't do. Until . . . well . . . Barney gets bored with himself, and New Order's obtuse misery, and our expectation of it. So, he talks to us directly, like an actor suddenly stepping out of a cinema screen. 'You caught me at a bad time,' he cautions, 'So why don't you . . . piss off.' There's no question mark there, because it's not a question. It's an under-breath mumble, an offhand, frivolous rejection of our endless reverence for his group. From that moment on, New Order were New Order, three Manc lads and a girl who liked gay disco and had a hard-man heavy metal bassist that made them different. They weren't the tragic survivors of Joy Division, or a group that had profound things to say, except that most surreptitiously profound of things – that

music was liberation and that popular music was about dancing and mixing your own thing with exotic other things, like maybe white northern English punk with Euro-queer electronica and black American dance music. It was a mix that invented the acid house aesthetic five years before acid house changed the cultural world, and gave a whole bunch of new electronic dance producers a rock group to be amazed by and to copy, as house and techno's pioneers all did. Indeed, 'Ecstasy' is an early rehearsal for the acid she-bang, and a reminder that New Order and the Factory label crowd were part of New York's cool clubland set, and that ecstasy was the American drug sensation way back at the turn of the '80s.

What this all had to do with power, corruption and lies is anyone's guess. But it was a smart title because its hint of 'meaning-of-life' depth and subtext obscured the fact that these former excavators of the despair of the human condition had become a cute, hedonistic disco group. In short, it kept the grey raincoat brigade on board. Marketing genius on a par with *Thriller*, which is perhaps why Jacko's producer/mentor Quincy Jones signed New Order to his Qwest label, and made 'Blue Monday' a hit again in the year of Our Acid, 1988.

BOYS DON'T CRY

THE CURE
PRODUCED BY CHRIS PARRY
FICTION/AUGUST 1983
UK CHART: 71
US CHART: DID NOT CHART
KEY TRACKS: 'Killing An Arab'; '10:15 Saturday Night';
'Grinding Halt'; 'Fire In Cairo'; 'Jumping Someone Else's Train'

You don't get anything for originality, not in the pop game. The first music by Blackpool-born, Sussex-raised Robert Smith and his Cure sounded like nothing before or since, yet even Smith himself has virtually disowned it. By the time this compilation of their early, funny kitchen-sink pop had been released in the UK (it had been around in America since 1980), the Cure were well on the way to being the planet's foremost alt-rock copyists, filling stadiums and major label coffers by taking noises made and poses struck by Joy Division, New Order and Siouxsie And The Banshees, buffing off the rough edges and disturbing bits, and pretending to be playful rather than cynical. Every doomy band coming out of America has a bit of Cure in 'em, so smartly did they create a template for being banal while appearing alternative.

But before all that, they made the music on *Boys Don't Cry*, which collected the best bits from debut album *Three Imaginary Boys* plus the first three singles and B-sides. Their A&R man Chris Parry created a unique sound palette for the group, an intimate, lo-fi pop fizz that used cheap sound effects, guitar solos and drummer Lol Tolhurst's rattling

cymbal-isms as shock tactics, ripping the garage-band fabric by mixing these interjections too high, or slightly out of time. As opposed to bedsit pop, it came on like pop made in a bedsit, transmissions from the hearts of the ultimate in morose sixth-formers, intellectualising their inability to get laid, lecturing prospective virginity-takers about how life's a sham, a lousy, hollow sham, and then dismissing them as sex objects when they decided to fuck their funny friend instead. It felt defined by Smith's voice and guitar becoming a dripping tap in a lonely room on the definitive you-really-should-get-out-more anthem that is '10:15 Saturday Night', and still inhabits a unique, unintentionally hilarious teen-angst boy world where the Buzzcocks' fuzzy melodies of romantic despair are twinned with a twatty Toytown existentialism, summed up by 'Killing An Arab', which is nothing to do with such mundane issues as the Middle East powder-keg, and is all about trying to file a musical essay on *The Outsider* by Albert Camus, which I read when I was about fifteen and thought was really deep and gave me insights that my stupid friends didn't have, unless they'd read *Nausea, The Catcher In The Rye, The Bell Jar* . . . I think you know what I'm getting at here. Like lots of boys who hover between working-class economics and middle-class aspiration, I was one of those self-righteous dicks who was finally cured (I think) by sex and dancing. Somewhere in the world, there is a student pseud talking down to a yawning girl every three seconds, you know, and the secret soundtrack which always plays is *Boys Don't Cry* – the most fun you can have without ever having a hope of taking your clothes off.

SWORDFISHTROMBONES

TOM WAITS
PRODUCED BY TOM WAITS
ISLAND/SEPTEMBER 1983
UK CHART: 62
US CHART: DID NOT CHART

Tom Waits has never been thought of as a political artist. But, in hindsight, his most famous album sounds like a protest against Reaganomics. Despite the facts of moving from LA to New York, of his new marriage to muse and collaborator Kathleen Brennan, of a new record label who understood that he wanted to move away from being a Tin Pan Alley-tributing cabaret act and invent a new kind of music that housed American blues and jazz melodies in textures pulled from various globally informed arthouse musics – a music made from hitting things, but carefully – despite all these happy excitements, *Swordfishtrombones* is an album about tired, angry losers from fucked-up neighbourhoods. It suggests that America was in such structural and psychological chaos that a rural backwater was no different to an inner-city ghetto. It was all broken dogs, and scrapyard cars, junk and the other junk, and people being driven insane by the American nightmare. The fact that Waits could find a song as funny as 'Frank's Wild Years', where 'His wife was a spent piece of used jet trash' who owns a Chihuahua with a skin disease, and Frank famously burns down the San Fernando Valley home and his Willy Loman life because he 'Never could stand that dog', doesn't mean he's not furious about why these people have no future. Just because 'In The Neighbourhood' is full of affection for a crushed area's inhabitants, dodging 'the newspaper sleeping bags' as they 'blow down the lane', doesn't mean it's just poetic imagery, grist to a master writer's mill. The more the songs laugh, and the bagpipes and brass bands and buckets, bones and bells weep and thunk and moan, the more anger they generate.

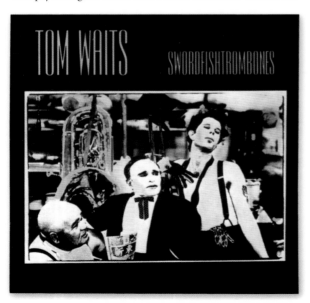

But, even if you can't be arsed with more potshots at the '80s Right, songs such as '16 Shells From A Thirty-Ought-Six' and 'Shore Leave' reimagine a blues fit for the modern world, where everything from avant-punk to smoochy mambo, from sea shanty to hillbilly lament, from Afro-Cuban percussion jam to beatnik poetry, gets injected organically into ancient blues chord changes, until they ooze atmosphere and sensuality. It's introduced by the stumbling flea circus of 'Underground', which makes the remainder of Waits' career clear when he barks, 'There's a big dark town/It's a place I've found/There's a world going on underground,' and makes us feel the crawl of a subterranean set of freaks who live beneath us while we sleep. From now on, Waits becomes the link between them and us, until we gradually realise that he's singing about us anyway.

There are fifteen songs here that shoot by in under forty-two minutes, in an ugly-beautiful blur of untethered textures and linguistic coups that made Waits the most respected composer of his age, and the writer of novelistic mystery plays that mean something different to everyone who falls under their spell. For me, it's hungry hobos performing threepenny ballet to the strains of a Salvation Army Band giving a recital in the rubble of a broken town with no station and a surplus of pungent mongrels. I didn't know I wanted to visit until Tom took me there.

SOUL MINING

THE THE
PRODUCED BY PAUL HARDIMAN AND MATT JOHNSON
CBS/OCTOBER 1983
UK CHART: 27
US CHART: DID NOT CHART
KEY TRACKS: 'Uncertain Smile'; 'The Sinking Feeling'; 'Giant'; 'This Is The Day'; 'The Twilight Hour'

Often, people approach me in the street and ask, 'Garry, pray tell me – what is your favourite pop chorus?' I like to keep these people waiting a little with a dramatic pause, largely because they are completely imaginary and I get lonely. 'It is from "The Sinking Feeling",' I finally reveal, 'which you will find located on the second album by The The, aka Matt Johnson, a sort of one-man alt-pop band from the Midlands, who was popular for a short while in the 1980s.' They leave satisfied, usually before I get the chance to actually sing them the chorus in question, the ungrateful imaginary bastards. But it goes like this: 'I'm just a symptom of the moral decay that is gnawing at the heart of the . . . country.' The pause before 'country' is the clincher, because it gives Johnson time to concoct a sweet harmony around the word, thereby undercutting the obvious melodrama and letting you know it's a joke. I used to dance round my room and sing it, with a certain defiant glee, and I suspect I wasn't alone.

Soul Mining is a concept album about being alone, in your room (probably the same bedsit full of good books and bad memories in a nondescript borough of a major British city that had been home to Edwyn Collins, Marc Almond and Robert Smith, and would later house Lloyd Cole, Jarvis Cocker and the patron saint of kitchen-sink pop trauma, Morrissey) and driving yourself insane. One suspects that Johnson was no stranger to the black dog of depression, because his internal discourse is surgically spot-on, and because he's one of the few pop depressives to understand how funny it can be, and how those laughs at your own expense often come at your most literally deathly moments. 'The Twilight Hour', especially, is so accurate about the maddening insecurities of self-obsessed men waiting for their girlfriends to ring, and interpreting silence, and completely losing it . . . Man, Woody Allen would've been proud.

So, yes, it is a bit like a grown-up version of the Cure's *Boys Don't Cry* (see p.158), but with the self-regard replaced by the benevolence of a good therapist. Many of the lyrics are in the second person, and feel like a big brother assuring you that you're not alone with these bizarrely self-lacerating thought processes. The album's major coup, though – apart from getting extraordinary guest contributions from the likes of Squeeze's Jools Holland and latter-day Orange Juice's Zeke Manyika – is the way it avoids the wallowing of a Joy Division by being musically optimistic, even sunny. Accordions, fiddles and African percussion work-outs keep very, very cleverly making clear the (or, at least, a) solution to the central character's self-loathing, fear and guilt. Get out there. Join with the others. Be alone less. Johnson lets the communal hoe-downs housed within the emphatic grooves advise this, knowing full well that people saying or him singing things like 'pull yourself together' falls on a depressive's deaf ears . . . even if it's fair enough, and it usually is. Meanwhile, *Soul Mining* is cheaper and funnier than therapy, and contains some of the richest groove and melody in British pop's history. It's a hidden masterpiece, which was probably too clever to enter the pantheon. Even Johnson himself just became another corporate rebel, far too interested in his own over-intense image to bother putting his arm around his listeners again.

Includes
"This Is The Day"
and
"Uncertain Smile"
EPC 25525
THIS STICKER IS REMOVABLE

Includes
a limited edition
12"of
"Perfect"
(new version)
EPC 25525
THIS STICKER IS REMOVABLE

£4.29
64785 A

SOUL MINING/THE THE

1984

THE SMITHS

PRODUCED BY JOHN PORTER
ROUGH TRADE/FEBRUARY 1984
UK CHART: 2
US CHART: DID NOT CHART
KEY TRACKS: 'Still Ill'; 'I Don't Owe You Anything'; 'You've Got Everything Now'; 'Reel Around The Fountain'; 'Suffer Little Children'

The Smiths made safe their early legend with a debut album about child abuse. The production was flat and dour, yet it succeeded in conjuring yet another Manchester-in-song, distinctly different from that of Ian Curtis and Mark E. Smith. In this Manchester, monsters corrupt the innocent on rainy cobbled streets that haven't changed since the early 1960s. It begins with 'Reel Around The Fountain' and a tale about how someone 'took a child/And you made him old'. It ends with a song about the most notorious murder of children in contemporary Britain. In 'Suffer Little Children', Morrissey went right ahead and blamed Manchester for Myra Hindley, Ian Brady and the Moors murders of the 1960s, and gave it no escape from its guilt. Death haunts *The Smiths*.

The sophistication and skill of Morrissey's lyrics and Johnny Marr's tunes and guitar still stun, but at the time The Smiths' impact on British pop was quietly cataclysmic. Our bands had spent the previous seven years slowly working their way from the 'no future' of the Sex Pistols' 'God Save The Queen' to a state of gung-ho optimism. But everything about The Smiths ran contrary to mid-'80s pop, from Andy Warhol star Joe Dallesandro on the cover to the restrained jangling of the songs, but mainly through Moz's dramatised disgust at sex, which here exists to ruin true love at best, and to ruin an entire young life at worst. You fell into the ten short, strange, sepia-tinged accusations of *The Smiths* and immediately felt on the side of the angels, as Marr framed

Morrissey's ribald accusations and fruity ripostes with a set of guitar lines that perfected the musical sigh. And there was something freeing – for gay men, straight men, and all men who aren't walking erections and never know whether that's normal or not – in 'Pretty Girls Make Graves', when Morrissey sang of being 'too delicate' to fulfill this pretty girl's needs. This song begins the ongoing fascination with whether Moz is straight, gay, bi or celibate, but what he sets out to do, with all the Carry On innuendoes that litter the album clashing with suggestions of abuse, rape and murder, is attack both rock and Blighty's obsession with the dirty joke and the lascivious wink as cover for our repulsed repression of real sexuality.

Among the creepy intimations of paedophilia in 'Reel Around The Fountain' and 'The Hand That Rocks The Cradle'; the rites of passage agonies of 'You've Got Everything Now' and 'What Difference Does It Make?', the fabulous smugness of 'Hand In Glove' and the horror of 'Suffer Little

Children', was an immortal line from 'Still Ill'. It went, 'England is mine/And it owes me a living.' All of youth's self-righteous defiance and optimism is contained with that line, and its echo of John Lydon's successful attempt to wake England from its dreaming. *The Smiths* was the first genuine 'like punk never happened' record, because it refused to accept that the same things shouldn't be said again and again, in more articulate and beautiful ways, until things change.

SWOON

PREFAB SPROUT

PRODUCED BY DAVID BREWIS AND PREFAB SPROUT
KITCHENWARE/FEBRUARY 1984
UK CHART: 22
US CHART: DID NOT CHART
KEY TRACKS: 'Cruel'; 'Couldn't Bear To Be Special'; 'Green Isaac'; 'Cue Fanfare'; 'Don't Sing'

My copy of Prefab Sprout's debut album is sadly fucked. Someone, many years ago, tipped coffee over the 'P's in my vinyl LP collection, and all the sleeves stuck together, and eventually ripped. I buy a CD replacement for a 'P' every now and again, but many of them are still there, because the music – by the Pixies and The Pogues and Prince – seemed to resist the sugary damp and stay clear and strong. I've had to get rid of so much of my vinyl down the years and it always breaks my heart, because, as Prefab Sprout's leader Paddy McAloon croons it in 'Cue Fanfare', 'the sweet sweet songs that cloud your eyes – nostalgia supplies.' *Swoon* makes me nostalgic about a time when pop was clever and proud of its intelligence and proud of our ability to keep up . . . a time before dumbing-down kicked in and the entire British educated class taught itself to drop its aitches and be fascinated by what it believed the working classes were fascinated by. In that pop culture, Paddy McAloon – like Green and Edwyn Collins and Momus and Luke Haines and Neil

Hannon – had to settle for being a worthy cult.

So *Swoon* breaks a cardinal rule of the mediocrity meritocracy – it's not a record that would appeal to everyone. It's a record that deconstructs pop songwriting, questions what it's for and why we want it. It's for pop fans who don't buy into that simplistic crap about pop being the province of the noble savage, that its genius is only instinctive. Every song on *Swoon* tries to be smart, and succeeds, through Steely Dan-influenced jazz chord-changes, virtuoso time signatures, constant surprise, musical in-jokes, literary references, nods to the Cole Porters and George Gershwins, and words about the writing of words. Its attack on the dull thinking of authenticity is contained in the wonderful 'Cruel', which insists, 'There is no Chicago urban blues/More heartfelt than my lament for you.' It's sure of its excellence, too, which is why it can afford to pretend that it 'Couldn't Bear To Be Special', a song where McAloon eschews the responsibility of being an object of desire, 'Who makes the cornball things occur/The shiver of the fur.' But the strangest and loveliest backing-vocal line this side of The Beach Boys has already shivered your timbers. *Swoon* is self-satisfied, precious . . . and so would I be, if I could bend melody and tempo like this. It also wants to be American, and dreams of being . . .

BORN IN THE U.S.A.

BRUCE SPRINGSTEEN

PRODUCED BY BRUCE SPRINGSTEEN, JON LANDAU, CHUCK PLOTKIN AND STEVE VAN ZANDT
CBS/JUNE 1984
UK CHART: 1
US CHART: 1
KEY TRACKS: 'Downbound Train'; 'Bobby Jean'; 'Dancing In The Dark'; 'Born In The U.S.A.'; 'I'm On Fire'

. . . this tough, this compassionate, this comfortable with the entire notion of rock 'n' roll masculinity. Springsteen's

BORN IN THE U.S.A/BRUCE SPRINGSTEIN

biggest album is also his masterpiece, and one lent extra resonance by its co-option by a shameless monster. Famously, on the campaign trail for his second Presidential term, Reagan appropriated Springsteen in a September speech as he talked of himself as the man who could make all of America's dreams come true. Reagan didn't mention the hit song 'Born In The U.S.A.' by name, but he didn't have to. Millions the world over had heard the screaming repetition of the chorus and the hammer-of-the-gods drums and figured it was a patriotic anthem from a man who'd done real well out of Reaganomics. Only those who'd heard *Nebraska* (see p.144) and listened to Springsteen's words, in 'Born Of The U.S.A.', of righteous disgust at the legacy – the murder and the lies and the neglect of the 'loser' veterans – of Vietnam, knew that Reagan was deliberately subverting one of the '80s' very few American anti-establishment songs.

Springsteen didn't rage too hard about it. He made a few wry speeches to his fans at his shows and made his own anti-Reagan allegiances clear. But Springsteen is a role model in terms of how to run a career in music; say what you mean, but allow others to make of it what they will, thereby both trusting your audience and avoiding direct punch-ups with those powerful enough to destroy you.

The music on *Born In The U.S.A.* applies the bright blunderbuss power of The E Street Band to many of the losers and lost boys of *Nebraska*. The theme this time was nostalgia. Reagan's presidency was based on making middle-America, still reeling from the endless upheavals and doubts of the '60s and '70s, believe that comfort and joy could be regained by believing in a mythical past where everyone knew their place and took pleasure in America's place as the leader of the world. Springsteen wrote a set of songs that conjured that shared myth of cars and girls in an eternally naïve and prosperous 1950s, and then undercut the spell by pointing out that this America could never come back because it had never existed in the first place. 'I had a job/I had a girl/Had somethin' goin', mister, in this world,' Springsteen mumbles in 'Downbound Train' with the beaten

voice of every American who's believed in the American dream and come to realise that even the most mundane aspects of that dream have no safety net, no ground on which to stand. Every character on this album looks back to a past which contained some optimism, then looks at the reality of now, and pleads only for the basics of home, love, survival. And, if 'I'm On Fire' makes you feel as if Elvis is alive and well and sick with nothing more deadly than sexual desire, then the rest of this extraordinary record is choc-full of daddies, real and symbolic, cool rockin' and real gone, castrated and rendered redundant by economics and the legacy of American military violence.

But, yeah, you're right . . . the video for 'Dancing in the Dark' does suck.

RUN-D.M.C.

RUN-D.M.C.
PRODUCED BY RUSSELL SIMMONS AND LARRY SMITH
PROFILE/JUNE 1984
UK CHART: DID NOT CHART
US CHART: 55
KEY TRACKS: 'Rock Box'; 'Sucker M.C.s'; 'It's Like That'; 'Wake Up'; 'Hollis Crew'

Springsteen may have been trying to distance himself from Reagan, but these harbingers of a musical revolution had no qualms. In 'Wake Up', from the first album by hip hop trio Run-D.M.C., rappers Joseph 'Run' Simmons and Darryl 'DMC' McDaniels are delighted to see that 'The President was chillin' at our show!' It's only a dream, of course, but one in which two black kids from Hollis, Queens, imagine themselves as Reagan's advisors, pointing the evil old cunt toward a Utopian vision, brought about by the awesome self-elevation involved in being a rapper.

It's hard to articulate how indescribably weird this record sounded in 1984. Its brutal 'beat-box' minimalism immedi-

'Beat It'-echoing masterstroke that was 'Rock Box', with thrilling metal guitar provided by Smith's friend Eddie Martinez, instantly revealed hip hop as the new rock 'n' roll, with all the boyish testosterone that that implied. 'Whatever happened to unity?', Run-D.M.C. asked, not unreasonably, on 'It's Like That', the trio's first recording which was remixed into a massive global dance hit by Jason Nevins in 1998. Even as Run-D.M.C. began rap's inexorable rise to being the planet's biggest musical money-spinner and most culturally influential pop tribe, this album contained clues to everything fractured and negative that hip hop would become.

PURPLE RAIN

PRINCE AND THE REVOLUTION
PRODUCED BY PRINCE AND THE REVOLUTION
WARNER BROS/JULY 1984
UK CHART: 7
US CHART: 1
KEY TRACKS: 'When Doves Cry'; 'Purple Rain'; 'The Beautiful Ones'; 'Take Me With U'; 'I Would Die 4 U'

Is the guitar solo from 'Purple Rain' a ludicrous ego-wank, a piss-take, or a thing of beauty? If you answered 'all three', then award yourself many Prince points, for you get everything gettable about pop. This, the first of a Stevie Wonder-like string of classic albums from the Minneapolis Mini-Maestro, was all our pop dreams come true, and the reason why we of the punk/disco generation didn't realise just how rotten '80s music was until much later. I mean, on the one hand, the boy was Little Richard, Hendrix, Jacko and August Darnell. But, on the other, he was Duke Ellington, Sly Stone, Elvis and a black Jagger. When The Pop Messiah arrives, of course, you have to believe he is just the first of many soon-come geniuses, rather than what he turned out to be, which is a complete one-off possessed of almost freakish amounts of talent.

ately made the likes of The Smiths and Springsteen sound like antique music. The electro beats and dislocated shouting of *Run-D.M.C.* was pure futurism, the echoing inner-city alleyways of Joy Division transformed into a robot funk landscape we will forever associate with boys spinning on their heads. It sounded sinister and dangerous, even though the rhymes of Simmons and McDaniels were cute, witty, conventionally moralistic and politically naïve. The crew's third member, Jason 'Jam Master Jay' Mizell, did little on the album. Early hip hop rhymes were about bigging up your DJ, and Mizell went onto become an accomplished beat-maker before his shocking murder in October 2002, outside a recording studio in his Queens neighbourhood.

The irony of Mizell's mysterious demise shouldn't be lost. Although Run's brother and manager Russell Simmons – hip hop's first superstar entrepreneur – guided hip hop's first credible group with smart caution, ensuring that the rhymes softened the sinister minimalism of Larry Smith's definitive beats, Run-D.M.C.'s sound undoubtedly predicted the future success of hip hop's violent undercurrents. The

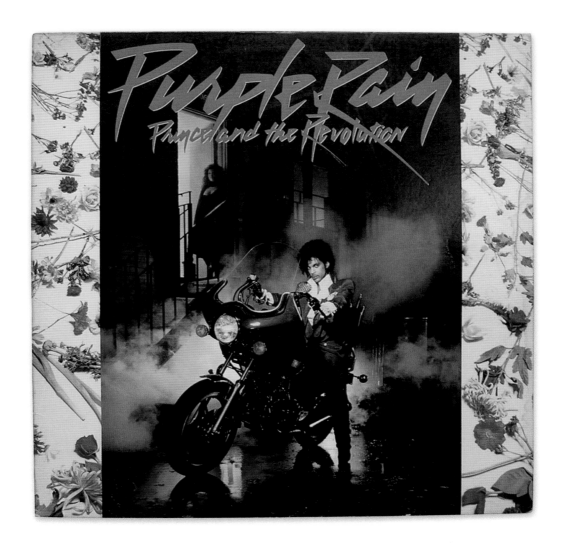

PURPLE RAIN/PRINCE AND THE REVOLUTION

Purple Rain is a movie soundtrack, but there's nothing that the film adds to the music. The sound is complete, from the moment our boy insists, on opener 'Let's Go Crazy', that, 'In this life . . . you're on your own,' and makes that sound like a promise of unimaginable future thrills. Indeed, between the years of 1982, when punk and funk were sent back to the margins, and 1987, when hip hop and house came to save us from A World Turned Beige (thanks again, Ms Burchill), pop was saved from death by misadventure by yer man here, plus The Smiths, Madonna, Springsteen, New Order and Pet Shop Boys. Hell, *Purple Rain* even got me through my worst break-up when, adrift and dumped in a hostile London, I just kept going back to the ballad melodrama deluxe of 'The Beautiful Ones', which was uniquely capable of making me laugh and cry at my self-pity at one and the same time.

True, 'Computer Blue' and 'Darling Nikki' (its slightly embarrassing to think we were once so shocked and titillated by the word 'masturbating') have dated horribly. But *Purple Rain* is still one of the all-time great albums about living for the moment under the ever-present threat of apocalypse, and it also effortlessly pulled off what the post-punks, Jacko and even Run-D.M.C. had only hinted cautiously at – a truly mixed-race pop fusion, where rock, jazz, soul and disco were morphed into a sexually androgynous high impact noise based in the ecstasy and agony of gospel. With a gloriously stupid title, to boot.

HALLOWED GROUND

VIOLENT FEMMES
PRODUCED BY MARK VAN HECKE
SLASH/JULY 1984
UK CHART: DID NOT CHART
US CHART: DID NOT CHART
KEY TRACKS: 'Country Death Song'; 'I Hear The Rain';
'Jesus Walking On The Water'; 'I Know It's True But I'm Sorry

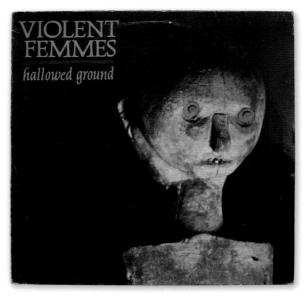

To Say'; 'Sweet Misery Blues'

It begins with a man throwing his daughter down a well and hanging himself in shame. This 'Country Death Song' is sung by a sneering, sardonic Bratvoice, the missing link between Lou Reed and The Pixies' Black Francis. Over punk rock skiffle. From Milwaukee. The '80s wasn't all bad.

The Violent Femmes comprised Gordon Gano (vocals, guitars, violin), Brian Ritchie (bass) and Victor De Lorenzo (drums). They were a pretty large cult band in their day, but have still never quite got their due props for punking up traditional American music long before the '90s alt-county/Americana boom, or sounding exactly like The Pixies if The Pixies had been hoe-down buskers. The Femmes were a vital lo-fi, DIY-style band sticking to their gutbucket guns while mainstream '80s pop bashed and crashed synthetically above their shaggy heads.

This, their second and best album, took the curious indie-punk kid on a whistle-stop tour through American roots music, reinterpreted by three obvious worshippers at the altar of The Velvet Underground. The dark terror at the core of so much American rural music fuels 'Country Death Song' (a modern murder ballad bettered only by Nick Cave), 'I Hear The Rain' and 'Never Tell', while 'Jesus Walking On The Water' revives a white take on (a strictly non-ironic) gospel, and 'Sweet Misery Blues' is a bravura update of drunken bar-room jazz. Gano's brattish, Lou Reed whine made these God-fearing noises into a kind of punk ... and an infinitely more entertaining and transgressive kind than the plaid-shirted 'cowpunk' typified by Femmes contemporaries such as The Long Ryders and Green On Red. The presence of avant-jazz saxist John Zorn as part of The Femmes' own brass section The Horns Of Dilemma is vital to their freshness. There's a thrilling balance here between reverence for the source material, and an arrogant disregard for following the old ways. Everything here is too fast, or too violent, or too sleazy – off-puttingly so on 'Black Girls', which manages to be both racist and misogynist without being as musically irresistible as its obvious spiritual ancestor, 'Brown Sugar'. It's a nasty blight on an otherwise immaculate record, and one of the decade's secret underground delights.

RATTLESNAKES

LLOYD COLE AND THE COMMOTIONS

PRODUCED BY PAUL HARDIMAN
POLYDOR/JULY 1984
UK CHART: 13
US CHART: DID NOT CHART
KEY TRACKS: 'Are You Ready To Be Heartbroken?';
'Charlotte Street'; 'Perfect Skin'; 'Forest Fire'; 'Four Flights Up'

There might not be that many albums from 1984 in this book. But the ones that have made it loom large. In March '84 I moved from Peterborough, where I had a settled life and a cosy job in a record shop, back to London, which may have been my birthplace, but was now a huge, unfamiliar, unfriendly place that had little interest in my desire to join a band and become a big rock star. I was jobless, hapless, and fronting it out to family and friends, because I wanted them to think that I'd always been Billy Big Bobs from London, rather than little Garry, from crappy Peterborough. The only things that made any real sense in this chaos and isolation were my records, and, for one of the few times in my life, I found myself settling on a few new albums and playing them endlessly, rather than my usual flitting about. They comforted me, and gave me some kind of sense that I was ready for the future. There are few things in this world that I have a deeper relationship with than *The Smiths*, *Born In The U.S.A.*, *Purple Rain* and the debut album by Lloyd Cole And The Commotions.

Rattlesnakes is the one it's hardest to be music-journo about, because it's the record that I listened to with the first two women I fell in love with, the one who left me to Prince's tender mercies, and the one who mended my shattered self and who is mother to my only son. These two women had nothing whatsoever in common, except for how much they loved *Rattlesnakes*. There are albums that I think have better music, or that I admire more. But no other record has soundtracked such a crucial and vivid time in my life.

And that relationship with *Rattlesnakes* – which, incidentally, is a twangy, melodic country-pop record refracted, in a completely different way than Violent Femmes, through a love of Lou Reed, and which still stands as the smartest, funniest and loveliest set of songs about being male, well-read, collegiate, and self-conscious about one's cultural references, yet completely obsessed with girls, and sex, and the dramatisation of every last glance at a gamine object of desire with 'cheekbones like geometry and eyes like sin' who's been 'sexually enlightened by *Cosmopolitan*'. This stand-out lyric from 'Perfect Skin' was made all the stranger by meeting someone years later who went out with the chubby-cheeked Elvis that was Mr Cole at the time, and who insists that all the songs are about her. No disrespect to her – lovely woman, honestly – but no one writes a line as great as 'Must you tell me all your secrets/When it's hard enough to love you knowing nothing?', from 'Four Flights Up', about any one person, no matter how extraordinary.

Anyway, you'll hopefully understand why *Rattlesnakes* still renders me unable to write rationally about, say, the outstanding bass chops of former Bluebell and future journalist Lawrence Donegan. 'Are You Ready To Be Heartbroken?' still brings me straight back to a moment when I realised I wasn't, and then another moment when I realised that no one ever is. It all just makes me cry and that's all that I can write.

HATFUL OF HOLLOW

THE SMITHS

PRODUCED BY ROGER PUSEY; DALE GRIFFIN; JOHN PORTER AND THE SMITHS
ROUGH TRADE/NOVEMBER 1984
UK CHART: 7
US CHART: NOT RELEASED IN USA
KEY TRACKS: 'How Soon Is Now?'; 'This Night Has Opened My Eyes'; 'William It Was Really Nothing'; 'These Things Take Time'; 'Girl Afraid'

Almost another go at a Smiths' debut album, *Hatful Of Hollow* compiled BBC sessions and early singles and B-sides for what is probably the most celebrated Christmas cash-in ever released. The sixteen tracks still sound like a Greatest Hits, which gives you some idea of just how stunning and fully formed the early Smiths were. Many prefer it to *The Smiths* (see p.164), simply because it's more varied in tempo and tone, and less relentlessly rainy.

The two most notable songs, sub-plot wise, centre on Morrissey's taboo-busting take on the pet subject of lost innocence. 'Handsome Devil' caused a minor tabloid furore in August 1983 (a full three months before 'This Charming Man' became their first hit) when the *Sun* suggested, in a typically lurid headline, that it was a 'Child Sex Song'. As Johnny Rogan examines in his definitive Smiths biog, *Morrissey & Marr: The Severed Alliance*, 'Handsome Devil' joined with 'The Hand That Rocks The Cradle' and 'Reel Around The Fountain' from the debut album to form a triptych of lyrics which allude to pre-pubescent sexuality. Although the *Sun* was attempting to demonise the group before anyone had even heard of them, 'Handsome Devil' remains a disquieting blend of nudge-nudge saucy ribaldry and a focus on the young summed up by the lines, 'A boy in the bush is worth two in the hand/I think I can help you get through your exams.' The lyric reads as a less coy, and therefore less creepy, take on the teacher-shags-pupil drama that

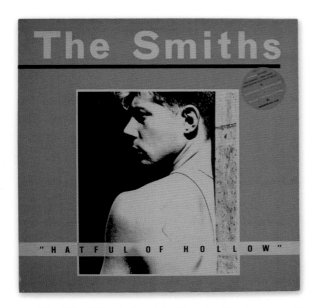

more clearly in the BBC sessions from the John Peel and David Jensen shows, where there's no time to ear-candy the recordings. The version of 'Reel Around The Fountain' here is all the more mesmeric for how close it is to falling apart, and how Marr keeps snapping it all back into focus.

was The Police's 'Don't Stand So Close To Me'. And it could all be from a female teacher's perspective. Except for the bit about mammary glands. Moz lyrics could and can be as confusing as they are accomplished. It comes down to whether you trust his motives or not. The reason I do lies in 'This Night Has Opened My Eyes', a sparkling ballad about a teenage mother abandoning her new-born baby (or possibly an aborted foetus), sung with an empathy for young women that was completely new to rock, and still would be, if any other male rock singers I can think of had displayed this much love and courage since, which they haven't. Morrissey's almost reckless bravery with subject matter wasn't preparing the pop audience for mainstream indie bands. He was the missing link between Johnny Rotten and Eminem. He simply chose to break those same barriers with gentler music. And neither Lydon nor Mathers were ever blessed with a musical partner like Johnny Marr, whose flowing arpeggios and graceful melodies are revealed even

1985

AROUND THE WORLD IN A DAY

PRINCE AND THE REVOLUTION

PRODUCED BY PRINCE AND THE REVOLUTION
PAISLEY PARK/APRIL 1985
UK CHART: 5
US CHART: 1
KEY TRACKS: 'Raspberry Beret'; 'Pop Life'; 'Paisley Park';
'The Ladder'; 'Around The World In A Day'

What you get if you mix kitsch psychedelia, peak-period Stevie Wonder, and muddle-headed politics. 'America' remains impossible to pin down as either piss-take or confused right-wing anthem, with its image of a black woman living in a 'One room jungle monkey cage' dealing merrily with being near death because 'she ain't in the red', that is, living in a communist country. It's probably not as offensive as 'Pop Life', a sumptuous strut that essentially tells the lis-

tener to shut up about not being as rich as the singer, and stop whingeing, and put up with your anonymous shitty life. If Prince wasn't the greatest artist of the '80s, he definitely was the great '80s artist who most closely followed the codes of the hell decade: purloining the language of '60s radicalism to backlash against liberalism, in a cake-and-eat-it fashion; much empty God-bothering in order to self-aggrandise; the use of Russia and the bomb as agents of fear and social control; and lashings of good, old-fashioned elitism and sexism. Having said all that, neither Thatcher nor Reagan spent too much time comparing their private bits to a 'Tamborine' (sic). The guy was both too gifted and too nuts to provoke much worry about his political perspective.

It's worth pointing out that this curious and risky '60s-rock tribute album was Prince's seventh in seven years, and that Warner Brothers gave this baby-faced Nelson six albums to underachieve with before hitting commercial pay dirt with *Purple Rain* (see p.168). After that one big hit, they gave him his own Paisley Park label to release largely dreadful albums by his mates on. All of this made his whole early '90s 'Slave' rebellion and TAFKAP symbol period completely bewildering, when he'd been given so much rope by a major label he'd already begun hanging himself with turgid funk work-outs and limp ballads.

You figure the guy's probably a prize wanker, and then you put on 'Raspberry Beret' and care not one jot.

LOW-LIFE

NEW ORDER

PRODUCED BY NEW ORDER
FACTORY/MAY 1985
UK CHART: 7
US CHART: 94
KEY TRACKS: 'Love Vigilantes'; 'The Perfect Kiss'; 'Sub-culture'; 'Sooner Than You Think'; 'Sunrise'

The third New Order album kicks off with the best single they never made. What possessed them to write an electro-disco country and western song remains lost in the mists of their deadpan Manc humour, but that is what 'Love Vigilantes' is. Barney Sumner plays a soldier who goes off to fight the patriotic fight for liberty. All he can think about is his wife and child. He gets leave and goes home to find that his wife has just received a telegram informing her of her husband's death. And . . . that's it. Everything here – drums, guitar, melodica and especially that Peter hook bass – literally shimmers with joy, giving the very deliberately uncool, almost ridiculous narrative a heartfelt substance, born of nothing more than the euphoria of the right melody rubbing against the right rhythm. The following 'The Perfect Kiss' makes no attempt to hide what a limited vocalist Sumner was and is, but it's that fragile non-voice that keeps New Order on the side of the angels, and away from candied perfection, where pop music so often dies. Ian Curtis could not have been the singer of New Order. He was too formidable a vocal presence to keep New Order's definitive 'indie dance' from falling into archness or inappropriate gloom. Most of us suspect that both music and dancing reaches into parts of us that words simply can't describe. New Order are the patron saints of that idea, and both Sumner's dumb words and non-singing are crucial to the surrender of the senses involved in listening to their best work.

Low-life is also the album that invents The Cure's post-'Lovecats' career (on 'Sunrise') and the best of the Pet Shop Boys (that would be 'Sub-culture'), and where Sumner's weird and wonderful way with a non-sequitur reaches its peak. The most infamous daft couplet remains 'Tonight I should have stayed at home/Playing with my pleasure zone', from 'The Perfect Kiss'. But my personal fave comes from the pre-Balearic disco of 'Sooner Than You Think': 'Your country is a wonderful place/It pales my England into disgrace/To buy a drink that is so much more reasonable/I think I'll go there when it gets seasonal.' Genius, of a pretension-busting, Ibiza-predicting kind, conveniently summed up by the boy

himself, in 'Sub-culture': 'These crazy words of mine/So wrong they could be right.'

STEVE MCQUEEN

PREFAB SPROUT

PRODUCED BY THOMAS DOLBY (EXCEPT 'WHEN LOVE BREAKS DOWN', PRODUCED BY PHIL THORNALLY, REMIXED BY THOMAS DOLBY)
KITCHENWARE/JUNE 1985
UK CHART: 21
US CHART: DID NOT CHART
KEY TRACKS: 'Appetite'; 'When Love Breaks Down'; 'Bonny'; 'Goodbye Lucille #1'; 'Faron Young'

Getting kind of repetitive now, isn't it? Look, people, I didn't make the mid-'80s into an arid musical wasteland . . . that was the death of punk and disco and the rise of the right-wing backlash and the elitist triumphalism of Live Aid, OK? Anyway, it's fun to follow a band like Prefab Sprout for a while, while they were at their best. Paddy McAloon's ongoing argument with America and machismo, and attempt to be the English Steely Dan, reached its peak on this untouchably precious thing, and kept thinking and doubting alive in a rock world that had lost its nerve and verve.

The marriage between McAloon's search for the perfect jazz-tinged pop melody and the sheeny electronics of producer Thomas Dolby proved prodigious; two men united in their contempt for the dirty end of rock. Although the album title fell foul of the legendary '60s/'70s Hollywood icon's family in the USA (it was changed to *Two Wheels Good*, in honour of the motor bikes on its self-deprecating sleeve), *Steve McQueen* was a great title, prefacing the fascinations of the *Loaded* generation by almost a decade, and giving an idealised counterpoint to McAloon's immaculately written studies of masculinity in crisis. No matter how smart or nerdy a (straight) boy is, no matter how puerile he

with six songs that are all slightly less interesting than the last. The five key tracks listed above represent the Paddy Plateau, and will delight anyone who can live with a record that includes, over really smug diminished chords, the line, 'I hear the songs of Georgie Gershwin' and has the cheek to remind us that 'sweet talk, like candy, rots teeth' . . . in the same song! That song, 'Hallelujah', is followed by 'Moving The River', which features the first use of the word 'break-dance' in a non-electro/hip hop context. Of such notable guff are nerdy pop obsessions made.

RUM SODOMY & THE LASH

THE POGUES
PRODUCED BY ELVIS COSTELLO
STIFF/AUGUST 1985
UK CHART: 13
US CHART: UNRELEASED IN USA
KEY TRACKS: 'A Pair Of Brown Eyes'; 'The Old Main Drag';
'The Sick Bed Of Cuchulainn'; 'And The Band Played Waltzing Matilda'; 'Sally MacLennane'

The characters, places and curses that populate the second album by the former Pogue Mahone deserve a book of their own. The bilious, bloody words of Shane MacGowan and the folk-punk music of his six-piece band raise armies of corpses to their feet and shake a defiant drunken fist at the devil. There were many directions for punk rock to take. But locating a key part of punk's afterlife in some hellish mix of Irish myth, abandoned folk song and the kind of drunken raising of ghosts contained with Bob Dylan and The Band's 1967 *Basement Tapes* was as unlikely as Geldof inviting Shane MacGowan to follow Queen at Live Aid. Now that Shane's face looks like a busted concertina, you can only wonder at how many of this record's most terrifying images were inspired by a glimpse of his own, increasingly forlorn, future.

knows machismo can be, he wants to be as sexy, as daredevil, and as impenetrably cool as Steve McQueen.

If you've never listened to Da Sprout and are thinking of it, be warned: this is proudly inauthentic music, unfashionable in a an era which believes that Radiohead have made the most emotional music because their singer always sounds like he's being very emotional. Surrounded by falsehoods, we grasp at half-truths. If you're allergic to irony, or think it begins and ends with The Darkness, you'll hate McAloon, because he's entirely about the juggling of ironies, and the honest acknowledgement that matters of the heart are complex, and won't be solved by growing a beard and wailing 'I'll fix yewww' like a gormless twat.

However, Paddy does, ironically, sport an immaculate beard on the cover of *Steve McQueen*, which does suffer somewhat from kicking off with five of the loveliest and saddest and slipperiest pop songs ever, and then continuing

RUM SODOMY AND THE LASH/THE POGUES

But The Pogues in 1985 were, live and on record, a fucking whirlwind of need and action, and London's only genuinely great group left. When MacGowan opened this album by modernising the Irish myth of the indestructible warrior Cuchulainn, by making him a dying drunkard who had 'Decked some fucking black shirt who was cursing all the Yids' and would 'Sing a song of liberty for blacks and paks and jocks', he brought centuries of Irish rebellion and years of London history slamming into the '80s here and now of rent boys, football hooligans, war veterans and the beggars which just a few years of Thatcherism had thrown onto the London streets.

Listening to Prince and Morrissey has been leading me to think a little about the nature of genius. Punk was a direct refutation of the idea that anyone – genius or not – was naturally any better than anyone else, and that's been something I've taken with me throughout my life. But 'better' is a loaded word. I think a genius is different from the rest of us, and seeing a recent documentary based around The Pogues' Christmas hit 'Fairytale Of New York' hit that feeling home. His work aside, Shane MacGowan is just this arse who used to bum drinks off me (and everyone) in Camden pubs at the turn of the '90s. I found him embarrassing, having worshipped his songs in the mid-'80s. But I soon learned that everyone on the Camden scene indulged him, despite the fact that he'd earned the sort of money that we'd never see. I'd ask why. 'Because he's a genius,' they'd reply. But I accept the point that someone who wrote this well, without any major scene of similar bands to provide context, was a genius, and didn't think the way most people do, and had earned some kind of right to be a prat, within reason.

Something very similar is happening around Peter Doherty at the moment, that endless indulging of his genius. His songs cover similar subjects . . . the viewpoint of the vulnerable outcast, an attempt to redraw society's flowers in the dustbin as heroes. But Doherty is nowhere near as talented as MacGowan. For a couple of years there, even Morrissey and Springsteen and Waits operated at a lower level, lyrically, than this Tipperary punk rock jester, and his fascinations with war, and self-destruction, and poverty, and the poetry of all that tough, surreal Irish literature that you know you ought to get round to reading, but never do. His words on *Rum Sodomy . . .* and his performances of folk standards such as 'And The Band Played Waltzing Matilda' and 'Dirty Old Town', reintroduced the pleasures of grimy reality to a generation in danger of zoning out completely. He conjured gods and devils, made London seem real, made us all want to get in touch with our inner Irishmen. And, just to cap it all, the band's female bassist, Cait O'Riordan, sang the traditional 'I'm A Man You Don't Meet Everyday' so beautifully that the producer up and married her. A fitting romantic PS to one of the greatest albums ever made.

DON'T STAND ME DOWN

DEXYS MIDNIGHT RUNNERS
PRODUCED BY KEVIN ROWLAND, HELEN O'HARA, ALAN WINSTANLEY AND BILLY ADAMS
MERCURY/SEPTEMBER 1985
UK CHART: 22
US CHART: UNRELEASED IN USA
KEY TRACKS: 'Tell Me What She's Like'; 'One Of Those Things'; 'I Love You (Listen To This)'; 'The Occasional Flicker'; 'Reminisce (Part One)'

More Irishness, and more singular lyrical and vocal genius, but without that cirrhosis-of-the-liver feel. Whereas The Pogues looked for beauty in ugliness, like buttercups peeking between paving stones, Kevin Rowland used the patron saint of Irish rock spiritualism, Van Morrison, as a jumping-off point for locating beauty of a purer, more obvious kind. In any other pop era, the third Dexys album would've been a huge critical success, and possibly a commercial one. But in 1985, its insistence on acoustic instruments, on arrangements that accentuated the relationship between textures and tones, its anger at England both liberal and conservative, its savage wit, its Pinter-esque spoken word interludes, and its sprawling, singles-pop-rejecting sense of scope became the end of Dexys and delivered a killing blow to the confidence of the man who'd made a global hit out of 'Come On Eileen' just three years earlier.

So . . . 'This Is What She's Like'. Got to start here, really, it being one of the most extraordinary pieces of music ever made in the name of love and politics. It begins with the band's guitarist, the heroic Billy Adams, turning up at a band rehearsal and asking Kev if he'd been talking about him. His paranoia reassured – and I have to stop here to say that the comedy throughout is all in the timing, as Kev and Billy fall gracefully into each other's pauses and idle thoughts, becoming a Wolverhampton Pete 'n' Dud in the process – he declares that he knows what they've been talking about, and demands an answer to the oldest and most vital question in this or any other book: What's she like?

So the music begins, softly and warily, an Irish lament, as Kev proceeds to try and tell Billy what she's like. And what Rowland tells him, over twelve minutes and twenty-three seconds of gradually evolving pop-soul-surf-jazz-folk loveliness, is everything that he hates, because everything that he hates is everything that 'she' isn't. And what better way to capture the impossible essence of all-enveloping love than defining it as everything you're against?

So what she's not like is the English upper classes ('thick and ignorant'), the Campaign For Nuclear Disarmament ('the scum from Notting Hill and Moseley', the latter being a bohemian area of Birmingham) and the entire nouveau riche ('peasants' and 'scumbags'). Having dismissed pretty much everyone except her, Kev needs some pretty heavyweight music to back up these claims. And, man, does he deliver. At exactly six minutes and fifty seconds in, a gently reverent lullaby of harmonies suddenly becomes . . . well, I guess the best Beach Boys impression ever, for a start. But so

emphatic, so startling, so utterly blissful and ecstatic that the song seems to turn in on itself. It's like breaking waves under a sun that's too bright and too strong. Tim Dancy's deep crunching drums slowly get the song back to its feet and, yeah, we're back in the stomping call-to-arms of early Dexys. We break again. This time it's violins that stagger back and . . . oh, bloody, bloody hell, that brass! Suffice to say, Billy gets what she's like. Kevin's reduced to speaking in tongues. He makes a joke about speaking Italian and concludes, softly, 'That's my story. The strongest I've ever seen.'

Now . . . that's one song. It's the best one, but not by much. A work of bloody-minded ambition by a man completely out of time and a band that follow him on the kind of multi-layered thematic and musical adventure that no one outside Mike Skinner remembers that albums ought to be. Apart from Morrison and Brian Wilson, Rowland raids Lou Reed, Warren Zevon, fiddle folk and a slew of deep soul weepies to put his point. So what is his point? Actually, simpler than you might imagine. In 1985, as the sublime 'Werewolves Of London' comic potshot at everything that is 'One Of Those Things' puts it as strongly as it can, everything sounded the fucking same. In 2006, as I write, everything sounds the fucking same. This isn't just about pop and how it could or should be better. It's about the middle-class, middlebrow cultural discourse, and how its complacency ensures that those who suffer, in Ireland, anywhere, keep right on suffering while our great and good pursue money, social acceptance and an invite to Elton's wedding. Like Shane MacGowan, Rowland was a punk through and through. And *Don't Stand Me Down* is one of the key albums that prove that punk is nothing to do with thrashing guitars.

One of the problems that this version of Dexys encountered was complete bewilderment at their look. Based on American Ivy League threads, it prefaced the British working-class adoption of Burberry by ten years, but somehow attracted more derision at the time than the dungarees-and-cow-dung look of the Too-Rye-Ay era.

DON'T STAND ME DOWN/DEXY'S MIDNIGHT RUNNERS

Don't Stand Me Down has been re-released twice on CD. The Creation label put a version out in 1996 that added two extra tracks (including the wonderful 'Reminisce (Part One)' where Kev embarks on a 'search for the spirit of Brendan Behan in the bars of Dublin', and absolutely rips the piss out of the Irish drunkard sentimentality that The Pogues thrive on) and had some fairly painful confessional sleevenotes from a Rowland still on the long road back from drug rehab. He explains that most of the songs are inspired by his pride in his Irish roots and his anger at the political situation in his native land, but that his lack of confidence at the time prevented him of making this as plain as it should have been. Hence 'Knowledge Of Beauty' is changed to its intended, pre-jitters title, 'My National Pride'. It's this version that provides the production credits and the basis of this review.

Then another version arrived in 2002. Released on EMI and sub-titled 'The Director's Cut', it featured a new opening track called 'Kevin Rowland's 13th Time' which laid into the middle classes again, inexcusably dumped 'Reminisce (Part One)' again, and had some stuff from SuperKev about there being less ear candy on the mix. All kind of confusing but all kind of fair enough, because *Don't Stand Me Down* is at least three times more individual than almost any other pop album made in England.

HOUNDS OF LOVE

KATE BUSH
PRODUCED BY KATE BUSH
EMI/SEPTEMBER 1985
UK CHART: 1
US CHART: 30
KEY TRACKS: 'Hounds Of Love'; 'Running Up That Hill (A Deal With God)'; 'The Big Sky'; 'Cloudbusting'; 'Under Ice'

So Irishness forms a key part of some of the best albums of 1985, and the Kate Bush album everyone liked makes that fact rather than opinion. *Hounds Of Love* featured 'Irish arrangements' from her brother Paddy, as well as contributions from master Irish folk musicians including Donal Lunny and Liam O'Flynn. Mind you, it also featured Youth out of Killing Joke, classical guitarist John Williams, king of the jazz-folk double bass Danny Thompson, and a sample of a helicopter from Pink Floyd's *The Wall*. And songs inspired by controversial psychoanalyst and rainmaker Wilhelm Reich ('Cloudbusting') and a B-movie called *Night Of The Demon* ('Hounds Of Love'). And a seven-song suite called 'The Ninth Wave', after a poem called 'The Coming Of Arthur' by Tennyson, which appeared to be the story of a woman drowning under ice, becoming an angel, rescuing drowning sailors and coming back to life. And the best song – the title track, again – about surrendering to love and sex that isn't sung by someone black and American. This girl's ambition knew no bounds (actually, after 2005's *Aerial*, that should read knows no bounds).

What *Hounds Of Love* achieved was the final refutation of the 'punk equals year zero' factor that had reduced pop-rock to cliché once the initial inspiration of punk wore out around 1982. Punk was a scorched-Earth policy, fashion-wise, with entire modes of music, dress, hair, speech and self-expression outlawed almost overnight. As one of the millions who was carried along by this, I can only testify to what a shock *Hounds Of Love* was: a record that obviously bore far more resemblance, in texture, influence and construction, to the Pink Floyd and Genesis records I despised . . . yet I was blown away by its scope, and poetry, and refusal to play along with anything I considered cool. When it became a huge mainstream hit and got critical cred, it was the beginning of a re-opening in adult-pop's imagination that has continued to echo in everything from Björk to Bright Eyes, and from Aphex Twin to Arcade Fire. In its biggest hit single 'Running Up That Hill', it contained an opening song that tied disco into white-bread pop with elegant discretion, and was also able to juggle love, death and God in direct, moving ways that Woody Allen can only dream about. Indeed, listening to *Hounds Of Love* at high volume is much like entering someone else's dream, and being scared, seduced and soothed by the storms it conjures. You'll believe a woman can control the weather.

RAIN DOGS

TOM WAITS
PRODUCED BY TOM WAITS
ISLAND/OCTOBER 1985
UK CHART: 29
US CHART: DID NOT CHART
KEY TRACKS: 'Rain Dogs'; 'Cemetery Polka'; 'Clap Hands';
'Singapore'; 'Downtown Train'

Swordfishtrombones (see p.159) part two, but longer, more varied and less horrified, and way more enamoured of itself. When I hear it I think of press gangs, and a Bob Dylan/Band song called 'Yea! Heavy And A Bottle Of Bread', and bones, and a diseased lounge bar where circus freaks hang out with drunken sailors and Waits does the music because he's the only piano player who'll work in this hell-hole, and how guitarist Marc Ribot has the only electric guitar style that could possibly fit this beautiful-ugly spawl, and how bits of it remind me of *Exile On Main St.* on welfare and barley wine and brewers droop instead of riches and smack and orgies, or maybe The Pogues if Shane MacGowan hadn't been unlucky enough to mean it. It's a menagerie, but a painless one, in which Waits can don disguises and show off his mastery of every roots music known to man. A great slumming album that doesn't leave a bad smell on your clothes.

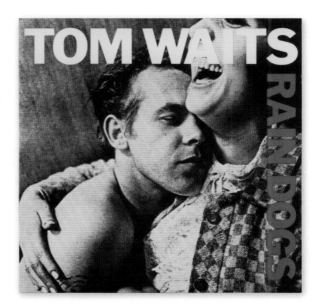

1986

A DATE WITH ELVIS

THE CRAMPS
PRODUCED BY THE CRAMPS
BIG BEAT/FEBRUARY 1986
UK CHART: 34
US CHART: UNRELEASED IN USA
KEY TRACKS: 'What's Inside A Girl?'; 'Can Your Pussy Do
The Dog?'; 'People Ain't No Good'; 'Aloha From Hell'; 'The Hot
Pearl Snatch'

As we begin to stagger slowly from the suspiciously sensible best albums of the horrid mid-'80s, it's time to reacquaint ourselves with rock 'n' roll, and being an idiot. Mind you, The Cramps' third studio album proper actually had, unlike the conceptual insanity of the works collected on *Off The Bone* (see p.154), some impressive guitar licks from Candy Fur and Poison Ivy, occasional bass, tunes that made some kind of linear sense, and the lyrics printed inside a most attractive sleeve, almost like a serious rock group. Sell-outs.

Never fear, however, when 'What's Inside A Girl?' begins with Mr Lux Interior delivering the immortal couplet, 'Whoa, there's some things Baby that I just can't swallow/Mama just told me that girls are hollow.' Prefab Sprout didn't pick up much airplay in the Interior household . . .

Despite the somewhat misleading title, *A Date With Elvis* has little to with The King, and everything to do with Da Laydeez, with a capital Sleeaz. Way before *The Vagina Monologues*, Interior and his main squeeze the luscious Ms Poison Ivy Rorschach created their own tender tribute to girl parts. You probably don't need me to explain the cunning subtext behind songs such as '(Hot Pool Of) Womanneed', 'The Hot Pearl Snatch' and 'Can Your Pussy Do The Dog?' But you do need to know that The Cramps, at this point, played garage-rock with more fuzzy abandon than an 800-pound goh-rilla, and spent the eleven songs here finding five thousand ways to say vagina, which always struck me as more useful than finding fifty ways to leave your lover.

The credits above tell a tale, though. Unreleased in USA. A persistent feature of the American music market is that the artists that sound most utterly American are the artists that can't get arrested in America. In the case of The Cramps, Lux probably still goes out every Saturday night and moons at police cars in an attempt to just get noticed and reviled, as he ought to be. Indeed, all the US bands who owe most to The Cramps – The Gun Club, Jon Spencer's Blues Explosion, The White Stripes, Rocket From The Crypt spring to mind – had to come to Blighty or Europe or Japan or just about anywhere that isn't America to get their varying degrees of success. Lack of irony? Disinterest in indigenous roots betraying national self-loathing? Not enough dates with Elvis? Maybe it's just as a chorus of munchkins insist on the tough-to-dispute 'People Ain't No Good' . . . 'People ain't no good/They never do what I think they should/People ain't no good.'

CANDY APPLE GREY

HÜSKER DÜ
PRODUCED BY BOB MOULD AND GRANT HART
WARNER BROS/MARCH 1986
UK CHART: DID NOT CHART
US CHART: DID NOT CHART
KEY TRACKS: 'Sorry Somehow'; 'I Don't Know For Sure';
'Dead Set On Destruction'; 'Crystal'; 'Don't Want To Know If
You Are Lonely'

Having given punk up for dead, this record came into my life and revived the idea of buying and adoring rock 'n' roll long-players. A punk rock power-trio from St Paul, Minnesota, Bob Mould (guitar, vocals, songs), Grant Hart (drums, vocals, songs) and Greg Norton (bass), began in the late '70s as an orthodox hardcore band before gradually slowing down and becoming genuine songwriters. The Beatles, The Byrds and British folkie Richard Thompson were among the mellowing influences on their Sex Pistols-tributing wall-of-

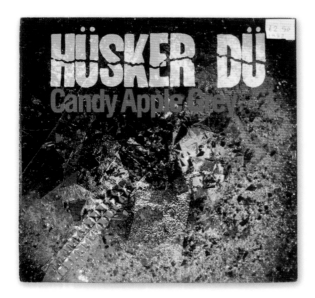

tal likes of 'Sorry Somehow', 'I Don't Know For Sure' and 'Dead Set On Destruction' are fizzing pop kiss-offs. The Dü found a way to blend The Beatles (especially 'I'm Looking Through You' from Rubber Soul), the Pistols and R.E.M., and forged an accessible US punk template for everyone from the Pixies and Nirvana to Green Day and The Offspring. The massive money-spinner that is twenty-first-century corporate punk, with its identikit laddish anthems and boy band vocals, all stems from here. What none of these bands could even conceive of is an album opener like 'Crystal', a blast of ranting rage that captures all the no-compromise outsider nihilism of the true punk rocker. It was Mould's everyman image and grainy lived-in voice that inspired a nation of nascent grungers to wear lumberjack shirts, celebrate the down-to-earth working man, and not worry that the lead singer was neither weird nor pretty.

Cool story about their name, too. It's Norwegian for 'do you remember?', and comes from a board game popular in the '60s. They began as a covers band, and were jamming a version of 'Psycho Killer' by Talking Heads (see p.24), and began hollering any foreign phrase they could think of to stand in for the bit in French that none of them knew. Of such random messages from punks past are legends made.

sound. *Candy Apple Grey* was their first album for a major label – they made just one more before splitting acrimoniously, with the most visible member Mould going on to form Sugar (see p.250).

Although three of the band's previous albums on Black Flag's SST label, *Zen Arcade*, *Flip Your Wig* and *New Day Rising*, gain more acclaim in critical circles, there's a tension in *Candy Apple Grey* that makes it the most colourful and accessible Hüsker Dü album. Whether down to the power struggle between Mould (gay, depressive, teetotal by this time) and Hart (heading into junkiedom), or the pioneering path they were clearing for the likes of Sonic Youth, The Replacements and Nirvana, the demands of making music on a corporate label which was still considered unacceptable to mainstream America and which had become unfashionable in Europe pulls at the harsh tones and despairing themes here. While 'Too Far Down', 'Hardly Getting Over It' and 'No Promise Have I Made' are bleak dirges, the immor-

PARADE

PRINCE AND THE REVOLUTION
PRODUCED BY PRINCE AND THE REVOLUTION
PAISLEY PARK/APRIL 1986
UK CHART: 4
US CHART: 3
KEY TRACKS: 'Girls & Boys'; 'Mountains'; 'Kiss'; 'Anotherloverholenyohead'; 'Do U Lie?'

By now, the little funker that could was making a full-tilt late stab at being the fifth Beatle, opening his albums with *Sgt Pepper*-style overtures such as 'Christopher Tracy's Parade',

A DATE WITH ELVIS/THE CRAMPS

PARADE/PRINCE AND THE REVOLUTION

chock-full of clashing off-kilter orchestras and crazy psyche-delic motifs. Excuse was given by *Under The Cherry Moon*, an inexcusably bad film (and by bad, I don't mean late-night laughable kitsch, I mean humungously dull and almost pathologically shallow) to which *Parade* was the soundtrack. Even as *Parade* was marking Prince's virtuoso pop high-point, the film was beginning the end of Prince's reign, by rather brazenly letting everyone know that the guy, without the cloak of music, was just a bit . . . well, boring.

Parade, though, is a blast. Considering the fact that the peripatetic Purple One was spreading his seed thin, produc-ing albums at his Paisley Park studio for every passing Tom, Dick and Sheena who took his fancy, *Parade* is both flamboy-antly eclectic and entirely flab-free, a forty-five-minute show-case of every kind of music that has ever been connected to God and the boudoir. There's almost a contempt for the rest of Planet Pop '86 within its grooves, a lofty disdain for com-petitors who couldn't hope to move from the sneering funk of 'Girls & Boys', through the playful faux-chanson of 'Do U Lie?' to the inspirational gospel-rock of 'Mountains'. No mat-ter how great the music is, though, what hits hardest is Prince's voice, touching Elvis Presley's level of teasing sexual humour, safe in the knowledge that it's the most lubricating instrument on God's funky green Earth. Maybe it wasn't all about him, though: this was the last album Prince made with The Revolution, the extravagantly talented band formed around the talents of Wendy Melvoin and Lisa Coleman. And, the fast approaching *Sign 'O' The Times* (see p.196) aside, the lack of great collaborators marked a rapid decline.

THE QUEEN IS DEAD

THE SMITHS
PRODUCED BY MORRISSEY AND JOHNNY MARR
ROUGH TRADE/JUNE 1986
UK CHART: 2
US CHART: 70

KEY TRACKS: 'There Is A Light That Never Goes Out'; 'The Queen Is Dead'; 'I Know It's Over'; 'Bigmouth Strikes Again'; 'Some Girls Are Bigger Than Others'

Before we move away entirely from the subject of pop Irishness, it's worth recalling that Morrissey, like John Lydon, Elvis Costello, Shane MacGowan, Kevin Rowland and Kate Bush, was from Irish blood. Awkward cusses, the lot of 'em, but none more so than Rotten and Moz, who trade blows against the empire across the decade that sepa-rates 'God Save The Queen' and 'The Queen Is Dead'. The latter, which opens The Smiths' finest long-player, dreams of 'Her Lowness with her head in a sling', and enters the body of one Michael Fagan, who caused a mini-constitutional cri-sis back in 1982 by breaking into the Queen's bedroom for a chat. Just as Lydon cackled manically at Blighty's 'mad parade', Moz finds madness and bleak humour in Liz's boudoir, searching not for the spirit of Brendan Behan (as

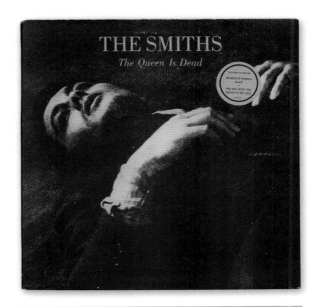

'Cemetry Gates' warmly informs us, Oscar Wilde was the Irishman that Moz related to), but for us, and a constituency that hated Britain's establishment as much he did, because 'it's so lonely on a limb'. He found us, of course. But all we insisted on doing about it was listening to his records and cheering a lot.

Johnny Marr makes 'The Queen Is Dead' into a jabbing flyweight version of the Rolling Stones, before filling the rest of this album with folky melody, music hall oompah and rockabilly flash. From the pettiness of 'Frankly, Mr Shankly' – a barbed shot at Rough Trade label boss Geoff Travis disguised as a précis of Keith Waterhouse's *Billy Liar* – to the deathly romance of the still-astonishing 'There Is A Light That Never Goes Out', The Smiths fill the world with beauty laced with bile, and a pox on new England. Possibly the best recorded argument against the truism that the words don't matter as long as the music's good, Morrissey's confidence in his lyrics echoes that of Prince's in his music, and listening to both in the mid-'80s felt like being a bystander at an unlikely pub argument – celibacy refuting sex, left refuting right, white folk-pop refuting black funk-pop, and, yeah, a Queen refuting a Prince. 'I'm the eighteenth pale descendent of some old queen or other,' Morrissey laughed on the title track, and literally made a mockery of our obsession with his proclivities. A subtext of this extraordinary record is an endless NO to the idea that any of us have betters, and that replacing the old betters of monarchy, aristocracy and boss with the new betters of anyone who gets on TV is surely the best argument against evolution one could muster. He was pissing in the wind, of course, but some of us still refuse to waste a single brain cell on fame unless it comes with talent and substance, and *The Queen Is Dead* is one of the very best reasons why.

While Prince inevitably alluded to death through his muddled Christianity, Morrissey made it so real – 'Oh mother/I can feel/The soil falling over my head,' he cried hard on 'I Know It's Over', welcoming that murderous double-decker bus with open arms on 'There Is a Light . . . ' –

that it breathed life and afterlife into rock, a genre which preferred to see death only as another level of decadence. The Smiths defied fashion and the coming age by defying both deliberate dumbing down and apathetic misery, and refusing to accept the way things are. Plenty of punks have done the same, but not with songs that are all persuasion and prettiness, passion and twinkling lights. 'It takes guts to be gentle and kind,' the bigmouth sang again on 'I Know It's Over', and the uncool truth made hard cases get all swoony.

LICENSED TO ILL

BEASTIE BOYS
PRODUCED BY RICK RUBIN AND THE BEASTIE BOYS
DEF JAM/NOVEMBER 1986
UK CHART: 7
US CHART: 1
KEY TRACKS: 'Rhymin & Stealin'; 'Paul Revere'; 'Fight For Your Right To Party'; 'Slow And Low'; 'No Sleep Till Brooklyn'

After several years of American movies and TV shows based around high school and the bullying stupidity of 'the jock', the joke behind the first Beastie Boys album now seems an obvious one. It's a forty-five-minute mickey-take of spoilt white brat puerility. Privileged New York Jewish college boy punks Adam 'MCA' Yauch, Mike 'Mike D' Diamond, Adam 'Adrock' Horowitz and their metal-fan producer Rick Rubin took this still new rap music, which was beginning to add violence and sexism to its early lead element of materialist bragging, and flavoured it with the immaturity of the middle-class jock and his favourite music of choice, heavy metal. And surely if you make blatant the fact that you are skinny young wimps who couldn't possibly cause the girls 'n' guns mayhem within the lyrics, and if you make the beats the deepest, leanest and meanest around, then the irony is made into great pop by the obvious groove expertise. Everyone will get it, right?

Well many millions did get it, but they maybe didn't get it. *Licensed To Ill* managed to unite everyone in self-righteous indignation, from British tabloids to left-wing feminist groups, from black rappers to white liberal critics. *Licensed To Ill* is the beginning of the second-half of this book, as the political correctness that dominated pop in the post-hippy and punk eras was shot down by the youth dollar and an increasing reliance on glibness disguised as irony. This record begat frat-boy punk, opened a market for gangsta, gave bands like the (early) Red Hot Chilli Peppers a chance to be meathead macho and boho cool at the same time. It's odd how little the Beasties are mentioned as influences on Eminem, but then, the speed with which hip hop became self-conscious about its blackness accounts for that. Eminem's career is *Licensed To Ill* with an injection of trailer-park anger.

What made a rap version of National Lampoon's *Animal House* strong enough to usher in the modern world? Two things. One is Rick Rubin, soon to be the producer most able to reinvent ailing careers from The Cult to the Chill Peppers to Johnny Cash. Rubin understood that the worst thing about '80s music was the everything-but-the-kitchen-sink thud and blunder, a dominant production style based in attempting to make obviously synthetic instruments sound 'real' and acoustic instruments sound electronic in order to create a radio-friendly sonic hegemony. Rubin, inspired by early hip hop producers Arthur Baker, Larry Smith and Schooly D, dispensed with such self-defeating fussiness and boiled everything right down to basics: a beat that clunked, a speaker-blowing subsonic bass that revolutionised dance production, guitar riffs and samples that were rude and intrusive, and voices which sounded all over the place, as if the rappers had just walked in pissed and started shouting obscenities.

Which brings us neatly to Thing Two, which is the rap voice of Adam Horowitz. Adrock brought a cartoon whine to hip hop which made plain all of pop's adolescent nerdishness and irritant factor, bringing a much-missed generation gap back into rock 'n' roll. Everyone over thirty hated that brattish bray, a coded insult to all the sensible music that had ruled the long-playing roost since 1982. The fact that there was nothing outrageous at all about the Beasties' liberal-baiting and thug parodies passed both their fans and their foes by entirely, and even made them into a very odd kind of public menace when they allegedly inspired a craze for stealing the metallic logos from cars and wearing them as badges.

Being very smart boys, they understood quickly that being too closely associated to both adolescence and novelty was already making sure that Run-D.M.C. (who lend their composition expertise to 'Slow And Low' and 'Paul Revere' here) had passed their zeitgeist peak. The Beasties bailed from the seminal Def Jam label, ditched Rubin, invented the sample-heavy toy box approach to making music on 1989's *Paul's Boutique*, and didn't appear to see any irony whatsoever when, many years later, they castigated The Prodigy for performing 'Smack My Bitch Up' at a festival. No defence of

MUSIC MADNESS/MANTRONIX

The Prod intended, but *Licensed To Ill* made 'Smack My Bitch Up' inevitable by convincing us that misogyny in pop was big and clever. There's more Beasties to come, because they're a musically brilliant group. But they are also hypocritical, holier-than-thou tosspots. It happens.

MUSIC MADNESS

MANTRONIX
PRODUCED BY KURTIS MANTRONIK
10 (SLEEPING BAG IN USA)/DECEMBER 1986
UK CHART: 66
US CHART: DID NOT CHART
KEY TRACKS: 'Who Is It?'; 'Scream'; 'Listen To The Bass Of Get Stupid Fresh Part One'; 'We Control The Dice'; 'Megamix'

Bass Bass Bass. The bass from *Music Madness*, the second Mantronix album, hurts my speakers, churns my guts and soothes my head. It's a major element of an album that amped up the musicality of hip hop, forged an early connection with the coming sound of house music, provided a missing link between the gauche naivete of the first rap records and all the rugged wordplays to come. Like Run-D.M.C., Def Jam, Rick Rubin and the Beasties, it came from New York, but represented an entirely different sector . . . the bridge-and-tunnel kids, white, black and Latin, who still worshipped at the altar of disco and the working-class upward mobility it had symbolised.

Kurtis Khaleel looked like a Latin matinee idol, but was a Jamaican-born production whiz who, as Kurtis Mantronik, revived Kraftwerk's idea of the musical *Man Machine* (see p.41) and gave it a shot of NY barrio funk. His early partner was Toure Embden, who, as MC Tee, provided motormouth rhymes concerned exclusively with what were the already 'old school' concerns of the laydees, the excellence of his DJ, and how much metaphorical mileage he could get out of the whole man-machine-rocks-the-party idea. His words were mostly incomprehensible. They were simply there to give some form of comprehensible focus to Kurtis's intimidating layering of electronic beats, distorted samples, back-flipping handclaps, stuck-record effects and general ground-breaking genius with computer and recording studio.

An album that encompasses every dance style of the '70s and '80s, from deep Jamaican dub to Latin-tinged disco, from winsome synth-pop to fledgling Detroit techno; from Bronx B-boy electro to Washington go-go, *Music Madness* is like some kind of NASA-approved blueprint for everything that was going to happen in black and dance music over the following six years. Largely instrumental but reaching its best moments every time Tee finds another cheery hookline, not only has it not aged . . . it still sounds as if all those glitchy post-techno and drum 'n' bass art records are struggling to catch up with it. Possibly because, unlike ninety-five per cent of dance and hip hop productions, it's never content to coast; even the greatest bassline or hook is altered after two bars or so, as if Kurtis – who garnered a rep as one of the earliest moody DJs – has no patience with anything that doesn't tell him something new every ten seconds.

Those of a rockist persuasion may be tempted in by the 'Megamix' and the snappily titled 'Listen To The Bass Of Get Stupid Fresh Part One', which use, as a starting point, a sample of 'Stone Fox Chase' by Area Code 615 – better known as the harmonica-driven theme from *The Old Grey Whistle Test*. You too will see visions of Whispering Bob Harris doing the electric boogaloo, and you will smile.

1987

I AGAINST I

BAD BRAINS
PRODUCED BY RON ST. GERMAIN
SST/FEBRUARY 1987
UK CHART: DID NOT CHART
US CHART: DID NOT CHART
KEY TRACKS: 'I Against I'; 'She's Calling You'; 'Sacred Love';
'House Of Suffering'; 'Return To Heaven'

The missing link between punk and hard rock that came to define nu-metal. This massively important, and criminally overlooked rastafarian punk band formed by Londoner Paul 'HR' Hudson (vocals), his brother Earl (drums), Gary Wayne Miller aka Dr Know (guitar, keyboards) and Darryl Jennifer (bass) in Washington DC remain the key influence on the agit-metal heroes Rage Against The Machine and System Of A Down, and one of the most extravagant examples of musicianly punk. They also forged a connection between the LA-based SST, the most successful US punk indie label, and Washington DC, where Ian Mackaye of Minor Threat and Fugazi was hatching dreams of a truly self-sufficient, no-compromise cottage industry label he would call Dischord, the global role model for punk rock integrity and achievable ideals. It was Bad Brains early move away from thrash toward a reggae and funk-inflected rock that inspired Fugazi's groovy noise, and invented what was later to be labelled emo-core – 'emo' short for 'emotion'. And, of course, there's the conversation a black band was bound to host between Hendrix, Bob Marley and the slam-dance transgression of LA hardcore punk. This is their third album and their best.

Title and keynote track 'I Against I' uses the Rastafarian 'I and I' and twists it to dramatise the fracture of self that's involved in our competition with others under capitalism. A throwback to the Gang Of Four and a development from their analysis of society to a new form of protest, the biggest message of punk in the post-hardcore age was the idea of humanity as one lifeforce, connected spiritually and mystically, which was being rent asunder by capitalism, shattering the self into competing fragments. Punk as a missing link between *Das Kapital* and *The Matrix?* Well, yeah, along with the best sci-fi, graphic novels, and the viral spread of anti-globalisation politics. *I Against I* is a key stepping-stone to a counter-cultural spirit we now take for granted, and Bad Brains, by choosing a music scene which was and will always be infiltrated and abused by the fascist right, were a vital '80s force for good in an America at war with itself.

What's more, *I Against I* features some of the most rhythmically mesmerising, sexy and mood-altering guitar music ever committed to good old-fashioned vinyl. This is persuasion rather than pure bludgeon, and an essential precursor to the black rock adventures of Body Count (see p.249) and The Dirtbombs (see p.346).

SIGN 'O' THE TIMES

PRINCE

PRODUCED BY PRINCE
PAISLEY PARK/MARCH 1987
UK CHART: 4
US CHART: 6
KEY TRACKS: 'If I Was Your Girlfriend'; 'Sign 'O' The Times';
'I Could Never Take The Place Of Your Man'; 'The Ballad Of
Dorothy Parker'; 'The Cross'

The great solo Prince double-album masterwork has a similar feel of anguished nostalgia to Springsteen's *Born In The U.S.A.* Indeed, if you cross that album with the 1972 murk-funk nervous breakdown that is Sly And The Family Stone's *There's A Riot Goin' On*, then this is what you get. The ominous single, opener and title track isn't actually that good a lyric – rap's Golden Age was coming to blow these kind of newspaper headline platitudes away once and for all – but the music carries the message, being the deepest funk of its time. The same goes double for the utterly out-of-character, Velvet Underground-style two-chord thrash that is 'The Cross'. Substituting the 'Ban the bomb' symbol for the 'o' or 'of' of the album's title shows that Prince was still obsessed with a Cold War that America's black community had no interest in anymore. There were more pressing problems on their doorsteps than remote nuclear nightmares. And yes, the way that 'Housequake' doesn't live up to its explosive chipmunk vocal intro, and the rubbish live pub-funk of 'It's Gonna Be A Beautiful Night' is a prediction of all Prince's anonymous funk jams of the '90s.

But the quibbles don't add up to a hill of beans in this crazy sonic world. 'The Ballad Of Dorothy Parker' is a late Prince entry into Waits/Dylan territory, a song about a waitress, 'Dishwater blonde, tall and fine', and a surreal thing regarding fighting with past lovers in 'a violent room', Joni Mitchell, and bathing with your pants on in a faint echo of 'Norwegian Wood'. It's completely baffling and one of the

man's most exquisite confections, starring a falsetto squeal towards the song's end that should come with a dangerous goosebump rating, and an overall feel that just beats D'Angelo (see p.331) in raising the Sly Stone stakes.

'Starfish And Coffee' joined with the best of *Around the World In A Day* to remind us that, as well as being the consummate post-James Brown soul man, Prince was the only major '80s artist who could tap into the charming, childlike pop psychedelia of The Beatles' most joyous post-*Rubber Soul* benchmarks, all Lewis Carroll and Edward Lear and the suggestion of a cultural joke that only the hippest of the hip could hear. 'Hot Thing' finds a post-electro funk riff big enough to encompass everything from the Stones to John Coltrane, Prince yet again making the most crass paean to fucking into a orgy of aural pleasure. It segued perfectly into 'Forever In My Life', a sacred/secular love song featuring Prince's hardest gospel voice backed by little more than a stiff rock beat. What was that line from 1985's 'Raspberry Beret'? 'Seems like I was busy doing something close to nothing/But different than the day before.' That's what Prince was doing in 1987, and making it sound like the thrillingest pop you'd ever heard. I mean, for 'U Got The Look' the guy got little Scots waif Sheena Easton – Britain's first reality MOR poppet – to sing the lines 'Sho nuf do be cookin' in mah book . . . Let's get to rammin'!!!', and somehow made it stick. Miraculous, frankly.

I firmly believe that all musical artists worth their salt have this shining moment when all the various stars and biorhythms and emotional resonances align, and they balance on the cusp of a peak of musical and thematic know-how before an inevitable slide toward cynicism or complacency, and therefore can do absolutely no wrong. This album was Prince's Top Of The World, Ma moment, and Prince's best was so much better – or, at least, broader – than everyone else's that he declined precipitously due to lack of anyone to measure himself against. The gender confusion sexplay of the towering 'If I Was Your Girlfriend' made old Bowie sound clumsy. Hell, listen again to the FM rock revival-meets-funky voodoo blues jam grin-fest that is 'I Could Never Take The Place Of Your Man', and you realise that it is, in fact, the most emotionally dishonest rejection of a single mother this side of 'Billie Jean'. Yet even getting that can't break the joy of it. There was simply nowhere for the boy to go from here but down.

YO! BUM RUSH THE SHOW

PUBLIC ENEMY
PRODUCED BY BILL STEPHNEY, HANK SHOCKLEE AND CARL RYDER
DEF JAM/APRIL 1987
UK CHART: DID NOT CHART
US CHART: DID NOT CHART
KEY TRACKS: 'You're Gonna Get Yours'; 'Timebomb'; 'Public Enemy No. 1'; 'Miuzi Weighs A Ton'; 'Yo! Bum Rush The Show'

The most stunning thing to happen to me culturally since the Sex Pistols, I can only imagine what Public Enemy felt like to an Afro-American youth in 1987. Coming out of Long Island, New York, and opening up a new chapter in pop and hip hop, Carlton Ridenhour aka Carl Ryder aka Chuck D brought the '60s militant black consciousness of Malcolm X, the Nation Of Islam and the Black Panthers into a nation that had convinced itself that such anger and defiance was ancient history. Taken one way, the first Public Enemy album made every white boy want to be just that little bit blacker. Taken another, it gave confidence to black men and women who knew that racism still bit hard, and wanted to make their non-compliance clear in public. Taken yet another, its evocation of black men above the law, and reflection of the US inner-city gangs that Prince had identified as part of the American problem in the 'Sign 'O' The Times' single, joined with the cartoon liberal-baiting of the Beasties to open the door to gangsta rap. The speed with which hip hop had moved from novelty pop to a culture

strong enough to affect the way the planet walked, talked and argued mirrored rock 'n' roll's journey from crazy mixed-race beat music to the global voice of change symbolised by The Beatles. This record rendered Prince's best album redundant in less than a month.

In simple terms, Chuck and bandmates William 'Flavor Flav' Drayton, Norman 'Terminator X' Rodgers and Richard 'Professor Griff' Griffin took the imperious brags of their labelmate LL Cool J and politicised them. But, even allowing for the presence on this debut of Beasties and LL Cool J producer and Def Jam co-founder Rick Rubin as 'Executive Producer' (there's going to be a whole lot of those from now on, and, after almost twenty years, I still don't have a clue what an executive producer does), the protest angle doesn't accurately sum up the shock of hearing PE for the first time.

Throughout the post-rock-'n'-roll years, black music had been the music of inclusion. The Holy Grail of the black entertainer was always to 'crossover' to white listeners because that's where pop's money lay. And it was accepted that, in order to crossover, black artists should only talk about race issues in non-accusatory terms. Sure, of course Stevie Wonder, Sly Stone, Curtis Mayfield and the other giants of the classic soul/funk era had written songs that pointed a finger at a wider world. But the anti-white power messages of soul were either subtly coded (for the definitive account of how soul's greatest composers pulled this off, check out Craig Werner's superb *A Change Is Gonna Come* published by Canongate), or written and performed to assure young liberal whites that they were on the side of the black angels, and that The Man was defined by his age and financial power rather than his race. Public Enemy destroyed this unified approach to black political pop at a stroke. Chuck D's torrent of words – enough words to make the gabby pop of the early '80s sound tongue-tied – raised a contemptuous finger at the entire notion of integration, not by railing at whites, but by bullishly addressing blacks and blacks only. Whether Chuck or Def Jam understood just how seductive that would be to white youth bereft of musi-

YO! BUM RUSH THE SHOW/PUBLIC ENEMY

cal rebellion in the late '80s – unless you count Guns 'N' Roses, in which case, you sure are in the wrong place, Buddy – it was bound to stir up a hornets' nest of buried racial conflicts. There are despicable things about Public Enemy (their championing of the segregationist Nation Of Islam, the talentless Professor Griff's anti-Semitism, which saw him sacked in 1990), and despicable things about this album (the bitter misogyny of 'Sophisticated Bitch'). But the music was so powerful, and Chuck's moralism and speed of thought so intimidating, that those of us who needed music to mean something, even (especially?) something difficult and divisive, were simply swept along by PE's force.

The key was in the beats. PE's Bomb Squad production team took metallic industrial beats and made them black and funky, mixing old soul samples, screeching white noise, clanging drums and ghostly snatches of traffic, party noise, guitar riffs and gut-punch bass drops into a noise that closed the gap between art-rock and soul-based dance music. The results on the likes of 'Timebomb' and debut single 'You're Gonna Get Yours' revived the visceral parent-baiting thrill of early punk, and ripped open the fabric of '80s music, making everything around it sound fey and compromised. It was a brutal, very male, very violent power, and it terrified as much as it delighted, just as Johnny Rotten's howl of rage had shown the world a glimpse of the abyss in 1977. Except that this time it was the rage of angry black men, and angry black men are what the world fears more than anything.

Despite PE's impact on music, ain't a damn thing changed.

SONGS ABOUT FUCKING

BIG BLACK
PRODUCED BY BIG BLACK AND JOHN LODER
BLAST FIRST (TOUCH & GO IN USA)/JULY 1987
UK CHART: DID NOT CHART
US CHART: DID NOT CHART

KEY TRACKS: 'Bad Penny'; 'The Model'; 'Kitty Empire'; 'Fish Fry'; 'Columbian Necktie'

So rap might now be scarier than rock. But that didn't mean that the occasional white boy couldn't try.

Steve Albini is, visually, the least likely reckless scourge of political correctness this side of David Baddiel. A stick-thin bespectacled dweeb from Evanston, Illinois, he went on to a career as the world's most visible arbiter of punk rock integrity, a man who thought calling a band Rapeman was a good idea, producer of the Pixies and Nirvana, and yet another recipient of the displeasure of Courtney Love. But before all this he was the leader of a coruscating punk rock trio called Big Black, who existed to wind up an increasingly self-righteous US punk rock scene, and had a drum machine where a drummer should be. They were evil and laughable in equal measure, and did the only good Kraftwerk cover version – 'The Model' – in recorded history.

Reviewing their second and final album of ringing din is tough, because everything is tinnily wrong, yet sounds absolutely right. I'm not sure I can better this, from the online *All Music Guide*'s reviewer, Andy Kellman: 'To sum up: yowl, ching, thump-thump-screech'.

Except to say that the album title – and luridly porn-par-dodying cover – is ironic. Like most great punk rock, *Songs About Fucking* is about sexual repulsion, as well as serial killers, Columbian modes of gangland execution, domestic violence, drive-by shootings and all that other gory stuff that nice middle-class geeks get all unnecessary over. It sounds like Quentin Tarantino's brain, without the blaxploitation funk bits. The revenge of the nerds was a-coming, and Big Black were a small but key element in the onward rush of new laddism, whereby white straight guys were allowed to feel OK again about their terror of everyone except . . . well . . . them. Albini's angle was simple, though. Just because we don't say the unsayable, doesn't mean we aren't thinking it. Healthier to get it out there, than to repress it through fear of not being acceptable. Wasn't that the whole point of challenging the racist, sexist, homophobic norm in the first place?

Hugely in debt musically to UK post-punk, especially Gang Of Four, *Songs About Fucking* also proved to be disquietingly girl-friendly. Apart from one Brit music journo, Kitty Empire, naming herself after one of its finest songs, a quick trawl through the net's punky netherworld brought this tribute, written very much in the vernacular of Albini's gratuitously unpleasant pulp inner sleevenotes: 'Drove goddam nearly 400 fucking miles to see these crab-crawling assholes fuckall if I didn't get a harden, stiff as a crowbar, and I'm a girl. Fucking shit.' Joy, Flipside 55, I thank you from the bottom of all our sexually confused punk rock hearts.

ACTUALLY

PET SHOP BOYS

PRODUCED BY JULIAN MENDELSOHN, STEPHEN HAGUE, PET SHOP BOYS, DAVID JACOB, SHEP PETTIBONE AND ANDY RICHARDS
PARLOPHONE/SEPTEMBER 1987
UK CHART: 2
US CHART: 25
KEY TRACKS: 'Rent'; 'It's A Sin'; 'Heart'; 'King's Cross'; 'What Have I Done To Deserve This?'

Three months after Margaret Thatcher won her third term, Neil Tennant and Chris Lowe released a magical album about the realities of being bought and sold. Despite the truth about pop life in a line from 'Hit Music' – 'It's all about love and it's about forgetting' – the Pet Shop Boys remembered everything that had been lost since the turn of the '80s, and made a long-player that forged a loving connection between escapism and political awareness, just as hip hop was doing for the same thing from a more macho perspective. Tennant was a former *Smash Hits* journalist, and the way he and Lowe blended the music hack's dream of pop subversion with a shameless desire to make radio and disco hits made flesh of the early '80s pop dream. There was something so pure about Tennant's voice and the ennui portrayed on *Actually*'s sleeve, an alignment of dry intellect with the simple seductiveness of the singer-keyboard boffin duo. Listening to this in 2006, it now strikes as an album that kissed the '80s a less than fond goodbye, and gave us back our pop, in all its gay disco glory. They really were the most dignified and undemonstrative of visionaries, were Chris and Neil.

Made with an army of collaborators, including soundtrack heavyweights Ennio Morricone and Angelo Badalamenti on AIDS elegy 'It Couldn't Happen Here', *Actually* plays like a Greatest Hits and houses a set of characters trying to make sense of a society based entirely round

ACTUALLY/PET SHOP BOYS

the dark sides of sex and/or economics. Fitting, then, that it sounds like the entire history of gay dance hedonism and pure pop melancholy concentrated into forty-eight joyful and broken-hearted minutes. So, just as 'Shopping' comes off as an ironic paean to a growing cultural obsession, yet is actually about the selling-off of public services in car-boot-sale Britain, the gorgeous closer 'King's Cross' sums up how PSB's alchemy was becoming prophetic at this point. A song about poverty and disillusion under Thatcherism, referring to the station that provides London's main gateway from the impoverished north, Tennant is talking about 'the smack of firm government' when he sings of 'Dead and wounded on either side'. Two months after *Actually*'s release, on 18 November 1987, thirty-one people lost their lives in a fire at King's Cross underground station. Many saw the disaster as a symbol of how London had declined under a government hostile to its multi-cultural politics, a sort of murder by neglect. The song seemed to see it coming.

There are few albums which sound equally lovely being concentrated upon through headphones, on a tinny portable while you wash up, and at ear-splitting clubbers' volume. *Actually* dances round God's handbag and then does something dirty to a stranger on its way back from the toilets. It's New Order with meaning and The Smiths that dances until dawn. And it does all that, and deals with the same doomed street urchin constituency as The Pogues as well. One of British pop's greatest achievements.

CRIMINAL MINDED

BOOGIE DOWN PRODUCTIONS
PRODUCED BY KRS-ONE AND SCOTT LA ROCK
B.BOY/SEPTEMBER 1987
UK CHART: DID NOT CHART
US CHART: DID NOT CHART
KEY TRACKS: 'Dope Beat'; 'South Bronx'; 'Poetry'; 'The Bridge Is Over'; 'Remix For P Is Free'

BY ALL MEANS NECESSARY

BOOGIE DOWN PRODUCTIONS
PRODUCED BY KRS-ONE
JIVE/JUNE 1988
UK CHART: 38
US CHART: 75
KEY TRACKS: 'My Philosophy'; 'Stop The Violence'; 'I'm Still #1'; 'Jimmy'; 'Part Time Suckers'

Seems like times were hard all over. The Pogues' 'Old Main Drag', PSB's 'King's Cross', and the area we'd soon come to know as the boogie-down Bronx had drugs and whores in common. 'The pussy is free/But the crack cost money,' a voice wailed over a mutant reggae beat that made Run-D.M.C. sound semi-orchestral. By the time we heard *Criminal Minded*, the record thought by many to be the first hardcore and/or gangsta rap record, one of its makers had been shot dead. Suddenly, the world's music-loving teen boys had genuine mayhem to become enthralled by.

Laurence Kris 'KRS-One' Parker was a teenage street kid from Brooklyn who had gotten himself together, largely through self-education and love of hip hop. Scott 'Scott La Rock' Sterling was a young social worker at one of the South Bronx hostels Parker stayed in, as well as a budding DJ and beat maker. By the time their first album was ready for release on the tiny B.Boy label (in itself rumoured to be a front for porn movie makers), Scott La Rock had attempted to intervene in a street argument and lost his life.

La Rock's death only made *Criminal Minded* more chilling, particularly housed within the first hip hop sleeve where the DJ and rapper were both holding guns. The lyrics of 'South Bronx' and the skeletal beats of 'Remix For P Is Free' and 'The Bridge Is Over' took hip hop right to its Jamaican roots, but most of the attention was attracted by 'The Bridge Is Over', a set of insults (mild by today's dissing standards) directed at MC Shan and Marley Marl, rapper and producer for the Juice Crew posse of MCs and DJs from the Queens area of New York. 'Sayin' that hip hop started out in Queensbridge?/Sayin' lies like that, Mon, you know dem can't live,' KRS declaimed in sing-song patois. From this point on, hip hop's battling culture constantly trod that thin line between death as metaphor and death as reality, and it was a matter of time before what came to be known as 'beef' between rappers and their entourages ended in the still-unsolved deaths of Tupac Shakur and The Notorious B.I.G.

Nevertheless, *Criminal Minded* was a fabulous record; less dense and arty than Public Enemy, stark and even fun in 'Dope Beat's sample from AC/DC's *Back In Black*. Kris Parker threw himself into his new major deal and a follow-up, and dramatically changed tack, inventing rap as 'edutainment' just a few months after laying the groundwork for gangsta.

By All Means Necessary took its cue from Malcolm X's call for Afro-American self defence in the 1960s, going as far as parodying the famous photo of Malcolm, armed, looking out of a window for potential assassins. Extraordinary pretension on KRS-One's part, and another key rap moment, as rappers grabbed the braggadocio that was key to rhyme battling culture, and reinvented themselves as gods, monsters, superheroes, indestructible gangsters . . . even martyred leaders. There was also an early version of rap's grave-robbing sentimentality, as the inner sleeve boasted a shot of Parker's slain partner as a toddler and the outer sleeve the credit, 'Overseen by DJ Scott La Rock'. It wasn't too long to 'I'll Be Missing You' and 2Pac being a more prolific recording artist dead than alive.

But By All Means . . . is an inspiring and timeless classic, which does its best to acknowledge Parker's own mistakes and show hip hop another direction. While keeping the battle rhymes as vicious, KRS-One made it clear, in 'Stop The Violence', 'My Philosophy' and 'Necessary', that this was verbal jousting and nothing more, and that hip hop provided an opportunity for black unity that had been missing from Afro-American culture since disco crushed 'message' soul and funk. What's more, the music took in digital dancehall reggae, ('Stop The Violence'), samples of Deep Purple's 'Smoke On The Water' ('Ya Slippin'), novelistic rhymes about the state's role in the drug trade ('Illegal Business') and the emergence, just before we got it from The Jungle Brothers (see p.209), of 'Jimmy' as a new word for 'penis', and rappers earnestly, but humorously, advising hip hop's growing youth male fanbase to wear a 'Jimmy hat' before sex. It's the breadth of KRS-One's concerns that signal the beginning of what hip hop diehards still call the 'Golden Age'. These two albums are vital in understanding why hip hop grew up so quickly, yet came to infantilise itself with even greater haste.

PAID IN FULL

ERIC B. & RAKIM
PRODUCED BY ERIC B. & RAKIM
4TH AND BROADWAY/AUGUST 1987
UK CHART: 85
US CHART: 58
KEY TRACKS: 'I Know You Got Soul'; 'Paid In Full'; 'Eric B. Is President'; 'As The Rhyme Goes On'; 'I Ain't No Joke'

From around about here, until around Spring 1990, this book is dominated by the best albums from what is usually referred to as the 'Golden Age' of hip hop. The rap of this period had such a profound effect on me that, by the time we'd hit the 1990s, I'd almost given up listening to anything else but hip hop. And I wasn't alone. Hip hop was seducing millions worldwide through its mixtures of aggression and low-tempo funk rhythm, of pro-black politics and punk fuck-you, of big voices full of character and substance, and that unique period in any music where a sound is being invented as it goes along, where rules haven't been set yet, and where every album you pick up holds the promise of a sound – in vocal, or bass, or drum, or in the whole mystery that was sampling and looping – you've literally never heard before.

remix of 'Paid In Full', for a single that rendered the album version redundant immediately, pointed out Barrier's limits as a beatmaker. But 'Paid In Full's sample of 'Don't Look Any Further' was deep enough to build another foundation of the Soul II Soul rhythm; 'As The Rhyme Goes On' provided future lyrics for Eminem's 'The Way I Am'; 'Chinese Arithmetic' made a rough template for the hip hop orientalisms of the Wu-Tang Clan. And, when all was said and done, there was enough deep, deep bass and enough deep, deep Rakim to make this a great debut, establishing the syncopation, authority and soulful texture of a rapper who had learned to 'hold the microphone like a grudge', and bring dimensions to that line – and to hip hop as a form of counter-culture – that would change Planet Pop forever.

Long Island, New York, had already given us Public Enemy and would give us EPMD. But, for now, meet Eric Barrier and William Griffin. As Eric B. & Rakim, they were the first rap artists to convince soul fans, rock fans and disco fans that hip hop truly was an art form rather than a strange dance novelty, and the hottest music in the galaxy in 1987. You heard Rakim rap on the legendary 'I Know You Got Soul', doing what we'd come to know as dropping science over Bobby Byrd and James Brown's already tough beat, but making it tougher, faster, interrupted by scratches that were violent enough to snap your head back, elastic enough to make your dancing feet do things they couldn't do. It was a masterpiece of dancefloor pop, yet, like Public Enemy, it had the rebellion of rock 'n' roll, in its arrogance, as much as anything else.

The debut album by Barrier and Griffin didn't all live up to that, and London DJ duo Coldcut's barrier-breaking

1988

GOIN' OFF

BIZ MARKIE

PRODUCED BY MARLEY MARL
COLD CHILLIN'/FEBRUARY 1988
UK CHART: DID NOT CHART
US CHART: 90
KEY TRACKS: 'Biz Is Goin' Off'; 'Albee Square Mall'; 'Nobody Beats The Biz'; 'Picking Boogers'; 'Vapors'

1988 is one of those big pop years: rap's Golden Age, the coming of acid house, rock albums that rediscovered the roll. But before all that, we have this: possibly the least serious album in this book, a hip hop album that existed for no reason other than to make some money out of harmless fun. It's here because its production sound is one of the best in hip hop history, and a sign that even the humblest rappers could find themselves backed by beats that were re-defining recorded music.

The beatmaker was one Marlon Williams aka Marley Marl, who came to prominence by making one of many 'Roxanne' records: a 1984–85 fledgling rap phenomenon whereby UTFO's 'Roxanne' single inspired an answer by every dodgy rapper and producer on the US East Coast. It was Marl's 'The Bridge', produced for MC Shan, a key part of Marl's Queens-based 'Juice Crew', that inspired 'The Bridge Is Over' by Boogie Down Productions, and the first high-profile rap feud. Although the smooth and verbally fearsome Big Daddy Kane (later a co-star in Madonna's *Sex* book) and the proto-gangsta Kool G Rap and DJ Polo were seen as Marl's heavyweight protégés, it was a plump, childlike part-time human beatbox called Biz Markie who somehow wound up with the best beats and most lovable songs of the Juice Crew era.

Harlem's Marcel Hall played hip hop strictly for laughs, going on to become one of New York's most enduring DJs and even a (rather embarrassing) star of one of those *Celebrity Fat Club* affairs. Imagine a more sane, less unpleas-ant Ol' Dirty Bastard and you get the idea. His debut album is one of those records which drags an ageing hip hop fanatic like myself back to a time when the explosion of new talent and experimental confidence inspired by Run-D.M.C.'s commercial success produced a rap classic a week. The key to this album's magic is an unlikely spark between Biz's rhymes – gruff, all over the place levels-wise, silly, teen-nostalgic, immature enough to include a song about the joys of picking one's nose, clinging to the innocence of chasing girls and never carrying a piece – and Marl's astonishing beats. Looping funky samples from James Brown through Dave And Ansel Collins to The Steve Miller Band, Marl made the bass churn your stomach, made hi-hats taste metallic, treated Biz's rhymes, vocal chants and beatbox throat tricks like another synthetic effect, crossing Jamaican dub's echoing space with a post-Mantronix, disembodied, robotic feel. The effect was dislocating, transformed your living room into a club with an enormous sound system, and provided one of the blueprints for that Soul II Soul rhythm that would soon transform British black music. All this on a completely daft novelty record which was fey enough to echo the Pet Shop Boys, as the Biz celebrated the wonders of his local 'Albee Square Mall' in Brooklyn, getting his singing partner TJ Swan to exhort us to 'Go shopping! Go shopping!' The gayest classic rap album ever, and that is, naturally, a compliment.

SURFER ROSA

PIXIES

PRODUCED BY STEVE ALBINI
4AD/MARCH 1988
UK CHART: DID NOT CHART
US CHART: DID NOT CHART
KEY TRACKS: 'Broken Face'; 'Bone Machine'; 'Gigantic'; 'Where Is My Mind?'; 'River Euphrates'

One of the first pop things I fell in love with was Marc Bolan. When you're getting your eight-year-old head injected full of hubcap diamond star haloes and metal gurus and raw ramps and Deborahs who move just like a zeborah, you get early prep in songs that are meaningless written down, but sound like the meaning of life when howled over the most sinful and unhinged of electric guitars. So when, now safely ensconced back working in a record shop, I managed to wrestle the deck away from the latest rare groove that was big in the Elephant & Castle, south London, and put on this record, attracted by the beautiful, flamenco-in-sepia Vaughn Oliver sleeve but expecting the usual 4AD sub-Cocteau Twins hip easy-listening drones, and this rhythm lurched and staggered in and everything screamed, and the singer sang: 'I was talking to preachy-preach about kissy-kiss/He bought me a soda/He bought me a soda/He bought me a soda and he tried to molest me in the parking lot/Yep, yep yep YEP!' . . . let's just say it was love at first listen, and pretty much the end of trying to love Stump and The Wedding Present.

Cuckolds, horse lard, incest, dresses soaked in blood, Spanish beach boys who can't find a beach, and more incest. Boston's Pixies took all the punk rock that had been building in the US hinterlands since the late '70s, and added mutant Spanglish, Old Testament sins, the old weird America the American punks had refused to engage with, The Cramps, the Violent Femmes and T. Rex, and gave rock 'n' roll back its madness and its mystery. Their first album proper (*Surfer Rosa* now comes packaged on CD with the excellent debut mini-album *Come On Pilgrim*) introduced us to a band who, on the one hand, had a lead singer called Black Francis and sounded *Addams Family*-unhinged, and on the other, had a smack-addled female bassist/singer (Kim Deal) who called herself Mrs John Murphy as if surrendering to an ancient idea of wife as chattel was the ultimate punk gesture, and they all behaved like utterly empty vessels as soon as they stopped playing. If any band were acting out all their neuroses, perversions and creepy thoughts entirely

through song, and then became your dull dumpy neighbour in the real world, it was these four Pixies, who turned out to be lightning conductors for punk's final co-option into mainstream entertainment.

Surfer Rosa reminds me of an interview I did a few years back with surrealist comic Harry Hill. I asked him which interview questions annoyed him the most. 'Where do I get my ideas from,' he answered, with barely a pause. 'I don't get my ideas from anywhere. That's what makes them ideas.' *Surfer Rosa* – the entire Pixies' catalogue – is a torrent of rock 'n' roll ideas which could have come from Charles Thompson/Black Francis/Frank Black's childhood, or comic book collection, or the time he spent living a hobo-esque life in Puerto Rico, or dark fantasies about the 'Broken Face' deformities of the offspring of incestuous union, or the *Bible*, or an atlas, a blindfold and a needle, or the famous advert with which he recruited his fellow Pixies, which asked for musicians into Hüsker Dü (see p.185) and ('60s pop-folk act) Peter, Paul And Mary. This incendiary, hilarious, physical and wild alchemy could come from all of these and other mundane things, or nowhere. That's what makes it a fucking great idea.

BARBED WIRE KISSES

THE JESUS AND MARY CHAIN
PRODUCED BY WILLIAM AND JIM REID AND JOHN LODER
BLANCO Y NEGRO/APRIL 1988
UK CHART: 9
US CHART: DID NOT CHART
KEY TRACKS: 'Upside Down'; 'Sidewalking'; 'Who Do You Love'; 'On The Wall'; 'Swing'

Injecting sex back into rock was too big a job for one band though. So, for Boston, Mass., read East Kilbride, Scotland, and two brothers whose incestuous union of masochistic sex songs and feedback-drenched guitars begat a beast dressed in black, one scary enough to cause riots at the band's early shows, and inky enough to be one of rock's best-loved exercises in postmodern murk. William and Jim Reid were so pale and studenty, with their pipe-cleaner legs and Robert Smith fright hair, but when they met in front of an amp and some freaky guitar pedals, it was moider.

For many years The Jesus And Mary Chain's debut album, *Psychocandy*, was an obligatory part of the All-Time Top Albums pantheon. But it has not dated well, being, when all is said and done, some Ramones songs with white noise dumped on top for shock value. And shock value it had, in a post-punk, pre-gangsta rap mid-'80s. But now? Not so much.

What makes this *Hatful Of Hollow*-like collection of singles, B-sides and demos a better record is its blend of the early Mary Chain din, and the narcotic goth they slid into after the early furore had died down. Possibly the most grim pair to ever dally with rock's mainstream, this was a punk negation with all politics stripped away, a long litany of horrorshow misery and wishful sexual thinking, made entertaining by the brothers' unerringly good taste in rock, and an ability to take all those Spector and Beach Boys and Velvets and New York Dolls and Johnny Cash and Eddie Cochran records they adored, and replace all of those vivid colours with BLACK, a vast, unending BLACK, in the manner of Charlie Higson's manic depressive painter out of *The Fast Show*. Understandable, then, that the only Mary Chain album that isn't a somewhat masochistic experience is a collection of bits and pieces which begins with an obvious joke – the nihilistic flipside of the Beach Boys that is 'Kill Surf City' – and never pretends to be doing anything other than playing with infinite slight variations on four minor chords for gothy youths.

But the Chain had innovations, too: the beatbox rhythm that hits home the swaggering 'Sidewalking' beat baggy by a couple of years; a version of Bo Diddley's 'Who Do You Love' more menacing than the original; and in the breathy demos at album's end, 'Swing' and 'On The Wall', they find a truly alternative rock classicism. *Barbed Wire Kisses* sounds like tired, wired sex, and that sounds as good as it should.

ACID TRAX VOLUME 2

VARIOUS ARTISTS
PRODUCED BY VARIOUS
SERIOUS/JULY 1988
UK CHART: DID NOT CHART
US CHART: DID NOT CHART
KEY TRACKS: Phuture Pfantasy Club – 'Slam and Spank Spank'; Maurice Joshua – 'I've Got A Big Dick'; Hot Hands Hula – 'Hot Hands' and '70th & King Drive'

HOUSE HALLUCINATES: PUMP UP LONDON VOLUME ONE

VARIOUS ARTISTS
PRODUCED BY VARIOUS
A & M/BREAKOUT/AUGUST 1988
UK CHART: 90
US CHART: DID NOT CHART
KEY TRACKS: Phuture – 'Acid Tracks'; Sleazy D – 'I've Lost Control'; Phuture – 'Phuture Will Survive'; Mr Lee – 'Pump Up London'; Maurice – 'This Is London'

1988 was, of course, the Second Summer Of Love. Acid house, one of the strangest and most influential trends to hit mainstream pop, hit and hit hard, and a plethora of cash-in compilations hit the UK record racks. These two were simply my favourites – the two that haven't dated or lost their ability to turn my home into a hallucinogenic disco.

Acid house was invented in Chicago by Marshall Jefferson, producer of 'Acid Tracks' by Phuture, which features on the *House Hallucinates . . .* album. The unique sound came from the bubbling, squelching noise generated when screwing around with the frequency dials of the Roland TB-303 bass sequencer. Legend has it that Jefferson stumbled upon the sound by accident. There are plenty of theories about the 'acid' tag, but the most likely is the most obvious – this sci-fi disco din sounded sufficiently out-there at high volume to gain comparison with the 1960s 'acid rock' of Hendrix, Cream and the psychedelic groups, even though ecstasy was the drug most associated this time around. In another echo of the '60s, the enthusiasm of British kids for this Chicago sound created an entire new genre of 'rave' dance music, just as British youth's love of Chicago blues created the beat boom that begat modern rock. And, just as before, the British adopted this key American sound well before the Americans themselves showed any interest.

These two collections are testaments to the disco apocalypse that was acid house. Treated horror movie voices, ludicrous futuristic lyrics, crunching drum sounds, overwhelming robotic handclaps, and that niggling, gnarly TB-303 sequencer, a true parent-baiter of its time and the precursor of everything from the dance sophistication of Basement Jaxx and Underworld to the various types of 'hardcore' which remain dance music's working-class anti-crossover music, the disco echo of punk's hardcore. And, even though the pop bandwagon hits of 1988 typified by D-Mob's 'Call It Acieed' ensured that acid house became uncool too quickly to grow into a single-artist album music, no music-loving home is complete without an acid collection or two.

These two are long out-of-print. But, if you do fancy tracking 'em down, *House Hallucinates* is the more 'classic' of the pair, due to its inclusion of acid's first two shots, Sleazy D's 'I've Lost Control' and the aforementioned 'Acid Tracks'. The Serious label collection is deliciously nuts, reaching an apex of tackiness with Maurice Joshua's 'I Got A Big Dick', the stupidest macho dance record ever made. You will be stunned at just how much fun a dance producer can have cutting up the phrase 'I Got A Big Dick' over and over

again, ripping the piss out of rap's penis-fixated excess before it truly got started. Because this music may be minimalist and repetitive, but dumb it's not, being a music that briefly united black and white, gay and straight, male and female on the dancefloor by neatly blending the pulse of synth-disco with the aggression and tastelessness of punk rock. It still sounds like no other music on Earth.

STRAIGHT OUT THE JUNGLE

JUNGLE BROTHERS
PRODUCED BY JUNGLE BROTHERS
WARLOCK/JULY 1988
UK CHART: DID NOT CHART
US CHART: DID NOT CHART
KEY TRACKS: 'Straight Out The Jungle'; 'On The Run'; 'Because I Got It Like That'; 'Black Is Black'; 'Sounds Of The Safari'

Michael 'Mike G' Small, Nathaniel 'Afrika Baby Bambaataa' Hall and Samuel 'Sammy B' Burwell came from the urban jungle of Brooklyn, New York, carrying the template for Afrocentric hip hop. Armed with an arsenal of classic funk samples and voices that invited everyone to the party, The JB's rhymes spoke of the slave mentality, of why black people shouldn't wear gold mined from Africa by white corporations, of the 'black is beautiful' vibe of civil-rights-era soul and black consciousness funk. They did the bohemian hip hop idea first and best, and then had to sit back and watch as Arrested Development, the Fugees and Black Eyed Peas watered down their best ideas and cleaned up.

Part of a rainbow coalition rap collective formed by old-school hip hop DJ and activist Afrika Bambaataa called *The Native Tongues*, which included the likes of De La Soul, A Tribe Called Quest and Queen Latifah, the Brothers' sonic tapestry depended on a deep funk that sounded live and spontaneous, and which blurred the boundaries between

STRAIGHT OUT OF THE JUNGLE/JUNGLE BROTHERS

sample-and-loop-heavy hip hop production and a traditional funk band sound. There was so much warmth and good faith in this brilliant debut record that it could encompass odes to the penis ('Jimbrowski') and their loverman abilities ('I'm Gonna Do You', 'Because I Got It Like That' and 'Behind The Bush') and not come off as anything but charming. Their look too – army fatigues, African medallions, safari headwear – had an enduring effect on hip hop's burgeoning underground, pointing the way towards an alternative to what came to be known as 'bling', establishing utilitarian soldier chic as the boho uniform for alternative men of all ages.

Destined to be overshadowed by Public Enemy's ferocity, De La Soul's surreal humour and A Tribe Called Quest's journey into jazz, the Jungle Brothers rarely get a mention in the hip hop pantheon. But for danceable entertainment performed with intelligence and sonic innovation – 'Sounds Of The Safari's cut-up of animal noises, Afro-percussion and vocal chants is still cutting-edge – there are few rap albums more loveable than *Straight Out The Jungle*.

IT TAKES A NATION OF MILLIONS TO HOLD US BACK

PUBLIC ENEMY
PRODUCED BY HANK SHOCKLEE, CARL RYDER AND ERIC 'VIETNAM' SADLER
DEF JAM/JULY 1988
UK CHART: 8
US CHART: 42
KEY TRACKS: 'Black Steel In The Hour Of Chaos'; 'Rebel Without A Pause'; 'Terminator X At The Edge Of Panic'; 'Don't Believe The Hype'; 'Bring The Noise'

So . . . how to sum up the most intimidating album in this book? To call it a concept album about black liberation is accurate, but doesn't explain why it's such a great party record, or why, sonically, it achieves a density and a sense of danger that still represents hip hop's peak. That's down to the funk, the strangest funk anyone ever recorded.

On the second Public Enemy album the group stepped up and became immortals. Over fifty-eight minutes and sixteen tracks – some little more than crowd noises recorded at a London show – PE invented the modern long-player. Designed for the longer playing time and sharper sound of compact disc, *It Takes A Nation . . .* had scope and depth beyond ordinary records. Anger was much of the reason – it sure helps if you make your art about something – but not the be-all-and-end-all. PE were a group that could turn disembodied screams into funk rhythms, make samplers sound like orchestras, mould a music that felt like it was always there, in the city street, waiting to be discovered. It was as if The Bomb Squad production team could shape air.

An album which defies the MP3 jukebox by demanding

to be heard from beginning to end, its tidal wave of words from Chuck D and Flavor Flav cover the evils of the press, being stalked by the FBI and CIA, the right to sample beats, Reagan and television, crack, a prison break and a great deal of beautifully articulated rage and equally thrilling inarticulacy. Chuck D had an unprecedented vocal authority – a statesman-like strength and über-masculinity that made his gibberish, of which there's plenty, sound as indefatigable as his wisdom – which led a music that attempts, like most great rock 'n' roll, to roll straight over those who would question its worldview, to take the young listener on a trip into a set of opinions, seduced utterly by the coolness of the noise and the band's imagery. Chuck was fond of saying how the US government saw PE as the ultimate threat. That never really materialised. Maybe someone in the military-industrial complex understood that parroting lines about Nation Of Islam leader Louis Farrakhan meant you could sign up to the hottest radical chic on the planet without having to do anything to back it up. That's rebel rock, and that's what people soon came to understand that PE were, as their black audience deserted them overnight at the turn of the '90s, but the white fans who saw them as a more exotic Clash remained loyal. The African flipside, perhaps, was more accurately covered by Flavor Flav, a bringer of visual and vocal chaos to Public Enemy's mix, the jester who carries the threat of bringing instinctive anarchy to your ordered world.

The prison break scenario of 'Black Steel In The Hour Of Chaos' convinced you that PE were above the law, a revolutionary force that no government could hold. But that was the dream, much as the '60s radicals believed that they could will revolution by sheer force of youth numbers, or punks believed they'd put paid to the corporate rock star. Groups as stunning as PE – who, again, can make a music that can make you believe that anything as possible – are one-offs who end up doing much of our liberation work for us. They allow us to believe that the morally righteous will prevail. On the other hand, I'm kinda glad that PE weren't as power-ful as they wanted to be. I mean, I agree with Chuck's '60s-radical mix of opinions, but I still don't think women, gay men, or Jews, or those of us of mixed race would've been seen as equals in this world. Why swap one set of racially obsessed tyrants for another? This was the point of PE, though: for the last time, a group made the conversation above seem worthwhile, as if they were a legitimate political party – a movement – rather than just a bunch of rappers. Don't know about you, but I'm sick of rappers. Especially when I've just listened to this.

INTROSPECTIVE

PET SHOP BOYS
PRODUCED BY TREVOR HORN, STEPHEN LIPSON, PET SHOP BOYS, LEWIS A. MARTINEE, DAVID JACOB, JULIAN MENDELSOHN
DEF JAM/JULY 1988
UK CHART: 2
US CHART: 34
KEY TRACKS: 'Left To My Own Devices'; 'It's Alright'; 'I Want A Dog'; 'I'm Not Scared'; 'Domino Dancing'

A big, fuck-off, risky dance album, where every track is an epic and all the lyrics are about being alone. It became the Pet Shop Boys' biggest seller, plugged by hit single after hit single, and kicked off by their masterpiece, 'Left To My Own Devices', where they hooked up with archetypal '80s producer Trevor Horn to make, as Neil Tennant calls it in the exhaustive sleevenotes for the 2001 CD reissue, 'a really up pop song about being left alone'. The PSBs are prescient men, and just as this album understands that house will forever be the basis of dance-pop from 1988 onwards, there is something in Tennant's fantasy twist on the single life and the childhood memory that taps right into the twenty-first century, where I suspect that most of us would just love to be left alone, to find somewhere where the world can't find you to tap you on the shoulder and remind you how many years of work and piles of money you owe it, for the privilege of being alive. Or maybe that's just me. But it isn't, is it? No one told us it would be this tiring and that so many bastards would have a say in our daily lives. 'Left To My Own Devices' finds a way of expressing that without rubbing our noses in it.

Anyway, *Introspective* is the high watermark of their wide-screen disco muse. 'I'm Not Scared' was taken into the singles charts by Patsy Kensit, while 'Always On My Mind' and 'It's Alright' were covers, of a country standard by Willie Nelson (famously covered by Elvis Presley) and a key uplifting house anthem by Sterling Void. Meaning they had their big LP success after writing four whole songs. It was just easy for Neil and Chris at this point, and this album oozes that ease, that absolute mastery of pop that plenty of producers but few performers get to reach. It reminds me of a key time – possibly a week, things were suddenly moving so quickly – when house was still a hipster's fetish, before, suddenly, it was everywhere, in every chart record, the youth on the terraces' music of choice, yet again our society's most homophobic blokes raiding gay culture for tribal choices . . . mod, northern soul and disco all over again.

FOLLOW THE LEADER

ERIC B. & RAKIM
PRODUCED BY ERIC B. & RAKIM
MCA/AUGUST 1988
UK CHART: 25
US CHART: 22
KEY TRACKS: 'Follow The Leader'; 'Microphone Fiend';
'Lyrics Of Fury'; 'No Competition'; 'The R'

> 'I'm here to break away the chains, take away the pains/
> Remake the brains, reveal my name/I guess nobody told
> you a little knowledge is dangerous.'

When you heard William 'Rakim' Griffin rap, you believed a tongue could fly, and you believed that that voice could break all your chains of bondage, if only you could understand everything he meant.

The long-playing peak fronted by the greatest rapper of all-time, its title track predicts the flows and themes of Tupac, Biggie Smalls, Method Man, Eminem, Jay-Z . . . aw, you know, it's like reeling off all the rock bands that owe Chuck Berry . . . it comes down to everyone. When Rakim declared his mic an untouchable 'third rail' – again in 'Follow The Leader' – he didn't need to back the threat with gunplay. The speed of thought and delivery, the juggling of complex metaphor and pop hook, makes Rakim the Hendrix or Coltrane of this rap thing. The guy declares himself God on 'No Competition', and it doesn't come as a surprise, never mind a blasphemy.

Not that Eric Barrier's beats were too far behind. *Follow The Leader* moves away from the straight funk of *Paid In Full* and hooks Rakim up to the kind of car-chase thriller beats which anticipate the re-evaluation of 'blaxploitation' funk by a fair few years. The musical interludes from Stevie Blass Griffin cleared a path for a music genre that was beginning to understand that sampling from other acts was no quick way to all that much rapped-about money. The scratching – that old manipulation of vinyl by DJs fell quickly from favour after rival acts clocked Public Enemy's bravura impression of an orchestra – dates some of this record, but Rakim's deliciously grainy voice, and his insistence on hip hop as a freeing from mental slavery, in a strictly post-Bob Marley way, never does. The back cover photo of KRS-One's Boogie Down Productions (see p.202) partner, the late Scott La Rock, is a signifier of the past, though. When tribute could be paid to a fallen hip hop soldier with some quiet dignity. Not an idea that could withstand the coming of Suge Knight and Sean Combs, sadly.

STRICTLY BUSINESS

EPMD
PRODUCED BY EPMD
SLEEPING BAG (FRESH IN USA)/NOVEMBER 1988
UK CHART: DID NOT CHART
US CHART: 80
KEY TRACKS: 'You Gots To Chill'; 'Strictly Business'; 'Get Off
The Bandwagon'; 'It's My Thing'; 'So Let The Funk Flow'

Mesmerising murk from Long Island, New York, taking the complete opposite tack to PE's 'Strong Island' noise terrorism. Erick Sermon and Parrish Smith hook up classic funk breaks from a wide variety of sources – from Kool & The Gang's 'Jungle Boogie' to Steve Miller's 'Fly Like An Eagle', from Zapp's 'More Bounce To The Ounce' to Eric Clapton's version of Bob Marley's 'I Shot The Sheriff' – and then spin offhand battle rhymes, while the music sticks with a swampy texture and head-nodding (out) tempo. The lyrics may not have mentioned dope, but this is where hip hop began to rock the joint – put the record on and weed is all you can smell, so laidback are the cruel slanders of Smith and the lisping, nasal Sermon, whose can't-be-arsed style became a rap cause célèbre, the antidote to Chuck D and LL Cool J's ranting, the connection between the grainy authority of Rakim and the apolitical insouciance of Snoop Dogg.

Strictly Business is one of the definers of hip hop's split personality, one minute threatening to shoot you over and over again on the title track, the next making merry sport out of parodying dance crazes, exhorting us to boogie like Steve Martin's white-boy-who-thought-he-was-black from his movie, *The Jerk*. It also predicted the pair's inability to follow such a shallow joy, with its final two tracks, the jazz-funk instrumental 'DJ K La Boss' and the throwaway 'Jane', among the worst songs tucked away anywhere within this book full of crackers.

BUMMED

HAPPY MONDAYS
PRODUCED BY MARTIN HANNETT
FACTORY/NOVEMBER 1988
UK CHART: 59
US CHART: UNRELEASED IN USA
KEY TRACKS: 'Performance'; 'Mad Cyril'; 'Brain Dead';
'Wrote For Luck'; 'Country Song'

And a great madness did descend from the north of England. It mixed the sniping of Mark E. Smith with the prophecies of John Lydon. It was Irish, like so many of the great English things were. It oozed with the nastiest drugs ever boiled in bedroom laboratories, and it was made by the lab's rats. It was like Hulme and The Hacienda in its native Manchester, but it was also like videos of films watched over and over again through dope and smack hazes, a *Performance* here, a *Get Carter* there. Mainly, though, it wanted you to dance, even if it was too fucked to join you, and it wanted you to dance to . . . post-punk. I mean, no one was gonna call it that, this time around. Madchester, baggy, indie-dance . . . anything, in fact, but post-punk. But there it was, with its Manc grime and scratchy, ringing guitars and funk beats that didn't pretend to be played by black drummers. It was A Certain Ratio (who did have a black drummer, actually – see p.353) and The Fall and PiL and Magazine, made by council-estate house-heads who you could safely add the 'on acid' soundbite too, because they were certainly on something. It wasn't until I heard Happy Mondays that I understood that there were probably drugs that were worse than smack or crack, things with street names like R2-D2, Geraldine and cake. It's not that the Mondays said anything about them. It's just that everything that came out of Shaun Ryder's mouth sounded like drug code. 'I say yes in every situation,' Ryder claimed on 'Bring A Friend', and you didn't have to see his drug-addled future to feel the truth of it, or see that we now had a singer-lyricist

BUMMED/HAPPY MONDAYS

who could bring a surrealist hip hop twist to the Irish exile and underclass testimonies of Shane MacGowan.

Ryder saw his future, though. Check 'Performance': 'One day he was admiring his reflection/In his favourite mirror/When he realised all too clearly/What a freakin' old beasty man he was/Who is?/You is/You is now, son.' His response? Same as anyone's: 'I took to dribblin' down my front.' Still makes me laugh. Still plays when I look in a mirror, notice that I've got just that little bit older ... But, in many ways, the second album by Salford's finest stars producer Martin Hannett and Mondays' guitarist Mark Day. Day is one of the most underrated players in Brit rock history, blending Manc post-punk funkisms with bluesy lines from Keith Richards and pop hooks from George Harrison, attaching this insane music to the ground. *Bummed* is where he's allowed to shine, with Joy Division and Factory house-producer Hannett knowing a ragged genius when he hears one, backing him with an old-fashioned wall of sound, and making the nastiness that underlies the Mondays into their chief element for the one and only time. Being able to rival the band for drug-hoovering probably helped him relate. Hannett died of drug-related heart failure in 1991, aged just forty-two. He was a vital part of British music, and his work on this, the greatest album by the best British band of their generation (The Smiths had split, The Stone Roses do not come close), was some kind of tribute. Meanwhile, *Bummed* continues to do its voodoo thing, with nursery rhymes, murderous threats, rude jokes and shimmering blues-funk, way, way ahead of its time.

ISN'T ANYTHING

MY BLOODY VALENTINE
PRODUCED BY MY BLOODY VALENTINE
CREATION/NOVEMBER 1988
UK CHART: DID NOT CHART
US CHART: DID NOT CHART

KEY TRACKS: Lose My Breath; No More Sorry; Soft As Snow (But Warm Inside); You Never Should; Nothing Much To Lose

There are many times when I feel frustrated at my lifelong unwillingness to learn how to play music – at my inability to introduce an element of musicology to my scribblings and musings. This is especially keenly felt in any attempt to write about My Bloody Valentine, or their creative leader Kevin Shields. One listen to this, the first MBV album proper, reminds you that he found a lost chord, a note completely his own. I scoured a little for an explanation, and this, from the online encyclopedia Wikipedia (www.wikipedia.com) is the best I could find of how he played guitar: 'Shields's unique guitar sounds lie in his approach to playing the instrument. Using Fender Jaguars and Jazzmasters, he manipulates the tremolo arm while strumming chords, which he claims contributes a lot to the overall sound of My Bloody Valentine. He combines this playing technique with excessive playing volumes (to produce better sustain), modulation effects (tremolo pedals), and reverb effects (specifically, reverse reverb).'

That still doesn't really explain the heartbreaking noise made when one of those overdriven, lysergic chords meets Bilinda Butcher's voice – sometimes no more than an 'ooh' or an 'aah' – at a place where the imagination meets the soul, or where your nerve-endings hit your tear-ducts. Is this actual magic? Is that why Shields supposedly spent half a million pounds of Island label money attempting to follow 1991's *Loveless* and producing zilch? Had he found something so special that even he couldn't locate it again?

Dunno. Do know that I love *Isn't Anything* far more than the legendary *Loveless*, where Shields's perfectionism almost bankrupted Alan McGee's Creation label, and which some people believe to be the greatest album ever. 'All I Need' here sounds like a practice run for *Loveless*, and I hate it for the same reasons I find *Loveless* unlistenable . . . it's all art din, and no bloody tune. Whereas, say, 'No More Sorry', sounds like a distillation of the very essence of human loneliness, and, say, 'Feed Me With Your Kiss' and 'Nothing Much To Lose', sound like the missing links between every great '60s sunshine pop anthem and every thuggish punk thrash, exercises in muscular musical miracle.

Kevin Shields was born in Queens, New York, and raised in Dublin, where he formed MBV with punk-Ringo drummer Colm O'Ciosoig. Since the Island label debacle, he's worked with Primal Scream, and made some precious music for the soundtrack of Sofia Coppola's movie *Lost In Translation*. 'City Girl' suggested what I still believe; that Shields's genius status depends not on guitar techniques, but in a unique way with melody, a mainline to inner sadness that neither the groups who most closely influenced him – Sonic Youth, The Velvet Underground – nor the legion of anonymously dull 'shoegazing' bands that have followed his trail can get close to. I wonder what it must be like, to find a Holy Grail, but only sometimes, and never when you need it.

FUGAZI

FUGAZI
PRODUCED BY TED NICELEY AND FUGAZI
DISCHORD/DECEMBER 1988
UK CHART: DID NOT CHART
US CHART: DID NOT CHART
KEY TRACKS: 'Bad Mouth'; 'Waiting Room'; 'Burning'; 'Glue Man'; 'Suggestion'

When emo meets straight edge. If you're going 'UHH?' at this point, you probably haven't been keeping up with those pesky niche genres, particularly those attached to American punk rock since the '80s. Don't blame you, frankly, but here we go . . .

Emo is short for emotion, and denotes an emotional – or, rather, a bleeding heart liberal – form of punk. Straight edge means that the members of the band are – and at least some of the band's lyrics will refer to being – teetotal. Washington DC's Fugazi are led by two men most often credited with inspiring these influential mini-genres. Considering that Ian MacKaye wrote a song in his first band, Minor Threat, called 'Straight Edge' about being drink- and drug-free, I think we have to label him guilty. MacKaye's fellow vocalist Guy Picciotto ain't so easy to pin down, with his first band Rites Of Spring one of many bands who may have started emo. I mean, how, exactly, do you measure emotion in punk rock, or when someone first showed it? Whatever way, the debut seven-track mini-album by Fugazi remains a thrilling chapter in punk's viral spread throughout the world, and down the generations.

It may have taken The Strokes to give permission to Brit

bands to re-discover post-punk, but Fugazi were one of those American bands who forgot to wait for music of passion and purpose to come back into fashion. And that, in a sense, is what Fugazi is about: using a groovy, funk and reggae-influenced rock, inspired by Gang Of Four, The Ruts, The Clash, The Pop Group, Wire, Wipers and Bad Brains especially, to question the band's ready-made audience. Both Minor Threat and Rites Of Spring had been recording for MacKaye's Dischord label and had played hundreds of shows to America's hardcore faithful. But turning up, having a good time, giving the bands a living – none of this was enough for Fugazi. They wanted their fans to question everything, including the scene's bone-head machismo ('Bulldog Front'), gender roles ('Suggestion'), addictions ('Give Me The Cure' and 'Glue Man') and apathy ('Waiting Room'). While drummer Brendan Canty and bassist Joe Lally laid down hip-snaking rhythms that, in keeping with the band's disapproval of the survival-of-the-biggest moshpit at punk shows, subverted the straight-ahead thrash of hardcore, and MacKaye splashed metal-influenced colours on guitar, Picciotto and MacKaye shredded their throats and our hearts, trying to convey their desire for new freedoms, and their dismissal of traditional, nihilistic or me-fixated rock 'n' roll rebellion. Since 1988, they have stayed on their own label, selling their albums and gig tickets at low prices, sticking so avidly to their guns that the very mention of their name is inclined to induce guilt-ridden squirming among the hordes of corporate US punk hacks, the majority of whom are not fit to handwash Fugazi's hair-shirts. The likes of Rage Against The Machine and System Of A Down are, but still owe Fugazi plenty.

You could boil down this record, and the Fugazi philosophy, to these celebrated lines from 'Bad Mouth': 'You can't be what you were/So you better start being just what you are.' It would be more than naïve to suggest that everyone who likes this band takes that advice to heart, but enough have to have inspired a self-sufficient, beneath-the-radar punk network that criss-crosses America, a lifestyle cottage industry that is sponsored by . . . The Kids. Fugazi is crucial to the spread of that message.

1989

TECHNIQUE

NEW ORDER

PRODUCED BY NEW ORDER
FACTORY/JANUARY 1989
UK CHART: 1
US CHART: 32
KEY TRACKS: 'All The Way'; 'Vanishing Point'; 'Mr Disco';
'Love Less'; 'Round & Round'

Technique is New Order's conquering heroes album. By early 1989, The Cure and the Pet Shop Boys had made much money adapting New Order's melodies and rhythms; acid house had vindicated the band's defiant love of queer disco; the students were all going indie-dance, flocking to a 'Madchester' built in the shadow of 'Blue Monday'; the ravers were all discovering Ibiza and a 'Balearic' sound that happily encompassed the dancier end of indie-pop. All Barney, Hooky, Stephen and Gillian had to do was make an album that did what they'd done for years, and it was bound to encompass almost everything happening in British pop. They did and it did. But they also decided to chuck in their loveliest melodies and a production style that hit their tracks home like the cleanest, toughest house. There's barely an album in this book that's more simply pleasurable to listen to than *Technique*.

Opener and neatly out-of-character hit single 'Fine Time' took the piss with its robot Barry White voice intoning 'You got lurrve technique', and its (acid house?) sheep baa-ing all over the fade. But it's still a fine time. 'All The Way' steals their tune back from The Cure, and gives Bob Smith the finger by making it one hundred times better, via a pristine three-chord guitar solo. 'Round & Round' steals their tune back off of the Pet Shop Boys, and doesn't make it better, but only because it can't. The backing vocal goes, 'Don't waste money, Baby!', and makes me laugh.

But, among all these casually despatched dance-pop gems, sits the most unlikely achievement of any New Order

album . . . a meaningful lyric. It formed the refrain of the album's best tune, the aforementioned 'All The Way'. It's sung really beautifully by Bernard Sumner, who had become a pretty good girlie-pop singer. It went like this: 'It takes years to find the nerve/To be apart from what you've done/To find the truth inside yourself/And not depend on anyone.'

I think that's true. I'm forty-three, still trying. New Order were a great group of the '80s because they were always striving to find the truth of something within their beats and melodies, just as their former vocalist Ian Curtis had tried to find the words to adequately express fear and despair. As the '80s reached an end that felt optimistic – the end of Thatcher, Apartheid, the Soviet Bloc – New Order's fifth album felt like the soundtrack to feeling good about yourself. It didn't sound smug. It sounded . . . independent.

THREE FEET HIGH AND RISING

DE LA SOUL

PRODUCED BY PRINCE PAUL AND DE LA SOUL
BIG LIFE (TOMMY BOY IN USA)/MARCH 1989
UK CHART: 13
US CHART: 24
KEY TRACKS: 'Say No Go'; 'Potholes In My Lawn'; 'Me Myself And I'; 'Eye Know'; 'The Magic Number'

An entire way forward for hip hop that was cruelly snuffed out four months later by Straight Outta Compton. Weelll . . . not exactly. From the moment both those albums were in the racks, and began that long, viral journey to word-of-mouth classic which never quite materialises in a big chart position, hip hop was, like pop and rock, a two-strand music. There was a mainstream and an alternative. What makes the debut De La Soul album a somewhat sad listen now is that this freewheeling ride around

TECHNIQUE/NEW ORDER

3 FEET HIGH AND RISING/DE LA SOUL

a planet of sound and a mountain of good faith became the alternative. Its good humour, broadmindedness, and lack of shame over liking women and being smart and hating violence . . . it sounds naïve. How could anyone hope to make a living doing this kind of black music, unless you've got the gall to become all pseudo-Marley like Wyclef Jean?

Beginning to realise that my hip hop entries are kinda sour. It's just that rap's Golden Age was just so . . . golden. Just the best music in the world, capable of encompassing any style, mood or texture without faking it, filled with that thrill of new discovery, broad enough to include De La Soul, Public Enemy and N.W.A. because they were all competing on the same stage, and no one had any idea which impulse would survive, and how much money each would make. Again, it feels naïve to ever think that the adventures of Long Island's De La Soul and Public Enemy – from in-jokey surrealism to radical politics, and both obviously middle class because, contrary to popular perception, a collegiate black middle class does exist – would outmuscle gangsta's blaxploitation. Hip hop must be one of the few cultures where working-class immediate gratification economically overpowered middle-class deferred gratification. And where that wasn't a good thing.

But, anyway, if you haven't heard *Three Feet High And Rising*, it's named after a line from a Johnny Cash song, it's over an hour long, it's sample-based and finds space for everything from funk and soul to country, folk and psychedelic pop. Its makers are Kelvin 'Posdnous' Mercer, Vincent 'Mase' Mason and David 'Trugoy' Jolicoeur. Like Mercer and Jolicoeur's nom de rhymes, it is bewildering, a day-glo explosion of short attention span popfunk which was perfect for compact disc, which had by now overtaken vinyl and cassette as the most popular music format.

The critics went crazy as they sorted the Steely Dan samples from the Hall & Oates quotes, clocking the progressive politics of 'Say No Go' and 'Ghetto Thang', pretending to get the slew of private jokes. In fact, the older the album gets, the less conceptually clever or amusing it seems, kicking off with a fake game show and never really making anything out of it. The delight was and is in the musical grab-bag nature of it all, and the impression that these were black men uniquely disinterested in appearing cool to other black men. 'Buddy' may not be the album's best track, but it remains the template for every male hip hop song that dares to like women. Plump and/or nerdish, taking the Afrocentrism of their Native Tongues friends (and guests, along with Q-Tip, on 'Buddy') The Jungle Brothers to Sloppy Joe extremes, the band seemed to recoil in horror from the public perception of them. After a slew of moody interviews where they made it as clear as possible that they were neither queers nor hippies, they followed this joyous tapestry with *De La Soul Is Dead*, an exercise in arty obfuscation featuring dead flowers on the cover. If N.W.A. vs. De La Soul was the fight for the heart of the hip hop nation, the Long Island boys quickly waved a white hankie pausing only to explain that it wasn't pink.

But they left this, and it's a very great thing. Their producer Prince Paul, if his subsequent work with The Gravediggaz and Handsome Boy Modelling School is anything to go by, had more to do with the album's scattershot wit than anyone wanted to let on at the time. A great many bohemian hip hop albums have been made in *Three Feet High . . .* 's slipstream, but none are as capable of changing the light of a room, nor so succinctly sum up an era of optimism.

DOOLITTLE

PIXIES
PRODUCED BY GIL NORTON
4AD/APRIL 1989
UK CHART: 8
US CHART: 98

KEY TRACKS: 'Monkey's Gone To Heaven'; 'Tame'; 'Hey';
'Debaser'; 'Number 13 Baby'

Meanwhile, this other plump, nerdy guy is perfecting ways to close the gap between horror and pleasure. The legendary opener to the second Pixies album, 'Debaser' is a celebration of Luis Bunuel's *Un Chien Andalou* and a neat way to say that boys find images of violence thrilling. The following 'Tame', a virtual template for the whole of Nirvana's career, could be a cruel slag-off of an uninteresting girl, or a rape, from the rapist's perspective. 'Wave Of Mutilation' could be about suicide, or ethnic cleansing, or going on a cruise. And on it goes. For our guy Black Francis's part, he just says the lyrics are meaningless, and most Pixies fans think the guy just smoked a lot of dope and wrote down the groovier B-movie thoughts travelling through his odd head. When he does explain, it's usually both cleverer and less deep than

you'd predict, such as with 'Number 13 Baby', which is about southern California biker culture where the number thirteen refers to the thirteenth letter in the alphabet, which is 'M', and M stands for . . . ho hum . . . marijuana. But surely 'Monkey's Gone To Heaven' is an eco-anthem, which insists, with memorable screaming intensity, that God is bigger than us and will therefore punish us for our cavalier ways with Mother Earth. Isn't it?

I'll never get tired of listening to puzzle it out. *Surfer Rosa* (see p.206) was a wild new shock, but *Doolittle* is something like the perfect rock 'n' roll album – vicious, androgynous, violent, stupid, curious, lost, warm, instinctive and deeply mysterious. It is, as we hacks like to remind you, about being Spanish, about quiet-verse-loud chorus-SCREAM!!!, about aliens and sci-fi movies and horror movies and inbreeding and weird 'did you know?' shit plucked from the *National Enquirer* and made into hit-and-run hooligan art. Even a throwaway sneer like 'La La Love You' – a band self-consciously excusing their obvious desire to be a big pop group – fits perfectly. And 'Hey' is just so painful, with the voices of Kim and Frank, who couldn't even bear each other most of the time, twinning in some beatific, almost religious way, like the unrequited love is theirs and is way above anything to do with the whores in anyone's head or bed. And 'Wave Of Mutilation', 'Gouge Away' and 'Here Comes Your Man' aren't even in the best five tracks here!

There is something unpleasant but compelling in this record concerning the human underbelly, about hell and teetering on the abyss, that no one line, song or scream can adequately sum up. They were an incredibly strange group of incredibly strange creatures. Here, they found their peak and talked to animals.

STRAIGHT OUTTA COMPTON

N.W.A.
PRODUCED BY DR. DRE AND YELLA

4TH & BROADWAY (PRIORITY IN USA)/AUGUST 1989
UK CHART: 41
US CHART: 37
KEY TRACKS: 'Straight Outta Compton'; 'Fuck Tha Police';
'Express Yourself'; 'Dopeman (Remix)'; 'Gangsta Gangsta'

Last night, aware that I was going to be writing about this album, I switched on the box and flicked onto *Film 2006* with Jonathan Ross. One of the featured movies was *Get Rich Or Die Tryin'*, the 'autobiographical' debut of one 50 Cent. Ross kept calling him by his slang name 'Fiddy' Cent, like some old biddy who'd just discovered that wild beat music they call rock 'n' roll. Anyway, they showed a couple of clips where this fucker – the biggest-selling recording artist in the world – barely managed to stay awake through the usual monosyllabic mumbling posing as street cool, and then Ross gave it a great review, slavering on about how Fiddy was as promising an acting talent as his mentor, Eminem. Ross's words began to blur and all I could hear was 'KER-CHING!!!KER-CHING!!!KER-CHING!!!' for every cunt involved. And then I remembered that I had to write about Niggaz With Attitude and realised that, after seventeen years of white people making money out of black-on-black violence, it's all *Straight Outta Compton*'s fault.

An obvious point to make from there is that if N.W.A.'s debut had been as mind-numbingly tedious as everything by 50 Cent except 'In Da Club' (refer to my Theory One from This Is Uncool: everybody's got one good single in them. How this becomes some kind of global mass hypnosis when coming to 'Fiddy' is someone else's territory) then we may never have heard of gangsta rap. But it wasn't. It was the stoopidest thrill-funk album of all times, the ultimate in liberal-baiting blaxploitation, providing the high-impact and easy-to-get antidote to the cries for action within both politicised rap and underground punk. This was rebellion without responsibility, and a black group grabbing back the adolescent fantasies of thirty-five years of white boy rock 'n' roll. It was the cleverest and most influential commercial idea of its generation, and the end of hip hop as a revolutionary music within the mainstream. De La Soul's daisies could do nothing but wilt. The title track took Public Enemy's sound, and the rest of the album stripped it of both political context and artistic complexity by mixing it with the parent-baiting of early Beasties and the amoral sex and violence of Philadelphia's Schooly D. Genius, really.

Nevertheless, 'I'm expressin' with my full capabilities/ Now I'm livin' in correctional facilities' (from 'Express Yourself') is funnier than anything on the De La Soul album. So let's take a look at the strange facts that surround this notorious debut and ponder whether this record was parody or unashamed misanthropy. N.W.A. was formed in Compton, Los Angeles, by Eric 'Eazy E' Wright, business-minded and jheri-curled son of Charles Wright, maker of the original 'Express Yourself' funk classic. Eazy got together

with manager Jerry Heller to essentially manufacture a sensationalist rap group, a West Coast Public Enemy with greater emphasis on sex and guns than revolution. His two most inspired discoveries were Andre 'Dr. Dre' Young and O'Shea 'Ice Cube' Jackson. The latter provided the most incendiary rhymes for *Straight Outta Compton* and left straight after this album became successful in a dispute over royalties. Dre left after the second album, same reason. Turned out that these two were the talented ones, as their subsequent success proved. Sadly, the idiot misogyny of Cube's 'I Ain't Tha 1' became the default artistic position of everything that spun off N.W.A., and almost every successful male rapper since.

Meanwhile, Eazy E was criticised for his loyalty to Heller, who was white and Jewish, and finally succumbed to AIDS-related illness in March 1995. By this time, everything in western culture had been irrevocably altered by the unprecedented success of Eazy, Dre, Cube, everything they touched and would touch including Snoop Dogg and Eminem, and this record, which is probably the least edifying in this book, but was (and remains) so irresistible that twenty-five years of progressive thought wilted under its pressure. What it revealed was that a large part of the planet had not been changed by the liberalism of counterculture. It had merely kept its mouth tactfully shut until a product came along that could adequately express its loathing of women, gays, men that weren't into violence and anything that believed in any form of unifying morality, and repackage that pessimistic conservatism as anti-establishment rhetoric, à la 'Fuck Tha Police'. Punk had always carried some of that as baggage. That redneck part of punk was co-opted by the extreme right and became known as OI! music. What N.W.A. proved is either: 1) That a black group could get away with what a white group couldn't, or: 2) That hip hop was a new enough artform to regenerate right-wing misanthropy, and render it cool. I'll offer up Dre's protégé Marshall Mathers, and go with ... a bit of both, sadly. In the meantime, this album rocks me and makes me feel guilty, all at the same time.

It's better than fucking Fiddy, though.

1990

EXTRICATE

THE FALL

PRODUCED BY CRAIG LEON, MARK E. SMITH,
COLDCUT AND ADRIAN SHERWOOD
COG SINISTER-FONTANA/FEBRUARY 1990
UK CHART: 31
US CHART: DID NOT CHART
Key tracks: 'Black Monk Theme Part I'; 'Bill Is Dead'; 'Sing!
Harpy'; 'Hilary'; 'I'm Frank'

458489 A-SIDES

THE FALL

PRODUCED BY JOHN LECKIE, IAN BROUDIE, GRANT
CUNLIFFE, SIMON ROGERS, CJ, MARK E. SMITH AND
SHAN HIRA
BEGGARS BANQUET/SEPTEMBER 1990
UK CHART: 47
US CHART: DID NOT CHART
KEY TRACKS: 'Big New Prinz'; 'Hit The North Part 1'; 'Rollin'
Dany'; 'Cruiser's Creek'; 'No Bulbs 3'

For a few years at the end of the 1990s, The Fall almost became a pop group. This was partly down to the period's obsession with Manchester; partly down to the melodic aesthetic brought by Mark E. Smith's Californian wife and guitarist Brix; partly down to some pretty cynical attempts at cover version hits while on the major label-funded indie imprint Beggars Banquet; and partly down to their drones being cleaned up in the studio and fitting in oddly well with the acid house inclinations of the time. They may actually have reached their peak too, by the way. There's nothing wrong with ambition when it comes to making music, and for a moment the definitive northern cult figure glimpsed *Top Of The Pops* and proper money, and went for it.

The *458489* singles compilation rounds up the Brix-era

perfectly; from the tough, reverent rockabilly and garage-punk covers of Gene Vincent's 'Rollin' Dany' and The Other Half's 'Mr Pharmacist', to genuinely adventurous art rockers, where Smith brings William Blake's 'Jerusalem' into the light of the present day ('It was the fault of the government!'), and attempts to make sense of the thirty-three-day papacy of John Paul I on the harpsichord-driven 'Hey! Luciani'. Before Brix Smith split to be with mockney violinist Nigel Kennedy – a runtish re-run of Jerry Hall dumping Bryan Ferry for Mick Jagger back in the '70s – she gave The Fall a wash and brush up that suited them. *458489 A-Sides* is chock-full of student disco floor fillers, and even a genuine Top 30 single in the (awful, it must be said) version of the R. Dean Taylor Motown/northern soul classic 'There's A Ghost In My House'.

Their new-found indie disco popularity gave Smith the chance to insist in the press that he'd invented acid house. Before anyone could ask what the bally heck he was on about, he'd signed his own Cog Sinister label to major label Fontana, and hired London mix pioneers Coldcut to give him his very own baggy hit. 'Telephone Thing' wasn't Smith's 'Blue Monday', but did form the centrepiece of The Fall's greatest album – the one that captures their obtuse art heart and their rockin' pop soul in perfect alignment.

Smith's love of a particular strain of cult music – The Fall are essentially a place where country, rockabilly, '60s garage and pop psychedelia, northern soul, reggae and art-rock typified by Can meet – makes *Extricate* the most come-hither of all Fall albums, despite fans' and critics' attempts to see it as one long slagging of his departed wife. If it was pain that provoked him to write – and deliver with utmost conviction – a Serge Gainsbourg-style paean to sex as unexpected as 'Bill Is Dead', then, hey . . . it's an ill wind. Elsewhere, dominant producer Craig Leon revels in how hard and hypnotically this endlessly gigging veteran band can play a good riff, and makes 'Sing! Harpy', the violin-flecked version of '60s punk rant 'Black Monk Theme Part I' and the unusually randy 'I'm Frank' full of muscle and good cheer, not allowing even the sub-Sonic Youth dirge that is 'Chicago, Now' to get too, well, dirgey. It all ends with 'And Therein . . .' further defining the warp and weft of Mancabilly, a gnarled and nutty genre which remains the province of one band. If you've always thought The Fall are just not a band you could learn to love, *Extricate* is the album that just might turn your head.

FEAR OF A BLACK PLANET

PUBLIC ENEMY

PRODUCED BY HANK SHOCKLEE; CARL RYDER, ERIC (VIETNAM) SADLER; KEITH SHOCKLEE
DEF JAM/APRIL 1990
UK CHART: 4
US CHART: 10
KEY TRACKS: 'Welcome To The Terrordome'; 'Fight The Power'; '911 Is A Joke'; 'Anti-Nigger Machine'; 'Fear Of A Black Planet'

Having allowed Professor Griff's sacking over anti-Semitic remarks to overshadow the release of their third album, Public Enemy had already passed their peak of influence, of trust from their audience. Just as well, then, that *Fear Of A Black Planet* was the most complete statement in hip hop's history, and one of the most complex yet accessible albums in music. With Chuck D's revolutionary fervour and slew of soundbites housed within a tapestry of found sound that appeared to play machines like avant-jazzers played sax, PE spoke of miscegenation ('Pollywanacraka', the title track), racist institutions ('911 Is A Joke'), and media paranoia ('Brothers Gonna Work It Out', 'Welcome To The Terrordome', pretty much everything that isn't hollering 'Power To The People'). Single 'Welcome To The Terrordrome' seriously pissed off anti-Semitism obsessives with some stuff about the 'so-called chosen' and how they got Chuck 'like Jesus'. Being of sound agnostic mind (and part-Jewish, part-Jamaican background), it didn't occur to me that such a typical piece of melodramatic rock martyrdom had any more sinister intent until journalists who couldn't give a real fuck either way started banging on about it, demanding resignations as if Chuck really was a government minister rather than, you know, a rapper. He says stupid things, for the sake of pop excitement, just like every other decent lead singer in a band.

As for that fear of a black planet, it sometimes feels as if hip hop culture is making that reality closer every day. This album is hip hop's most directly rebellious and politically charged tract – a final coherent call for something other than the triumph of the individual. No matter how brilliant musically, there was too much here to follow, even for now.

GOO

SONIC YOUTH

PRODUCED BY SONIC YOUTH WITH NICK SANSANO AND RON SAINT GERMAIN
GEFFEN/JUNE 1990
UK CHART: 32
US CHART: 96
KEY TRACKS: 'Kool Thing'; 'Tunic (Song For Karen)'; 'Dirty Boots'; 'My Friend Goo'; 'Mildred Pierce'

So Chuck gets a call from some arty New York rock band. They want him to guest on their track, want some of that black radical chic that he and PE have exclusively revived. They're making some damn, droning noise . . . sung by a chick, too. So, hell, do the bare minimum, Chuck: 'Word up! Yeah! Fear of a female planet! Tell it like it is!' Heh. Money for old rope. Maybe Chuck should've listened, though, when that middle-class white girl took your pathetic non-engagement and made it the answer to this: 'I just wanna know, what are you gonna do for me? I mean, are you gonna liberate us girls from male white corporate oppression?' Yeah! Word up! Etc! What a dick . . .

The rest of the album lives up to these two big songs by way of a set of rattling, charging rock-action guitar drives that form the missing link between The Who's 'I Can See For Miles' and Franz Ferdinand's 'Take Me Out'. Sure, post-punk is a big influence on Franz and all the other crappy laddo chancers who've sprung up in their suited and booted wake. But every indie-rock band has a little of Thurston Moore and Lee Renaldo's off-kilter six-string ring in it. Again, much like *Extricate* by The Fall (see p.228), this is the sound of a veteran art pin-up band getting some major label money and having fun with it, seeing no shame in reaching out a little to the pop masses. It's better than their more critically acclaimed stuff, because it has better tunes, and more of them.

BEHAVIOUR

PET SHOP BOYS

PRODUCED BY PET SHOP BOYS AND HAROLD FALTERMEYER
PARLOPHONE/OCTOBER 1990
UK CHART: 2
US CHART: 45
KEY TRACKS: 'Being Boring'; 'Jealousy'; 'My October Symphony'; 'To Face The Truth'; 'This Must Be The Place I Waited Years To Leave'

Not Neil and Chris's most popular album, but perhaps their most admired. While everyone else raved and vibed off new-decade optimism, PSB almost seemed to mourn. The ten songs here mine an endless seam of sadness. But then, no matter how cruel the 1980s had been – and this album's anthem, 'Being Boring', captured the grief caused by AIDS better than any other pop song – Tennant and Lowe were key '80s winners. Why shouldn't the passing of time, and the eternal dichotomy of being a pop star and being over thirty, be captured and mourned too?

On *Behaviour* Tennant became increasingly accom-

Sonic Youth had been New York's most celebrated art-noise band for almost ten years before they signed to a major label, shocking US punk's holier-than-thou wing and famously helping to broker Nirvana's deal with Geffen. They took the chance and made their best record; a bravura tethering of their off-kilter modal guitar drones with tough rock 'n' roll melodies and a proto-riot-grrl feel dominated by bassist/vocalist Kim Gordon. On the song discussed above, 'Kool Thing', Gordon expertly juggles Chuck D's ego, perceptions of black male potency, the lingering phenom of radical chic, and her own admitted crushes on early rappers like LL Cool J, and ends up revealing something funny and discomforting about all those things, and humanity's apparently unending horror about race. Not bad, considering she's already done the same for anorexia nervosa and Karen Carpenter on 'Tunic (Song For Karen)'. Possibly inspired by Todd Haynes's 1987 movie *Superstar*, which uses Barbie dolls to tell the tragic story of the honey-voiced MOR star, Kim gives Karen her place in the Great Rock Band In The Sky. Again rubbing up against the unintentional comedy of cliché, Gordon avoids it by hitting truth early in the song, as she speaks in Carpenter's voice; 'I feel like I'm disappearing/Getting smaller every day/But I look in the mirror/I'm bigger in every way.'

plished at counting the emotional cost of gay male promiscuity, amusingly so on the single 'So Hard'. A lyric such as 'To Face The Truth' could, of course, be sung by anyone to anyone else who cheats. But Tennant and Lowe were about the balance between celebrating gay nightlife and counting the cost – to self-esteem, to health, to your lover's heart – in the morning. On the other hand, Tennant insists, on the album's 2001 reissue sleevenotes, that 'To Face The Truth' is 'a heterosexual story'. He knows better than anyone that once a song is out there, it's whatever the listeners want it to be. But I like the way he plays with critics' perceptions of his themes and image, knowing how our minds work from experience. No doubting the intentions of 'How Can You Expect To Be Taken Seriously?' though, as Neil lays into the pretensions of rock stars in a lyric that should be tattooed onto the inside of Bono and Chris Martin's eyelids.

The visionary bit, though, is in Neil and Chris deciding that cheesy '80s 'Axel F' producer Harold Faltermeyer was absolutely the right man to make their most musically sophisticated and accomplished album. *Behaviour* is a sumptuous symphony that bathes you in the pair's wise melancholy, making an imaginary stage musical out of bittersweet nostalgia, fear of age and loneliness, and . . . well . . . behaviour. I wonder just how many long, painful, paranoid nights 'Jealousy' has soundtracked?

Mozzer's very own *Hatful Of Hollow* (see p.172), *Bona Drag* collects gems from an early, risky solo career. Bemused and hurt by the end of The Smiths, Morrissey threw himself into work but was unable to find a settled line-up of musicians, nor an entirely satisfying writing partner. He settled for writing extraordinary lyrics and occasionally brilliant vocal melodies over a less exciting version of The Smiths. Again, just as it had with the early Smiths (and their only real contenders in mid-'80s British rock, The Jesus And Mary Chain), the prolific narrowness of style suited singles and B-sides best – at least until *Vauxhall And I* (see p.262).

Tackling subjects that no other high-profile rock star would go near, Morrissey established his cult by way of a song such as 'November Spawned A Monster', where a deformed child is almost drowned by Moz's strangely graphic sympathy, entirely squirm-worthy until the final lines, where he pleads only for the girl to be allowed to 'be walking your streets in the clothes that she went out and

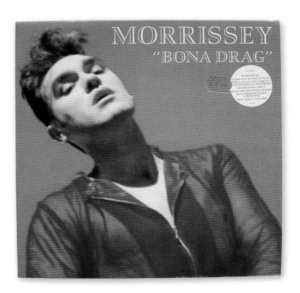

BONA DRAG

MORRISSEY
PRODUCED BY CLIVE LANGER, ALAN WINSTANLEY
AND STEPHEN STREET
HIS MASTER'S VOICE/EMI/OCTOBER 1990
UK CHART: 9
US CHART: 59
KEY TRACKS: 'The Last Of The International Playboys';
'Everyday Is Like Sunday'; 'He Knows I'd Love To See Him';
'Hairdresser On Fire'; 'Suedehead'

chose for herself'. It is so utterly different to the average rock lyric, not just in subject matter, but in the complete lack of melodramatic self-regard in its love for a 'poor, twisted child'. No wonder, then, that listeners clocked Morrissey as a rent boy in 'Piccadilly Palare' or a psychopathic Kray Twin groupie in the glorious glam-rock of 'The Last Of The International Playboys', and found themselves unable to believe that the man wasn't always singing about himself. Pop lyricists play with fire every time they fall into writing in the first person, as so many of us are so much more interested in the star than his or her work, we find ourselves baffled that the star themselves might find someone else's feelings or life more interesting than their own. If they sing 'I', then that must be precisely what they mean. It was all brewing trouble for Moz, who would attempt to sing from the point of view of a racist in 1992's 'National Front Disco', and come a right old No. 1 cropper.

But *Bona Drag* represents a master singer and lyricist when he was still pretty much toast of the town, and able to waste wonderful tunes such as 'Hairdresser On Fire' and 'Disappointed' on B-sides. The former is a magnificent riff on rich west London, shallow vanity, and that ever-present homoeroticism, featuring the lines, 'You may be repressed/But you're remarkably dressed.' The latter revives the self-deprecating boy who laughed at his own voice on *The Queen Is Dead* (see p.189): 'This is the last song I will ever sing,' Moz sighs. A crowd cheers. 'No,' he decides, 'I've changed my mind again.' The same crowd 'ahhs' with disappointment. It's simple, but it's funny, Jack, and in a world where The Kaiser Chiefs passes for wit, it's Groucho sodding Marx.

Meanwhile, 'He Knows I'd Love To See Him' still sounds like a tender sigh towards Johnny Marr, and 'Yes, I Am Blind', 'Hairdresser . . . ' and ' . . . International Playboys' reveal what is rarely said about Morrissey: that he was/is a wonderful, innovative vocalist with an instinctive ear for both hook and the aesthetically pleasing vocal tick and twist, and especially in this period straight after The Smiths, when he had a

great deal to prove. The album title, incidentally, means 'nice outfit' in palare, or polari, the gay subcultural slang which reached its peak of use in Britain in the late '50s and '60s, particularly amongst gay and Jewish theatre folk.

THE LA'S

THE LA'S
PRODUCED BY STEVE LILLYWHITE, MARK WALLIS AND BOB ANDREWS
GO! DISCS/OCTOBER 1990
UK CHART: 30
US CHART: DID NOT CHART
KEY TRACKS: 'There She Goes'; 'Way Out'; 'Lookin' Glass'; 'I Can't Sleep'; 'Freedom Song'

Those who know the strange, truncated tale of Liverpool's La's may already have noticed the crystal-ball nature of their only album's first lines: 'If you want I'll sell you a life story/About a man who's at loggerheads with his past all the time/He's alive and living in purgatory' . . . and there, for most intents and purposes, lies our perception of Lee Mavers.

Named after the Scouse slang for The Lads, The La's were a quartet who reinvented classic English guitar pop over the course of one twelve-track album. Their leader Mavers wrote perfect lost Merseybeat anthems, shanties and bierkeller waltzes, sang like every great swinging '60s lead singer, and looked like mod-jazz organist Georgie Fame, because even Lee's face was THE SIXTIES. Problem was, our twenty-eight-year-old likely La was too obsessed with the Golden Age. Every sound that his band recorded – every last note and jangle and harmony – was picked over and over and over in a damned search for the utterly authentic beat-pop sound in Mavers's head. When Mavers sings, like a bruised choirboy with a Chicago soul gene buried deep in his golden throat, 'The melody always finds me' on 'Timeless

THE LA'S/THE LA'S

Melody', it now seems like a cry for help rather than an expression of the joy found in song.

Add hard drugs, and the outcome remains one of Britpop's great enigmas. His Go! Disc label put out this record despite his protests that it was unfinished. He rubbished it in the press, despite critics being genuinely stunned by its offhand magic. And . . . that's it. No follow-up, ever. His bassist John Power got bored of waiting for his mad leader and formed arch dadrockers Cast. A story would emerge occasionally; Mavers was locked in various garages, doomed to search for this sound only he could hear, babbling incoherently, the Brian Wilson who never got as far as his *Pet Sounds* or 'Good Vibrations' before becoming a casualty of the genius-equals-madness equation. Once every five years or so, there's a rumour of a La's reformation, they play one show, it's a disaster, the mystery deepens, with fewer fans bothering to care. At the time of writing, Mavers and Power are rumoured to have reconciled, and how great would it be if Mavers had made a great record before this book hits the shelves? Hold. Breath. Don't.

But *The La's* is what it is: the best retro guitar pop album ever made. The Stone Roses? Forget it, Pal. Everyone from Oasis to The Coral to the Arctic Monkeys owes this record a living, because it captured, with exquisite grace, simplicity and weird sadness, what we'd lost in the years since the optimism of the mid-'60s. Whereas the coming Britpop, which The La's invented, largely pastiched The Beatles, The Kinks and The Who, creating a template for English guitar pop's empty nostalgia and continuing inferiority complex about the Great British Invasion, the melodies, guitars, vocals and words of this blessed and cursed man felt deeply real, as if Mavers simply couldn't live in the 1990s without his total belief in the '60s promise of freedom for all the young of the world. It's blissful because it's so horrified, because art only reaches those peaks when it looks into the abyss and resists the temptation to recoil. 'Turn the world around,' Mavers sang, soaring, weightless, on the album's closing epic 'Lookin' Glass', and when the world refused to answer, you imagine, Mavers could only retreat from his own shamanistic raising of dead hope.

Or maybe he just had a way with a tune and took too much acid. Bloomin' scallies.

PILLS 'N' THRILLS AND BELLYACHES

HAPPY MONDAYS
PRODUCED BY PAUL OAKENFOLD AND STEVE OSBOURNE
FACTORY/NOVEMBER 1990
UK CHART: 4
US CHART: 89
KEY TRACKS: 'Kinky Afro'; 'God's Cop'; 'Holiday'; 'Dennis And Lois'; 'Loose Fit'

And scallies in bloom. Are there lovelier, happier moments in pop than when the easy funk of 'Dennis And Lois' suddenly climbs, and the Italian house pianos get chunky and Shaun Ryder hollers 'RIIIDE!!! Ride on ride on!'? Or when, in the same song, the band casually toss in a Beatles standard middle-eight, and a horde of Shauns ask, 'Honey, how's your breathing?/If it stops for good we'll be leaving'? While Mavers mourned the past, his Manc cousins lived entirely for this second, got house DJ Paul Oakenfold to clean up – ha! – their funky act and revelled in being the most unlikely pop stars of the new decade. Its one thing being a bunch of drug fiends in casual clothes; it's entirely another screaming the facts at the world. It was a genuinely strange moment when a homophobic comment by Bez in an *NME* interview effectively killed the Mondays' career. 'Cos, obviously, we'd thought they were such right-on boys. Oddly, the same big brave journos stayed well away from all the black men . . .

Anyway, what the previous album *Bummed* (see p.214) hadn't told us is that these thug-ugly gits could be sexy. Apart from the frisson that Rowetta's soul backing vocals brought to the show, 'Bob's Yer Uncle' was almost in the

Barry White class. But this was the Mondays' gift: like most British working-class boys, they were soul boys. This embarrassment about sex that infects indie-pop – that informs a 'naughty' album like *Songs About Fucking* (see p.199) – well, this band were no more embarrassed about fucking than they were about their drug intake. The most important thing in their lives was pretty much revealed in the closing 'Holiday'/'Harmony' segue, a ludicrous, hilarious and actually very sweet epic made about the indignity of being prevented by Customs officers from smuggling drugs into foreign countries. I would've written to my MP, but I was too busy singing, 'I'm so nice I'm so nice I'm so nice . . . Man, I'm so niiiice!'

As for what this dayglo dirty dancing version of all the best riffs of The Beatles and the Stones actually meant, well, at times it sounds like a manifesto for an alternative nuclear family, one where, as long as you skin up, roll up and fuck up, your commitment to family values is assured. But the boy Ryder can speak for himself, from 'Donovan' (why Donovan? You know . . . why not?): 'I've been umpteen different people and no one else can tell,' but, 'Oh sunshine shone brightly through my asshole today.' Yes it did. That smarts after a while.

The inside sleeve is taken up with notes by a critic, one Gene Sculatti. He writes very nicely, in an obvious everything's-brilliant-because-they're-paying-me kind of way – something which every music hack has done to make a living. That's not what's interesting. What's interesting is that it's there at all, as if a woman who had ended the '80s as the biggest pop star on the planet still felt she lacked legitimacy, and still depended on, of all people, a music journalist to persuade the buyer that they were purchasing quality.

There's a lot of good things about Madonna. One lousy thing is how responsible she is for our current cake-and-eat-it-too culture, whereby the rich and famous seem to have decided that riches and fame is never enough, and insist on running after us or breaking down our fucking doors screaming, 'I'm a serious musician! And a thespian! And an earth mother! And a great humanitarian! Don't you dare think that there's even one damn thing in the totality of human experience that I cannot master! ADOORRE MEEEE!!!'

What this seventeen-track double album does prove, though, is that she always made brilliant pop singles, most of which you can dance to. She's a really good pop star. But she's shit at everything else, and I wish she'd discover dignity in her old age and accept it.

THE IMMACULATE COLLECTION

MADONNA
PRODUCED BY VARIOUS PRODUCERS
SIRE/NOVEMBER 1990
UK CHART: 1
US CHART: 5
KEY TRACKS: 'Like A Prayer'; 'Papa Don't Preach'; 'Into The Groove'; 'Like A Virgin'; 'Borderline'

And no one was smarting more in 1990 than Ms Ciccone. This sublime Best Of contains a giant clue to just how much Madonna wanted to be taken seriously for her, like, music.

1991

RETRO TECHNO/ EMOTIONS ELECTRIC

VARIOUS ARTISTS
PRODUCED BY JUAN ATKINS, DERRICK MAY, KEVIN
SAUNDERSON AND MARK KINCHEN
NETWORK/FEBRUARY 1991
UK CHART: DID NOT CHART
US CHART: DID NOT CHART
KEY TRACKS: Rhythim Is Rhythim – 'The Dance'; Model 500
– 'No U.F.O.'s'; First Bass – 'Seperate Minds'; Cybotron –
'Clear'; Rhythim Is Rhythim – 'Strings Of Life (Unreleased Mix)'

Detroit techno producers were intense dudes. This definitive compilation of the genre's key '80s records features quotes from the makers about each track. Clock this one, from the legend that is Derrick May, about an instrumental called 'R-Theme': 'Nobody really cares. This song had the potential to initiate change and it didn't do that. Before I had shared my life with a woman I was so full of emotion. I think you can hear that.' Now that's how to review your own record, tedious I-wanna-be-adored guitar berk!

Techno is a genre built around an inversion of the twentieth-century pop norm: a music invented by African-American men pilfering from white European music. This stunning twelve-track comp collects the best early techno tunes from The Belleville Three – students at Belleville High School near Detroit, Michigan, who began making music in their bedrooms that went on to change the nature of global dance music. Kevin Saunderson, Juan Atkins and the aforementioned 'Mayday' May took inspiration from a local radio show, Midnight Funk Association, where DJ Charles Johnson played cutting-edge funk by George Clinton and the new electro coming out of New York alongside European synth-pop – Depeche Mode, New Order, Gary Numan, Giorgio Moroder and, of course, Kraftwerk. Seen as a '90s phenomenon, it's sobering to note that Juan Atkins made techno's first record, 'Clear' by

Cybotron, in the winter of 1982. It took five years of local Detroit innovation and club activity, and some exchange with the early house music pioneers of Chicago, before Europe got to hear what these futurism-obsessed black men had done to our song.

The fizzing hi-hats, undulating synths and neo-classical motifs of techno were based on a romantic view of what these pioneers perceived Europe to be, through the records that they loved. Derrick May again: 'Perhaps I have an idealised image of Europe and its music. I have a certain way I see it in my mind. I feel I should be there. I know I'd feel right there.' I should point out here that one of the many wonderful things about this record is the sleevenotes. Journalist John McCready's essay does what the bumph on *The Immaculate Collection* has no interest in – gives a potted history of this music, puts it in context, teases out its influences. Like, did you know that 'Magic' Juan Atkins named his music techno after reading the phrase 'techno rebels' in Aaron Toffler's book *Future Shock*? Nope? McCready's essay led me to go find out, and it's joined by a set of quotes from The Belleville Three (and the set's only other featured producer Mark Kinchen, the man behind 'Seperate (sic) Minds', who insists that he would 'rather listen to computer games than any music') that feature all kinds of anger, frustration, intelligence and passion. So, apart from imploring you to track down this mood-elevating, era-defining thing, I'll leave the redoubtable Mr May to get to the core of the sadness and soul at the heart of this music. 'Why do people connect with my music? I think it's because the world has made them bitter. They have deep emotional feelings and no way of expressing them . . . They're out on the floor dancing, but in their heads they see themselves walking on clouds . . . My music makes me cry sometimes.'

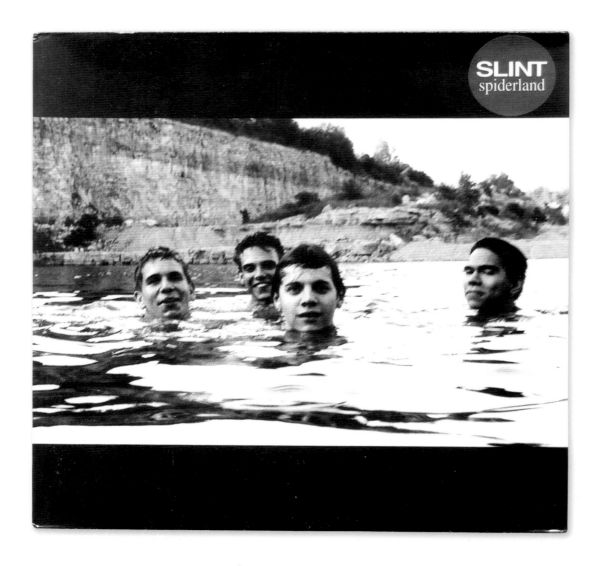

SPIDERLAND/SPLINT

SPIDERLAND

SLINT
PRODUCED BY SLINT AND BRIAN PAULSON
TOUCH & GO/MARCH 1991
UK CHART: DID NOT CHART
US CHART: DID NOT CHART
KEY TRACKS: 'Good Morning, Captain'; 'Nosferatu Man';
'Don, Aman'; 'Washer'; 'Breadcrumb Trail'

An inspired exercise in creepy cleverness, listening to *Spiderland* alone in the dark is like watching the last thirty minutes of an art-house horror movie, maybe George Sluizer's *The Vanishing* or Takashi Miike's *Audition*. You know what's coming is almost unbearable. You know you could be doing something altogether more uplifting. But you can't tear yourself away.

So legend has it, every member of Slint had to be institutionalised at various points through the recording of this massively influential six-track album. Knowing the way rumours snowball in the rock world, it all probably amounts to one of the poor waifs getting his hair-shirt stuck in the tumble-dryer, but it's a testament to the record's dark intensity that you're willing to believe the tale. Like a deathly quiet, neo-classical (again!) inversion of doomy metal bands, Louisville, Kentucky's Brian McMahan, David Pajo, Ethan Buckler and Britt Walford invented, on their two long-players, an indie mini-genre called post-rock. Bands that this much-admired album inspired include Tortoise, who have included guitarist Pajo in their line-up, and Scots Blur-botherers Mogwai.

If you've never heard Slint, imagine an insomniac American librarian reading out favourite passages from obscure novels about the sea, princesses and existentialist paranoia over a heavily concentrated blend of early Cure, Wire, Pere Ubu, Sonic Youth and a less happy My Bloody Valentine, if that last thing is remotely possible. It's the kind of stuff that generally bores me to tears, and that's my recommendation . . . it's so bleak and arty and self-conscious and miserabilist and obviously deeply suspicious of fun, yet its intensity is emotionally purging, its ability to tease new directions out of gloom-rock remarkable, and its scariness impressive, especially considering there's a really cute picture of them on the sleeve (taken by a young Will Oldham, beardy cult fans!), neck-deep in water where they look so fresh-faced you'd expect them to sound more like Haircut 100 than a Black Sabbath who are trying not to wake up the neighbours, which is how they sound, occasionally. They split up after this, ensuring that the album became an enduring art-punk legend, and one of those records that you have to like before the nerds will let you in chess club. I'm not doing much of a PR job here, am I? Really, it's brilliant, and scary and a little bit funny, in a post-'Death Disco' manner.

OUT OF TIME

R.E.M.
PRODUCED BY SCOTT LITT AND R.E.M.
WARNERS/MARCH 1991
UK CHART: 1
US CHART: 1
KEY TRACKS: 'Belong'; 'Near Wild Heaven'; 'Losing My Religion'; 'Texarkana'; 'Shiny Happy People'

There's something charmingly club-footed about R.E.M. launching their big album with a song about bad radio featuring a guest rapper, who, being a black man, can claim their moral high ground for them. KRS-One is almost as cynical about the exercise as Chuck D was on Sonic Youth's 'Kool Thing' (see p.229), but the Youth had the good grace not to try and play funk. R.E.M.'s monochrome thunking and how seriously Stipe takes this 'fun' track is the reason why they – and bands like them – become so huge. They have that middlebrow gift for making a little knowledge seem like a substantial thing.

Nevertheless, *Out Of Time* is a great album, and one of those records where you can hear the band very deliberately going for massive mainstream success, and it doesn't come off too nakedly compromised or greedy. The unsung reason why is a New Orleans string arranger and producer called Mark Bingham who, every time the band threaten to wander back into mumbly, enigmatic college rock, whatever that is, finds an Arthur Lee via Lloyd Cole orchestral bit and takes them up to the clouds again. How many lovelier male harmony pop songs have you heard, since the pomp of The Beach Boys, than 'Near Wild Heaven' and 'Belong'? Very few, and you suspect it's because R.E.M. adore a pretty melody far more than their peers, and have no indie-rock shame about it. The only puzzle about R.E.M.'s rise to superstardom is that it took them so long to step up to the plate. But then, consider the stick they took for something as pretty and direct as 'Shiny Happy People' – because, by this time, we'd all become so cynical about the popular arts that we suspected a song recorded by a 'credible' rock band for no other reason than that people might like it was obviously laughing at us. For the rest of this book, the albums that aspire to greatness are the ones that cut through this suffocating second-guessing of any genuine emotion that isn't expressed as sensationalism or melodrama.

For Michael Stipe, though, connection was the mission. If ever the way a singer sang a line changed a band's standing, then it's the way Stipe chews yet hollers the words, 'And I don't know if I can do it' on 'Losing My Religion'. Whether the song was about stardom, homosexuality, insanity or fear of commitment, that line was sung with such a heart-tugging balance between a childlike plea for help and an entirely adult knowledge of life's agonies, it opened up a hole in the radio, big enough to bathe in, warm enough to give succour to the lonely. For me, that is Stipe's great gift as a singer; the humility with which he makes an outstanding singing voice feel like the testimony of an everyman. There is almost no ego in his singing, only the desire to own the notes and the words, and to plant their roots into the ground.

At the same time as Nirvana were convincing the planet that punk rock had been pop-metal all along, R.E.M. produced a perfect adult rock, a sound steeped in American guitar-band history, but entirely lacking the Fear Of Music, smug-references element that generally holds back record-collector rock. It sounded like it had gone a few rounds with God, yet had a lack of bitterness, an energy taken from the sheer beauty of popular song. The more you go back to *Out Of Time*, the more you hear that it brought an innocence and a swing back to old-fashioned rock, and the more you understand that that couldn't fail.

BLUE LINES

MASSIVE ATTACK

PRODUCED BY MASSIVE ATTACK AND JONNY DOLLAR
WILD BUNCH/CIRCA/APRIL 1991
UK CHART: 13
US CHART: DID NOT CHART
KEY TRACKS: 'Unfinished Sympathy'; 'Daydreaming'; 'Safe From Harm'; 'Hymn Of The Big Wheel'; 'Blue Lines'

The debut from this ever-shifting Bristol collective is now part of the Classic Album pantheon. Long forgotten is the dropping of the word Attack from the band's name, due to it being seen as insensitive in the midst of the first Gulf War. Was it really only fifteen years ago that we actually noticed wars, and had sensitive feelings about them?

Opener and single 'Safe From Harm' felt like succour from Scud missile realities, while bringing hostilities into the realms of the strictly personal: 'If you hurt what's mine/I'll sure as hell retaliate,' the quivering voice of Shara Nelson sang, and although 'baby' could've been lover, it felt like the growl of a mother forming her own human shield to protect her child. This is what *Blue Lines* did, and encouraged others to do – make a warm, moody low-tempo music, all spliffy relaxation and soon-come vibe, that had teeth. Anger and paranoia bubbled closed to the surface, just like that packed basement party you go to that thrills because violence is just one misplaced look away: 'I was looking back at you to see you looking back at me . . . '

Blue Lines has a big cast who all need to be flagged up: the three permanent band members Robert '3-D' Del Naja, Andrew 'Mushroom' Vowles and Grant 'Daddy-G' Marshall, plus rapper Adrian 'Tricky' or 'Tricky Kid' Thaws, female vocalist Nelson, veteran Jamaican vocalist Horace Andy, producer Jonny Dollar, executive producer Cameron 'Booga Bear' McVey and a great many classic funk and rare groove samples. The sleeve namechecked PiL among the acknowledged influences, but, for this first album, the collective fused hip hop, reggae and rare groove, aiming for a British multi-cultural soul that stank of weed but sounded just as good on caffeine, nicotine or a pint of Scruttocks Old Dirigible. It, of course, features 'Unfinished Sympathy', a strong contender to be considered among the most perfect records ever made, a combination of fizzing portent and ringing misery, a music that weeps as it dances. Nelson pleads for an agonising romance that goes way beyond the bounds of girl-pop masochism, and Dollar's orchestra opens black holes of self-laceration. Nelson and Dollar find the centre of the universal love-pain-pleasure connection, and break us into pieces.

Massive Attack grew out of the Wild Bunch, an '80s sound system collective in Bristol that also featured a pre-Soul II Soul-producing Nellee Hooper. In that sense, the first Massive Attack album stands as a tribute to the funk, reggae and early hip hop that made them popular DJs and led to a record deal. The rap voices of 3-D, Daddy-G and Tricky gave an entirely new voice to hip hop, whispering rather than yelling, stoned and strong, British and Jamaican with no shame about the accent. Massive Attack would go on to make better records. But it's genuinely hard to imagine the last decade of worthwhile black British music without this record's singular vision.

BAZERK, BAZERK, BAZERK

SON OF BAZERK FEATURING NO SELF CONTROL AND THE BAND

PRODUCED BY HANK SHOCKLEE, KEITH SHOCKLEE AND THE BOMB SQUAD
MCA/MAY 1991
UK CHART: DID NOT CHART
US CHART: DID NOT CHART
KEY TRACKS: 'One Time For The Rebel'; 'Bang (Get Down Get Down!)'; 'Change The Style'; 'The Band Get Swivey On The Wheels'; 'J Dub's Theme'

Made from the same breadth of reference in a hip hop context as *Blue Lines*, but coming to an opposite musical conclusion, *Bazerk, Bazerk, Bazerk* remains the greatest-ever hip hop album that no one's ever heard of. Featuring Timothy 'Son Of Bazerk' Allen on lead vocals and the Public Enemy production team on an arsenal of scattershot samples, buttressed by bass, guitar and keyboards, the explosive, hilarious *Bazerk* . . . effectively forges the template for the later adventures of OutKast (see p.341 and p.363) and N*E*R*D by refusing to accept any musical boundaries whatsoever. On this record, funk crashes into Led Zeppelin riffs, which segue straight into a snatch of doo wop, which jerks into dancehall reggae, which somehow finds itself back inside early '90s hip hop noise. The whole thing comes over like relief for its genius producers – a playpen record with no political point, unless, of course, you count doing exactly what you like within any modern creative business as political, which you should. It's no surprise that the album's only boring track is 'Lifestyles Of The Blacks In The Brick' and its half-hearted attempt to be Public Enemy.

The album's dressed like James Brown's *Please Please Please* debut, all postmodern self-promotion and flash nostalgia, presenting Allen and his cohorts Daddy Rawe, Almighty Jahwell and Sandman as a dapper old-school vocal group, with a stray imaginary Shangri-La, Cassandra aka

MC Halfpint, there to provide fabulous Flavor Flav style interruptions at helium pitch. Much of the album's unique thrill is dependent on juxtaposing old-fashioned soul or reggae male vocals with a frantic, avant-funk backing, brilliantly exposing the links between the The Bomb Squad's artrock-referencing modernity, and the beautiful strangeness at the heart of soul and reggae. Each track, from the minimalist 'N-41' to the insane distillation of eclecticism that is 'Change The Style' carries the persistent thrill of being absolutely impossible to predict. Could do without some of the proto-pimp rhymes of 'What Could Be Better Bi . . . ' and 'Are You Wit Me', but when they get boorish, Bazerk and his band are overwhelmed by the astonishing leaps of compositional chutzpah from The Shocklees and Gary G-Wiz, thirty years of soul, reggae, funk, metal and avant-garde experiment compressed into thirteen shots of pop vandalism. And when Bazerk has to find a rhyme to set a track off, he does. The breakaway club hit 'J Dub's Theme' is nothing more than an old-school reggae sound system chant until Bazerk grunts his way into it – a little Bobby Byrd, a little Chuck D – and makes the whole thing surreal and serrated.

Bazerk, Bazerk, Bazerk stands at a key point in hip hop. Firstly, it's the last truly great thing that Public Enemy and The Bomb Squad were involved in. Secondly, everything about the album is confident of its success. There was a belief, after hip hop's extraordinary creative and commercial leaps of 1987–91, that this new audience would accept anything – the more left-field and self-evidently smart the better. This album bombed, like a great many records which took their cue from PE and De La Soul rather than N.W.A. and Ice-T, and we soon realised that hip hop had passed through exactly the same phase that rock had done between 1977–80 . . . A phase where everyone in the biz, the media and much of the music fanbase were too bemused by developments to demand tailor-made product. If the music changes every day, you can't define what you want because you're subconsciously aware that today's cutting-edge could be redundant tomorrow. But *Straight Outta Compton* (see

p.224) had taught a lot of young rap (and rock) fans that what they really wanted was lurid tales of black men dying and black women being abused. They also wanted this over a beat that sounds roughly the same for fifty minutes. *Son Of Bazerk* didn't stand a chance, in hindsight. If you manage to track down this long-deleted album though, you will be amazed that any record could throw so much music into a pot, and stir it with such jovial glee, until it tasted spicy and secret. Fifty million gangsta rap fans can be wrong, and usually are.

THE LOW END THEORY

A TRIBE CALLED QUEST
PRODUCED BY A TRIBE CALLED QUEST AND SKEFF ANSELM
JIVE/SEPTEMBER 1991
UK CHART: 58
US CHART: 45
KEY TRACKS: 'Check The Rhime'; 'Buggin' Out'; 'Excursions'; 'Jazz (We've Got)'; 'Scenario'

By now there was an 'urban' dance music called jungle, which was being politely re-branded 'drum 'n' bass'. But if you want drums and bass, you need to get *The Low End Theory*, the second album by Queens hip hop trio Jonathan 'Q-Tip' Davis, Malik 'Phife' Taylor and Ali Shaheed Muhammad. A dark, deep but entirely accessible exercise in giving depth to the long muzak-ified jazz-funk, it's an album of almost nothing except great rhymes over sonorous upright bass and a crackling funk drum sound. Like Massive Attack, ATCQ were interested in finding our pulse beat, connecting us up to head-nodding and hip-shaking sex-funk, much doped-up contemplation, the left-field jazz which remains a shorthand for the Afro-American arts and a 'low end' that sounds like it's straight out the jungle, just like their mentors, The Jungle Brothers (see p.209)

THE LOW END THEORY/A TRIBE CALLED QUEST

Q-Tip aka The Abstract was and is blessed with the cutest, girliest voice in rap, but escapes criticism from the immature side of the idiom by being much better than almost everyone else. Phife's jumpier, simile-stuffed, pop-referencing style was unafraid to rhyme 'thanks', 'banks' and 'Shabba Ranks', and was always the supporting act to Q-Tip's irresistible articulacy, which also, being a trebly vocal sound, cut through the bassiness of Ali Shaheed's beats. The DJ's contrast between acoustic subsonic bass, and snare drum both high in tone and volume, is still default position for all 'jazzy' hip hop bands who fancy themselves a bit right on because one of them has a beard, or something.

Of course, back in the early '90s, right-on groups would still feel it their job to wander into difficult subject matter and come out smelling of roses, even though they're knee deep in shite. I've been listening to 'The Infamous Date Rape' for fifteen years now, and still don't know what Q-Tip and Phife are getting at, so intent are they on keeping male and female fans happy. It ends with Q-Tip's foot in his mouth, trying to appease the victims of rape by saying that he understands that women feel bad once a month, you know, 'cos she has 'a bloody attitude'. Like this has anything to do with consensual sex, and . . . fuck, I don't know where to even start with this shite . . .

It was about this time, after three or four years where I listened to little else but hip hop, that I began to realise that rap wasn't going to be the benign revolution that I'd also dreamed punk would be. Man, even the right-on, boho ones with the girlie voices just became complete fucking idiots whenever trying to say anything to a woman or about a gay man (no one in hip hop ever talks to a gay man). It became kind of . . . dispiriting. I refuse to believe that black men are more bigoted than white men. That just doesn't make any historical or geo-political sense. I realised that hip hop's worst crime wasn't violence or sexism or greed per se. It was that it lied about what black men were and how they felt, because it wanted to present sensation as truth. Sensation isn't truth. It's showing your willie at a bus stop.

Not sure why that all turned up in a Tribe Called Quest review, of all groups. 'The Infamous Date Rape' just annoys me. The rest of this album is one of hip hop's deepest hits.

1992

CYPRESS HILL/CYPRESS HILL

CYPRESS HILL

CYPRESS HILL
PRODUCED BY DJ MUGGS
RUFFHOUSE/COLUMBIA/JANUARY 1992
UK CHART: DID NOT CHART
US CHART: 31
KEY TRACKS: 'Hand On The Pump'; 'How I Could Just Kill A
Man'; 'The Phunky Feel One'; 'Pigs'; 'Hole In The Head'

So having got on my big fat high white liberal horse over A Tribe Called Quest, I'm now gonna wax lyrical about the most stupid, irresponsible and cynically childish album in hip hop history. Oh, OK, no it isn't. But it comes off like it straight after ATCQ's jazzy Afrocentrism.

Other people's musical guilty pleasures appear to involve going to discos to dance to 'The Pina Colada Song'. My guilty pleasure is the debut album by Louis 'B-Real' Freese, Senen 'Sen Dog' Reyes and Lawrence 'DJ Muggs' Muggerud, out of Cypress Hill, Los Angeles. Fifty minutes of claustrophobic dope, guns and fighting in the streets, it's the ultimate explanation of why hip hop became the most popular music in the world by embracing directionless violence. For the same reasons that boys who know better will always tell you that the best gangster movie is *The Godfather* or *GoodFellas* or *Little Caesar*, when they actually get the greatest pleasure from watching a wildly mugging Al Pacino holding an enormous machine-gun like a giant penis and screaming, 'SAY 'ELLO TO MY LEEDLE FRIEND!' in Brian De Palma's gaudily immoral remake of *Scarface*, a group such as Cypress Hill sound not like incitement nor shock, but absolute escapism, the post-toddler equivalent of all those Sam Peckinpah slow-motion carnage moments that small boys have together in play before they realise that there are more . . . uhh . . . moist things to do with all that testosterone.

The sound hinges on three men doing three very specific things over and over again. DJ Muggs makes a music that crosses the dope-smoking treacle claustrophobia of EPMD with Public Enemy's rock 'n' roll intensity by taking '60s soul and R&B guitar riffs and drum breaks, cutting them into fragments of screech, drone or twang, and then forcing them into a sonic box as small and intense as Speedy Gonzales. Speaking of which, the second element depends on rapper B-Real, and a high-pitched cartoon whine that pulls all those baby faced killer rabbits out of old film noir hats, a voice that laughs at mayhem. The third element belongs to Sen Dog, who occasionally repeats the hookline of a tune like an animated dawg. That's it. It's fucking awesome, too.

And what makes the first album so much better than the twelve-teen dozen identical albums they've made since, as they famously wowed the rap-metal crossover crowd, with their skateboards, big shorts and goatees, is that Cypress Hill has a semblance of a point, and it's contained within just a few lines from two of the best songs. The opener 'Pigs' is Cypress's anti-cop song, de rigeur for rap artistes since the success of N.W.A.'s 'Fuck Tha Police', about to head into proper grown-up trouble with the furore surrounding 'Cop Killer' by Body Count (see p.249-50). 'Pigs' is pure come-and-have-a-go taunt, but there is real anger at the L.A.P.D. here, and you can feel B-Real's contempt when he spits, 'This pig's steady eating doughnuts while some motherfucker's out robbing your home,' a nod to Public Enemy's '911 Is A Joke', a thrust in the direction of everyday black and Latin (and, in the case of the mixed-race Cypress Hill, both, in America, are just 'niggas') realities in ghetto America.

But one of my favourite verses in hip hop is unleashed by B-Real within 'How I Could Just Kill A Man', one of a choice few violent rap lyrics both written and performed with such skill and power that you understand, immediately, that this is American folk song, the blues, the place in working-class folk art where myth and reality collide, and become reportage built to last. B-Real stops bragging about his murderous abilities for a few seconds, and, well aware that it's middle-class kids who are set to make this music a license to print money, and also aware of the pressures constantly put on black public figures to set a good example (or else), asks us to put ourselves in his place. 'Say some punk tried to get you for your auto/Would you call it one time and play the role model?/No! I think you'll play like a thug.' More gunplay, linguistic and rhythmic fun with magnums and gats, before: 'How do you know where I'm at/When you haven't been where I've been . . . understand where I'm coming from?/While you're up on the hill in your big home/I'm out here risking my dome . . . Just to stay alive, Yo!/I got to say fuck it!/Here is something you can't understand/How I could just kill a man.'

Admittedly, it ain't as good written down as it sounds when that sick, twisted voice hits Muggs's wailing, siren guitar. But it's the reason why gangsta rap exists, why new British acts such as Plan B and Eighteen 18 are reviving the genre for twenty-first-century English realities, and why the colour of the rapper is becoming ever less important. Rap said lines like the lines above, for an underclass that rock – even punk – had long abandoned. And even though that's meant a whole lot of lies and misanthropy for rap profit, someone still has to speak up for those we find unspeakable. What hip hop taught us, like no other music, is that, if you get this stuff right, it's just the most thrilling noise you can make. And those who can't discern between the good and the bad, who simply react against all of it in self-righteous ignorance, are just hiding their cowardice behind fake liberalism.

Cypress Hill, meanwhile, were never that great after this. But I can forgive much of a group who chanted, like playground warriors, 'I'm heading up the river in a boat with no paddle,' and put every doomed gangster in your head, all those unrepentant tough guys, all like Humphrey Bogart's Roy Earle, from *High Sierra*, 'just rushing toward death'.

DIVINE MADNESS

MADNESS
PRODUCED BY CLIVE LANGER AND ALAN WINSTANLEY
VIRGIN/FEBRUARY 1992
UK CHART: 1
US CHART: DID NOT CHART
KEY TRACKS: 'Embarrassment'; 'My Girl'; 'Our House'; 'House Of Fun'; 'Yesterday's Men'

One of the best things about constructing a book chronologically and including Greatest Hits albums is the complete change of mood a treasure like this provides. Madness made some good albums, but a compilation of singles is where they're at, and this kind, friendly pop provides a welcome contrast from all those sweary rap fellers and their dense sonic collages. The British public appeared to agree in '92, when, a good eight years after the Camden Town crew's sales began to dip, and six after Madness split, they upped and made this collection of all the singles No. 1, and the kind of hardy Best Of perennial that sticks around long enough to be reissued in 2005 with a DVD of all those much-loved promos.

I think what strikes hardest now about Madness is the musicianship. Punk's non-musician attitude had an effect on the way all its fellow travellers were perceived, and there were never too many words wasted on this band's mastery of ska, reggae, soul, jazz and '60s beat pop. Every pop git did a Motown tribute song in the early '80s, but no one captured the rhythms, but reinvented the feel, in the way that Madness did on the immortal 'Embarrassment'.

Of course, 'Embarrassment' was about something important – about a mixed-race couple and the enduring horror, for some, at the prospect of a mixed-race baby. By the time *Divine Madness* was around, 'Embarrassment' felt like a song about the distant past. The 2-Tone vibe had been absorbed into the mainstream of pop culture, with even the most defiantly black element of music, hip hop, already broad enough to encompass a group as 2-Tone, in every department, as Massive Attack. Madness, I think, were key in this, even though, unlike The Beat or the Specials, they didn't have any black band members. The left-liberalism of the band's themes gelled beautifully with a working-class past – music hall, the swing-derived dance band, kitchen-sink drama, the first skinheads' love of ska – and helped modernise the unreconstructed British male. This isn't to say that racism has disappeared – just pick up today's paper and I'm sure you'll find proof that its alive and kicking. Merely that the Britain I grew up in was jammed full of racist meatheads and hate criminals, largely tolerated by the establishment as long as they just kicked the shit out of young gig-goers and clubbers, and left the adult world of 'tolerance' well alone. I've always hated that word 'tolerance' when applied to race. What have groups of powerless people of a different culture done to you, exactly, that you must force yourself to 'tolerate'?

Madness's songs spoke of a gentler world where fun could still be had, and were deft enough to be musically nostalgic and thematically progressive simultaneously. It's a wonderful (but unsurprising) thing that their pop outlived the diseased sub-skinhead culture that tried to attach itself to them. The disquiet that runs from the surprisingly depressive likes of 'Grey Day' and 'Tomorrow's Just Another Day', through later, much under-rated singles such as 'Yesterday's Men', '(Waiting For The) Ghost Train' and 'One Better Day', was the necessary balance to the circus knees-ups their music invoked. Suggs's grin was always a sarcastic grimace, the legendary jolly japes in the videos always undercut by the feeling that they were forced. This is why Britain loved them: they were how we like to see ourselves. They were stoical. All the time, you knew that an enormous sadness at the state of the world infused every note of the group's best pop, but they literally grin, and bear it. Played one after another, these twenty-two hits contain the nearest our generation needs to get to the spirit of the Blitz. Still,

mustn't grumble, and you don't have to be mad to work here, but . . .

BODY COUNT

BODY COUNT
PRODUCED BY ICE-T AND ERNIE C
SIRE/MARCH 1992
UK CHART: 26
US CHART: DID NOT CHART
KEY TRACKS: 'Body Count'; 'KKK Bitch'; 'Cop Killer'; 'There Goes The Neighbourhood'; 'Momma's Gotta Die Tonight'

. . . I'm mad as hell and I'm not gonna take it anymore. At least, that's what LA's very own Ice Muthafuckin' T wanted you to think when he came up with the wizard wheeze of forming an all-black heavy metal band and making a single

called 'Cop Killer'. Old Tracy Marrow was and is a hustling kind of guy, and who knows whether this was sheer cynicism or reckless protest against the pictures of Rodney King being beaten by police, and background for the riots that followed. But our hero was soon getting death threats. His family, too. And staff at Warner Brothers records, who owned his Sire label. He withdrew the offending track from both single and album, and left Sire soon afterwards. His credibility among 'hardcore' hip hop fans never recovered. Perhaps the mistake was sneering, towards the end of 'Cop Killer', 'Don't be a pussy . . . Have some muthafuckin' courage.'

So why did 'Cop Killer' cop all the flak from the LAPD, Charlton Heston, the Parents, Music Resource Center, etc, rather than N.W.A.'s 'Fuck Tha Police', Cypress Hill's 'Pigs' or KRS-One's 'Sound Of Da Police'? Ice's theory, I think we can safely assume from *Body Count*, his interviews and the following *Home Invasion* album, was that when Ice-T made rock music, the establishment suddenly realised that it was their very own corn-fed darlings who were gleefully listening to this gangsta stuff. This may seem ridiculous to you, considering how infamous N.W.A. were at the end of the '80s. But the American right believe in the colour bar in a way that we Brits just don't. One suspects they were as pissed off with him playing their good ol' boy metal as they were at him hollering, 'I'm 'bout to dust some cops off' and 'I know your family's grievin' – Fuck 'em!'

So far, so sensational. But believe me, the first Body Count album is not waving its willie around at a bus-stop. It's the best punk-metal album of the early '90s bar none.

If you're someone who keeps up with hard rock, you'll know Rage Against The Machine and System Of A Down (see p.348), and how their punk, rap and world music-informed riffage has made metal a music of protest, of one sort or another, in the twenty-first century. When *Body Count* came out, metal was Guns 'N' Roses and silly poodles with trust-fund drug habits. Marrow understood both the inherent comedy in the doomy side of metal and the aggression politics in the hardcore end of punk. He understood absolutely

that gangsta rap had quickly come to be black pop's first taste of the profits available from boys who like rude things. He also loved Bad Brains (see p.195). So he shoved punk, metal and rap together, inventing the next fifteen years of US stadium rock/rap crossover, and delivered the political side with the bad taste wind-up attitude of an Alice Cooper, predicting the coming of Marilyn Manson and Eminem.

On 'KKK Bitch', where Ice satirises rap misogyny and the extreme right by imagining he and his band fucking Nazis' daughters at Klan rallies ('We show them how to really work the white sheets'), he finds an appropriately stupid music and scenario to ridicule the stupidest people on the planet. As a genuinely shocking balance, 'Momma's Gotta Die Tonight' sees Ice's character recognise that his black mother is racist. So he sets fire to her. No one believed – or cared – that Ice or his fans really wanted to set fire to black women who didn't like whites and Koreans. But, in the wake of the LA riots, some very powerful people understood how useful it would be to take Ice's cartoon lyrics out of context, and distract from the obvious everyday brutality of sections of America's police force by convincing parents that their child wanted to be a big black man with a big black gun, just indiscriminately taking out cops. And it worked.

All I can say in Ice-T's defence – because the lyrics and the style of music did give the media far too many easy targets – is that Body Count is up there with the Led Zeps and Sabbaffs, metal-wise, as far as I'm concerned. Mainly 'cos Ice-T is very, very funny, brave as hell, and his attitude to that ever-present fear of a black planet spot on. Watch out for the drum solo, though.

COPPER BLUE

SUGAR
PRODUCED BY BOB MOULD AND LOU GIORDANO
CREATION/SEPTEMBER 1992
UK CHART: 10

US CHART: DID NOT CHART
KEY TRACKS: 'Changes'; 'The Act We Act'; 'A Good Idea';
'Fortune Teller'; 'The Slim'

The Mould for all those post-Green Day 'punk' records. Sure, don't blame you if you'd like to move on at that point, but the odd thing is that it was contrived by a man so bleak and grim that his previous album was called *Black Sheets Of Rain*. A major label gave Bob Mould money for that. Then he left Virgin for our own, at that point unsullied indie, Creation, and decided to make the power-pop record that the legendary Hüsker Dü had always threatened to, but hated each other/themselves/pop music too much to get around to. Fifteen months after this first Sugar album came out, Green Day remade it with all the interesting bits sucked out by a big corporate sucking machine and called it *Dookie*, and the rest is a legion of spotty middle-class Yanks called

Son Of Geek or Bad Daphne or Gurls Smell or whatever who now define what most of the planet knows as punk rock. Ho bloody hum.

Copper Blue didn't need a huge adjustment from the old Hüsker Dü model to score a surprise Brit hit, in the grunge hangover years before Britpop. Mould just made his guitars beefier, hired solid sidemen in Dave Barbe (bass) and Malcolm Travis (drums) who wouldn't complain about the endless overdubbed riffage, and slowed down just enough to take the whiff of hardcore punk away. What emerged was one of those rock albums that's just . . . satisfying. It does all the right, Beatles-meets-Pistols things in all the right places, and if you're thinking, hang on, that description could easily be applied to those Oasis chappies, well . . . let's just say that McGee and Creation's flights of fancy with the likes of My Bloody Valentine and Primal Scream almost bankrupted the label, whereas Mould appeared to walk across the Atlantic, plug in, and make a profitable hit unadorned by even a hint of self-indulgence. So sure, Oasis sounded like The Beatles and the Pistols and T.Rex. But they also sounded more than a little like Creation's one pre-Oasis straight-ahead rock hit. Funny no one mentioned it at the time. Didn't fit into the whole 'Brit' marketing thing that we rock journalists like to convince you that we're not a part of, one supposes.

Anyway, if you haven't heard this record, but have a soft spot for either Oasis or Blink 182, you'll find plenty to love in *Copper Blue*, and be made to believe that there is a link between these two basic forms of modern rock.

The lyrics? Oh man. Completely depressing. And not terribly good. Luckily, Bob Mould has a fabulous singing voice and an amp he can turn right up to eleven.

HOLLYWOOD TOWN HALL

THE JAYHAWKS
PRODUCED BY GEORGE DRAKOULIAS
DEF AMERICAN/SEPTEMBER 1992

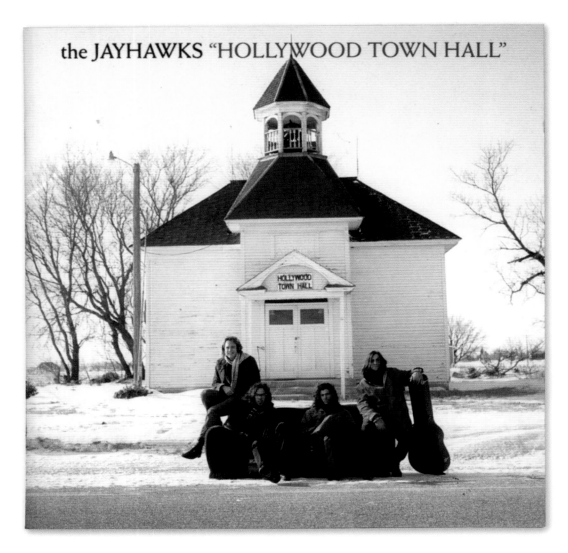

the JAYHAWKS "HOLLYWOOD TOWN HALL"

HOLLYWOOD
TOWN HALL

HOLLYWOOD TOWN HALL/THE JAYHAWKS

UK CHART: DID NOT CHART
US CHART: DID NOT CHART
KEY TRACKS: 'Crowded In The Wings'; 'Take Me With You
(When You Go)'; 'Settled Down Like Rain'; 'Wichita'; 'Nevada,
California'

Throughout the '80s, a revisionist country-rock revival grew in America. Labelled cow-punk, then alt-country, then No Depression after a fanzine named in tribute of a 1990 album by key group Uncle Tupelo, finally the press and record shops seem to have settled on Americana, a name that suggests that hip hop and house music aren't made by real Americans, but . . . it makes its point. Americana is music that wears a plaid shirt and its hair long, and aspires to the 'cosmic American music' of solo Gram Parsons, and his work with The Flying Burrito Brothers and The Byrds.

Much Americana smacks of a student-friendly, cool re-branding of sexless, stodgy old dadrock . . . the Yank variety. But there were exceptions, and the best of these is *Hollywood Town Hall*, the third album by The Jayhawks, a Minneapolis bar-band who became more than that, due to the natural high harmonies and twanging twin guitars of leaders Mark Olson and Gary Louris.

Producer George Drakoulias was proving a dab hand at retro-rock with The Black Crowes, and *Hollywood Town Hall* is an unashamed throwback to the late '60s – a beefed-up but rugged enough amalgam of Dylan, Neil Young, the Stones (onetime Stones pianist/organist Nicky Hopkins was the star guest here) and the aforementioned tragic rock Godhead Parsons. There was almost certainly a cynicism here, which is probably why the sweet-voiced Olson quit to make DIY country in the desert with his wife, Victoria Williams, whose multiple sclerosis has prevented them both from touring the world. Louris and various Jayhawks continued, rather anonymously, with their connection to the country-rock soil apparently severed. Meanwhile, this beautiful record exists to delight all those of us who can't resist beardy boys who harmonise as if joined at the heart, and guitars that jangle, and keys that go all minor just as everything's getting too jaunty, and words that mean little written down but seem to all be looking death in the face and waving loved ones a tortured farewell, when borne on those harmonies. But 'Clouds' seemed to say something real, about what this new form of country-rock tries to say and why it never goes away: 'God of the rich man ain't the God for the poor/Autumn ending the state hospital is closed/And wouldn't you know/Winos and office girls in the park . . . Can your diamonds talk to you?' As pleas for economic justice go, that sure is a purrty one.

AUTOMATIC FOR THE PEOPLE

R.E.M.
PRODUCED BY SCOTT LITT AND R.E.M.
WARNERS/OCTOBER 1992
UK CHART: 1
US CHART: 2
KEY TRACKS: 'The Sidewinder Sleeps Tonight'; 'Everybody Hurts'; 'Drive'; 'Ignoreland'; 'Find The River'

It really was all fields around here in 1992. All these sensible, square-jawed rockers, trying their best to provide some pastoral respite from urban music's relentless . . . urbanness. Aww, maybe Stipey, like Bob Mould, isn't that square-jawed. Which does remind me: why did he take so long to come out?

R.E.M.'s *Big Kahuna* album begins with the saddest song yet written about rock 'n' roll rebellion. 'Drive' is 'Smells Like Teen Spirit' with the irony turned off and no place given to release the misery. America's being 'bushwhacked', Oliver 'Ollie' North gets off free, and the kids are convincing themselves that they're free, largely because they can go to rock shows. No one has ever sung the word 'baby' with so much resigned pessimism, in what is yet another Stipe vocal masterclass. Stipe may not have had much courage in the sexuality stakes, but R.E.M. released this eerie dirge as a single, believing that their audience wasn't waiting for any more 'Shiny Happy People's. Which was the kind of brave thing a band does when they know it's their time, and they can do no wrong.

Automatic For The People is the album the word 'moody' was invented for. A sadness pervades, and even the japery of 'The Sidewinder Sleeps Tonite' plays with its quote from 'The Lion Sleeps Tonight' by allowing Stipe to unleash one of the most startling howls this side of Diamanda Galas. By now, mandolins, accordions and pianos have become every bit as vital to the R.E.M. muse as Buck's rock-historical guitar jangles, and the likes of 'Monty Got A Raw Deal' and 'Ignoreland' sound, as songs and performances, like ancient treasures unearthed, a world away from the generic rock of a musically barren time. 'Ignoreland', particularly, is a fascinating attempt to write a different kind of protest song – one that simply flags up the frustration without pretending that the singer has a solution for you. The early verses rant with vivid rage at the Reagan presidential campaign of 1979, before Stipe takes a deep breath and sings, 'If they weren't there we would have created them/Maybe, it's true/But I'm resentful all the same/Someone's got to take the blame/I know that this is vitriol/No solution, spleen-venting/But I feel better having screamed – Don't you?' That would be the nub of the crux of ye olde protest rock, but Mr Stipe is still being sly. He doesn't scream. We don't scream to R.E.M. He, and we, don't feel better at all. As for that coming out query, 'Monty Got A Raw Deal' is Stipe's obvious stab at comparing himself with Montgomery Clift, the screwed-up '50s movie icon who tried to keep his homosexuality a secret, and failed miserably. No wonder he's so elegiac about a simpler past, as he so gently is on 'Nightswimming'.

But 'Everybody Hurts' remains the heart of this record, and from its stoicism, four guys made a record that felt like it was on everyone's side, and that there was a morality, a good that's better than bad, and that one didn't have to scream about it when you were sure. *Automatic For The People* shows its listeners a lot of love. I'm not sure how much more you can achieve, in a material pop world.

1993

THE CHRONIC

DR. DRE

PRODUCED BY DR. DRE
DEATH ROW/INTERSCOPE/FEBRUARY 1993
UK CHART: DID NOT CHART
US CHART: 3
KEY TRACKS: 'Let Me Ride'; 'Nuthin' But A 'G' Thang'; 'Wit
Dre Day (And Everybody's Celebratin')'; 'Lil' Ghetto Boy';
'Deeez Nuuuts'

Kicking off with N.W.A. producer Dre's new protégé Snoop
Doggy Dogg insulting Dre's former bandmates and label by
way of his trademark bizzle fo' shizzle wordplay, *The Chronic*
was so irresistible it killed hip hop as a subversive mainstream
art form. Celebrating the most damaging stereotypes of black
men, glorying in a view of black women as whores to be
pimped, inviting the whole planet out for a gunfight at the

Compton corral, *The Chronic* took gangsta from a blaxploitation gimmick to rap's commercial default position in the time
it took to establish its first laconic bassline. Based sonically
around the catchiest hooks and sleaziest rhythms of George
Clinton's Parliament and Funkadelic, Andre Young trumped
what De La Soul and EPMD had done with P-funk by
stripping everything down to basics, mixing classic samples
with 'interpolations' played by musicians in the studio. It prevented the low-tempo rhythms from becoming bland, and
meant giving away less of the booty. Speaking of which, a skit
such as 'The Doctor's Office' (a woman begs for her appoint-
ment with Dre the shag doctor) was ridiculous enough to
convince floating liberal voters that it was all self-parody. No
one buys records that make them feel guilty. The success of
the tactic set the scene for the chauvinistic sigh of relief that
was 'New Lad' culture, and your local newsagent selling
demeaning images of women just above *The Beano*.

Whereas Cypress Hill presented LA street life as a *Boy's
Own* nightmare from a noir western, Dre took their obsession with 'chronic' weed, guns and gang warfare and made it
erotic and aspirational. If Cypress were 'heading up a river
with a boat and no paddle', Dre and Snoop were cruising
along the bank in a gleaming jeep, doing that weird bouncing thing with the suspension, pissed and stoned and convincing otherwise sensible women to switch off their feminist sensibilities and take a ride with the superbaaad black
men their mommas warned them about. By now, those of us
attracted to hip hop for its anti-establishment reportage
qualities were wincing at the homophobia and misogyny,
but resigning ourselves to Dre's mastery of deep funk, a
noise so seductive it made all musical competition sound
castrated and uptight. Hip hop's leftist revolutionary qualities were reduced to a chalk drawing on the sidewalk.

Snoop escaped a murder rap, dropped the Doggy, and
became more loved – by women as much, if not more, than
men – the more he played the amoral pimp. Give or take the
odd Fugee or Black Eyed Pea, Dre and Snoop proved there was
no profit in reviving a gospel-derived, Civil Rights-era morality

for the rap age. As another Los Angeles resident once sang it, in what seemed like ancient punk history . . . all crimes are paid.

MODERN LIFE IS RUBBISH

BLUR
PRODUCED BY STEPHEN STREET, STEVE LOVELL, BLUR AND JOHN SMITH
FOOD/MAY 1993
UK CHART: 15
US CHART: DID NOT CHART
KEY TRACKS: 'For Tomorrow'; 'Starshaped'; 'Miss America'; 'Chemical World'; 'Blue Jeans'

What we'd been waiting for.

It was only when you heard the second Blur album, with its edge and melody and sharpness, that you remembered how much you missed British guitar pop. Yep, there'd been plenty of British guitar rock since the split of The Smiths. But *Modern Life* . . . grabbed energy and innovation from post-punk, and, as Franz Ferdinand, Kaiser Chiefs etc have since proved, post-punk was a pop impulse, an attempt to realign the electric guitar and pop's cutting edge and find the spirit – not the sound – of mid-'60s Beatles, Stones, Who, Kinks, Syd Barrett-era Pink Floyd, as well as the key US alternatives within The Velvet Underground, Love and Captain Beefheart. The idea was simply that, if Beefheart and Barrett were ahead of their time, then it was high time to find out if time had caught up. Blur did the same for the late '70s. *Modern Life Is Rubbish* should've been subtitled 'Like The '80s Never Happened'.

At least, that would've worked for the music, brilliantly crafted from stray bits of XTC, The Kinks, Syd Barrett, The Teardrop Explodes, Wire and Bowie. But this album attempted to take on the weight of the '80s, and the consumer culture it had established, and all those of us who'd tried to buy in and found that our lives were no different to the rebellious wage-slaves in all those Angry Young Novels from the rationing

years. *Modern Life* . . . could've been 'Billy Liar – The Musical', so vividly did it capture the frustration of the ordinary man, and the stuff we cling onto when hope is draining away. The sleeve's gift shop paintings of a steam train and the band themselves further established Blur as a lost gang of mods, hatching their refusenik plots over cups of sugary tea in rural Places Of Interest. Of course, they were all just taking Class A drugs and becoming alcoholics in Camden. But the sugary tea-mod thing was much more loveable.

It also takes putting on this sepia-tinted, suited and booted album again to see how it enabled pretty much all the guitar pop we're listening to in 2006. Damon Albarn reclaimed the right to sing in his own English lower middle-class accent, and Graham Coxon reclaimed the right for guitars to do the unexpected, and scrape away at the surface of a pop song. It took a decade and the false start that was Britpop for British pop musicians to get it. But now they have, *Modern Life* . . . sounds like all those indie things' best ideas squared.

The record even found time for an intermission, two-and-a-half minutes of nightmare circus waltz, a prophecy of *The League Of Gentlemen*. A track such as 'Oily Water' gave Dave Rowntree and Alex James the space to relocate the dub-funk rhythms of post-punk and, in return, the drummer and the bassist gave Albarn space to learn to sing. Because, even though that bluff yap was needed at the time – especially with that yelping berk Brett Anderson around – it took years of great records before Damon realised what his voice was, and to free himself from a self-imposed Essex Boy tone that began to grate. 'Turn It Up' seemed beamed from another band in another country at another time, a top youth-club pop tune that felt almost embarrassed to be so simple.

But some of the most exciting albums – *Fear Of Music*, *Heaven Up Here*, *The Clash*, the first Love album, Van Morrison's *TB Sheets*, off the top of my head – are made by bands that are obviously a work-in-progress, who haven't learned too much yet. The coming *Parklife* may be a more complete musical and thematic record, but *Modern Life . . .* is one of those albums that never quite unpeels all its layers, and where the tension between Coxon's love of frazzled indie-punk and Damon's early desire to be a more commercial Andy Partridge is at its most precariously and enjoyably balanced.

And the double-edged title was right, too. Still is.

DEBUT

BJÖRK
PRODUCED BY NELLEE HOOPER AND BJÖRK
ONE LITTLE INDIAN/JULY 1993
UK CHART: 3
US CHART: 61
KEY TRACKS: 'Venus As A Boy'; 'Violently Happy'; 'Come To Me'; 'Human Behaviour'; 'Big Time Sensuality'

Some didn't agree. For Björk Gudmundsdottir, former lead singer of wacky Icelandic indie-popsters The Sugarcubes, modern life meant modern machines, machines that liberated visionary female singers from having to arse around with drummers and shouty blokes. Cue phase two of the retooling of adult-pop, following Massive Attack's *Blue Lines*, with more Bristol disco science courtesy of former Wild Bunch member and Soul II Soul producer Nellee Hooper. He and Björk decided to make an album that evoked seventeen types of joy. Maybe eighteen. Who's counting?

Björk also made it easy for we journalists. One of the tracks is called 'Big Time Sensuality' and that is what *Debut* is about. Having, like so many British-based musicians, had her life changed by the club scene, Björk sets out to find that big ol' ecstasy buzz and make it intimate, dragging it away from the communal to the sexual and romantic. Exhibit one: 'Venus As A Boy'. A contender for the most beautiful thing ever made by human hand and voice.

I think it's high time we reclaimed the word 'beautiful', you know? It's like, last night – it's a digression, but stick with me – I was watching *ER*, of all things, and the last poignant image was soundtracked by 'Beautiful' by James Blunt. Now, setting aside the potential for obvious rhyming-slang fun – what the fugg is every fugging fugger doing? Why are people playing, buying, supporting this farrago of pish? Do people not see the ugliness inherent within the terminally banal? Do they not feel chunks of their soul being chipped away by the faux-innocence of this mewling ponce's egregious screech? If they don't, then . . . I just want to play them 'Venus As A Boy' and see if it won't wash their brains, like an Icelandic pixie baptism under torrents of fragrant lady ju . . . you see where I'm going here. Ahem. But people are largely unhappy in this world and I don't understand why they can't see the correlation between their fear and despair, and listening to James Blunt. They need 'Venus As A Boy'. On the NHS. Now. It will save millions in the long-run.

MIDNIGHT MARAUDERS

A TRIBE CALLED QUEST

BJÖRK/DEBUT

PRODUCED BY A TRIBE CALLED QUEST
JIVE/OCTOBER 1993
UK CHART: 70
US CHART: 8
KEY TRACKS: 'Oh My God'; 'Electric Relaxation'; 'Award Tour'; 'Sucka Nigga'; 'Clap Your Hands'

As much unlike your Cypress Hills and Dr. Dres as they could get without taking up the fiddle and banjo, Queens' finest purveyors of jazz-inflected hip hop made a third album masterpiece which bravely went against the prevailing antagonistic hip hop wind. Housed in a sleeve that featured just about anyone who was and had been anyone in hip-hop wearing headphones and looking relatively happy, ATCQ's idea of marauding revolved around making late night grooves for music lovers . . . and lovers who like to do it to music. The drums cracked, the bass boomed, and Q-Tip, Phife, and Ali Shaheed held up hip hop's soulful end by making a tough record without insulting anyone, and a sweet record without ingratiating themselves. As hip hop became huge enough to support an underground as well as a mainstream, it was Quest, along with a resurgent Beastie Boys, who gave that underground its shape and attitude: an understanding that battle-rhyme culture was about speed of thought rather than size of weapon, a template for musicality that didn't depend on sampling familiar hooklines, a way of discussing sex that neither dehumanised nor patronised women. That's a really long way of saying that I love this group, and that their split in 1998 after five intelligent yet vibrantly funky albums has not changed the fact that they probably just edge out Public Enemy as the greatest rap group of all time, on the grounds of versatility and come-hither vibes.

Q-Tip even found time and space to write the best recorded contribution to the debate around hip hop's controversial and constant use of the word 'nigger' (you can put an 'a' at the end of anything: it still is what it is). 'Sucka Nigga' puts both sides of the argument within a few lines.

This time I just have to let these lines stand alone, and explain themselves:

> See, nigga first was used down in the Deep South
> Fallin' out between the dome of the white man's mouth
> It means that we will never grow, you know the word dummy
> Other niggas in the community think that it's crummy
> But I don't, neither does the youth cause we
> Embrace adversity it goes right with the race
> Yo, I start to flinch as I try not to say it
> But my lips is like the oowop as I start to spray it

His lips is like the 'oowop'. The man takes it right back to the bebop, because that's where this reclamation of hate language began. The same song ended with a robotic female voice intoning: 'You're not any less of a man if you don't pull the trigger. You're not necessarily a man if you do.' *Midnight Marauders* is the essence of sweet reason.

1994

VAUXHALL AND I

MORRISSEY
PRODUCED BY STEVE LILLYWHITE
PARLOPHONE/MARCH 1994
UK CHART: 1
US CHART: 18
KEY TRACKS: 'The More You Ignore Me, The Closer I Get'; 'I Am Hated For Loving'; 'Hold On To Your Friends'; 'Now My Heart Is Full'; 'Speedway'

A love letter to his own persecution complex, Morrissey invokes the works of Graham Greene ('Now My Heart Is Full') and Herman Melville ('Billy Budd') to give his fourth solo album proper some serious Judy Garland melodrama, informing us that 'I Am Hated For Loving'. Still, if the references to 'twelve years' in 'Billy Budd' are still mourning the death of his partnership with Johnny Marr, it can't be coincidence that the most Smiths-like of his solo songs advises us to 'Hold On To Your Friends'.

By this time, the various 'Is Moz a racist?' furores surrounding comments about reggae and black bands on *Top Of The Pops*, the attempts to take on British race relations both past and contemporary in 'Bengali In Platforms', 'Asian Rut' and 'The National Front Disco', and wrapping himself with a Union Jack as skinhead dickheads didn't know whether to riot or cheer while supporting Madness at a 1993 show at Finsbury Park, had made Morrissey a figure of abuse in the music press that had helped make him an '80s icon. So, even though Moz had more claim than most to be the very essence of the burgeoning Britpop scene, he became Banquo's ghost at the English guitar revival feast. He hired a former rockabilly revival act The Polecats to be his backing band and fellow songwriters. He hired quintessential '80s rock producer Steve Lillywhite. He wrote songs that all seemed to look with endless self-pity at his court battles with his fellow Smiths and his treatment at the hands of the *NME*. And, bizarrely, the album went to No. 1 – as the music press world I'd only just entered did its best to ignore it, the closer it got. I'd just begun writing about music, largely hip hop and the whole acid jazz/trip hop thing, so no one was asking me to write about Mozzer, in defence or condemnation. Good job, too. I was bemused by the whole affair, and still am.

What hindsight allows is the acknowledgement of a beautiful forty minutes about feeling ostracised, misunderstood, alone. 'Don't rake up my mistakes', he crooned with an offhand majesty on 'Why Don't You Find Out For Yourself', 'I know exactly what they are.' But Vauxhall And I was fundamentally resigned rather than defiant, and elegantly embarked on the commercial and critical decline that suddenly ended with 2004's *You Are The Quarry*, as we ended his incredibly strange exile as a superstar in Mexico, of all lazy sunbathing places, by realising that we missed singers who looked good, and gave good interviews, and wrote great lyrics and behaved like stars are supposed to do, and stopped self-righteously accusing him for all the dark dislike of black people that permeates our culture in our cake-and-eat-it England. The final 'Speedway' with its barely bearable list of accusations and bitter self-references, was a fitting temporary goodbye, as the Britpop era made it as clear as it could that 'Brit' meant white, and that that was something to be celebrated. Really, grab a listen to, say, 'Asian Rut' from 1991's *Kill Uncle* again ('I'm just passing through here/On my way to somewhere civilised') and tell me that Moz didn't see that coming, and wasn't right – and proudly anti-racist – all along.

PARKLIFE

BLUR
PRODUCED BY STEPHEN STREET ('TO THE END' PRODUCED BY STEPHEN HAGUE, JOHN SMITH AND BLUR)
FOOD/APRIL 1994
UK CHART: 1

US CHART: DID NOT CHART
KEY TRACKS: 'This Is A Low'; 'Girls & Boys'; 'Tracy Jacks';
'Badhead'; 'Parklife'

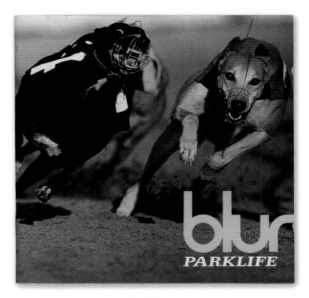

Meanwhile, Morrissey's former collaborator Stephen Street produced the album that kick-started a new era. From now on, there was no such thing as British alternative music: every punk/indie/art-rock/alt-pop band had to go platinum, or piss off back to the office . . . or the Trust Fund, increasingly. None of this was Blur's fault, though. They just did the overdue right thing and made an album about a Britain that had gone to the dogs.

Parklife is a whole set of pop culture dots that were just waiting to be connected. It's quite a list. Here goes.

Since the '60s, there was a class somewhere between working and middle, but that didn't mean we were, as John Major had it, 'a classless society'. We were increasingly lacking in class, though, and pop should be able to look at those facts, and critique. Those of us who had hip hopped and raved didn't necessarily hate guitar pop. We were just happy to be at a disco until someone found the instruction manual for how to do it properly. There was a line of typically English pop song, that went Beatles–Kinks–Small Faces–Syd Barrett–Bowie—Buzzcocks–XTC–Smiths, and why should we be ashamed at loving that? You could be a bit of a lad yet not mean women, gays, etc any harm. There was a way to play guitar noise that didn't mean grunge – see the list above. You could make an ostensibly cheery record out of sadness and satire, you could even throw in songs as fundamentally bereft as 'Badhead' and 'This Is A Low', because sadness makes the English happy. There was something out of control about lottery-call-centre-package-holiday-shopping-mall-binge-drink Britain, and it's pop music's job to talk about such matters. And – and this is very key to the anti-Blur backlash, and the way the band got out from under it – irony is not the same as glibness. Glibness – making a joke of everything shite in order to re-sell it, and everything amoral so no one has to organise, politicise and stop it. Irony

– the very substance of British humour, stoicism and art. Simple, really. And that's all I have to say, except that I've occasionally read recently that this album has dated. Some members of my profession are deaf and measures should be taken to help them.

LET LOVE IN

NICK CAVE AND THE BAD SEEDS

PRODUCED BY TONY COHEN AND THE BAD SEEDS
MUTE/APRIL 1994
UK CHART: 12
US CHART: DID NOT CHART
KEY TRACKS: 'Do You Love Me?'; 'Red Right Hand';
'Nobody's Baby Now'; 'Ain't Gonna Rain Anymore'; 'Do You
Love Me? (Part 2)'

Hell's bells. They ring throughout the first indisputably great album by former Birthday Party singer Cave and his ever-growing Seeds; pealing at the horror of the all-consuming love that makes men into killers and victims. Cave has had to put up with many indignities in his life – being dismissed as a junkie, being accused of inventing goth, living in Hove. But none burns like the agony of falling in love, and asking the question 'Do You Love Me?', and hearing the bells of the chapel go jingle jangle, because the answer, 'Yes', is the worst answer of all. If you are a man who has loved and ended up losing all direction and sense of self until the only answer becomes writing poetry about she-devils and occasionally looking at your increasingly gaunt reflection in a cracked mirror, and pointing and laughing hysterically, then *Let Love In* is the cuddly fun-packed album for you.

Hard to find a favourite bit, apart from those bad bad jingle bells, of course. It may be when Nick searches for answers in the twangy '60s balladry and the 'holy books', of the 'poets and the analysts' to find out why his love is 'Nobody's Baby Now', and decides to tell us of 'Her wild feral stare/Her dark hair/Her winter lips as cold as stone'. Ooh, Nicky, you must invite her round for a cup of tea. Or maybe it's the bit in 'I Let Love In', when he describes his darling as 'the punishment for all my former sins'. Suffice to say that nice girls are not his type, unless they are sucking the marrow from his very bones and torturing with him curling tongs and the bones of old folk singers.

'Red Right Hand', however, is not about a girl, despite it starring the best bell this side of Colin Bell, the former Manchester City and England midfield general most notable for his extraordinary levels of stamina. It's a spook B-movie in six mesmerising minutes, as Cave paints a picture of a bloody handed stranger who might be Satan, or drug dealer, or dream weaver, or death itself. It proved that Cave and the Seeds – Mick Harvey, Martyn P. Casey, Blixa Bargeld, Conway Savage and Thomas Wydler – were now so suave and sure that they could uniquely traverse the thin line between boy horror and human truth, as Cave embarked on a seemingly infinite future of finding tales to tell, metaphors to conjure, black jokes to deliver, all based somewhat around the image of a stick-thin preacher in a Godforsaken swamp-bound small American town untouched by modern science, where ghoulish women push men to murder while the undertaker leads the local church army in an ironic chorus of 'Jesus Wants Me For A Sunbeam'. What's not to like?

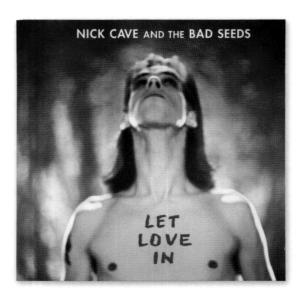

ILLMATIC

NAS
PRODUCED BY VARIOUS PRODUCERS
COLUMBIA/APRIL 1994
UK CHART: DID NOT CHART
US CHART: 12
KEY TRACKS: 'The World Is Yours'; 'Halftime'; 'It Ain't Hard To Tell'; 'Represent'; 'NY State Of Mind'

A welcome return to the sharp focus of the forty-minute rap album, the legendary debut by Nasir Jones of Queens, New York, is a key hip hop milestone. West coast gangsta rap had been spanking east coast rap commercially since the turn of the '90s. A slew of star producers including Gang Starr's DJ Premier, Pete Rock and Q-Tip provided backing tracks for this twenty-one-year-old son of jazz and blues musician Olu Dara, and the east coast-based rap media hailed him as a Second Coming for hip hop – the implication being that, whatever those cynical Californians were doing, it wasn't 'real' hip hop. It was around this time that 'keeping it real' became a rap catchphrase, and *Illmatic*, with its rough, articulate, and politically aware street reportage rhymes over claustrophobic and scratch-reviving beats was what the self-appointed arbiters of hip hop integrity meant.

Much of this was a whole bunch of greedy fuckers taking their art way too seriously. But, even twelve years later, the moment when Nasty Nas proclaims his ability to 'cause mass hysteria' over the smokey sleigh bell funk of 'Halftime', and embarks on a lyric that merges battle-rhyme, Afrocentric consciouness-raiser, ghetto testimony and stand-up comedy routine, makes tingles run down the spines of everyone who loved the first glorious wave of hip hop. The finest track, 'The World Is Yours', took great care over that 'yours' rather than lesser rap's wearying 'mine'. While G-funk was like a greasy takeway you couldn't resist but sat in your gut spreading poison, *Illmatic* tasted like soul food. With its sophisticated and sexy jazz and soul backdrops, and its lyrical air of effortless street-level authority painting a picture of Afro-American life, which came off as neither sensationalist nightmare nor materialist wet dream, the album marked the passing of hip hop's peak. From now on, it was just the black equivalent of MOR country, with the occasional genius adrift in an ocean of bottom-feeder shite. Listen to *Illmatic* and you'll know why hip hop influenced the world, and why so few – not even Nas himself – had the artistic energy to match this standard, when there was really no financial incentive to try.

MUSIC FOR THE JILTED GENERATION

THE PRODIGY

PRODUCED BY LIAM HOWLETT AND NEIL MCLENNAN
XL/JULY 1994
UK CHART: 1
US CHART: DID NOT CHART
KEY TRACKS: 'Poison'; 'No Good (Start The Dance)';
'Voodoo People'; 'Break & Enter'; 'Full Throttle'

You know that 1994 was the best year for albums since 1981, because so many of the best albums are No. 1s. That's when culture is at its most thrilling – those rare times when the innovations are the best-sellers, when a major section of the audience for art picks up on each other's desire for change, and votes with wallet, as well as head and feet. Makes all those barren years worth ploughing through, don't it just?

The second Prodigy album was a hit that few saw coming. Initially the Essex-based maker of novelty rave singles, Liam Howlett saw a convergence of possibilities. The politicisation of dance fans, in opposition to Michael Howard's Criminal Justice Act of 1994, which sought to crack down on raves on open land, as well as squatters and campers. The lack of a credible live rave act. The obvious connection between the gonzo 'I'm mad, me' qualities of metal, hardcore punk and hardcore house. Howlett joined the dots, magnificently.

The inner sleeve painting by Les Edwards was extraordinary, too: not because it was great art, but because of the societal schism it depicted. A part of the English countryside is split by a ravine. On the left, massed ranks of riot police and a sky blackened by factories belching eco-destruction. On the right, the sun shines on a towering sound system and a group of partying ravers, apparently oblivious to the dark forces ranged against them. The ravine is traversed by a rope bridge, and one man – looking less like a raver and more like a '70s hippy – raises his middle-finger to the cops. In his left hand is a sword, poised to cut the rope that keeps the bridge

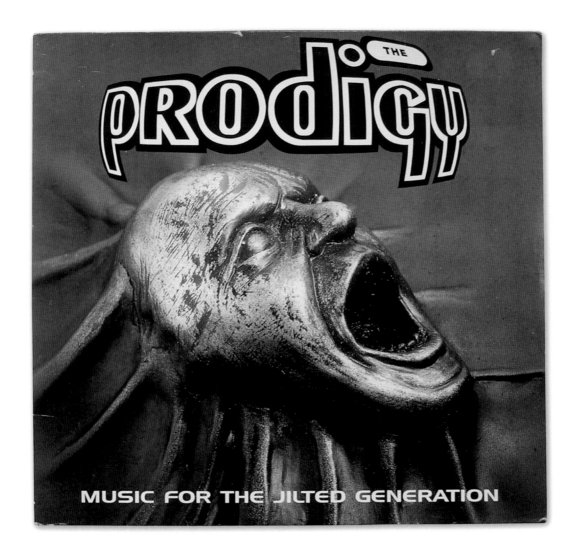

MUSIC FOR THE JILTED GENERATION//THE PRODIGY

suspended. According to The Prodigy, raving youth and their new age hippy fellow travellers wanted to cut themselves adrift from society completely, leaving us to the rule of 'Their Law' and a sky full of red raw 'Poison', lost in the communality and innocence of The Dance.

What struck hardest when you heard the album is how loud, hard and sophisticated this machine music was, a sound busy and abandoned enough to raise that defiant middle finger. But this was no hippy feelgood dance-rock – 'Poison' and 'No Good (Start The Dance)' were suffused with dread and sonic prophecies of apocalypse, honestly representing, in a manic but multi-layered tone poetry, the hard drugs and violence that had splintered the house club scene.

Music For The Jilted Generation, unlike the cartoon punkisms of The Prodigy's later, lazy and laddish bitch-smacks, still sounds like a landmark in hooligan art, an album that connected the loneliness inherent in bedroom electronica with a community of youth rapidly turning towards a new kind of anti-globalisation politics. It has more in common, then, with the nu-metal of Rage Against The Machine, and easily located the British equivalent of that huge potential audience, who'd been waiting for a rebel music that sang a different tune to the trad-rock gangs of yore. For one brief moment it presented the possibility of a radical agit-prop based around the dance scene. It never materialised, for material reasons. A Utopian ministry of sound turned out to be a branded nightclub that looked just like the dark, Satanic factories in the painting. Hippy guy should've cut that rope.

DEFINITELY MAYBE

OASIS
PRODUCED BY OASIS, MARK COYLE AND OWEN MORRIS
CREATION/AUGUST 1994

UK CHART: 1
US CHART: 58
KEY TRACKS: 'Cigarettes & Alcohol'; 'Supersonic'; 'Live Forever'; 'Slide Away'; 'Rock 'N' Roll Star'

What's left to say about this record? I guess I should start by saying I love it much more now than I used to. At the time, the first Oasis album was just too ubiquitous, and hit me as much too samey. You'd think a Ramones and acid house fan might have seen the advantages of repetition more clearly, eh?

What I love most now about *Definitely Maybe* are the guitars. Noel's shameless regurgitation of every old, basic twelve-bar riff and distorted dirty lick takes a slight tune like 'Shakermaker' into the realms of true trance music, an irresistible shorthand for communal excess, for good-bad but not evil behaviour. The bleeding and chopping and swaggering that ends 'Supersonic' – refusing self-indulgence and experimentation at every turn! – is one of the very greatest minutes of rock 'n' roll ever recorded, up there with Chuck Berry and the Stones and the Pistols at their most wizardly.

Noel is echoed by Liam's love of singing. Not one for smiling and betraying his crucial cool, the grin is all in his love of vowels, the way he can take a 'me' or a 'be' or, of course, a 'soon-sheeyine' and inject every ounce of his desire, his anger, his triumph and his ambition into the most prosaic grab for The Moment. The way these brothers egged each other on sonically, two working-class brothers from a background where showing emotion equated to weakness, putting all their love and tears into the strip mining of trad-rock gold dust, made this one of the very few rock 'n' roll albums that rivalled dance music's grasp on the bliss of communal freedom. I don't think there is another pair of rock musicians who could write and perform a song about the individual glories of being a 'Rock 'N' Roll Star' and make it belong to their audience, make it our collective dream, and make it feel possible. All the walls of sound that they summon – from the serious rebel powers of the Pistols and Neil

Young's Crazy Horse to the undervalued glam party stomps of Slade and Marc Bolan – are erected to immerse us in a warm ocean of noise. What makes *Definitely Maybe* most unusual – and an influence on British rock that was, inevitably, reductive in the hands of lesser talents, on rock dullards who wanted and needed this less – was that the more noise it made, the less 'difficult' it became. They didn't really sound anything like The Beatles. But they tapped into a buried memory of the way The Beatles had united every-one who wanted more from life in an age of change, and enabled it to feel possible without having to engage politically. No wonder, at all, that New Labour was so keen to use them. And no wonder, at all, that many who were carried along by its millennial euphoria still cling to *Definitely Maybe* as the greatest album of all time, a symbol of hedonist optimism that each generation increasingly understands is only avail-able inside music.

Because the truth, sadly, is that while 'Is it worth the aggravation/To find yourself a job when there's nothing worth working for?' is the key question that rebel music always asks, and Noel was a genius for asking it so directly and getting his bruv to make it hurt, the answer is always 'No . . . but you have no choice'. For the fifty-two minutes that *Definitely Maybe* lasts, you believe you do. The ninety-five per cent of humanity owned by money can ask for nothing more from a long-playing record.

GRACE

JEFF BUCKLEY
PRODUCED BY ANDY WALLACE
COULMBIA/AUGUST 1994
UK CHART: 50
US CHART: DID NOT CHART
KEY TRACKS: 'Grace'; 'Lilac Wine'; 'Lover, You Should've Come Over'; 'So Real'; 'Hallelujah'

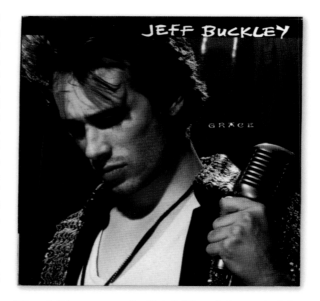

When I did my promo for This Is Uncool, I was asked the same question every time. And every time, I was caught off-guard. 'So, in the end,' the kind soul who was helping me sell my list book about singles would ask, 'what's your favourite single of all time?' I would cavil, splutter, umm and arggh . . . and I gave a different answer every time. What's more, I'd end up blurting out something from the '60s, which rather undercut the whole premise of the exercise, about people banging on about the '60s to the detriment of the music of our own generation. For some inexplicable reason I figured people would just accept my chronological order schtick and not do what we all do when raised in a system based on competition, and seek the World Champion single that ren-ders all other singles also-rans on the great playing-fields of the art of pop. So this time I'm prepared. Always have an answer. Say the same one every time. Make it one in the book, you twat.

Except . . . pop music isn't football. There isn't a winner.

DEFINITELY MAYBE/OASIS

What's more, once released, a record belongs to its listener and it becomes what we make of it. Which means that we need different music for different moods, and a record's qualities rise or fall on whether the listener is looking for soundtrack or mood enhancer, sympathy or fantasy, escape or advice, succour or big sexy fun. The best thing about writing this book is being forced to listen to records I've taken for granted down the years, and being ripped apart by them all over again. So I started the book thinking that my favourite albums were set in stone – *The Clash*, *Entertainment!*, *Metal Box*, *The Queen Is Dead*, *It Takes A Nation Of Millions To Hold Us Back* – and found myself stunned by, and now possibly preferring, *Armed Forces*, *Marquee Moon*, *Bummed*, *Isn't Anything*, *Cypress Hill*. But maybe that was all down to that hour of that day. You see my problem.

What all this has to do with *Grace* is that I approached it thinking that it might be the album I say is my fave of all time, if anyone's daft enough to care this time around. But, I'm listening to it now, and . . . it's not really doing it for me. And I think I know why. Everything bad in the rock of now is *Grace*'s fault. All those mewling public school choirboys with their soft-rock melodies over minor chords, hovering up the cash of total suckers by giving substance to twenty-first-century Britain's resigned and inarticulate and apolitical disappointment. All those banal lickspittle cynics lining up to meet Bono and Geldof, pretending that their sensitive hearts bleed for the world, on their way to boning an actress and buying a mansion with a moat to keep the lower orders away from Pater's millions. You know who I mean. And the weird, sick thing about it is that if Jeff Buckley hadn't died in Memphis in a freak swimming accident in May 1998, you suspect that his continued existence and work and brilliance and beauty and originality would have just made them all look so pathetic compared to the Real Thing, that they would've gone off and traded pork bellies and left music well alone.

But another day I'll come back to *Grace* – probably on my MP3 jukebox, 'cos its random nature is really good for this sort of thing – and it will sound like the rock album that most successfully aspires to gospel music, and a spirit that connects music, God, love and community at a level that, like *Definitely Maybe* in a very different way, makes the injustice and harshness and waste of the world go away, and remind you that people are capable of better things than the things thrown in our faces, in a way that music, and only music, can tell us.

So, if I do get asked, I might still say *Grace*.

DUMMY

PORTISHEAD
PRODUCED BY PORTISHEAD AND ADRIAN UTLEY
GO! BEAT/AUGUST 1994
UK CHART: 2
US CHART: 79
KEY TRACKS: 'Sour Times'; 'Glory Box'; 'Biscuit'; 'Roads'; 'Pedestal'

Not sure what was in the water in August 1994, but the first Portishead album completes a triptych of albums that changed pop. If Oasis and Jeff Buckley set the tone for twelve years of rock and counting, Bristol's Beth Gibbons, Geoff Barrow and Adrian Utley made a record that immediately established a hip hop that had nothing to do with rap or its black cultural concerns, and the commercial possibilities of dance music you couldn't dance to. The Britpop era is always referred to as an optimistic period, defined by Blair's accession to the Labour throne and national feeling that the end of Tory rule was just around the corner. But *Dummy*, like *Grace*, was one unhappy fucker of an album, and we Brits lapped up its miserable insularity, its air of bereavement.

The deluge of wine bar/coffee-table/dinner party ambient dance albums that followed in *Dummy*'s wake obscure what a powerful sonic shock a first hearing of Portishead was. Decorating low-tempo heartbeat hip hop, strongly influenced by fellow Bristolians Massive Attack, with motifs from spy movie soundtracks and the saddest voice since Ian Curtis departed much too soon, Portishead fashioned a white English blues that owed nothing whatsoever to the '60s beat boom, and seemed to have stumbled upon an entirely new musical language. Sometimes resembling hip hop on a life-support machine, at others a late-night jazz set from the subterranean factory tunnels of David Lynch's *Eraserhead*, maybe even De La Soul drowning in squid ink, and more than occasionally the inner body sounds of someone deciding whether to fuck or slit their wrists, there is still not an album in all of that half-assed genre labelled trip hop that gets near its level of intensity and private grief. That it apparently became a sort of bourgeois lifestyle accoutrement in the manner of stripped pine and chrome kitchenware is one of the most unlikely glitches in British pop history. But it did prove that, somewhere among the

supposed optimism of Britpop and 'Cool Britannia', there was a profound feeling of dread. It was almost as if we decided to mourn the inevitable New Labour comedown early. 'Can't anybody see/We've got a war to fight/Never find our way/Regardless of what they say,' sang Beth Gibbons with brittle deliberation in 'Roads', and it sounds, now, like she'd glimpsed all our tomorrows, and was desperate to make us act, instead of meekly accepting.

On a lighter note . . . well, actually, there isn't one. Except to say that there's an ongoing conversation about when British hip hop will get as good (meaning as profitable) as US hip hop and, with no disrespect intended to Roots Manuva, Dizzie Rascal, Lady Sovereign, Sway, et cetera, *Dummy* was better hip hop than anything coming out of America by 1994, and the fact that it didn't have rapping and there was no one black in the band wasn't the point. The point was and is that hip hop is a broad culture that includes a form of music, that beats, scratching and reinventing old records was a bigger part of that music than banging on about the size of your uzi/jewels/posse/nuts, and that it was in desperate need of some input from nerds and breathtaking female singers.

If you've not listened to this for a long time 'cos of those sucky trip hop records, stick it on. You'll be stunned anew.

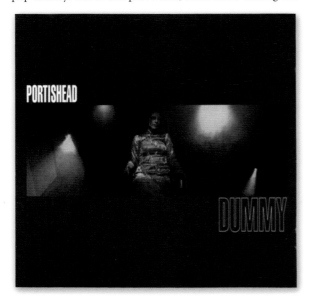

PROTECTION

MASSIVE ATTACK
PRODUCED BY NELLEE HOOPER AND MASSIVE ATTACK
CIRCA/SEPTEMBER 1994
UK CHART: 4
US CHART: DID NOT CHART
KEY TRACKS: 'Karmacoma'; 'Protection'; 'Sly'; 'Euro Child'; 'Spying Glass'

When Tracey Thorn sings the title track of this album, I

never find myself dwelling too much on the gender-swapping boy-girl aspects of the lyric. I just feel gratitude for the warmth and sincerity the Everything But The Girl chanteuse brings to the lines, 'I'll stand in front of you/Take the force of the blow.' The line embeds itself within the womblike depth of the beats and softly circling piano, and sounds like music itself singing. Because that's what music this good does – it gives you shelter from the blows of life. The swish of rain that ends the song is perfect – if you, like me, feel most secure when inside, in the warm, listening to something sad but strong, as the rain falls outside.

Upon its release, 'Protection' felt like a blanding out of the promise of *Blue Lines* (p.240), and in hindsight that was because it was both benign and mellow compared to *Dummy*. But this is an album that grows as time passes, as Massive Attack endeavoured, in their unprolific way, to encompass as much of what they loved about art-rock as black music. Protection sounds as if these sonic cocoons came easy to them, and they could make albums like this like other people push pens or plan holidays. Which they could. Which is presumably why they didn't. What an uncynical bunch.

The showcases they gave to Tricky, Nicolette and Thorn were generous, too, even though Tricky moaned in public about his treatment at Massive Attack's hands. The problem inherent in the kind of collective that 3-D, Mushroom and Daddy G pioneered is that, when Shara Nelson and Jonny Dollar pulled off an 'Unfinished Sympathy' or Tricky lit up a record with his contributions to 'Karmacoma' and 'Eurochild', there was plenty of scope for the featured artist to feel credit unfairly given to the brand name. The same sort of bad feeling was generated by how much singer Caron Wheeler contributed to the best of Jazzie B's equally influential Soul II Soul. I'd imagine Horace Andy, a reggae vocal genius largely obscure to those exposed to British adult-pop, might have a different perspective on the nebulous nature of how much is given and how much taken in. What I do know is that the crossover between Massive Attack and Björk –

Hooper production, Craig Armstrong string arrangements, Tricky and Björk dating for a while in what would have provided a great basis for an eccentric trip hop pixie sitcom – pointed the way forward for a lot of British musicians who wanted to blend jazz and hip hop, but couldn't figure out how without just bolting together a break beat, a rapper and a sax player. It was *Protection* rather than *Dummy* that drew up the blueprint for the muzak end of hip hop/trip hop. What all the chin-stroking copyists left out was Massive's love of Public Image Ltd, Talking Heads, the Specials and The Slits, lending even the sweetest Massive Attack tune a shadow of loss and anger. In short, they made better music because they had better taste in music.

Still can't explain the bloody awful version of 'Light My Fire', though. Nobody's perfect, will have to do.

CRAZYSEXYCOOL

TLC
PRODUCED BY VARIOUS PRODUCERS (EXECUTIVE PRODUCTION BY ANTONIO 'LA' REID, KENNETH 'BABYFACE' EDMONDS AND DALLAS AUSTIN)
LAFACE/ARISTA/NOVEMBER 1994
UK CHART: 4
US CHART: 3
KEY TRACKS: 'Waterfalls'; 'Creep'; 'Sumthin' Wicked This Way Comes'; 'Kick Your Game'; 'Diggin' On You'

The most cohesive R&B girl group album ever was made by the most fractious and doomed of trios. Tionne 'T-Boz' Watkins, Rozonda 'Chilli' Thomas and Lisa 'Left Eye' Lopes were formed in Atlanta, Georgia, in 1991, and shaped by '80s R&B singer Pebbles and producer Dallas Austin. *CrazySexyCool* made them superstars, but showed up all the cracks in the façade. Just before the album's release, rapper Lopes was arrested on arson charges after she burned down the house of her boyfriend, NFL football star Andre Rison.

Watkins was battling sickle cell anemia. All three fell out with Austin, who had just had a child with Thomas. The next album took five years to make. Then all three began publicly slagging off each other's lack of talent and/or commitment before the big comeback tour. And then, in 2002, shortly after Left Eye had signed a solo record deal with Suge 'Death Row' Knight, of all people, she died in a car accident in Honduras, at the age of thirty-one.

Until someone gets round to making the biopic, we'll have to make do with this definitive modern girl-group album. Admittedly, the version of Prince's 'If I Was Your Girlfriend' both removes the original's sexual complexities and sounds as if they sang over the original. But by that time 'Waterfalls' has forged the missing link between Prince and the coming nu-soul of D'Angelo and Erykah Badu, and provided an anti-gangsta lyric of such unpretentious wisdom, that only a great album could avoid being completely overshadowed by its splendour. 'Creep' is an even better infidelity song than Destiny's Child's 'Jumpin' Jumpin', 'Sexy' is memorably obnoxious at the expense of the male ego, and this buttery soul-funk 'Interlude' keeps appearing (co-produced by a bloke who still called himself Sean 'Puffy' Combs) and making other peoples' proper songs sound lame.

The tendency to give girl groups a ton of limp, obsequious ballads for their albums is resisted. Instead, the album ends with both accusation and a plea for Civil Rights-era unity in the tough, doomy 'Sumthin' Wicked This Way Comes'. A pre-stardom Andre Benjamin of OutKast provides the first verse for a reinvention of gospel that Stevie Wonder would have been proud to have written and produced. Having also produced 'Waterfalls', the Organised Noize production team share top billing with our three talented, tragic heroines.

1995

TO BRING YOU MY LOVE

PJ HARVEY

PRODUCED BY FLOOD, POLLY HARVEY AND JOHN PARISH
ISLAND/FEBRUARY 1995
UK CHART: 12
US CHART: 40
KEY TRACKS: 'Working For The Man'; 'Down By The Water'; 'Meet Ze Monsta'; 'C'mon Billy'; 'To Bring You My Love'

What do you get if you cross Grace Jones and the psycho preacher from Charles Laughton's 1955 movie *Night Of The Hunter?* You get 'Working For The Man' by Polly Harvey, the weirdest, sexiest song of the whole goddam '90s, and a tune that'll make you believe a woman can truly be Iggy Pop. Is it from the perspective of a woman picking up boys? A man picking up girls? A priest picking up hookers? It's a mystery I don't care to solve while I can hear that purr rub up against that bassline, never quite giving sweet relief, making the potentially evil sound like holy rapture.

Moderately famously, the third album from Yeovil's finest Patti Smith tribute act was made while Polly briefly stepped out with Nick Cave. From his side, the relationship inspired *The Boatman's Call* (see p.292), a deeply moving set of broken-hearted love ballads. In Ms Harvey, it inspired the nearest a woman's ever got to a cock-rock album. It's easy to hear who wore the trousers in that coupling.

But I'll stop poking fun at Polly's poking fun, because this is a sublimely sensual record, and there are so few of those in rock any more that electric guitars should come sponsored by bromide. Harvey has a striking penchant for switching between a male and female perspective, and 'Down By The Water' and 'Send His Love To Me' mainline the suffering-sex-ballad side of Cave's work and attach it to the strident earth mother yearning of Patti Smith until you realise that PJ is a truly mighty hermaphrodite, and a defiant proclaimer of that unpopular truth about the basic impulses, desires and needs of men and women not being that different, if everyone stopped hiding behind chick flicks and lad mags, and hen nights and dadrock, and just let the truth stand naked, or at least in one of those riot grrl frocks Ms Harvey drapes around her skinny frame. I'm not sure she has anything profound to say except Gimme It!!! But, in the case of *To Bring You My Love*, she reaches Kate Bush heights of life-affirming perv-love. And that's just enough.

MAXINQUAYE

TRICKY

PRODUCED BY TRICKY, MARK SAUNDERS, KEVIN PETRIE AND HOWIE B
ISLAND/FEBRUARY 1995
UK CHART: 3
US CHART: DID NOT CHART
KEY TRACKS: 'Black Steel'; 'Overcome'; 'Ponderosa'; 'Aftermath'; 'Abbaon Fat Tracks'

Speaking of Ms Bush, the title track from her 1982 album *The Dreaming* (see p.141) is the secret influence on Bristol trip hop. Check it out again and then listen to the rhythm track of Massive Attack's 'Karmacoma'. See?

The opener to the first Tricky album – yet another unlikely 'coffee table' hit – takes Tricky's rhymes from 'Karmacoma' and puts them into the mouth of singer Martina Topley-Bird for 'Overcome'. It took some time before the release of her 2003 album *Quixotic* brought the Londoner due respect for her vocal gifts, but the on-off musical and romantic partnership sparked much of Tricky's earliest and finest music. Inputting even more gnarly post-punk into a multi-textured mix of hip hop and dub, *Maxinquaye* sounded like what all those early '80s punk-funksters had been trying to achieve all along – a music that defied all pigeonholes, scrambled norms of gender and race, and presented Tricky/Adrian Thaws as a fly in the Britpop ointment. Sampling the Specials, Shakespears Sister and Smashing Pumpkins was unpredictable enough, quoting from David Cassidy's 'How Can I Be Sure?' and getting The Pop Group's Mark Stewart to quote from Japan's 'Ghosts' uncovered buried pop memories, but getting mixed race Martina's teasing cockney voice to sing Public Enemy's 'Black Steel In The Hour Of Chaos' was evidence of an inspired mind. The definitive black male rap, with its cinematic fantasy of a prison break (where the only guard that actually dies is female), is turned inside out by Tricky's heavy-metal-in-a-box and Martina's voice, making it sound like a true cry for freedom rather than race war. Meanwhile, 'Hell Is Round The Corner's use of a sample of 'Ike's Mood' by Isaac Hayes echoed Portishead's 'Glory Box', and increased the suspicion that the whole Bristol crowd plus Björk and Martina were part of a subtle conspiracy to transform pop, sharing whispered secrets, speaking in codes, occasionally letting us into their spliff ambience.

Although *Dummy* was colder and sadder, *Maxinquaye* balanced seduction and struggle, bouncing between sophisticated ambience and something that felt like disease and dirty needles, often in the space of a few bars. And it had a Boomtown Rat on the bass guitar. Strange, great pop times.

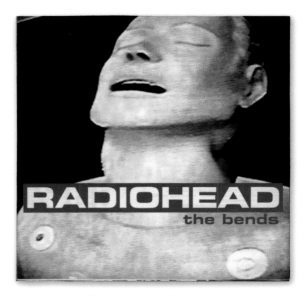

THE BENDS

RADIOHEAD
PRODUCED BY JOHN LECKIE, RADIOHEAD, NIGEL GODRICH AND JIM WARREN
PARLOPHONE/MARCH 1995
UK CHART: 6
US CHART: 88
KEY TRACKS: 'Fake Plastic Trees'; 'Planet Telex'; 'Just'; 'Bones'; 'My Iron Lung'

The Bends is the major reason why I can't get into Nirvana. For this listener, the second Radiohead album presented all the desperate alienation that Cobain symbolised for so many, and gave it a melodic and thematic sophistication that only Jeff Buckley could match. Indeed, Thom Yorke recorded the vocal for the heartbreaking 'Fake Plastic Trees' after the band had been to see Buckley perform. Originally a 'guide' vocal, meant to be re-recorded later, Yorke hit the emotions so hard he burst into tears. That's a wrap, Buddy. Apparently inspired by the strange netherworld that is London's Canary Wharf, Yorke somehow gets from there to the still jaw-dropping pain and regret in the line, 'If I could be who you wanted all the time,' and we were suddenly faced not with an indie-rock band, but a singer who could draw blood from the rockiest stone.

The Bends is now an acknowledged classic, but was a huge surprise at the time. Radiohead were seen as a fake plastic grunge band, angst on a major label as summed up by their 1993 hit 'Creep'. The title refers to the decompression sickness the band suffered from the sudden success of

'Creep', and 'My Iron Lung' exposes every doubt of every musician who isn't necessarily in it for fame, by way of The Beatles, Queen, Nirvana and an almost vomiting disgust. Throughout the album, first and second person clash and merge in the face of Yorke's furious bewilderment, so that, by the time you reach 'Just's famous sneer, 'You do it to yourself, you do/And that's what really hurts,' the line hits as one of rock's very greatest notes to self, and the key moment in a masterful album about depression, self-loathing and being horrified by the prospect of getting what you've always wished for. Yorke has said that closing track 'Street Spirit (Fade Out)' ' . . . has no resolve. It is the dark tunnel without the light at the end'. It's a strange observation, about such a pretty tune that, despite the imagery of cracked eggs and dead birds, asks the listener to 'Immerse your soul in love'. But then this is why Radiohead have done more harm than good to rock, despite their talent. They take themselves too seriously, and, like Pink Floyd, seem to have convinced adult rock fans that intelligence and lacking a sense of humour are precisely the same thing.

Still . . . they have an extraordinary facility for finding magical chord sequences. No disrespect intended to bassist Colin Greenwood and drummer Phil Selway, but *The Bends* is carried by Yorke's voice and the concise-history-of-heavy-rock guitars of Jonny Greenwood and Ed O'Brien. Occasionally, on 'Fake Plastic Trees', say, or 'Sulk', it all sounds like a '70s power ballad by The Hollies called 'The Air That I Breathe'. Which fits that *Bends* concept pretty well.

ME AGAINST THE WORLD

2 PAC

PRODUCED BY VARIOUS PRODUCERS
INTERSCOPE/MARCH 1995
UK CHART: DID NOT CHART
US CHART: 1

KEY TRACKS: 'Dear Mama'; 'Me Against The World'; 'If I Die 2Nite'; 'So Many Tears'; 'It Ain't Easy'

If Thom Yorke thought being a rock star or going back to Oxford was a bleak choice, perhaps he should've spent a week or two in Tupac Shakur's shoes. By 1995, the Brooklyn-born but west-coast-raised son of a Black Panther single-mother had survived a slew of arrests, a sexual assault charge and a bullet in the bollocks. By September 1996, the violent death he fantasises about throughout *Me Against The World* had come to pass. By this time, it was hard to judge who was the most horrible – the various rappers, rap moguls and hangers-on that would drive Shakur and his east coast nemesis Biggie Smalls to their deaths, or the rap fans and media who jerked off over this stuff. Increasingly, no new rapper would be accepted unless they could convince us of their thug credentials. 2 Pac simply became the most high-

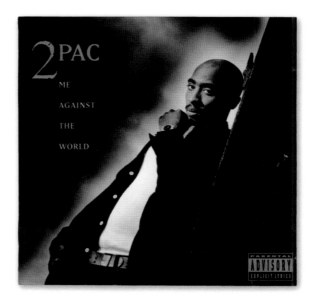

profile victim of the exploitation of black-on-black violence.

The interesting thing about Shakur's third and best album is that you can block out the raps, and what you know about the man, and listen to it as an old-school, mellow, soul-funk album. The various producers blend a set of 'quiet storm' samples with just enough post-Dre G-funk to update the sweetness. Shakur's lyrics run through many of the familiar gangsta-isms, but with an existential despair and political awareness that his rivals simply weren't interested in. 'Dear Mama' grabbed most of the attention for its heart-felt maternal sentiments, 'Old School' invented the rap roll-call from hip hop's past, and 'If I Die 2Nite' and 'Death Around The Corner' ended up being transformed by events into something more than melodrama. Dressed in smart-casuals and even glasses on the sleeve, there is a picture where Shakur is smiling, and he looks so charismatic and healthy that it's easy to imagine the parallel universe where, having got something like 'So Many Tears' off his chest (where that sing-song rap style, somehow resigned and defiant at the same time, intones 'Don't shed a tear for me/Nigga I ain't happy here/I hope they bury me and send me to my rest/Headlines readin' murdered to death, my last breath'), he slays his demons, forsakes guns and the macho dare, and becomes a kind of reformed gangsta soul man. Instead, a drive-by and the longest posthumous recording career that the owners of a barrel of scrap could possibly scrape.

You did it to yourself, it's true, and that's what really hurts.

POST

BJÖRK
PRODUCED BY BJÖRK, GRAHAM MASSEY, NELLEE HOOPER, TRICKY AND HOWIE B
ONE LITTLE INDIAN/JUNE 1995
UK CHART: 2
US CHART: 32

KEY TRACKS: 'Hyper-ballad'; 'Isobel'; 'I Miss You'; 'Possibly Maybe'; 'You've Been Flirting Again'

Restless and recklessly individual, Björk followed *Debut* with an album of wildly differing moods. Aggressive and dismissive on the throwaway opener (made for the *Tank Girl* movie) 'Army Of Me'; a dreamy earth mother on the awesome 'Hyper-ballad'; a reborn Siouxsie Sioux, declaiming through industrial din for 'Enjoy'; the fifth Beatle for the plaintive intimacy of 'You've Been Flirting Again'. Purple patches in pop are as much down to the buying public as the artist, and the popularity of the bewildering range of sounds, styles and themes on *Post* showed how much dance music, hip hop and the Bristol bunch had opened up our ears to sonic adventurers as the mid-'90s became music's best period since the late '70s.

Björk's ability to blend an elemental world of forests and mountains with a fascination with the beats and flows of the human body enabled her to conjure sensuality without ever selling her sexuality. The contrast between the deliberate pronunciation of each gleefully masticated word, and her surreal images and fairy-tales of mystery defies literal interpretation. But when you travel with her (and her male producers, who all suppress trademarks to search for the unexpected) through these eleven songs, and their virtuoso mutations of electronica, classical, country, big-band swing, the more left-field moments of Kate Bush and an ever-present tang of girl group pop, and then she sings, on the penultimate 'Cover Me', 'I'm going to prove the impossible really exists,' you can do nothing except believe her. Her impossible dreams include 'The Modern Things', where Björk posits a theory that technology always existed, locked inside a mountain, seeing off the dinosaurs, waiting to take over the world. 'It's their turn now,' she calls, and fear and delight are indistinguishable in her voice.

The closing, corpuscular 'Headphones', dedicated to the album's main producer 808 State's Graham Massey, sees Björk and Tricky define the rules of this new pop game, and

POST/BJÖRK

its desire to mix the production wizardry and musical wanderings of the early '70s progressive rock era with a punk ethic shorn of ego. 'Sounds go through the muscles/These abstract wordless movements . . . these cells are virgins waking up slowly/My headphones – they saved my life.' And mine, doll. And mine.

IT'S GREAT WHEN YOU'RE STRAIGHT . . . YEAH

BLACK GRAPE
PRODUCED BY DANNY SABER, STEPHEN LIRONI AND SHAUN RYDER
RADIOACTIVE/AUGUST 1995
UK CHART: 1
US CHART: DID NOT CHART
KEY TRACKS: 'Shake Your Money'; 'In The Name Of The Father'; 'Reverend Black Grape'; 'Little Bob'; 'Tramazi Parti'

An unlikely comeback, and a brief one. No one expected Shaun Ryder and Bez to be given another chance after the messy dissolution of Happy Mondays, but Black Grape were irresistible. When asked why he called the band Black Grape, Ryder pointed at co-vocalist and former Ruthless Rap Assassins MC Paul 'Kermit' Leveredge, and replied: 'Because he's black, and I like grapes.'

But it wasn't all giggles round at Ryder's place. Despite insistence at the time that this debut album's title was sincere, Kermit was as out of it on Class A drugs as Ryder, and 'Tramazi Parti' was a love letter to 'downer' drug Tamazepam. The sleeve featured a Warhol-coloured pop art treatment of notorious Venezuelan anti-Israeli '70s/'80s terrorist Carlos the Jackal aka Ilich Ramirez Sanchez, contrasted, on the back cover, with a similarly treated snap of a young and Afro'ed Michael Jackson. And then, the lead single 'Reverend Black Grape' featured, among its funk-rock party beats and sneering references to Reebok (a bit of a

Black Grape sub-plot, sportswear watchers) the immortal lines, 'Old pope he got the Nazis to clean up their messes/In exchange for gold and paintings/He gave them new addresses'. This was presumably a reference to the 1933 Concordat between Hitler and Pope Pius XI. The implication missed out the same Pontiff's 1938 denunciation of anti-Semitism and some Catholic groups got offended. Ryder might have played the fool throughout his career, but there was a darkness in his worldview, and it wasn't all about drugs.

Having said that, this surprise No. 1 album's best song, 'Shake Your Money', took James Brown's 'Sex Machine' instruction to 'Shake your money maker' and added, ' . . . into little airtight bags'. *It's Great . . .* pretty much sounds like a drug orgy where a band play funk versions of Rolling Stones songs while the guests get royally monged. Because of Shaun and Bez's embarrassing slide into pre-Doherty celebrity drug addict status, Black Grape have been almost wiped from Britpop history. Which means you'll be able to pick up this contrarily triumphant album cheap, and strangely cheerful.

SCREAM, DRACULA, SCREAM!

ROCKET FROM THE CRYPT
PRODUCED BY JOHN REIS JR
ELEMENTAL (INTERSCOPE IN USA)/DECEMBER 1995
UK CHART: 40
US CHART: DID NOT CHART
KEY TRACKS: 'On A Rope'; 'Born In '69'; 'Middle'; 'Young Livers'; 'Burnt Alive'

The finest pure rock 'n' roll band of the mid-'90s suffered from being both ten years too early and twenty years too late. A six-piece punk rock showband out of San Diego, California, Rocket From The Crypt's mix of positivity, irony and old-school showbiz may well have done fine in a rock world that gets The White Stripes. But back in the '90s, only

SCREAM, DRACULA, SCREAM!/ROCKET FROM THE CRYPT

a small (but rabid) section of The Kids were ready for a band that sounded like a mix of *London Calling* Clash, early Springsteen and Hüsker Dü, and looked like a '50s revival band. Add a brass section, reckless use of glockenspiel, a love of '60s pop vocal harmonies and '60s soul showmanship, and a promotional soundbite insisting that 'Rocket From The Crypt are contradiction and lies', and you had a band that some would die for and most would be bewildered by. Although it was as a blistering, impossibly intense and entertaining live band that RFTC truly made sense, their fourth album captured enough of their breakneck spirit to delight any fan of punk rock and/or danceable old-school rock 'n' roll.

Named in tribute to Rocket From The Tombs, the short-lived '70s Ohio band that morphed into Pere Ubu (see p.38), the band was led by Speedo aka John Reis Jr, a slick barrel-chested cross between Elvis and a motorcycle mechanic, the kind of guy you believed when he sang, in his grainy growl, 'My hands were just untied/So I'm using my fists to buy me time' in the excellent 'Young Livers'. *Scream, Dracula, Scream!* saw Reis lead his gang through fourteen manic yet tune-packed slices of garage deluxe, kicking off with a one-minute song called 'Middle' that simply asked 'Are you broke?' and 'Are you down?' and 'Are you broke down?' and got an air-punching 'YEAH!!!' each time, in a distant echo of the opening seconds of the first Dexys Midnight Runners LP (see p.91). The high-speed riffage slapped and whirled you hither and thither, and the stage was set to re-dress Springsteen ('Used'), The Beach Boys ('Misbeaten') and The Temptations ('Come See, Come Saw') in punk duds, while hitting paydirt with the screw-you underclass party anthems listed above. One of those key tracks, 'Born In '69', has a chorus which hits like a punch in the breadbasket and declaims, 'I want it! I need it! I feel it! Awlright!', as girl soulie singers harmonise and the geetars hammer out morse code on yer wildly shaking head. But even though it all feels like a winning rumble, the band know it ain't that simple, even as they make their best moves. Like I said, there's irony in this spe-cial group, a knowledge that punk and rock 'n' roll never give all that they promise. 'Young Livers' is a neat booze pun, and a two-minute rock history lesson, and more, as the line about Speedo's fists is followed by a fleeting dream of power, and then a truer prophecy of oblivion: 'We're so strong and we're so feared/They're gonna look back . . . and never knew we're here.'

The band got dropped, split up, we're gonna look back and never knew they're here.

1996

MURDER BALLADS

NICK CAVE AND THE BAD SEEDS

PRODUCED BY NICK CAVE AND THE BAD SEEDS,
TONY COHEN AND VICTOR VAN VUGT
MUTE/FEBRUARY 1996
UK CHART: 8
US CHART: DID NOT CHART
KEY TRACKS: 'O'Malley's Bar'; 'The Curse Of Millhaven';
'Stagger Lee'; 'Song Of Joy'; 'Crow Jane'

'Parental Advisory: Explicit Lyrics' hollers the now familiar black and white label on my copy of this CD. Man, you think? The lyrics of 'O'Malley's Bar', 'The Curse Of Millhaven' and this album's version of the ancient American folk-blues song 'Stagger Lee' are so profane I don't want to write them down. Not out of embarrassment, exactly (although the difficulties of picking the nastiest/funniest/most relevant out of the buckets of blood is another factor). It's just that there are lines from this album which, taken out of context, will just come off as sensationalism and gratuitous shock on both mine and Cave's part, and that would be a grisly crime. *Murder Ballads* is at a level of lyricism, both verbal and musical, that popular music seldom aspires to, let alone reaches. Besides, the CD has a lovely illustrated booklet with every horrifying, hilarious word contained within, and Cave was a great singer by now, and is up high in the mix on every song, so's you can't miss a single shot, wound or burning. Ain't the art-consumerism interface grand?

The commercial success of *Murder Ballads* was less to do with the blood and swearing, and more to do with the presence of Kylie Minogue and her starring role on Cave's one hit single, 'Where The Wild Roses Grow', where Nick bashing sweet Kylie's head in with a rock shot this rilly wunnerful new boy/girl duo to No. 11 with a, erm, bullet. Cave's onetime paramour Polly Harvey guested too, on the next single 'Henry Lee', and avenged poor Kylie with a penknife. No one suggested a happy house remix of 'O'Malley's Bar', a fourteen-and-a-half-minute orgy of slaughter which is possibly the greatest lyric ever written and very possibly the secret influence on the writing style of Marshall Mathers, beating, as it definitely does, all those gangstas at their own game. You feel excitement battle a creeping unease as you realise that Cave is making you cheer his murderer on, and, of course, you become culpable as you understand your own addiction to the imagery of violence. Was it Jean-Luc Godard who once said that all you need to make a movie is a girl and a gun? *Murder Ballads* is a short film about killing, and it's the love of language, the close readings of madness, Cave's refusal to ease up and wink at the listener, or admit to a moral stance while still making his self-parodies apparent, not to mention the stunning, cinematic swamp-blues playing of The Bad Seeds, that makes this album mesmerising, and deeper than a guilty pleasure.

CASANOVA

THE DIVINE COMEDY

PRODUCED BY DARREN ALLISON AND NEIL HANNON
SETANTA/APRIL 1996
UK CHART: 48
US CHART: DID NOT CHART
KEY TRACKS: 'Something For The Weekend'; 'Becoming More Like Alfie'; 'A Woman Of The World'; 'Through a Long And Sleepless Night'; 'Middle Class Heroes'

I love this record for many reasons. But one of them is a fond memory of my son, ten at the time and just getting serious about pop, demanding I play Neil Hannon's one real hit 'Something For The Weekend' by shouting 'Woodshed! Woodshed!!!' repeatedly, in a delighted and breathless manner. Some of you will recall that the song in question tells the tale of a girl asking her boyfriend to go down to the woodshed, because something wicked that way lurks. The bloke laughs at her, with appropriate condescension, insisting that 'There's nothing in the woodshed/Except, maybe, some

CASANOVA/THE DIVINE COMEDY

ODELAY/BECK

wood'. Finally he relents, to put her sweet, stupid fears to rest. There is something. It's the girl's gang. They beat him up and steal his car and money. All you need is a girl and a gun . . .

It's a fitting beginning for a concept album about the joys and dangers inherent in thinking with your cock. Hannon, from Londonderry, Northern Ireland, was, and still is, somewhat adrift in contemporary pop, being very clever, intellectually and musically, and insisting on showing it off without shame. It means that, even on this his third and best album, there are moments, such as 'In And Out In Paris And London' and 'Charge' that overdo the smart-arse comedy, tip over into smugness. But it's forgivable, because when he gets it right, he's a sharpshooter.

A deft arranger and composer of orchestral pop strongly influenced by Scott Walker, Jacques Brel, Michael Nyman's classical repetitions, and the odd lilting Irish waltz (this album contains 'Songs Of Love', the vocal version of his theme for sitcom *Father Ted*), Hannon dresses his anger at lazy thinking in deceptively sweet Radio 2-lite pop. *Casanova* arrived amidst the 'new lad' era ushered in by Oasis, Chris Evans, 'Three Lions', *Loaded* magazine et al, and, by reviving historical randy git Casanova and '60s bird-shagging anti-hero Alfie (played in the film by new lad icon Michael Caine), set out to satirise it, from the perspective of a man who knew better, but largely didn't care. Whether being dumped by 'The Frog Princess' (a female equivalent to the laddish male chauvinist), or railing at the conformity of bourgeois parenting (and interior décor) in 'Middle Class Heroes', Hannon crooned melodramatically and loftily, and laughed his nuts off at all our '90s absurdities. The music was a sneaky foil, being a jaunty MOR that stood at odds with the search for authenticity implicit in the popular dadrock of Oasis, Weller, The Verve, et al. The bloke media briefly fell for the irony of ' . . . Weekend' and ' . . . Alfie', then realised, perhaps subconsciously, that they were the butt of the joke. Some of those of us who felt out of place amid the recidivist lumpen twattery of lads and laddettes appreciated someone satirising the times, from the perspective of someone more than tempted

to join in and be damned. The grandiosity and bitterness was the sweet and sour icing on the cake. Hannon had to settle, like so many besuited orchestral satirists before him and since, for being Big In France.

ODELAY

BECK
PRODUCED BY BECK HANSEN, THE DUST BROTHERS, MARIO CALDATO JR, BRIAN POULSON, TOM ROTHROCK, ROB SCHNAPF AND JON SPENCER
GEFFEN/JUNE 1996
UK CHART: 18
US CHART: 16
KEY TRACKS: 'Devil's Haircut'; 'Hotwax'; 'Jack-Ass'; 'Where It's At'; 'The New Pollution'

An album so postmodern that the CD actually features, between tracks seven and eight, a stylus being picked up, and put back down onto a vinyl record. I feel somewhat guilty for having nothing else to say about it, or Beck Hansen. But *Odelay* is a set of carefully chosen but empty Dylanesque phrases put to some cool people's immaculate collection of hip hop, pop, funk, rock and country records, and that's all it is. It makes a seamlessly fantastic noise because it can't help it. The more it tries to, you know, fuck things up, by making something all distorted or abruptly changing tempo, beat or genre, the more seamless and ambient it becomes. Even the five key tracks above are interchangeable from any other five. It communicates in fragments because that can replace truth in this gliberated age, but it does have a winning air of confidence about its insistence that American folk imagery and American hip hop imagery are natural bedfellows in gnomic meaninglessness. The only boring track is 'Ramshackle' because it's the only one that sounds sincere. The rest is just so . . . so . . . here it comes, can't escape it . . . cool.

Oh yeah ... the picture on the front is of a peculiarly moplike dog called a Komondor leaping over a mini-hurdle. I think that's what the youth of today would call 'random'.

IF YOU'RE FEELING SINISTER

BELLE AND SEBASTIAN
PRODUCED BY BELLE AND SEBASTIAN
JEEPSTER (ENCLAVE/CAPITOL IN USA)/NOVEMBER 1996
UK CHART: DID NOT CHART
US CHART: DID NOT CHART
KEY TRACKS: 'The Stars Of Track And Field'; 'Judy And The Dream Of Horses'; 'The Fox In The Snow'; 'Like Dylan In The Movies'; 'Seeing Other People'

Album cover clues to a band's aspirations. *Definitely Maybe* had a picture of the grand pop composer of the '60s, Burt Bacharach. It lent a band who had no intention of sounding like Dionne Warwick an instant, quasi-Rat Pack cool. The second album by Scots indie-popsters Belle And Sebastian featured a carefully positioned copy of *The Trial* by Franz Kafka. It told you that they were tortured students, while they set about sounding like a school band re-interpreting the tunes of Burt Bacharach. As their leader Stuart Murdoch put it, in 'Get Me Away From Here, I'm Dying', 'Play me a song to set me free/Nobody writes them like they used to/So it may as well be me.'

Belle And Sebastian were formed in Glasgow and named after a '70s children's show about a boy and his dog. It wasn't a Komondor. It was a Pyrenees mountain dog. Murdoch, a one-time boxer, and DJ, and heavy metal fan, and church janitor and committed Christian chorister, began the band as part of the music course at Stow College. The group's air of nostalgia, calmly expressed frustration, and anti-rockism is perhaps explained by the fact that Murdoch had much of his late teens and early twenties taken by illness. There is a

witty bitterness, or, at least, a self-deprecating and sexualised envy of those who enjoyed the energy of their youth in his writing summed up by the spectacular opening track of this album, 'The Stars Of Track And Field', as he accuses one of the star girls in a school he's never quite left: 'You liberated/A boy I never rated/And now he's throwing discus/For Liverpool and Widnes.'

Traces of Morrissey there alright, and the music attracts equal amounts of starry-eyed adoration and anti-twee loathing from those who chatter about pop by pitching Murdoch's choirboy vocals over a pop-historical mix of late Velvet Underground, Arthur Lee's *Love*, Nico, The Byrds, Simon And Garfunkel, Nick Drake, Bacharach and his country equivalent Jimmy Webb, with a wee smidgeon of arch and literate Scots jangling by Lloyd Cole and Orange Juice. Like Kathryn Williams (see p.328), Murdoch makes a vocal virtue of refusing to act out emotions, his warm calm remaining constant whether bitching, joking or, as on the title track, dismissing his religion with poetic disdain. His songs are populated by recorders and trumpets and girls who are into 'S&M and Bible classes' and who are smart and needy and vulnerable and suicidal and indestructible and who, in another resounding echo of The Smiths, are forever doomed to be disappointed by Murdoch's passive celibacy, like the heroine of 'Judy And The Dream Of Horses': 'We can do whatever you want,' he coos, so preciously, yet with power that jolts, 'But you will be disappointed/You will fall asleep with ants in your pants.'

There's been no downhill from here, exactly, with Belle And Sebastian. They're one of the few groups I can think of who've yet to make a bad record. *But If You're Feeling Sinister* flushes with amazement and pleasure of getting this far from such modest beginnings, and strikes an alchemical balance between compositional and thematic sophistication and basic musical technique. The record is a torrent of images from a now ancient 1970s seen through the eyes of a child, and equally mourned, celebrated and laughed at. But now is very much here, and carries an anti-modernity Health Warning, felt hardest in 'Like Dylan In The Movies', from an album that really wants to go further back and inhabit an innocent, imaginary, perfect 1960s: 'If they follow you/It's not your money that they're after, boy . . . It's you,' Murdoch sings soft but strong, stalked by harsh and fragmented modern times.

UNCHAINED

JOHNNY CASH
PRODUCED BY RICK RUBIN
AMERICAN/NOVEMBER 1996
UK CHART: DID NOT CHART
US CHART: DID NOT CHART
KEY TRACKS: 'Rowboat'; 'Southern Accents'; 'Spiritual'; 'Memories Are Made Of This'; 'I Never Picked Cotton'

The search for authenticity was well underway by 1996. Step forward Johnny Cash – a man whose life was a movie and whose voice possessed depths that felt like the ground beneath our feet. And with him, Rick Rubin, a producer who has made a career out of taking acts that were losing their way – early Beastie Boys, Red Hot Chilli Peppers, even The Cult – and stripping them down until the listener could hear real people and what they wanted to be and to do.

Unchained was well-named, and Cash and Rubin celebrated their second collaboration and the resulting 1997 'Best Country Album' Grammy by putting a full-page ad in US industry mag *Billboard*, featuring a big thank you to the country music industry and a much bigger picture of a grinning Cash raising his middle finger to the lot of them. Cash was just another old country has-been when Rubin had the inspired idea, in 1993, of letting the man sing, true, unadorned. The resulting *American Recordings* was all acoustic darkness and rock of ages, and reinvented Cash as an icon of Mount Rushmore cool for the MTV Unplugged generation. This follow-up album, with his failing and, of course, therefore all-the-more-moving voice backed by a revelatory Tom Petty and his Heartbreakers, dramatised death and fear of eternal damnation whether begging Jesus for mercy on Josh Haden's 'Spiritual', or squeezing dry the sentiment of the cheese-fest that is 'Memories Are Made Of This'. A version of grunge-metal band Soundgarden's 'Rusty Cage' rattled with defiance and explained Cash to a new generation of rock youth who had a greater acceptance of veteran musicians, as rock's generation gap began to freeze over.

The best song, though, was the opener 'Rowboat', an ancient folk song, pulled from the dusty pages of a barely legible scroll found by an itinerant hobo in 188 . . . uh, no, actually. Written by Beck. Yep, glib little Beck Hansen. This old man, counting down the days, brought the best out of everyone, and gave a song integrity just by doing it. Some of us figured we'd bypass dadrock, and go straight back to Old Father Time.

1997

BLUR

BLUR
PRODUCED BY STEPHEN STREET
FOOD/PARLOPHONE/FEBRUARY 1997
UK CHART: 1
US CHART: 61
KEY TRACKS: 'Country Sad Ballad Man'; 'Song 2'; 'You're So
Great'; 'M.O.R.'; 'Beetlebum'

The album that wrenched Blur from under Britpop was their least coherent. Whoo, and, indeed, hoo, because sometimes, just sometimes, an album that sounds like a band splitting asunder strikes sparks from the tension. With Damon Albarn and Graham Coxon getting down to fisticuffs, all four either on or recovering from addictions to drugs and/or booze, and the band's biggest-ever hit a parody of grunge angst bashed out while they sat around waiting for some posh bit of equipment to arrive, *Blur* is a celebration of chaos.

So, some facts, and assumptions. 'You're So Great' is entirely Graham, and its beautiful, wayward lo-fi sound and sophistication successfully presented as avant-punk, twinned with the Beatles-mainlining 'Beetlebum' and set off reverberations of *The White Album*.

'M.O.R.' sounds so much like Bowie's 'Boys Keep Swinging' that the band decided to cut out the lawyers and give him and Eno a co-credit.

Many reckon that the 'heavy metal' and 'pins' and 'needles' of 'Song 2' are about heroin. Weren't Damon and Justine prim and proper, in retrospect, compared to Pete and Kate?

'Death Of A Party' isn't about Britpop or a lonely teen, but about AIDS.

'Beetlebum' is about Liam Gallagher/Justine again/heroin/acid/The Beatles/cocaine/sex.

'Country Sad Ballad Man' is the moment when Damon Albarn became an outrageously good singer, producing a falsetto and a sense of vocal abandon that nothing in Blur's previous career had even hinted at. Graham follows him every step of the way, egging him on with his most breathtaking guitar crashes and imaginings. The way it all resolves into a tribute to XTC is typical of an album which wears all its art-rock influences proudly.

But none of it sounds like Pavement.

And just how good is an album where 'Strange News From Another Star', 'Death Of A Party', 'On Your Own', 'Look Inside America' and 'Movin' On' aren't the top five? And 'Movin' On' sounds like The Fall and Mott The Hoople, which is scientifically impossible.

But 'Essex Dogs' sounds like Can, and I really admire the line: 'In this town we all go to terminal pubs.'

It's lovely, the way 'M.O.R.' gives it a bit of 'all for one and one for all' in the surviving-Britpop-and-being-mates stakes. Rousing. But wishful thinking, as it turned out. You can hear both Graham Coxon's solo career and Damon's Gorillaz begin on this album, arm-wrestling to the death. It makes a great noise out of comedown, ennui and the dance of two people who have just discovered that they have nothing whatsoever in common. Which two people? Any.

BADUIZM

ERYKAH BADU
PRODUCED BY VARIOUS PRODUCERS (EXECUTIVE
PRODUCTION BY KEDAR MASSENBURG)
KEDAR/UNIVERSAL/MARCH 1997
UK CHART: 17
US CHART: 2
KEY TRACKS: 'Appletree'; 'On & On'; 'The Otherside Of The
Game'; 'Next Lifetime'; 'Certainly'

In 1995 a young prodigy called D'Angelo (see p.331) made a successful album that changed the rules of American R&B, and offered a way back to soul. Modernising classic soul by way of the deep beats and jazz influences of A Tribe Called Quest, strongly influenced by the ingestion of marijuana and prepared to deal with the violence and sexual aggression of what hip hop had become while suggesting more conciliatory alternatives, D'Angelo's *Brown Sugar* album was dubbed nu-soul. A Memphis poet, choreographer and actress called Erica Wright listened hard, and presented a female version that killed us softly with its songs.

Baduizm came off like Billie Holiday reborn as an Afro-American princess of the hip hop streets, and taking the soul-starved listener on a low-end-heavy journey through all the most loving and strong impulses of twentieth-century black music. 'On & On' and 'Appletree' made inky purple hues out of being broke, and hanging out with friends respectively, expressing a gratitude for living and loving that felt hard-won, even radical compared to the flabbiness of (non) competitors. But, for all the quotes from muso blues, jazz and soul, being anti-hip hop was none of the point. Like the conscious soul era it invoked – the Stevies, Slys and Marvins and Curtis Mayfields of the early '70s – its politics and social comment strived to be inclusive, to understand why a vicious, materialist attitude had permeated black culture since the Reagan '80s.

'Otherside Of The Game' made the point as clear as (Lady) day. Badu plays the loving wife of a criminal – it's not made explicit that he's a drug dealer, but the implication is unavoidable. Over the sparest of blue funk, the wife and pregnant mother frets about her man's 'complex occupation'. Her powerlessness overpowers the danger her man is in. 'Whatcha gonna do when they come for you/Work ain't honest but it pays the bills.' She tries to explain further: 'It ain't that he don't have education/'Cos I was right there at his graduation.' By bringing it back to school and the image of these two as childhood sweethearts, the story of how they got here fills the space in the soft music, shows those of us who don't live in the American projects some rhyme and reason for the destruction and cruel choices. She gives up trying to persuade him to give up this life. But she's smart enough to see this is all part of a historical struggle, that this is not just about her unborn child or her man, and that society is punishing those who fight, no matter which way they choose to battle. 'Peace out to revolution,' she mumbles, caustically. 'But we paid though.'

The generosity and intelligence of 'Otherside Of the Game' opens up the album's sundry delights; the feminist kiss-off of 'Certainly', the extraordinary 'Next Lifetime', where another Badu character (and it's important to understand her playing of roles) turns down an extra-marital shag in a voice and language that would have any man laying down his life for a kiss, even as she walks away, giggling coyly. 'Drama' fully revives Marvin Gaye's 'What's Going On' and its air of looking down over a world in chaos, and implores us to look to God for the answers. But it's the least convincing tune on the record. 'It's hip to be spiritual this year,' the regal Ms Badu told me in an interview for *Time Out* later in 1997, with all the fearlessness of someone who had no moral ground to claim, and had no intention of faking one when confronted.

All this coded fury and weighty debate, yet the music fashioned by various producers including A Tribe Called Quest engineer Bob Power and live hip hop group The Roots makes this record work as seduction soundtrack, Saturday night chill-out, Sunday morning church replacement. The success of her masterpiece briefly threatened to inspire a new era in conscious soul. But only Lauryn Hill (see p.309) and D'Angelo (see p.331) were at her level. Baduizm stands alone, a missing link between '70s street funk, basement jazz, bohemian hip hop and the blues reinventions of Portishead.

THE BOATMAN'S CALL

NICK CAVE AND THE BAD SEEDS
PRODUCED BY NICK CAVE AND THE BAD SEEDS AND FLOOD

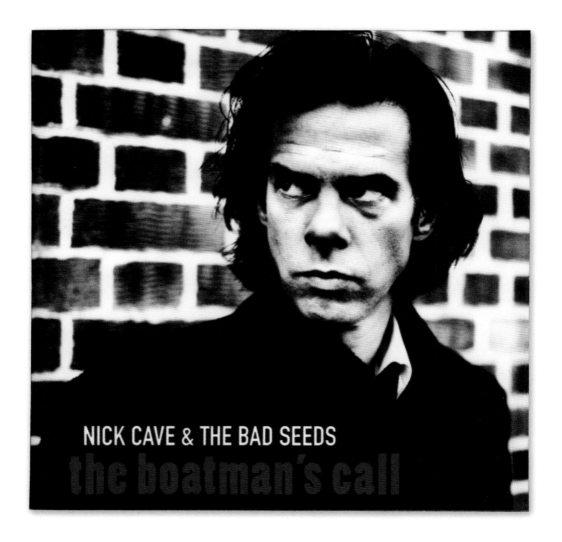

NICK CAVE & THE BAD SEEDS
the boatman's call

THE BOATMAN'S CALL/NICK CAVE AND THE BAD SEEDS

MUTE/MARCH 1997
UK CHART: 22
US CHART: DID NOT CHART
KEY TRACKS: '(Are You) The One That I've Been Waiting For?'; 'Into My Arms'; 'Far From Here'; 'People Ain't No Good'; 'Brompton Oratory'

As first lines of an album go, it don't get no better than 'I don't believe in an interventionist God'. Particularly as the rest of the record continually insists that he does. Maybe.

An album made from a crisis in faith, in God, in people, in love, *The Boatman's Call* is heavily influenced by Leonard Cohen and by Bob Dylan's divorce masterpiece *Blood On The Tracks*. It represents the most drastic mood change between Cave albums, from the blood, guts and character comedy of *Murder Ballads* (see p.284) to a set of acoustic ruminations dominated by gospel piano, and lyrics about his relationships with Polly Harvey and Viviane Carneiro. Cave was also, despite calming much of the suicidal wildness that characterised his time with The Birthday Party and the early Bad Seeds, still struggling to quell his heroin habit. *The Boatman's Call*, then, is an ultimate quiet storm, with the air of a man writing and singing to make sense out of inner turmoil. The music's sense of rolling calm – like the lull after, rather than before, a storm at sea – sets each word in classic songwriting stone. It was powerful, deep and bereft enough to cut right through the gossip side of the Cave/Harvey relationship, and take away the last vestiges of the singer's 'goth' image.

There is cruelty at real people's expense in 'People Ain't No Good' (no relation to the Cramps' song), 'Far From Me' ('You were my brave-hearted lover/Who at the first sign of trouble went running back to mother') and 'Green Eyes', but that's why you believe it when he compares the same people to God and Christ. There are more than a few people I know who keep this album close, believing it to contain more truth about love, loss, abandonment, faith and the black horror at the heart of losing yourself in love affairs that are doomed to fail than almost any other work of art. The music is made from folk song, shadows of rockabilly and hymn, and grim self-deprecating humour and stunned silence, and it soothes as it agonises.

LADIES AND GENTLEMEN WE ARE FLOATING IN SPACE

SPIRITUALIZED
PRODUCED BY J. SPACEMAN
DEDICATED/JUNE 1997
UK CHART: 4
US CHART: DID NOT CHART
KEY TRACKS: 'I Think I'm In Love'; 'Broken Heart'; 'Come Together'; 'Ladies And Gentlemen We Are Floating In Space'; 'Electricity'

On the other hand, when you get dumped, you can reaffirm your love affair with heroin, employ The Balanescu Quartet and the London Community Gospel Choir, and blast-off into orbit. This is what Rugby's Jason Pierce, guitarist, singer and former member of lysergic droners Spaceman 3, opted for, when his keyboard player Kate Radley ran off and married Richard Ashcroft out of The Verve. Just in case anyone was in any doubt about how you were dealing with your broken heart, you could dress initial copies of the CD in a pharmaceutical pill packet. And then complain when anyone asks you about drugs in interviews.

To be fair to Pierce, asking him about drugs was pointless. 'Love in the middle of the afternoon/Just me, my spike in my arm and my spoon,' he groaned breathily in 'I Think I'm In Love'. What could he mean? Even allowing for this towering album's sonic ambition, and the layers of bluesy cosmic shimmer and fanfare needed to blend Phil Spector, the Stones, The Stooges, Aretha Franklin, and free-jazz space-bothering legend Sun Ra, you didn't really need any more information, short of every copy coming with a free inflatable Jason, jacking up in living colour in your living room.

So, while Cave dug deep and stripped heartbreak bare, Pierce took a similarly male and drug-fuelled self-pity and made it into the best wall of rock 'n' roll sound of the whole damn 1990s.

Putting the eternal triangle aside, the main controversy surrounded the estate of Elvis Presley refusing to allow an interpolation of The King's 'Can't Help Falling In Love' to be used in the opening title track. Suffice to say that there's plenty here to soften the blow of the Elvis no-show. Free-jazz skronking and cosmic boogie. Epic pop rubbing up against avant-garde mastery. Cinematic orchestras and New Orleans voodoomeister Dr John's guest piano on the manic seventeen-minute space-jazz-meets-John-Prine audience tester that is 'Cop Shoot Cop'. The Good Lord's own backing vocals. And a-weepin' and a-wailin' fit to beat the band playing at the last tearooms of Uranus. When the boy staggers through the line, 'I've been told that these things heal . . . given time,' only carried to some kind of continuance of breathing by the powerful shoulders of a swelling orchestra on 'Broken Heart', I swear your own heart will pause for a second's silence out of respect for its dead brethren. If albums like this and *The Boatman's Call* don't bring the woman back, we can safely assume, boys, that a bunch of flowers ain't gonna fly.

SUPA DUPA FLY

MISSY 'MISDEMEANOUR' ELLIOTT
PRODUCED BY TIMBALAND
THE GOLD MIND INC/EASTWEST/JULY 1997
UK CHART: DID NOT CHART
US CHART: 3
KEY TRACKS: 'The Rain (Supa Dupa Fly)'; 'They Don't Wanna F*** Wit Me'; 'Hit 'Em Wit Da Hee'; 'Sock It 2 Me'; 'Don't Be Commin' (In My Face)'

Sex on wax. In virtual space. On a giant bouncy castle.

Melissa Elliott came bounding out of Portsmouth, Virginia, after contributing tracks to Aaliyah's not dissimilar *One In A Million* and rapping with Boyz II Men, with hip hop's first whiff of a brand new sound for years. The 'Dirty' South was transforming black American music, by virtue of being able to avoid the whole east vs. west, playas vs. gangstas mess, and its young artists and producers were intent on pushing the rap/R&B envelope. Missy was everything the hip hop doctor ordered: a big, beautiful woman who could flip between aggression and romance, sex and nonsense, materialism and imagination, without batting one outrageously spidery eyelash. Her producer Tim 'Timbaland' Mosley was the perfect foil, eschewing samples for a bump 'n' grind electronica, strongly influenced by the digital rhythms of dancehall reggae (and maybe mindful of Massive Attack and Portishead, too, both much-respected cult artists among black American musicians), but rounder, fuller, fatter. There was no room for skinny lattes once you sunk into the warm folds of this sound. 'My hormones jumpin' like a disco,' Missy sang (because she uniquely sang and rapped equally well) on the blaring hook of the party-hearty 'Sock It 2 Me', and *Supa Dupa Fly* was one of those rare albums that transformed your living-room/car/headphones into a sweaty, writhing, grinding basement nightclub, as soon as . . . what is the compact disc equivalent of needle hitting groove, anyway?

Lyrically, Missy is more often part of the problem than the solution. 'Pass Da Blunt' bigs up dope because everyone else does, disses other 'bitches', and supports gold-digging in a self-confessed 'this pussy costs' manner. On the other hand, it makes the chorus taken from Musical Youth's 'Pass the Dutchie' into funk gold, so what can you do but dig it? The bling-bling era was well under way, and *Supa Dupa Fly* is a key prophecy of the dominant twenty-first-century black pop. The proudly synthetic, all bass-and-treble music anticipates ringtones. The titles anticipate text messaging, by way of Prince. The themes are all money and sex, but with-

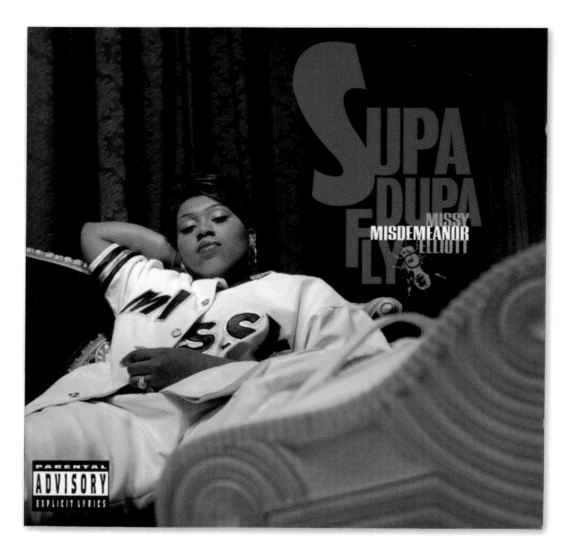

SUPA DUPA FLY/MISSY 'MISDEMEANOR' ELLIOTT

out the brutalism and violence that had made hip hop appear terminally sick at heart. The double-entendre in 'Don't Be Commin' (In My Face)' was entirely intended, and Timbaland unleashed this bizarre woody boing noise, just to add punctuation. The guy raised the production bar, brought back creativity to urban hit making, got rid of all those who just threw a breakbeat under a funk sample almost overnight, and invented The Neptunes and Kanye West.

Missy and Tim would make better individual songs (the epochal singles 'Get Ur Freak On', 'Work It' and 'Pass That Dutch' . . . no, the themes didn't change much), but never again such a coherent, irresistible long-player. The likes of Lil Kim, Aaliyah, Busta Rhymes and Da Brat guest, and you barely notice. You just want to hear that thrilling drawl or thrilled trill hit the next freaky freaky beat.

WHEN I WAS BORN FOR THE 7TH TIME

CORNERSHOP
PRODUCED BY TJINDER SINGH, DAN THE AUTOMATOR AND DADDY RAPPAPORT
WIIIJA/SEPTEMBER 1997
UK CHART: 17
US CHART: DID NOT CHART
KEY TRACKS: 'Brimful Of Asha'; 'Good Shit'; 'We're In Yr Corner'; 'Sleep On The Left Side'; 'Butter The Soul'

'My full name is Tjinder Singh Nurpuri. I used Tjinder Singh so my family wouldn't know that I was in a band. It was a bit of a cultural thing. It wasn't a good thing to speak about to the neighbours.'

Tjinder Singh of Cornershop is one of many of us who don't quite know where we belong. Born in Wolverhampton, forming the slyly named Cornershop at Preston University in 1991, and from Sikh parentage, he's turned that questing for identity into a vital influence on British alt-pop. Going from the raging punk noise of their racist-baiting beginnings, to finding increasingly organic ways to input the Punjabi into Britpop, Cornershop are a national treasure, no matter what nationality you define yourself as on this funky island.

Released while a horrible band called Kula Shaker, who featured a singer who nicked Asian licks and then spouted pseudo-mystical right-wing claptrap in the music press, were having their fifteen bewildering minutes in the post-Britpop sun, Cornershop's third album was a surprise to anyone who thought them just noisy agit-proppers. Blending Jonathan Richman-style pop minimalism with post-Beasties hip hop, South Asian classical music with laid-back dope-fuelled funk, Panjabi folk song with The Beatles, *When I Was Born For The 7th Time* is a virtual template for the global mish-mash of the two Gorillaz albums, right down to using underground hip hop producer Dan The Automator.

'Brimful Of Asha' reached No. 1 in the charts, of course, after getting a fizzy Norman Cook remix. But the original is a more beatific treasure, a paean to singles culture finding a missing link between Marc Bolan, the Trojan reggae label, and various Indian artists including legendary Indian playback singer Asha Bhosle. The playback singer sings the tunes from Bollywood movie musicals while the actors mime, yet sell millions of records in their own right. Whether those who bought and danced to 'Brimful Of Asha' learned that or not, the song entered the British cultural body on a viral level, kicking off the mainstream acceptance of Bollywood as fodder for movies and stage musicals.

The band was part of something dubbed 'New Asian Cool'. Cynics sneered at yet another media fad, but Asian actors, comedians and musicians are accepted in twenty-first-century Britain as never before, and Cornershop's sumptuous Asian punk-funk has as much to do with that as *East Is East* and *The Kumars*. It's hard to overstate just how violent and vile anti-Asian racism was in the England I grew up in. In order for Brits to accept a foreign presence, two things have to happen. Firstly, they have to lose a few street-fights, and various pastings for skinheads in Southall and Bradford began that process. Then, it's all about clothes, cool, sex and, especially, music. This album is key to Britain being a better place, most of the time, than it was.

Elsewhere the album featured beat poet Allen Ginsberg's last recorded performance, a poem about death recited over a recording of a Punjabi band playing in an Indian street recorded just weeks before he passed away; and a deadpan cover of The Beatles' 'Norwegian Wood (This Bird Has Flown)', sung in Punjabi, bringing one of the first uses of Asian art in British pop culture right back home. The biggest compliment you can pay *When I Was Born For The 7th Time* (which Singh and his creative partner Ben Ayres denied was anything to do with reincarnation) is that The Beatles don't provide anywhere near the best song.

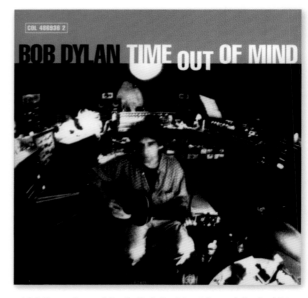

TIME OUT OF MIND

BOB DYLAN
PRODUCED BY DANIEL LANOIS AND BOB DYLAN
COLUMBIA/OCTOBER 1997
UK CHART: 10
US CHART: 10
KEY TRACKS: 'Not Dark Yet'; 'Tryin' To Get To Heaven'; 'Make You Feel My Love'; 'Highlands'; 'Love Sick'

Shortly after recording this, his first album of self-penned songs since 1990, Bob Dylan was, in the spring of 1997, hospitalised with a life-threatening heart condition. Although he recovered quickly, critics noted the deathly tone of *Time Out Of Mind* and concluded that it was the musings of a man approaching that final curtain call. Dylan pooh-poohed the idea, and had the evidence of dates and good health on his side. But this has been Dylan's way since his

mid-'60s peak saw him hailed the Messiah, and freaked him out. He says that every word he sings has been misinterpreted, but offers no alternative interpretation at all. It's a big part of why Dylan retains a presence, a mystery, a public perception of depth that his fellow '60s rock gods have long since lost. Many of us just can't help suspecting that he has the answers. The question is all that's missing.

So *Time Out Of Mind* sounds like a man reaching the end of a dark road, voice crackling with ill health and bad feeling, casting doubt on humanity, beauty, hope and God, but mainly on love which, in a strikingly similar if less florid way than *The Boatman's Call* (see p.292), is expressed as life's obsession, the way of greatest pain, the source of all souls' decay. Whereas the Johnny Cash American albums take all that same pain and fear of the void to present a man resigned but going down fighting, *Time Out Of Mind* is hopeless, bereft and weary of finding, to borrow the quote that Martin Scorsese used to title his recent Dylan documentary, 'no direction home'. If the record did remind you of his '60s peak, it was only in a loud echo of 'Like A Rolling Stone', and a feeling that all the things the victim of that famous song had been so cruelly exposed to and accused of had now, in old age, befallen the arrogant young singer.

The music here is essential to making this a mesmerising blues album, rather than the soul-sapping well of misery it surely could've been. Apparently plucked from chaotic sessions effectively featuring two bands playing simultaneously, the masterful Daniel Lanois fashions his trademark cosmic swampiness, a rootsy ambience that owes something to post-*Swordfishtrombones* Tom Waits (see p.159), and much to an appreciation of the spaces between. Every time the album seems to be content just to play an elegant form of the blues, a twist, like the stunning chord that builds the bridge in 'Tryin' To Get To Heaven', brings levels of sad beauty that effortlessly carry the music towards the grand and timeless. Everything weeps, but with the restraint of someone for whom bitterness and fury have become mutually exclusive. It's also more modern than Dylan's endless fascination for traditional American folk-blues might lead you to hear. 'Love Sick', for example, carries elements of R.E.M.'s 'Drive' and a maudlin, Sandinista-era Clash.

But it's the voice, mainly, and the deceptively simple lyrics, occasionally, that do the damage. They reinvent the love piano ballad on 'Make You Feel My Love', the dehydrated crack of Dylan's throat giving the cheesy, I'll-give-you-the-moon-and-the-stars lyric a devastating edge of panic and grief. But nothing prepares for the final song 'Highlands', sixteen minutes of shuffling rockabilly bewilderment with a lyric that briefly, but memorably, coalesces around an encounter with a waitress in a diner in Boston. It's a shock return to the old Dylan: the master wordsmith, juggling opposites, presenting conversation as post-Beckett misunderstanding and mordant satire. My fave bit is when she mistakes him for an artist and implores him to draw a sketch of her:

I make a few lines and I show it for her to see
Well, she takes her napkin and throws it back
And says, 'That don't look a thing like me.'
I said, 'Oh, kind Miss, it most certainly does.'
She say, 'You must be jokin'.'
I say, 'I wish I was.'

As to whether the pained testimonies to haunted, lost love were aimed at ex-wives Carolyn Dennis or Sara Lowndes or someone else entirely, well, I rang Bob, and he just said, 'The curtains hang the judges, but the bread, it just don't shave,' and hung up. I also can't do the 'this was his best album since . . . ' routine, because I hadn't listened properly to a Dylan album since 1976's *Desire*. He seemed, to me, just another persistent relic, and I had my own messiahs to be disappointed by. But *Time Out Of Mind* hit – hits – me hard, its pessimism a strange source of strength in the face of accepting pain, old age, mortality. It makes me want to go back and listen to all those albums that everyone said sucked, and work out how this man got to the point of singing, in the most honest and human voice I think I've ever heard, in 'Not Dark Yet': 'Well, my sense of humanity has gone down the drain/Behind every beautiful thing there's been some kind of pain,' and not make me laugh nor turn my back.

PORTISHEAD

PORTISHEAD
PRODUCED BY GEOFF BARROW, ADRIAN UTLEY, BETH GIBBONS AND DAVE MCDONALD
GO! DISCS/OCTOBER 1997
UK CHART: 2
US CHART: 27
KEY TRACKS: 'Humming'; 'All Mine'; 'Only You'; 'Western Eyes'; 'Half Day Closing'

You are pretty much screwed in pop if you come up with a

completely original sound. The story goes: make first record, people stunned, becomes word of mouth hit and therefore ubiquitous, but not necessarily reflected in chart position, sales being spread over months, even years. Make second record, media hype goes into overdrive, fans buy ensuring high chart entry, but . . . it's like the first one. Where's the novelty? Quality is basically ignored and artist criticised for not coming up with original sound again. Record goes down as career suicide, or somesuch.

People, ignore such desperation for The New at all costs, and get *Portishead* if you got *Dummy*, because it's the same, but more John Barry-meets-spaghetti-western cinematic, with twangier guitars, darker hues and even more extraordinary singing from the ball of fearful tension that is Beth Gibbons. It often sounds like Shirley Bassey on a drip interpreting the works of Joy Division. The Portishead sound is a wintry, sensual and dangerous thing, and has a pessimistic old-world bluesiness that wouldn't be a stranger to old crackin', cracklin' Bob. Plus it's so grim that, like Dylan and Cave, it has a gallows humour vibe, even when they make a true post-punk spook tune called 'Half Day Closing' which sounds exactly like the creeping horror of waking up in an English town 'Where money talks and leaves us hypnotised' and 'Underneath the fading sun/The silent sum of a businessman/Has left us choking'. By the final 'Western Eyes', it's making like a zombie lounge group playing an eternal residency in a ghost town.

Hmmm . . . Nick Cave, Spiritualized, Dylan, Portishead . . . maybe we should have that New Labour election party round at Missy's house.

1998

MOON SAFARI

AIR

PRODUCED BY JEAN-BENOÎT DUNCKEL AND NICOLAS GODIN

SOURCE/JANUARY 1998

UK CHART: 6

US CHART: DID NOT CHART

KEY TRACKS: 'Sexy Boy'; 'Kelly Watch The Stars'; 'La Femme D'Argent'; 'Remember'; 'All I Need'

An optimistic yet wistful, dance-derived counterpoint to *Spiritualized* (see p.302), Versailles-born and Paris-based duo Jean-Benoît Dunckel and Nicolas Godin also made a retro-nouveau debut album proper that made us feel like we were floating in space. Defining the '90s electronica/alt-dance scenes' fascination for pre-digital synths, soundtracks and easy-listening music from the late '60s and early '70s, Air pulled off the trick of making music that reflected their name, but with melodic ambition and enough muscle under the dreamy surface to pull away from conventional chill-out music. It became another in a lengthening line of dance-influenced 'coffee table' albums, a cool modern soundtrack for happening thirtysomethings.

The big hit, 'Sexy Boy' used vocoders – a distinctly old-school robotic vocal effect – to obscure its homoeroticism, and its lyrics, translated from French, are a dream of being a dreamboat: 'One day I too will be beautiful like a god,' the pair whisper creamily, and the song unveils as a male counterpoint to Kraftwerk's 'The Model' (see p.41), a paean to catwalk and celebrity prettiness with an undertow of ironic sneer. Elsewhere, they sing in English for the balmy thrill of 'Kelly Watch The Stars', among instrumentals that conjure half-buried memories of early '70s Radio 2, of key Gallic mood music legends Serge Gainsbourg and Jean-Jacques Perrey, of the stately pop melancholy and strangeness of Pet Sounds-era Beach Boys, of Burt Bacharach songs that back-drop Paul Newman doing tricks on a bicycle. Yet the meaty, deep, yet lyrical basslines of 'La Femme D'Argent' and 'New Star In The Sky' and the somnambulant skyward glide of guest vocalist Beth Hirsch's chorus on 'All I Need' are pure post-Portishead and Massive Attack, attaching the past to the present with an all-important tang of '70s futurism, the world of flying cars and walking on the moon we imagined when we watched James Burke and *Tomorrow's World* on TV, and read magazines such as *World Of Wonder*, and believed that science fiction, was, in the end, a force for good, rather than music boiled down to ringtones on a crowded bus, or a CCTV camera watching you pick your nose. All gurgling Moogs and twinkling Fender Rhodes pianos, *Moon Safari* was the emollient panacea for pre-millennial dread, and it's still one of the kindest listens when feeling overwhelmed by digital chaos.

RAY OF LIGHT

MADONNA

PRODUCED BY MADONNA, WILLIAM ORBIT, MARIUS
DE VRIES AND PATRICK LEONARD
MAVERICK/MARCH 1998
UK CHART: 1
US CHART: 2
KEY TRACKS: 'Ray Of Light'; 'Skin'; 'Frozen'; 'The Power Of
Good-bye'; 'Nothing Really Matters'

The only Madonna album where the music overwhelms the Madonna-ness of it all. Having become, since 1989's *Like A Prayer*, more famous as a symbol of celebrity sex, attitude and power than an actual singer, Madonna sounded almost humble as she allowed Brit techno/pop producer William Orbit to carry her airborne on bubbling electronics, and make her sing properly. Whether her increasingly settled relationship with movie director Guy Ritchie, parenthood, or her signing up to the teachings of Kabbalah – a kind of Judaism for those who don't actually want to sacrifice anything for their spirituality or follow any rules, a very modern celebrity religion mix of traditional piety and New Age me-orientated laissez-faire – inspired such an earth mother approach is Ms Ciccone's own considerable business. For the listener, it was a shock delight, a delicate, sweet and strong trade-off between the left-field experiment of Björk and the pure disco-pop Madonna we knew and loved.

Not that you necessarily believe the poor little rich girl theme introduced in the opening 'Drowned World/ Substitute For Love'. But by the third and title track, her sincerity is not the issue, because it never has been: it's always been about her ability to make pop that encapsulates the joy of dancing and its relationship with sexual display. So, even though we get an ode to Baby in the 'orrible 'Little Star', it's the one misstep in a multi-layered dance-meets-ambient adult party set, with just enough genuine emotion – and when you listen to 'Ray Of Light' or 'Skin' you get a blissful reminder that pleasure and sexual desire are emotions too, and often more honest and generous ones than twenty-first-century adult rock's endless whining eunuch sadness about nothing specific – to make you feel that she actually feels. If 'Nothing Really Matters' is a manual for guilt-assuaging airy-fairy Hollywood karmic gobbledegook – don't you just adore obscenely rich people who advise that 'love is all we need?' – then its roots in old-school orchestral disco force you to stop questioning the substance, and buy into the joy. Even 'Ashanti/Ashtangi's Indian chic is sung and produced with enough detail and gusto to grind your cynicism into dust. Indeed, *Ray Of Light* comes across as a key text in the western middle classes' quest for the organic and authentic . . . rendered in appropriately cute but superficial style from a Queen of Masks.

MEZZANINE

MASSIVE ATTACK

PRODUCED BY MASSIVE ATTACK AND NEIL DAVIDGE
CIRCA/VIRGIN/APRIL 1998
UK CHART: 1
US CHART: 60
KEY TRACKS: 'Inertia Creeps'; 'Risingson'; 'Angel'; 'Black
Milk'; 'Group Four'

When everyone on the planet is copping your licks, how do you stick with what you're doing but take it too far to be buried in the avalanche of trippity-hoppity shuffling? Easy. You find a two-note bassline, deep like breath, set to the rhythm of a body in sleep. You hire the most androgynous voice in reggae, the great Horace Andy, to sing about angels and love in as soothingly pained a voice as he can produce, and then, at two minutes and twenty-four seconds (now that's one advantage of CD) you thwack two solid snare beats and . . . unleash a churning thrum of heavy metal power chords. All the good taste boffins disintegrate, the

RAY OF LIGHT/MADONNA

song's blood boils, and the mood is set for your greatest album and one of the very best covered in this book.

Named after that floor in the hotel, which is neither here nor there, perfumed by brain-scrambling skunk, and feeling like the after-effects of a bacchanal gone-very-wrong, *Mezzanine* defines Massive Attack's art of dread-fuelled parties. Everything here drums and drones like a heartbeat, yet finds melody out of pain. Tracks from the album were and are used all over soundtracks, from Guy Ritchie's *Snatch* to *The Matrix*, from *Pi* to *24*, an immediate shorthand for something-wicked-this-way-comes.

Fingers literally on the pulse, the band tellingly made the album available as a legal MP3 download on their website months before release. Even more tellingly, the gnarly power-rock guitars appeared to be a post-punk influence too far for Andrew Vowles aka Mushroom, who left soon after the release of *Mezzanine*, amid much public bickering. Daddy G even plundered a line, 'Please send me evenings and weekends,' from Gang Of Four's 'Return The Gift' for the very PiL-like title track – a reminder that Massive Attack and Blur were hugely influenced by post-punk long before it became a fashionable genre to plunder, and that a major theme of their music was the wage-slave life, and our conformity to the most soul-sucking of norms and conventions. Yet G, aka Grant Marshall, has been on some sort of Bristolian hip hop equivalent of gardening leave ever since, leaving Robert '3-D' Del Naja and this album's co-producer Neil Davidge effectively to carry on as Massive Attack.

So, naturally, one looks at *Mezzanine* as an album wrenched out of internal tension. I was out in a bar in Brighton a few weeks before writing this entry and, after an hour or so of your common or garden trendy bar beatz for da headz, *Mezzanine* came on. And sure, the warm bass and the dragging tempo and the stoned sophistication fitted the bar ambience criteria, but . . . it sliced through the fabric of the room, just too hard, angry, murky and strange to sit politely in the background. 'We need a little love to ease the pain,' the oddly light and poppy vocals of Sara Jay insist on 'Dissolved Girl' before being crushed by ten tons of metal riffage. But *Mezzanine* feels like pain and love arm-wrestling, and pain winning every time.

Nevertheless, the musical pleasures of *Mezzanine* are boundless. Daddy G and Del Naja's mumbled horror and sardonic amusement at the celeb party on 'Risingson', the graceful gossamer folk melodies The Cocteau Twins' Liz Fraser finds inside 'Teardrop', 'Group Four' and 'Black Milk', the brooding moonwalk that is 'Inertia Creeps'. And, for good measure, they mix Horace Andy, Led Zeppelin's drums and a sample of The Cure for yet another extraordinary version of John Holt's noisy neighbour classic 'Man Next Door', following in the footsteps of The Slits and Dr Alimantado (see p.47), finding the universal in its plea for personal space and peace of mind, which is far more pressing a concern for most of us than world peace.

Love is not all we need. Never has been. *Mezzanine* uses that knowledge and creates a magisterial world of interior darkness, a rudder to grab on to in a sea of the banal. It also connects music with roots in Africa, and music with roots in the British inner-city, more naturally and unpretentiously than any other album outside of *Metal Box*. It possibly makes tea and knits its own yoghurt, too. I'm just too worried about it taking over my house to find out.

ANGELS WITH DIRTY FACES

TRICKY
PRODUCED BY TRICKY
ISLAND/MAY 1998
UK CHART: 23
US CHART: 84
KEY TRACKS: 'Broken Homes'; '6 Minutes'; 'Money Greedy'; 'Demises'; 'Singing The Blues'

Tricky's third album concludes, yet again, that all we need is love. Admittedly, it's the last line of a last song called 'Taxi', which plays around with the idea that he and vocal foil Martina need a white girl or boy because, 'Now I can get a taxi,' before mumbling distractedly, 'The only disease in our blood/We need is love.' Love comes from dark places in Bristol, it seems.

The various fractious relationships in Massive Attack came further to the surface on this dank, disturbed beast of a record, as Adrian Thaws addressed his occasional former bandmates thusly, on opener 'Money Greedy': 'Remember we used to sit at The Brits/Never won any awards/That's not what we used to look towards/Money greedy.' Exactly why almost everyone who began with Massive Attack ends up so pissed off with everyone else is a story that will presumably emerge over time. What was certain was that Tricky's success was not making him a happy bunny. He raps about 'Standing in government lines' for benefits on 'Money Greedy' with twisted pride, almost as if he misses it. It's the appropriate way to kick-off an album that defied fashion, dumped trip hop, wheezed like a toothless wino on Woodbines, and talked to itself about society's decay, poverty, absent fathers, racism, fame, the music business and overpowering stress. Everyone seemed to hate it but me. Punk rock dies hard.

By now, Tricky had been wretchedly unpleasant to some of my fellow journalists, and rumours abounded about drugs, Martina, drugs, violence and drugs. If he wanted to make an album that confirmed that he was being driven insane by something, then he shot, he scored. Using a live band who essentially begin every song playing a mutant rock/hip hop/drum 'n' bass hybrid riff and . . . well, that's about it, give or take the odd turntable scratch or looped whoop, eerie fiddle or pipe . . . Tricky headed too far into the heart of darkness to ever completely return. Changes of chord or key or melody line bring surprise, delight and relief to a music listener. *Angels With Dirty Faces* has none. It's so horizontal it's drowning in a puddle. What I loved was what I missed in all those post-punk records from the late '70s . . . an artist laying bare their furies and night terrors, and find-

ing a sonic dislocation of the norm to match. Tone poetry, basically, but it was understandable that radio and the general public weren't too keen on fourteen aural sonnets that smelt of rat-infested alleys and had nothing – with the possible exception of Polly Jean Harvey's gospel-blues chorus on the single 'Broken Homes' – in the way of a tune. 'Talk To Me (Angels With Dirty Faces)' didn't even have a regular beat, just drums like dead men walking and Tricky incanting over a cast-adrift Martina Topley-Bird's shoulder, in a suitably creepy way.

Like Shaun Ryder and Shane MacGowan, Tricky had been to bad places, met bad people, and possibly done worse. Unlike that pair of lovable rogues, he came over like the neighbourhood threat. Some of that can be put down to his colour and the truth that most white people are, despite all liberal protests to the contrary, more scared of black men than white men. But most has to be put down to his inability to leaven his art with humour. There are no smiles here . . . although having a spot-on rant at the violence in hip hop and calling it 'Record Companies' perhaps counts as a grimace. Or maybe 'Peyote Sings', and its stumbling grumbles about fame and media intrusion, counts as a curled lip, when Tricky, being both envious inquisitor and his poor old self, growls sleepily, 'I don't like your voice/That's OK, neither do I/The only difference between me and you is that I get by.'

This is probably the one album in this book which I understand to be a very personal pleasure, and which I wouldn't make a try-it-you'll-love-it argument for. But it sounds like no other record I've ever heard, and that strikes me as an almost impossible achievement. Captain Beefheart's *Trout Mask Replica* broke every rule of pop music and still lives, almost forty years after its making, on the love of the adventurous listener. Indeed, the musical *mise en scène* of *Angels With Dirty Faces*, with its broken-bone percussion and desire to take the blues right back to the African bush, inhabits some singular dwelling between the junkyards of post-*Swordfishtrombones* (see p.159) Tom Waits and the

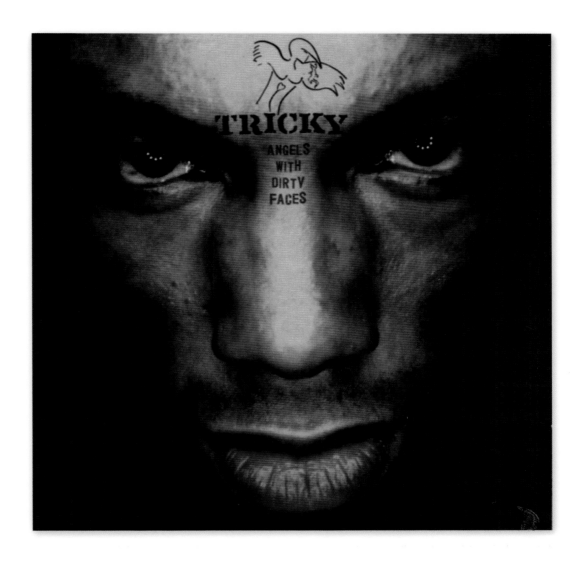

ANGELS WITH DIRTY FACES/TRICKY

jungles of *My Life In The Bush Of Ghosts* (see p.110). Maybe, one day, *Angels With Dirty Faces* will get a similar rep, because its evocation of an underclass world of dirty needles, abused children, and broken bones is brave and unique and more accurate about Britain and the paranoia of the poor and disenfranchised than rich white men whining about nasty computers and being watched by the CIA. Most of this planet would love to be watched, if only someone would give them money, shelter, parental love, acknowledgement of their existence. Switch on the TV, see the poor in all their shame. *Angels With Dirty Faces* is about them. Tricky still felt like one, trapped, weary, seething.

THE SINGLES 86–98

DEPECHE MODE
PRODUCED BY VARIOUS PRODUCERS
MUTE/SEPTEMBER 1998
UK CHART: 5
US CHART: 38
KEY TRACKS: 'Personal Jesus'; 'A Question Of Lust'; 'Never Let Me Down Again'; 'Behind The Wheel'; 'Stripped'

THE SINGLES 81–85

DEPECHE MODE
PRODUCED BY DANIEL MILLER, DEPECHE MODE AND GARETH JONES
MUTE/OCTOBER 1985
UK CHART: 6
US CHART: DID NOT CHART
KEY TRACKS: 'See You'; 'Get The Balance Right'; 'New Life'; 'Just Can't Get Enough'; 'Everything Counts'

Thirty-six devilishly catchy and enormously influential nuggets of electronic pop. Having made the decision to hold back the Basildon bondagemeisters' collection of 1981–85 hits, which was repackaged and reissued to tie in with the 2-CD set of more recent singles, I now get the pay-off of a couple of hours in the company of unlikely English pop genius, beginning with the unmatchably fey and naïve 'Dreaming Of Me', going through their lovable social commentary phase in 'Everything Counts', 'Get The Balance Right' and 'People Are People', and ending with . . . well, actually, ending with a pointless live version of 'Everything Counts' tacked on the end of 86–98 . . . but let's ignore that and end with 'Little 15', a beat-less, goth-orchestral ballad about – I think, because the other theories are frankly unpleasant – a mother wishing more for her teenage daughter than she feels she got from life, and which is crying out to be covered in an R&B style. The difference, apart from seventeen years, is that Vince Clarke wrote the early frothy singles before leaving for Yazoo (see p.139) and Erasure, and Martin Gore took over, and gradually turned the ultimate in gimpy synth poppets into stadium-trashing, drug-guzzling purveyors of S&M pervery and air-punching misery.

In *This Is Uncool* I bigged up 'Get The Balance Right' as the best Mode single, but have since fallen hopelessly in love all over again with 'See You', their fourth hit from 1982, and the very first that Gore wrote. It reminds me of a particular girl, but it's better than that; there's something in its neediness that sums up teen boy love angst beautifully, and it has a kindness very rare in songs of its kind.

But the overall best thing about the Mode is their understanding of the everyman nature of Dave Gahan's voice, and how that deadpan English croon could make themes of depression, decay and dominatrixes sound like dance-pop, rather than tiresome old goth. The guitar on 'Personal Jesus' makes up for pretty much any pop mistakes they made, and these two albums prove that they were few and far between. Nevertheless, anyone who manages twenty more years of successful songwriting after penning the line, 'People are people so why should it be/You and I should get along so awfully?' might have to thank their own personal Jesus once in a while.

THE MISEDUCATION OF LAURYN HILL

LAURYN HILL
PRODUCED BY LAURYN HILL, CHÉ GUEVARA AND VADA NOBLES
COLUMBIA/SEPTEMBER 1998
UK CHART: 2
US CHART: 1
KEY TRACKS: 'I Used To Love Him'; 'Ex-Factor'; 'To Zion'; 'Forgive Them Father'; 'Lost Ones'

If ever an album sounded like an ecstatic release of tension, it's this, the first solo album from sometime Fugee, Lauryn Hill. Yet, after seemingly exorcising the demons left behind by child-prodigy-dom, worldwide success with The Fugees, and the notoriously acrimonious affair and break-up with bandmate Wyclef Jean, the terrifyingly talented Ms Hill seemed to settle into permanent unsettlement, veering between self-righteous preaching and unlistenable songs for a bizarre and deadly dull MTV Unplugged album, withdrawal from music followed by reforming The Fugees, and an ongoing attempt to be the world's most bemusing earth mother/religious spokeswoman/wearer of hair-shirts since Sinead O'Connor. It's weird . . . the woman I interviewed for *Time Out London* in 1999 was easygoing and self-deprecating and . . . fun. It's still difficult to listen to what is the best soul album of its era without looking for clues to the maker's mental health. On the other hand, you can just feel the joy of the reggae-meets-girl-group intro of feminist self-help anthem 'Doo Wop (That Thing)', or the Wyclef-bashing authority of the dancehall-subverting 'Lost Ones', or her ability to write a song to Baby ('To Zion') that compares him to a god and yet somehow manages to convey every last bit of the joy and pain in parenthood.

A deserved winner of five Grammys and carrying a title inspired by Carter G. Woodson's book *The Miseducation Of The Negro*, this record constantly crosses the line from righteous to self-righteous, and drew a court case from producers and musicians involved for being denied full credit for their work. But it transcends all of the bad faith and ill-feeling that it carries as its baggage, blending hip hop, soul and reggae with both good taste and adventurous spirit, and features a set of melodies and lead vocals that are as transcendent as peak-period Stevie Wonder. When, on 'Superstar', Hill begins, 'Come on baby light my fire/Everything you drop is so tired/Music is supposed to inspire/How come we ain't getting no higher?', you want to stand up and fucking cheer, because the music and the courage of the themes throughout this record back up her stance, and put every lame and cynical manufactured rap and R&B album, with their soul-sucking and self-serving obsession with material gain and the power that comes with celebrity status, right back in their place. Because Lauryn can out-sing and out-rap and out-write and out-arrange the lot of them . . . even if was just . . . uh . . . one time.

But, even though the songs are great, the arrangements wonderful, the guest appearances by D'Angelo, Carlos Santana and Mary J. Blige well-judged and gimmick-free, the lyrics ferociously moral . . . it's the Hill voice that lifts your heart, and breaks it, too. When she raps or speaks, her voice is thick and cool, confident and androgynous, the voice of an old, old soul in the body of a twenty-two-year-old woman. When she sings, she reclaims the throaty, roaring melismatics of gospel singing from all those wailing Mariahs and Whitneys, and blends them with a Jamaican influence with such natural flair and call-and-response clarity that you sometimes feel she could move mountains using nothing but the things that her vocal cords do to her deepest emotions.

True, the between-song classroom kiddie 'skits' are trite and patronising and make the album a shade too long. And the record company's insistence on tacking on a lazy cover of 'Can't Take My Eyes Off Of You' and the nice but irrelevant 'Sweetest Thing' only go to show why singular artists like Hill

So we've still got the soul. But where, oh where, is the rock and the roll? Well, truth be told, it was largely absent in 1998, recovering from Britpop and post-grunge, and largely in need of a respirator, what with all its wheezing and groaning. So we have to rely on a lost gem for the thrill of great long-playing rock 'n' roll, not to mention the sex and the drugs. Coming out of Denver, Colorado, based in the then-intact city of New Orleans, and somewhere at the polar opposite of priorities to the Clean-Up Woman Ms Hill, it's one Greg Dulli, an old school, flat-nosed rock slugger who believed that rock was about bleeding guitars, discreetly funky beats, a classy suit, and songs about fucking, and fucking up. He was the leader of The Afghan Whigs, and *1965* was his band's final and finest album.

Dulli may not be able to sing like Lauryn, but soul music is his passion, and The Whigs developed from a mediocre late'80s grunge band into the most unusual American band of their age, reviving organs, orchestras, female soul backing vocals, horns and songs about wanting to be saved by the love/lust of a good woman, which looked back less to the titular year, and more to early '70s Rolling Stones. In fact – and despite the fact that Dulli was not as technically good a singer as Jagger – *1965* resembles some Great Lost Album the Stones made in between *Exile On Main St.* and *Goat's Head Soup*, buried because Mick was going through an unlikely period of self-loathing and vulnerability.

Dulli's fellow Whigs, Rick McCollum (guitar), John Curley (bass) and Steve Earle (not that Steve Earle – drums) played unlike anyone of their generation, producing, by *1965*, an effortlessly funky soul-rock hybrid without ever descending into the retro pastiche of Kravitz, Black Crowes, et al. It was American music writ large, but sleazy, damaged, and quite brilliantly erotic, by virtue of Dulli's ability to balance the straight-talking loverman come-on with the novelistic testimonies of a man who just had too much guilty bag-

become so disillusioned with The Biz. And the religion? Well, I'm an agnostic bordering on atheist, but I love good gospel music, and know that great soul is predicated on balancing the sacred and the profane, and, on that level, The *Miseducation Of Lauryn Hill* belongs with the best moments of Aretha Franklin, Sam Cooke and Al Green. If Ms Hill wants to tell me that this divine sound comes from a Divine Being, then she can take me to church anytime she likes.

1965

THE AFGHAN WHIGS
PRODUCED BY GREG DULLI
COLUMBIA/OCTOBER 1998
UK CHART: DID NOT CHART
US CHART: DID NOT CHART

gage to carry, who sought sex not as trophy, but salvation. On 'Neglekted' – not even in the best five tracks, people, and a near-masterpiece! – Dulli opens by confiding 'I met a girl/Extraordinary/Suggested something/Unsanitary'. By verse three, our boastful hero is on his knees to the same extraordinary girl, pleading, 'You can fuck my body, baby/But please don't fuck my mind.' The band were occasionally described by critics, accurately, as film noir set to music, and the mix of sleaze, humour, hope and inevitable disaster made lines like the above hit home, as Dulli constantly traded off between swaggering and suffering.

The band's frame of references was staggering, with the final epic segue of 'Omerta' and 'The Vampire Lanois' equally at home quoting from rapper Nas (see p.264) and The Beatles, over a wall of weeping noise that owes as much to the free jazz of 1965 as it does to anything in the rock canon. With the world in 2006 fairly open to '70s nostalgia, The Whigs may well have got the success that always eluded them.

In 1998, they were a complete anachronism, sharing similar tastes to Spiritualized (see p.294) but with short, sharp pop songs, and a suited and booted, muscular glamour that made them too arty and adult for the charts, and too dirty and direct for indie kids. But *1965* is one of the few sexy rock albums made since punk, shot full of love, pain and expensive bourbon.

1999

THE SLIM SHADY LP

EMINEM

PRODUCED BY DR. DRE, MARSHALL MATHERS,
MARKY, JEFF BASS, MEL MAN, R. MONTGOMERY, M.
BASS AND J. BASS
AFTERMATH/INTERSCOPE/APRIL 1999
UK CHART: 12
US CHART: 2
KEY TRACKS: '97' Bonnie & Clyde'; 'Role Model'; 'Guilty
Conscience'; 'My Name Is'; 'My Fault'

My clearest memory of first hearing the second Eminem album (his first, 1997's *Infinite*, was a 500-copy self-release) was laughing. Admittedly, the chortling came with a great deal of open-mouthed 'did he really just say that?' amazement. But hip hop's major selling-point had become its unrelenting grimness, as if a joke or a smile was a sure-fire sign of faggotty weakness on the part of the rapper. Marshall Bruce Mathers III rediscovered the cartoon side of gangsta rap that had been inside N.W.A. and Cypress Hill, and relocated and developed the satirical wit that had briefly made Ice-T America's favourite bogeyman. Mathers understood that being pretty and white, while a distinct disadvantage at the underground freestyle battles in Detroit, Michigan, where he cut his lyrical teeth, would enable him to discuss America's worst nightmares without terrifying the establishment. He had the personality to be pop, the rhyme skills to be credible on the rap scene, and themes sophisticated enough to draw florid tribute from the liberal-intellectual intelligentsia. His flow, too, was something new in rap, using assonance and stunning staccato patterns to give that light, childish and entirely non-Afro-American tone a strange kind of strength, more akin to the nerdish patter of Woody Allen than any rapper. With Dr. Dre, the man who had already made N.W.A. and Snoop Dogg, in his corner, the music worked too. It had to. No matter how clever/hilarious/shocking the lyrics were, no matter how defined

the cheekbones, the Eminem themes demanded a new kind of hip hop . . . synthetic, jokey, infectious, taunting. The album began with a US news announcer proclaiming the ultimate in cake-and-eat-it-too disclaimers . . . 'The views and events expressed here are totally fucked, and are not necessarily the views of anyone,' an instant rebuttal of gangsta rap's insistence that it reflected reality. At the finish of the sweary litany of disclaimers, the announcer asks Mathers/Eminem/ Slim Shady if he wants to add anything: 'Yeah,' he whines, with perfect offhand comic timing . . . 'Don't do drugs.'

Of course, we Brits continue to labour under the assumption that the country that produced Jack Benny, Bill Hicks, Larry David and *The Larry Sanders Show* doesn't 'get' irony. Mathers gets away with murder – on as many levels as you can bear – on *The Slim Shady LP* through nothing else but heavily loaded sarcasm, way above and beyond anything that pop lyrics had considered possible or desirable previously. Yet, unlike, say, Biggie Smalls or Jay Z, Mathers provides context outside of himself and the real hard-knock life that rap has turned into yet another form of exploitation, and presents a form of fictionalised autobiography in the likes of 'Brain Damage' and 'My Fault' that thrives on weakness and inadequacy and builds a cogent critique of the American underclasses, and why it – and rap music, in particular – seethes with so much loathing, misanthropy and violence against itself. Bullying, child abuse, neglect and poverty create little monsters, and Mathers is one of the few lyricists who make you feel the horror of that, even as he makes you laugh at capitalism's chaos. Amongst the curses, insults and gross-outs, 'Role Model' makes the point about what we should and shouldn't take from the popular arts, as Mathers makes himself into nothing but a symbol – 'How the fuck can I be white? I don't even exist!' – and then goes into a hilarious list of exaggerations of rap (and rock) gimmicks of transgression, asking the children he knows will adore his naughtiness, 'Now don't you wanna grow up to be just like me?' The point isn't what they or we want. The

THE SLIM SHADY LP/EMINEM

point is that they already have and are, and that forces more powerful – economic, parental, societal – than pop songs make it so. It struck me as the most moral and truthful thing anyone had ever said in pop.

Nevertheless, *The Slim Shady LP* loses its way. It is, like so many hip hop albums from the period, too long, and from the repulsively homophobic 'Ken Kaniff' onwards, genius increasingly gives way to the mundane survivalism of 'Rock Bottom' and gratuitous, and often boring, sexual disgust. The major tribute I can pay to a scenario – a murder ballad, straight from ancient country and blues – as complete as Eminem's notorious short-story about murdering his child's mother, '97' Bonnie & Clyde', is that it and the album's best material overwhelm the album's most despicably lazy and unpleasant moments. But much though I wince at his willingness to shock in the most conservative of ways, I suspect that the album – and therefore, his future work – wouldn't have worked without the shite. The joke about hiding behind a character called 'Slim Shady' was that it was no character. The ensuing soap opera of court battles with his mother and assaulting Kim's boyfriend and raging at the press destroyed Eminem's work eventually, turning him into just another celebrity fuck-up, taking the art out of his music. But, at this point, the album only hit home if you understood that this boy (he was twenty-seven but sounded like a verbally precocious fifteen-year-old) was both a hateful idiot and the conscience of a nation. In millennial America, they could be one and the same thing. It is, after all, an era dominated by Stupid White Men.

REMEDY

BASEMENT JAXX
PRODUCED BY BASEMENT JAXX
XL/APRIL 1999
UK CHART: 4
US CHART: DID NOT CHART

KEY TRACKS: 'Jump 'n' Shout'; 'Same Old Show'; 'Red Alert'; 'Rendez-vu'; 'U Can't Stop Me'

Writing this on the greyest February morning. Put this album on. The first four-to-the-floor beat and vocal chant kicked in . . . and the sun began to shine. *Remedy* is putting it mildly, being a S.A.D. bastard at heart. And the only place where I don't believe in coincidence is brilliant dance music.

The first true disco album to pop up here since Madonna's *The Immaculate Collection*, the debut album from London's Brixton-based production and DJ duo Felix Buxton and Simon Radcliffe gathered all the splintered tribes from the rave era and reminded you that the greatest dance music is always a fusion. Taking every bit as much from 2-Tone (in the Brixton-goes-to-Ibiza clarion call of 'Jump 'n' Shout' and the Selecter-sampling sensuality stomp that is 'Same Old Show') and the 'acid jazz' scene of the early '90s (the sophisticat meldings of Latin and funk through-

out) as it does from hip hop and house music, finding sounds that replicated the feel of a frantic, feelgood basement party without stooping to actual party noises, *Remedy* decides to take the inner-city chaos that artists as far apart as Tricky and Eminem present as a bringer of paranoia and insanity, and make it into the essence of joy under pressure.

There are glimpses of the shadow, the city sickness, that brings everyone to this manic disco. The squelchy acid epic 'Don't Give Up' lets you know what's at stake here, advising, 'Don't pull the cracks in your mind apart . . . Why feed on bitterness?' 'U Can't Stop Me', features Yvonne John-Lewis negotiating the stumbling, broken beats and hysterical noises off with sweet determination, describing the stress of coping with London, of charging through its realities, knowing stopping to look – to worry – is to stop surviving. 'I got sixteen seconds and I don't want to stop . . . I got a fast food store selling poison, selling rocks/Spaghetti Junction in my head – I'm living in the aftershock.' And then 'Red Alert' slams in, where tropical birds and machine-gun digital squeals give a harder edge to the oldest, most swishily feminine disco, where a scratchy string quartet is shot down and trampled by a Funkadelic dance troupe, and Blue James happily exclaims, 'Don't panic/Ain't nothing' goin' on but history,' and you feel the history of weekend hedonism of swing bands in draughty dancehalls and black girls grinding their butts at a Miami beach rave and all points inbetween, and you are put in your place, in the very best way, as just another struggling human joining the ecstasy of the dance, and the dance of life, because these moments, where isolation is beaten by communal bliss, are what you're living for.

Remedy does this fourteen times, before chilling out with its baby on the final, fitting 'Being With U'. The album is never crass enough to mention the millennium by name. But it is the album that embraced the fear of Y2K and danced exactly like it was 1999.

FULL CLIP: A DECADE OF GANG STARR

GANG STARR
PRODUCED BY DJ PREMIER
COOLTEMPO/JULY 1999
UK CHART: 47
US CHART: 33
KEY TRACKS: 'Who's Gonna Take The Weight?'; 'Tonz O' Gunz'; 'The ? Remains'; 'Take It Personal'; 'B.Y.S.'

The studio albums made by Brooklyn hip hop duo Chris 'DJ Premier' Martin and Keith 'Guru' Elam all have something to commend them. But this thirty-two-track double CD is really all you need. Making immaculate choices from the six previous long-players, *Full Clip* . . . is like a hip hop operators' manual, a summing-up of everything positive, complex and extraordinary about the most popular music in the world. The fact that the misguidingly-monikered Gang Starr were never among hip hop's most popular practitioners is one of the many reasons why this album rocks so hard.

Hitting their stride on their second album, 1991's *Step In The Arena*, Gang Starr found their voice and concentrated on making it tougher, ignoring the desperate search for trend that turned hip hop in on itself in the '90s. Premier came up with a musical backdrop consisting of dense collage built from soul, funk or jazz sample, often set on fire by spectacular, and now 'old-fashioned', turntable skills for a chorus hook. And then Guru would dispense what can only be called street wisdom in a deep, deadpan tone, rejecting gangsterism for reportage and warning, using rap cliches such as 'Yo!' and 'crazy phat' like others used rap cliches such as 'bitch' and 'motherfucker'. The fact that Premier and Guru stuck to their uncommercial guns, staying clear of misanthropy and exploitation of the gangsta and materialist norms, gave authority to Guru's already authoritative tones. Like A Tribe Called Quest, Gang Starr were crucial to establishing a hip hop alternative, a grounded, old-school-respecting scene that continues to operate as a smarter, more experimental, and less amoral parallel to chart rap. Diving into the molasses-thick wall of music on *Full Clip* . . . tells you what real hip hop is about – and believe me, as someone who thinks notions of authenticity are usually little more than dull thinking, easily suckered, and who didn't grow up spinning on my bonce in the South Bronx, I don't chuck about phrases like 'real hip hop' lightly.

Guru, a bubbly, positive kind of geezer, deserves much praise for remaining completely unimpressed by the verbal trickery that, with endless MCs seemingly unable to rap on a beat and routinely praised for their self-indulgence, replicated the pre-punk-rock obsession with technical virtuosity over substance. He also didn't swallow the line that society creates helpless thugs and that hip hop's exploitation of that idea was, in fact, reality. He believes in individual responsibility, that we have a choice. His straight-talking flow and attitude is summed up in 'Discipline':

Yo! Just because I want to it don't mean I will
And just because I'm angry it don't mean I'd kill
And just because she looks good it don't mean I'd hit it
And just because I'm horny, it don't mean I'm with it . . .
I got discipline baby, and I use it a lot

Man . . . doesn't take much to cut through all this bollocks, does it? It's tempting to paint Guru as the anti-Eminem, but that would be a backhanded compliment to both. When Mathers is at his best, his ironies, once juggled, are not dissimilar to the words above. When Guru is at his best, he's capable of conjuring imagery that lays bare every reason why many ain't taking his moralising on board. 'Tonz O' Gunz' is an anti-gun rant, but understands that the imagery of men with firearms is a thrill, and not just to kids. 'I don't glorify/'Cos more guns will come and much more will die,' he glowers, admitting he has no solution. And he knows he gets his cake and eats it because his partner is among hip hop's greatest producers.

Premier's beats are a legend, and rightly: no hip hop producer has so consistently walked the line between muscle and musicality. His music is enveloping, narcotic, elegant, strong and deep as Dr. Dre's pockets. Mixing a '70s soul-funk aesthetic with avant-garde juxtapositions of jazz, orchestral soundtrack and far eastern music, using sudden breaks and repetitions as extra rhythms, Premier backs his rapper like one of those all-important posses backs their crew member: you laugh at Guru's moralising, the music knocks you flat on your ass. This is one of those rare compilations that comes off like a concept album, so focussed and complete is Gang Starr's undervalued mastery of this hop they call hip.

PICTURES FROM LIFE'S OTHER SIDE

JOHNNY DOWD

PRODUCED BY JOHNNY DOWD AND MATTHEW SACCUCCI MORANO
MUNICH/AUGUST 1999
UK CHART: DID NOT CHART
US CHART: DID NOT CHART
KEY TRACKS: 'God Created Woman'; 'Mystery Woman'; 'Worried Mind'; 'Hope You Don't Mind'; 'No Woman's Flesh But Hers'

The shocking and extraordinary Johnny Dowd began his recording career at the age of fifty. Born in Texas, spending time in Memphis and Oklahoma, and now still running a trucking and removals firm in Upstate New York, his first album, 1998's *Wrong Side Of Memphis*, was an exercise in all-American psychosis, tales of true crime and dementia, over stark, guitar-led country-blues, sung by what sounded like a depression-era hobo waiting on Death Row for blessed release from mental torture. It picked up enough acclaim and sales to start one of the most singular recording careers of the twenty-first century. This, his second album, added a

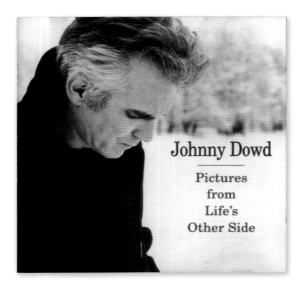

Johnny Dowd

Pictures from Life's Other Side

full band, textures drawn from a Tom Waitsian voodoo-junkyard blues with added fairground sickness waltzes, and Dowd's secret weapon, the sweet, high, ethereal voice of Kim Sherwood-Caso. Murder, she sang.

Dowd is one of those performers who defies the very notion of black comedy. Is he serious, when he sings, in a southern drawl so old, fragile and reptilian on brooding, bereft cuckold testimony 'The Girl Who Made Me Sick', 'Some birds like to sing/But not my friend, the crow/What's he got to sing about/When desolation's all he know'? My only real clue is the first time I saw him play, in 1999 at the Water Rats in London, when he sang a particularly grand guignol line from this album's 'No Woman's Flesh But Hers', the cheery tale of a man singing to his comatose wife, and someone down the front laughed. This mean-looking, but handsome, grey-haired and wiry man spun away from the mic and pointed his guitar at laughing boy like a sub-machine gun. 'You think this is FUNNY??!!,' he roared, and

crashed into a guitar solo plucked straight from the fires of one of his character's private hells, staring homicidally at the man who dared to laugh at the horror. I've seen a lot of rappers up close, giving it the hard-man dare. None of them got close to how unhinged Dowd looked, for maybe less than a minute, but quite long enough.

The title of this album is plucked from the opening Hank Williams cover, 'A Picture From Life's Other Side', a legendary live-fast-die-young country renegade's plea for the underclass, the lost ones corrupted by love and money and too little of both, transformed into a rumbling punk-blues. Dowd's pre-rock references ('Worried Mind' is also a Williams cover) and advancing years not only draws his work into the same old-time Americana and murder ballad world as Johnny Cash, but gives the impression that his characters' ravings – all Nick Cave fear of an Old Testament god, but on the same level of analysis of mental illness and misanthropic pessimism as the king of pulp insanity, novelist and screenwriter Jim Thompson – are drawn from experience. Of course, if he'd actually done the things some of his songs describe, he wouldn't be free to make weird pop records. But Dowd's preoccupation with crime and punishment, and merciless refusal to sweeten any pill he prescribes, has you wondering just what his life has been like, even as you realise that the things he sings are the things you think, at your most desperate, disturbed moments. But the wavering voice is an effect, and one used superbly, like the strangled falsetto – so wrong, so absolutely right – that sinks into the fabric of 'Bad Memories', and its Tom Waits-goes-goth mambo, and cries, 'You can't make love without spilling some blood.' Brrrr.

Ms Sherwood-Caso, the aforementioned secret weapon, isn't just much-needed sugar. She gives the female objects of his fear, longing and hatred a voice. On 'God Created Woman', a graphic depiction of a very male strain of self-pity, and an examination of the roots of misogyny as pungent as anything by Eminem, Sherwood-Caso trills the chorus, the essence of innocence, inviting the tortured lover to level three of a parking lot, because, 'There's something you've just gotta see,' and every corrupt anti-hero and femme fatale from every great film noir – I'm particularly thinking Edgar G. Ulmer's bizarre, brilliant Detour – slams into your brain, and chills you to the bone.

On an acoustic waltz of brutally honest self-laceration, Dowd describes himself as 'One more victim of the sexual wars'. This rubs up against the likes of 'Hope You Don't Mind' – which sounds like a slightly strained love ballad until you realise the singer is stalking a schoolgirl – and makes a compelling argument for separatist feminism. You suspect that the unsettling and magnificent Mr Dowd would be the first to welcome his gender's extinction if it stopped the voices in his squirming brain.

AVENUE B

IGGY POP
PRODUCED BY DON WAS
VIRGIN/SEPTEMBER 1999
UK CHART: DID NOT CHART
US CHART: DID NOT CHART
KEY TRACKS: 'Shakin' All Over'; 'Nazi Girlfriend'; 'Façade'; 'I Felt The Luxury'; 'Miss Argentina'

A not dissimilar record from another ancient mariner. *Avenue B* was an odd proposition, Iggy Pop's first downbeat confessional album. But Dowd came without baggage. When you listen to James Osterberg singing about his 'Nazi Girlfriend' over Radio 2 acoustic balladry produced by Was (Not Was)'s Don Was, it's with full knowledge of Iggy Stooge, big-dicked Godfather Of Punk, the most reckless rock 'n' roll death-wisher this side of Keith Richards, and Keef needed his entire blood supply changed in order to keep up the narcotic abuse, the panty-waist. We knew that Iggy had, literally, forgotten more than we'd ever know. Hearing him do lugubrious, post-divorce meditation on 'considering the circumstances of my death' over lounge and soundtrack atmospherics was . . . different.

Avenue B strives to present Iggy as a 'bookish' (his word, spat out memorably) fifty-two-year-old, sitting alone in his New York study, sifting through the debris of all his many mistakes, mainly with women. Much like Dowd, it's hard to tell just how much of this is autobiographical, and how much is storytelling, but if it had been plainly the former, it would have been unbearable. 'Nazi Girlfriend' doesn't make clear whether this girlfriend was real, whether she was actually a fascist, or whether 'the desert in her stare' leads Iggy to describe her as a Nazi. But it does tell you that this girlfriend is not as young as the girls he invites into his life elsewhere, but still 'has ways to make me talk', which is pretty funny. When a pop performer sings the word 'I', the assumption, on everyone's part, is that this is the unexpurgated truth, straight from the heart. It isn't, necessarily. This is why pop music isn't a self-help manual. What this album is, to me, is a slyly funny set of self-justifications for an old man's preoccupation with young women, and an acknowledgement from the source that that way lies self-delusion, loneliness, grief. With acoustic guitars, Angelo Badalamenti-style sinister orchestrals backdropping spoken-word interludes, jazz and Latin tinges, and a great deal of seedy, smart poetry. I'm sure there's lots of fact here. But not enough to get in the way of a good, true story.

The parade of girls looking for father figures, and Iggy's sad laughter at himself for buying in, undercuts rock's bog-standard leering. This is why, I imagine, that the album was met with derision by male reviewers who revere Iggy as an unreconstructed relic, and don't want to be confronted by mortality by a man who, infamously, 'survived'. 'The façade falls down,' as the weary, broiling, self-lacerating final track 'Façade' puts it.

In amongst the spoken-word passages and the wry tributes to young women who he'd used and been used by, stand two more recognisably Iggy moments, which throw a light on the supposed confessionals. 'Corruption' is what it says, a hard-rock purging of the corruption Iggy (or the character he plays on this record) believes rules his soul. Before that there is a glowering, dance-metal version of 'Shakin' All Over', the first truly great British rock 'n' roll record, made by Johnny Kidd And The Pirates way back in 1961. But the vocal is not strong, deep Iggy, as evinced elsewhere. It is sick, old and desperate, still clinging to an addiction to young flesh, the butt of a cosmic joke, flailing and drowning in the wall of power-chords.

You can understand why no one wanted to hear someone so successful with women – someone whose fame and money, apart from any other qualities, could continue to attract women young enough to be his granddaughter – make an album that made the connection between fucking youth and an old man's decay. The guy reformed The Stooges, got on with being a cartoon. Pearls before swine, frankly.

LE TIGRE

LE TIGRE

PRODUCED BY CHRIS STAMEY AND LE TIGRE
WIIIJA (MR LADY IN USA)/OCTOBER 1999
UK CHART: DID NOT CHART
US CHART: DID NOT CHART
KEY TRACKS: 'Deceptacon'; 'Hot Topic'; 'What's Yr Take On Cassavetes'; 'Friendship Station'; 'Let's Run'

An interruption of the guilt-ridden old geezers. No interruption, however, to a run of pre-millennial albums that no one bought.

Le Tigre are an all-female trio formed from the ashes of riot grrl band Bikini Kill, whose Kathleen Hanna was based in the feminist/alt-pop sanctuary that is Olympia, Washington, but relocated to New York and found girl group-garage-post-punk-pop fun! Hanna is blessed with a paint-stripping, post-Poly Styrene voice of both strident power and melodic soul, and her new band sought to veer away from the shouty punk of Bikini Kill, and make turn-of-the-'80s-style rainbow disco-pop, all hooks, danceable drum machines, meaty basslines, girl-group chants and a machismo-baiting slyness culled all the way from The Slits (see p.71), the best of Ze Records (see p.119) and Talking Heads spin-off Tom Tom Club. In 2006, 'Deceptacon' and 'Hot Topic' may well have been hits; instead they had to be content with cult indie-club fave status, giant girl-pop hits waiting in vain for a chart to accommodate them.

So, on Le Tigre's first album, you get defiantly plastic pop in an '80s mode, and joyous reinventions of '60s femme-pop, and feminist sloganeering rendered subversive by melody, disco pleasure and good jokes. 'What's Yr Take On Cassavetes' is as much a gag at the expense of their own, perennial student scene as it is male taste in cult movie directors, as the trio (Hanna joined by film-maker Sadie Benning and fanzine writer Johanna Fateman) simply ask

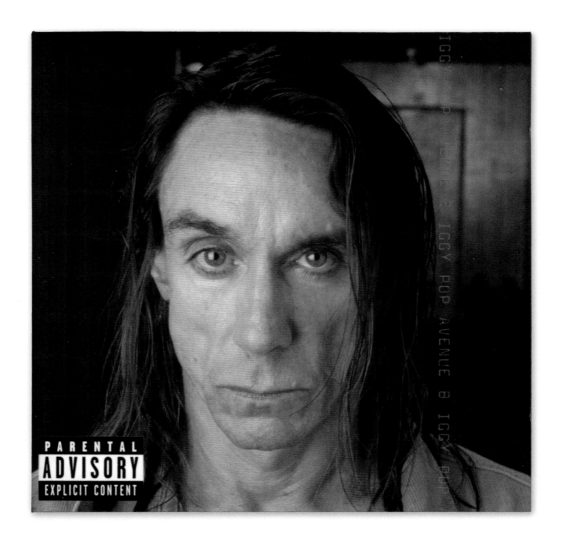

AVENUE B/IGGY POP

what you think of the legendary John Cassavetes: 'Misogynist? Genius? Alcoholic? Messiah?' Don't bother to vote, because the real point is contained within one hollered question: 'Hey! Where's Gena?' Cassavetes' wife Gena Rowlands that is, hidden from history while the guys debate other guys.

Elsewhere, 'Hot Topic' asks you to sing along to a handy list of feminist heroines, 'Deceptacon' lets us know that blokes in tediously dull rock bands 'took the Ram from the ramalamadingdong', and savages a particular kind of unreconstructed male fake on 'Dude, Yr So Crazy' . . . all with bouncy grooves, big grins and infectious melodies. 'Slideshow At Free University' is something like the perfect mixture of mood music for adverts and a satirical dig at bohemian higher education.

Oddly, having found an ideal sound to reach far beyond the underground in a few years time, Le Tigre decided to get so poppy on their following two albums that they lost the guts of their sound. Shame. Nevertheless, *Le Tigre* is one of the great buried gems of the late '90s. Sure, it wants to cut your balls off, Jack. But you won't feel a thing.

SAVE YOURSELF

MAKE UP
PRODUCED BY BRENDAN CANTY
K/OCTOBER 1999
UK CHART: DID NOT CHART
US CHART: DID NOT CHART
KEY TRACKS: 'Hey Joe'; 'The Bells'; 'White Belts'; 'Call Mommy'; 'Save Yourself'

Just as Le Tigre sought to smuggle their feminist polemics inside sparky pop music, Make Up (sometimes known as The Make-Up) quit the shouting and scraping of leader Ian Svenonius's former band Nation Of Ulysses and, by the time of this, their fifth album, were a sexy soul-influenced garage-

punk band. Building a sound where bongos, electric pianos, vibraphone and bass were equally as important as guitar and Svenonius's delirious yelp of a post-Pere Ubu (see p.38) voice, this Washington DC quartet kept the retro-garage flame alive, as raucous and cult-popular fellow travellers of Jon Spencer Blues Explosion, Rocket From The Crypt (see p.280) and The Gories, preparing the youth indie-rock ear for the coming of The White Stripes.

Save Yourself is pitched somewhere between The Stooges, the more soulful, sensual blasts of The MC5 and Jack White's favourite '80s swampabillies The Gun Club, with a vital seasoning of soul, funk and steals from The Doors and Love. It was unashamedly nostalgic rock 'n' roll, but, in 1999, it came to sound thrillingly modern among rock's plunderings from The Beatles and Pink Floyd, that blustery desperation for the epic. *Save Yourself* is intimate, up-close and live in your living room, touched with the maverick impulses of toy pianos and shimmering tambourines, like a dream of a sleazy '60s go-go club, in a blue-light basement. Svenonius's lyrics eschew agit-prop for an eccentric take on

sexual politics, imagining himself giving birth on 'Call Me Mommy', spinning circle-of-life metaphors for doing the wild thing on 'C'mon, Let's Spawn', pleading for love's cleansing in torrid, florid style on 'Save Yourself' and '(Make Me A) Feelin' Man'. The pièce de résistance though was a closing, epic version of 'Hey Joe', as most famously performed by Jimi Hendrix. Make Up rejuvenate the song by turning it into a three-act play, and dispensing with the murder ballad element. The early verses are a Pixies-style spook-lament, the guitars go into Stooges overload for the break, and then a phone rings, and bassist Michelle Mae asks her Joe to come back home from Mexico Way. Joe's keen. Guitars explode in excitement, raging against the original's violence. The ancient traditional death song is transformed into a celebration of sex as an almost celestial life-force. Rock 'n' roll subverts the blues, yet again.

BLACK ON BOTH SIDES

MOS DEF

PRODUCED BY VARIOUS PRODUCERS (EXECUTIVE PRODUCERS: MOS DEF AND SHAKA)
RAWKUS/OCTOBER 1999
UK CHART: DID NOT CHART
US CHART: 25
KEY TRACKS: 'Ms Fat Booty'; 'Umi Says'; 'Rock 'N' Roll'; 'Brooklyn'; 'Mathematics'

For many, The Native Tongues collective symbolised the Golden Age of hip hop. Colourful and bohemian, experimental yet mellow, espousing the discovering of African roots and various forms of spirituality as a way to make the black nation rise, De La Soul, The Jungle Brothers, A Tribe Called Quest, Brand Nubian and the pre-Hollywood Queen Latifah made an inclusive hip hop – non-violent, anti-misogyny, and, if not exactly pro-queer, then at least classy enough to leave the sisters alone. As the '90s progressed,

gangsta and its materialist heirs crushed The Native Tongues and their fellow travellers for the same reason that no one buys papers for the good news. But good ideas never disappear, and politically conscious, come-hither, non-exploitative hip hop based on traditional rhyming and production skills gathered its strength on the . . . ahem . . . downlow, waiting for enough punters to get bored of the white sponsoring of black-on-black violence as popular entertainment. Enter Dante Terrell Smith, an actor, singer, musician, producer and rapper from Brooklyn, New York.

After flagging up the return of Afrocentric rap with 1998's Black Star alongside partners Talib Kweli and Hi-Tek, the endearingly old-school renamed Mos Def made a debut solo album that contained enough confidence and focus to level trees, never mind grumbly gangstas. His voice was deep, appropriately stoned, and hit the beats and the themes hard, riding a set of jazzy, basement backdrops that blended ATCQ, The Jungle Brothers and Nas's *Illmatic* (see p.264) with just the right amount of modernism to avoid worthy nostalgia.

Black On Both Sides is truly an album of both sides. You can switch off the brain and nod your head to the pretty beats, or you can engage and get your head fed. 'New World Water', for example, compares environmental disaster and corporate poisoning of natural resources with the psychological damage done to oceans by their transport of slaves. Does water have a sensitive psyche? Does it make any less sense than our endless waste? For Mos Def, everything he feels strongly about is connected, physically, spiritually. 'Mathematics' connects the billions of dollars spent on defence in the USA to the paltry royalty rate he receives for making a tune. On 'Mr Nigga', he wonders why the horror at what Michael Jackson might have done with children is not equalled by the horror of Woody Allen marrying his own adopted stepdaughter. Yep, that would be a black thing. Sadly, his singling out of Allen became tainted on the follow-up to this album, 2004's *The New Danger*, where an anti-corporate rap parody of Jay Z's 'The Takeover' called 'The Rape

Over' insisted that 'Some tall Israeli is runnin' this rap shit', reviving an unpleasant and self-defeating anti-Semitism that runs through pro-black hip hop from Public Enemy onwards. By 2005, Mos Def was rapping on adverts for gas-guzzling SUVs in America. I trust the car firm was black-owned.

The album's most argumentative track, 'Rock 'N' Roll', uses an eerie Afro-funk-reggae hybrid to reconnect black people to the rock they invented; 'Elvis Presley ain't got no soul,' he contends, understandably but incorrectly, 'You may dig on the Rolling Stones/But they didn't come up with that shit on their own.' Of course, this is a cake-and-eat-it-too era, so 'Brooklyn' bases its opening hook on 'Under The Bridge' by the Red Hot Chilli Peppers, a massive white rock band who may have appropriated more of their fair share of black moves. Whaddya think? Benefit of the doubt concerning irony? Your call. Meanwhile 'Rock 'N' Roll', inevitably, breaks with a short Hendrix lick into a Bad Brains-style punk thrash. I'm glad someone else heard that Son Of Bazerk album (see p.241).

So, no, I don't always agree with Mos Def's views, but then I'm not sure I agreed with Johnny Rotten's view of abortion on 'Bodies', either. *Black On Both Sides* is stoned soul music that provokes debate, and, as an old punk rock-er, that's exactly what I think the best pop art should be. Angry, yet mournful, possessing the current affairs and his-torical details that only an activist brings to the lyrical table, *Black On Both Sides* is a key moment in hip hop's realign-ment, as it slowly became a music, again, that could blend the bohemian with the bling, and be popular, as OutKast and Kanye West went on to prove. It's also a genuinely sexy album. Its best moment, 'Ms Fat Booty', pulls off the impos-sible, kicking off with a predictably sexist title, yet making a seduction dance tune which sees the object of Mos Def's desire as a real, living, breathing human being, therefore being honest about male objectification while letting us know that the love game is not, in the end, about the fat ass. Which brings us neatly to . . .

AMPLIFIED

Q-TIP

PRODUCED BY JAY DEE, Q-TIP AND DJ SCRATCH
ARISTA/NOVEMBER 1999
UK CHART: DID NOT CHART
US CHART: 28
KEY TRACKS: 'Breathe And Stop'; 'All In'; 'Let's Ride'; 'Vivrant Thing'; 'End Of Time'

. . . the King of this boho rap thing, taking time out from moralising and giving it the full-on party sex symbol vibe he always threatened.

A Tribe Called Quest had split at the top, with a US No. 3 album *The Love Movement*. For his first solo album, Jonathan 'Q-Tip' Davis looked and sounded like a man breathing a sigh of relief, released from the burden of being hip hop's conscience throughout the gangsta era. That androgynous drawl is in a permanent grin as he paints a series of scenarios about chatting up beauties at the dance. And, although he'd been the appropriate guest on Mos Def's anti-racist rant 'Mr Nigga' (based on Q-Tip's former band's 'Sucka Nigga', see p.???), while Mos Def got on with forming an all-black rock supergroup Black Jack Johnson, the previ-ously rockphobic Q-Tip name-checked Led Zeppelin on 'Let's Ride' and drafted in dodgy Caucasian doom funk-metal band Korn for 'End Of Time', the album's strangely energising goth-hop closing track. There's an air of 'screw it – cross me over' to *Amplified*, which, presumably, didn't sit well enough with his major label or his good self. The fol-low-up was shelved, Q-Tip disappeared into the world of occasional guest spots, and only now, in 2006, is a second solo album apparently set for release. In the unpleasant, labyrinthine world of hip hop/major label politics, it's the mature, conscious artists – the Lauryn Hills, Q-Tips and D'Angelos – that seem to break under pressure, who end up missing in action. The boy gangstas just churn out the same record, year after year, building their mansions in areas well away from the 'niggaz' they dis on vinyl. Something's very sick in hip hop, in case I hadn't made that point so far.

Meanwhile, any compromise of integrity on *Amplified* is trampled underfoot by the subsonic basslines, staccato, stumble-funk beats and reggae and jazz textures of Q-Tip, Scratch and the now sadly-deceased Jay Dee. It's the best intelligently empty hip-grinding hip hop party album of the modern era.

BEASTIE BOYS ANTHOLOGY: THE SOUNDS OF SCIENCE

BEASTIE BOYS

PRODUCED BY BEASTIE BOYS, MARIO CALDATO JR, SCOTT JARVIS, RICK RUBIN AND DUST BROTHERS
GRAND ROYAL/CAPITOL/NOVEMBER 1999
UK CHART: 36
US CHART: 19
KEY TRACKS: 'Intergalactic'; 'Sabotage'; 'Get It Together'; 'Three MCs And One DJ'; 'Song For The Man'

I know, I know. Too much hip hop. Too much subtext about white boys appropriating black music. Not enough singing. And, actually, too much Q-Tip (he's on this album's 'Get It Together'). Honestly, it's just the way the classics fall. Something very different next, if you're getting bored. Promise.

The Beastie Boys reinvented their brattish PC-baiting old selves and drew much praise for their albums *Paul's Boutique*, *Check Your Head*, *Ill Communication* and *Hello Nasty*. The last of those albums aside, it was over-praise, a knee-jerk reaction to their smart appropriations of various geek-chic elements into their presentation, and the very '90s enthusiasm for music that reflected a perceived low attention span amongst the young. In truth, what you wanted was something that pulled in all the best bits – including choice cuts from their low-key excursions into shouty hardcore punk – and left out all the self-indulgent mood-breakers. Here it is.

Having been every bit as vital as Tarantino to the re-evaluation of mullets, smartarse dialogue with no real point, wah-wah blaxploitation and dodgy '70s MOR-pop records and everything else we now bracket as ironic, self-referential postmodernism, the Beasties make surprising amounts of mindlessly great tunes. Buy in to their trust fund kid at the Buddhist jumble sale schtick or don't – when they shout a stupid LINE!!! at the same TIME!!! there is barely a more joyous, innocent sound in pop music, a distillation of the boys-having-fun aesthetic that built our fascination with rock bands. Their ability to blend, rap, punk, funk, jazz, Latin, lounge and metal into something instantly recognisable as beastly is a feat you can only pull off if you are instinctively intelligent composers, producers and players, and this two-hour, forty-two-track album is one of the very few endlessly long albums that never gets boring, whether giving it the police chase garage-funk whammy for 'Sabotage', or getting Biz Markie (see p.206) to take the piss out of Elton John on their affectionately duff cover of 'Benny And The Jets'. Best of all, though, is the way the group fuel their music with a dream of a truly multi-cultural (not just black and white, but Latin, Asian, Jewish and all points inbetween) New York, living, laughing and dancing together, and work to make that dream real, in their fatback grooves, in their Rainbow Coalition verbal tics, in the whole spicy urban stewiness of it all. It also includes a love song to an old lady called 'Boomin' Granny'. Sure, it's a joke. But done with exquisite taste, because, at a Beasties' party, it's those always left out who head the guest list.

BEASTIE BOYS ANTHOLOGY
THE SOUNDS OF SCIENCE

THE SOUNDS OF SCIENCE/BEASTIE BOYS

2000

LITTLE BLACK NUMBERS

KATHRYN WILLIAMS

PRODUCED BY KATHRYN WILLIAMS AND HEAD
CAW/JANUARY 2000
UK CHART: 70 (WHEN REISSUED IN SEPTEMBER 2001
ON EAST WEST)
US CHART: DID NOT CHART
KEY TRACKS: 'Jasmine Hoop'; 'Soul To Feet'; 'Toocan'; 'We
Dug A Hole'; 'Stood'

There is great beauty in anger and cruelty, ain't it true? And nowhere is that as plain as in the songs and voice of Liverpool-born, Newcastle-based guitarist/singer Kathryn Williams, and her ongoing project to revive an English pastoral vocal folk-pop missing, in any soulful and meaningful way, since the untimely deaths of Nick Drake and Sandy Denny. Her voice is the essence of sweetness, calm and innocence. Her music is soothing, softly sad and lullaby-warm. But her words spit venom at fakes and false lovers, fair-weather friends and the endless prattle of the chattering world. 'We dug a hole,' she trills, so fragile, so strong, on the opening track of this, her second, self-financed album, 'To keep everything out of view . . . Hoped it was big enough.' It's that escape from the (un)real world with a lover/co-conspirator, as much a Weller or Morrissey preoccupation as that of the Van Morrisons or Joni Mitchells her acoustic song is compared to, that colours her short, sad slices of magic.

Evocative of both rain-soaked cobbled streets and sun-dappled fields, her songs swell and swoon like ruminations, but lyrically are confrontations; abrupt conversations with people she feels she's seen through, and feels betrayed by. Some may be sexual partners, others family or friends. But it's the impatience with the hypocrisies and self-delusions that strikes home, in music that unravels like scrunched tissue paper, slowly, with a faint rustle. Upright jazzy bass, brushed drums, rough brass, a little tango, mournful cello and the occasional swell of an organ. Oh behave. A Hammond organ, like on those '60s records.

At times, in the depths of isolation, she sees something from the natural world, something, perhaps, as cold and hard as the bird flying into the glass of her window in 'Toocan', and she makes a leap from there to her, sees herself 'Changing my life to fit myself to it', and she moves you to tears. It's the stillness in her voice, making any tiny change of emphasis a profound hit of emotion. There is a bleakness here. But it's leavened by the keen-ness of her observation, her refusal to be fooled. It embodies the idea that happiness only comes having paid the price of suffering, from, as Jonathan Richman put it all those pages ago, being able to 'take this world and take it straight' (see p.4).

This album gained a Mercury Music Prize nomination, and gave her a brief, unhappy dalliance with a major label. There was always something too pure and true about this music for that kind of crossover to work, particularly as you could apply any of her most scalpel-sharp lyrics to almost anyone in the corporate music world. Kath is one of those precious few pop stars to whom that world has no relevance. You should buy all of her albums, a dozen times so she can keep on digging that hole, right through to a less tainted world.

EXTERMINATOR

PRIMAL SCREAM

PRODUCED BY VARIOUS PRODUCERS
CREATION/JANUARY 2000
UK CHART: 3
US CHART: DID NOT CHART
KEY TRACKS: 'Blood Money'; 'Exterminator'; 'Accelerator'; 'Insect Royalty'; 'Shoot Speed/Kill Light'

So – what's the missing link between acoustic, pastoral Kath Williams and the digitalised electro-thrash of late period Primal Scream? Oddly, the answer is Alan McGee. The Oasis mentor has backed all of Primal Scream's triumphs and follies, and later went onto manage Ms Williams through, and beyond, her major label traumas. *Exterminator* (also known as *Xtrmntr*) was also the final album released on McGee's Creation label, and fittingly so. It was a big, fuck-off noise, featuring production help from just about everyone who'd ever been a mate of the Scream or the Creation label, including The Chemical Brothers, future Gorillaz collaborator and underground hip hop producer Dan The Automator and occasional Scream member Kevin Shields, formerly of My Bloody Valentine. It's an in-crowd album that aims to be the antidote to the dadrock that McGee had helped create, a speaker-trashing electro-metal, Dylan-quoting, agit-propping, hippie-slaughtering reaffirmation of punk rock, modernised for the millennium. Bizarrely, they pulled it off.

All the various post-punk quotes from The Strokes and The Rapture and Franz Ferdinand and LCD Soundsystem and The Killers and Interpol and on we go . . . *Exterminator* was the album that brought all those buried memories of PiL, Joy Division, Suicide, DAF and Gang Of Four back to the fore. What's more, being closer to the age of the original punks than to yer young whippersnappers, they remembered that this wasn't just about mutating rock, funk, reggae and pop . . . it was about anarcho-leftist politics. So *Exterminator* rages at The Man, dragging slogans from Noam Chomsky and Naomi Klein blinking into the half-light of a rock world that couldn't be arsed, frankly, attracting ridicule for daring to don radical chic while hanging out with Kate Moss (yep, the Scream's Bobby Gillespie started that trend, too), glorying in a strange lyrical preoccupation with syphilis. There are many things Primal Scream can be accused of. Subtlety was never one of them.

But, God bless 'em, because *Exterminator* was exactly what the rock doctor ordered at the beginning of the twenty-first century – a big, ballsy rant that found a connection between metallic garage punk and pro-tools-informed digital disco. Gillespie's voice may never . . . well, it can't really be classed as a voice, in the final analysis. But hearing the guy, wasted and disgusted, just hollering 'Sick! Fuck! Sick! Fuck!' on 'Pills' makes me happy. It's rock 'n' roll, kids . . . the seriousness is beneath the stupidity, and that's how the omelette gets made.

Nevertheless, an hour of crunching noises would have been too much/not enough, so the Scream draft in cinematic funk producer David Holmes for a tune, 'Blood Money', that manages to revive PiL, Was (Not Was), Miles Davis, John Barry and Metalheadz-era jungle in one seven-minute instrumental journey into the heart of dark dance majesty. Bobby was probably out blowing up an arms factory and catching syphilis at the time. Syphilis comes up (grooo!) again in 'Keep Your Dreams', which encapsulates all the floaty bits from their 1991 hit *Screamdelica* in five-and-a-half minutes, so you don't have to keep pretending to like the most over-rated album of the post-rave era.

Oh, alright. Let's not be backhanded, shall we? There is sonic genius in every lope, boom and click of 'Insect

EXTERMINATOR/PRIMAL SCREAM

Royalty'. And, *Exterminator*, in its entirety, is like a whizz-bang trip through every boy-cool record collection, whipped into an aimless frenzy, yet intense and defiant and played and produced as if the music had been found under an old road paved with the very best intentions. It's one of the best rock 'n' roll albums made in Britain since the long-lost 1966 radical garage classic URGGGH!!! by Sick Phyllis And Thee Running Pustules, and no mishtake.

VOODOO

D'ANGELO

PRODUCED BY D'ANGELO, DJ PREMIER AND RAPHAEL SADDIQ
EMI/JANUARY 2000
UK CHART: 21
US CHART: 1
KEY TRACKS: 'Devil's Pie'; 'Chicken Grease'; 'Untitled (How Does It Feel)'; 'Feel Like Makin' Love'; 'The Root'

The greatest soul album of the modern era is a spook-fest. Taking its cue from the title, the back cover picture features a shot of a young black woman, eyes rolled upwards, in speaking-in-tongues mode, looking as if she's about to pull an innocent sacrificial chicken apart, limb-from-limb.

D'Angelo's debut album *Brown Sugar*, a sexy, melodic reinvention of Stevie Wonder, Al Green and Marvin Gaye, was widely credited with kickstarting the conscious R&B genre known as nu or neo-soul. But the follow-up, delayed for five years due to the enigmatic singer and multi-musician's management and label problems, rendered the debut redundant. Gone were conventional song structures and soul's familiar play-off between church and bedroom. *Voodoo* came from an altogether darker, more primitive spiritual plane, sounding, with its reliance on drums, bass and bubbling rhythms, laid back so far that their off-beatness veered toward the avant garde, as if D'Angelo was try-ing to burrow through the New York earth to find his way back to Africa, and a truly ancient bush of ghosts. D'Angelo's ability to replicate Al Green's chewy, androgynous and fearful sex-vocal tics remained, particularly on a Green-tributing cover of Roberta Flack's 'Feel Like Makin' Love'. But the major influences this time were the pessimistic, haunted deep funk jams of Sly Stone's 1972 paranoid masterpiece *There's A Riot Goin' On*, via the deeper, weirder elements of peak-era Prince.

Born Michael Eugene Archer in 1974, in Richmond, Virginia, D'Angelo had, like the majority of soul greats before him, begun his musical career in the Pentecostal church, where his father was minister. But Archer was also a child of hip hop, gaining attention as a rapper before being signed as a singer-songwriter. So, like Erykah Badu and Lauryn Hill, D'Angelo bears the weight of the violence, infighting, drug celebration and materialism of rap within the

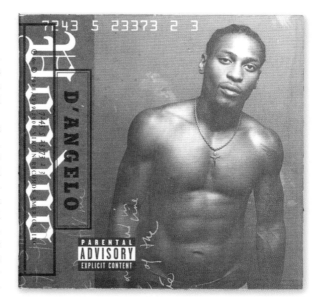

molten, concentrated grooves, largely fashioned here by ?uestlove, drummer of live jazz-influenced rap group The Roots. This bears the sourest fruit on the album's defining track, 'Devil's Pie'. Boiled down to a funk skeleton by Gang Starr producer DJ Premier, mumbled by D'Angelo as if the mic had picked up his internal nightmares, the lyric lays into the materialism and envy of hip hop specifically, of contemporary black culture generally, and leaves us in no doubt that the owner of this pie is Whitey. It makes reference to the 'Five Per Cent' strain of Nation Of Islam thinking, whereby eighty-five per cent of humanity is 'dumb and blind', ten per cent, which, of course, includes the 'white devil', have the knowledge and power to exploit the eighty-five per cent, while the remaining five per cent are 'poor righteous teachers', which means blacks gaining 'knowledge of self' in order to free the eighty-five per cent. Five Per Cent theology, largely discredited within Islamic circles, enjoyed a particularly high popularity among rappers from the late '80s onwards, possessing, as it does, that heady mix of self-obsessed will-to-power, occasional anti-white and Jewish racism coded in such a way as to escape protest, and the casting of black men – and we are, in the end, talking men, as usual – as both Chosen Ones and superheroes, with that built-in failsafe that anyone who argues with all this gobbledegook is simply dismissed for having not attained 'knowledge of self', or of protecting the privileges of their racial tribe, take your pick.

So the intense, almost post-punk 'Devil's Pie' is presented as an argument between righteousness and temptation. D'Angelo may fancy himself as one of the five per cent, but confesses: 'Who am I/To justify/All the evil in our eye/When I myself feel the high/From all that I despise?' As a footnote to that, we still await a third D'Angelo album, as the six-packed genius disappeared, re-emerging in early 2005 to receive suspended sentences for driving while intoxicated and possession of marijuana and cocaine. He is still recovering from a September 2005 car crash.

How much all this holy spookery throughout *Voodoo* actually means probably depends on how seriously you take the various self-help cults that American entertainers like to sign up to, to justify their grotesque wealth and status. What I do know is that D'Angelo makes powerful medicine from a sensualised, ominous sense of dread. The tone of the record so closely resembles the aforementioned *There's A Riot Goin' On* that it almost sounds like a long-delayed sequel. *Riot* represented Sly Stone's drug-addled peak, beginning a long slide into mediocrity, addiction and silence. I hope that lightning is not striking twice, because, much as I despise everything separatist cults stand for, I want to hear more fathomless funk from the most talented musician of his generation. But maybe my agnosticism is misplaced, and Sly and D'Angelo dabbled in something beyond the holier spirits. Music is powerful voodoo.

KALEIDOSCOPE

KELIS
PRODUCED BY PHARRELL WILLIAMS AND CHAD HUGO
VIRGIN/FEBRUARY 2000
UK CHART: 54
US CHART: DID NOT CHART
KEY TRACKS: 'Mafia'; 'Suspended'; 'Roller Rink'; 'Caught Out There'; 'Mars'

Six years is a long time in pop. On the release of this debut album by Harlem's Kelis (pronounced Ker-leese) Rogers, The Neptunes' production team were just another up-and-coming set of rap/R&B backroom boys, unknown outside of black American scene-watchers. Now, after a few years of getting his kit off on every passing rap video, and becoming the coolest man in the world for a few months while gently massaging the same staccato beats, Pharrell Williams finally put out a solo album at the end of 2005 and the world yawned, having moved on to the just as egotistical but apparently more versatile and politically articulate Kanye West. I supposed we should have known that an unbearable ego had landed, when playing this perfect black pop album and having to plough through Williams's interminable intro, where he mumbles away witlessly about finding Kelis as a baby while travelling through a far-off galaxy. God bless the CD skip button.

Still, at this pre-Justin Timberlake, Snoop Dogg point, Williams and his more modest Asian-American partner Chad Hugo were simply the writers, musicians and producers of this key femme R&B long-player which, rather oddly, barely sold a bean. Its clarion-call, of course, was 'I hate you so much right now! WAARRGGGH!!!', the chorus of 'Caught Out There', a scream of rage at cheating guys, a memorable call-to-arms to the sistas, penned entirely by two blokes. Guess it takes one to dis one.

Kelis neatly treads the line of brassy, ultra-modern hip-hopped R&B, and the neo-soul impulse. While her voice is pure, crystal-clear pop, and The Neptunes's sparse, playful beats reference as much '60s psychedelia and '70s mellow funk-rock as hip hop or soul, the feel is retro, from the brilliant twinning of electronic drum and bass with acoustic guitar and piano melodicism, to the sleeve photo of a kaleidoscopically body-painted Kelis in huge orange Afro-wig, a throwback to black hippie soft-porn imagery of the '60s/'70s, and specifically to Betty Davis, sexually aggressive beanpole feminist funk singer and, for a short, unhappy time, Miles Davis's wife as well as Jimi Hendrix's mistress. The unusual references struck a chord in Europe, where she's been fairly popular over three great albums, but has bewildered the American audience, who like their bling ultra-bling and their alternatives churchily authentic. *Kaleidoscope*, however, is gnomic, contradictory and weird, an album that came over as feminist but includes Williams occasionally whispering 'bitch'; an album that sounded entirely self-possessed yet was almost entirely conceived by The Neptunes; an album that used rootsy retro ideas while implying the cosmic. But some of us were delighted by the

politically and socially confused mixed messages; happy-clappy for the memorably dippy 'Roller Rink', furious for 'Caught Out There', both in one song for 'Ghetto Children'. The album's two most beautiful moments see Rogers floating between love as transcendence and black despair on the lovely ballad 'Suspended', and defiantly in love with a gangster (not 'gangsta' this time) on the extraordinary, brilliantly written 'Mafia', her voice as pregnant with airy menace as the object of her desire. She's buoyed all the way by the hungry, adventurous Neptunes, who find soft melody within hard, sparse rhythm with miraculous regularity, making the cosmic conceits of their Star Trak Entertainment concept not just bearable, but believable, so subtly do they suggest a calmly lysergic inner-space.

Easily the most imaginative black female pop album of the modern era, *Kaleidoscope*'s wonders are not dimmed by my meeting Williams twice and finding him to be a complete tit.

NIXON

LAMBCHOP

PRODUCED BY MARK NEVERS AND KURT WAGNER
CITY SLANG (MERGE IN USA)/FEBRUARY 2000
UK CHART: 60
US CHART: DID NOT CHART
KEY TRACKS: 'The Distance From Her To There'; 'Up With People'; 'The Old Gold Shoe'; 'Grumpus'; 'The Book I Haven't Read'

Lambchop make music that forever suggests a friendly, wise and slightly cynical and potty-mouthed uncle, possibly called Uncle 'Grumpus', chewing over life's funny sadness to a friend, on a front-porch in a rural part of Texas, while leaves rustle in the breeze, a dog falls over, and flies buzz around a single porch-light. Once you enter Kurt Wagner's country-soul world, so fundamentally decent and true, so

NIXON/LAMBCHOP

self-deprecating and proudly old, you can't help but love everything he and his ever-expanding band have done over the space of eight albums since 1995's *I Hope You're Sitting Down*. He's the Nashville-born-and-bred antidote to everything modern Nashville has become, with its cowboy-hatted scoundrel patriots who don't play anything that resembles country. Although, having said that, by the time of this, their sixth and most accessible and expansive album, Lambchop had become closer to a Curtis Mayfield-tributing blue-eyed soul group than anything C&W.

As gnomic as fuck and, you suspect, wryly amused by our inability to work out exactly what he's on about, Kurt Wagner, a floor-layer by trade, titled the album in homage to the disgraced former American President, and even suggests a Nixon-related reading list on the album's inner sleeve. Yet there are no clear references to Nixon in the lyrics – they are, as usual, a set of jumbled, poetic observations of life's minutiae, which occasionally slam into focus, before blurring again, jauntily. The album's minor hit, and centre-piece, apart from enabling Wagner to make a band containing upwards of thirteen members into a full-time job and leave the floor-laying trade, might offer some clues, though.

'Up With People' takes its name from an American youth organisation formed in the 1960s. Up With People aimed to focus the increasing anger and radicalism of American youth into an all-embracing humanist positivity, all happy-clappy songs, slogans, and touring youth performances. The group became a strong enough part of the American fabric to inspire piss-takes by both *The Simpsons* and *South Park* in recent years, but were at their most prominent during Nixon's controversial presidential tenure of the late '60s and early '70s. The song employs a female choir and a light gospel bounce, as Wagner quietly grumbles that 'We are doing/And we are screwing/Up our lives today!', with as much offhand relish for the truth as he can muster. Zero 7 remixed the song into a surprise club hit later in 2000.

The unsung heroes of the album are string arranger Lloyd Barry and The Nashville String Machine, who, even in the light of Wagner's affectionately strangled falsetto vocals on the Curtis Mayfield co-write 'What Else Could It Be?', lovingly recreate the lush, romantic orchestral counterpoints of '70s Philadelphia soul and the loverman likes of Barry White and Isaac Hayes.

There's an alt-rock dread factor to Wagner's muse too, in the closing, out of character, traditional suicide balladry of 'The Butcher Boy', and a silly, endearing sense of wordplay humour, as evinced in the Granddad-plays-The-Cure curio that is 'The Petrified Florist'. But Lambchop hit hardest when Wagner haltingly delivers shy, sly ballads about what he calls, for this album's finest song, 'The Distance From Her To There'. As the music weeps and shimmers, a tone painting of nightfall and fireflies, Kurt sings a lament for his 'sad old bone', as he boozes in the yard, unable to traverse the yawning chasm between he outside and her indoors, some mysterious, and familiar, invisible barrier keeping him from getting and giving the love they both need. As always, resignation is the tone. Which is as near to anything to do with Richard Nixon as I can fathom.

THE FACTS OF LIFE

BLACK BOX RECORDER
PRODUCED BY BLACK BOX RECORDER AND PETE HOFFMAN
NUDE/MAY 2000
UK CHART: 37
US CHART: DID NOT CHART
KEY TRACKS: 'The Art Of Driving'; 'The English Motorway System'; 'The Facts Of Life'; 'French Rock 'N' Roll'; 'Straight Life'

Two musician males make the music and put words in the mouth of a beautiful female lead singer. On the face of it, Black Box Recorder is an old-fashioned manufactured pop idea, a white middle-class English echo of Kelis and The Neptunes. But, as ever with Luke Haines, leader of The

Auteurs, there is a twist. He and former Jesus And Mary Chain member John Moore aren't content to write catchy ditties that would suit any singer, and Sarah Nixey is no mannequin diva. Nixey, an actress by trade, tells her musical partners (she was soon to marry Moore) stories from her past, a childhood and post-pubescence, one can only imagine from the themes of this second Black Box Recorder album, that involved much precocious taunting of horny boys, and many internal arguments about whether to be the suburban wife and mother, or whether to break out and run. Her voice, turned right up in the mix, is a plummy English whisper, an echo of Deborah Evans, the posh girl who satirised the coming economic clampdown on The Flying Lizards' 1979 hit version of 'Money'. It is Roedean and bored smoking and a promise of sex as a spoiling of the perfect English Rose. She makes ennui sound both alluring, and like the only sane way to face life. The impression you're given is of the bright, insular girl looking at human horror – perhaps even causing it – with sociopathic dispassion, a siren luring leering boys to death on the rocks beneath Beachy Head. 'Write your name in blood across your shirt/Prove to me that I'm the only one,' she breathes on 'May Queen', and you know the boy is doomed, a bug dissected on a petri dish.

Her blank savagery absolutely fits a group named after the 'black box' flight data recorder, the device that tells you why the plane crashed. They love to sift the gory details of life. There is an obsession with childhood, with driving, with leafy England and with accidental death. The music is a slow, quiet European pop. Sweet washes of melody, electronic without quoting from either '80s synth-pop or '90s trip hop. Haines and Moore are witty, precise writers who appear to relish finding their inner woman; there are few better car-sex metaphors than the parade that illuminate the opening 'The Art Of Driving', as Moore attempts to trap Ms Nixey, only to be met by her freezing cool: 'You've got the hang of steering/Now try stepping on the brakes.' And if he doesn't take her advice? He'll simply become, 'Another dead boyracer/Cut out from the wreck.'

Irony, in its genuine sense, rather than the post-'80s, so-bad-it's-good excuse for being shallow, is the stock-in-trade of Haines and Moore, who take great pleasure in chanting the words 'Rock 'n' roll,' on 'French Rock 'N' Roll', over a stately Serge Gainsbourg-meets-Blondie ballad that couldn't be any less like rock 'n' roll if it was played entirely on a tuba. The glam '70s of Haines's youth is always a background companion on his journeys into human crapness; 'Straight Life' is a sly parody of Roxy Music's 'Street Life' and 'In Every Dream Home A Heartache', replacing Ferry's arch views of urban rush and shagging inflatable dolls with a detailed, deadpan depiction of suburban marriage, all DIY and day trips to 'sites of local interest' and static flight from 'alternative culture' and 'transient people'. The trio never show their hand in terms of judgement of this straight life. They understand that the nature of the adult alternative pop world they inhabit means that the majority of listeners will hear it as a nightmare even though it's the life they're living. Our delusions that we're somehow different are the killing jokes.

Single 'The Facts Of Life' was a surprise mini-hit, but BBR

make a kind of pure pop that radio and public won't accept as such. Like Morrissey and Jarvis Cocker, or, less successfully in commercial terms, Momus, Lawrence from Felt/Denim and Neil Hannon of The Divine Comedy (see p.337), they are smart excavators of Britishness, purveying the sort of wry intelligence and insight that makes many feel they're being laughed at. And, in Black Box Recorder's case, we probably are. Sarah Nixey makes it into a masochistic pleasure.

THE MARSHALL MATHERS LP

EMINEM

PRODUCED BY DR. DRE, EMINEM, MARK BASS, JEFF BASS AND THE 45 KING
AFTERMATH/INTERSCOPE/MAY 2000
UK CHART: 1
US CHART: 1
KEY TRACKS: 'Stan'; 'Kim'; 'The Way I Am'; 'The Real Slim Shady'; 'Who Knew'

Nope – these days, if you want to get Transatlantic No. 1 albums from home truths, you have to kick off your second album by threatening to rape and kill your own mother. Then, after 'Kill You' has set the rules of engagement, fail to prevent a fan murdering his wife, rail at your own fans for bothering you in public, and scream primal blue murder at your baby's mother. Sly irony doesn't really stand a chance.

Not that Mathers, at his best, is not one of the great ironists of his times. Difficult though it is to forgive 'Stan' for inflicting Dido upon us, it remains a dark, cruel, true masterpiece, a time capsule for future historians striving to understand why humans of the twenty-first century believed that the famous were not just more important than their friends, families and selves, but how we made them into Gods, having killed off all the traditional Gods and replaced them with the moral vacuum of money. 'Stan' revealed to all those who figured that Eminem was just an anti-PC exploitation machine that there was a point to all the splenetic savaging of the same old targets. 'Stan' was followed here by 'Who Knew', a sequel to 'Role Model' where Mathers veers between defiant shock-value transgression and frightened pondering of his effect on young ears, trying to negotiate a world where violence as entertainment and parental neglect shape potential Columbines without castrating his muse. 'Kim', however, is a washing of personal dirty linen rendered as a still shocking rage . . . but it taps with absolute accuracy into the primal misogyny unleashed within men by sexual rejection. Did we want or need to hear this particular truth? You may as well ask if we want or need art.

If you're one of those who believe we're living through the decline of the American Empire, a society striking out as it turns on itself, then the stress and conflict, the crisis of masculinity and its effect on still-unequal woman, the working-class male terror of homosexual feelings and the violence it breeds, the black humour and hysterical anger, the selfish depression and private trauma as public drama, then the fear and loathing and misanthropy within the torrent of words and the itchy, ringtone irritant music of the first two Eminem albums is the grist to your mill. He's just a symptom of the moral decay that's gnawing at the heart of his country.

ESG: A SOUTH BRONX STORY

ESG

PRODUCED BY ED BAHLMAN AND ESG
UNIVERSAL SOUND/MAY 2000
UK CHART: DID NOT CHART
US CHART: DID NOT CHART
KEY TRACKS: 'Moody (Spaced Out)'; 'Dance'; 'You're No Good'; 'UFO'; 'Erase You'

Just as the post-punk/punk-funk/mutant disco impulses were beginning to re-emerge in pop, this compilation appeared on a small London label, a timely reminder of all that was best about the polyglot fusions of late-'70s/early-'80s New York. It revealed the hidden history of a group led by Afro-American sisters that, by a set of happy accidents, largely involving attempting to be James Brown and The J.B.s on a breadline budget, made a noise that sounded like Public Image Ltd reinterpreting the best of Tamla Motown. Its makers supported PiL, The Clash, Grandmaster Flash and Gang Of Four in New York, were flown to Manchester to play at the opening night of the legendary Hacienda, and were worshipped by the DJs and dancers at the Paradise Garage, The Gallery and The Warehouse – the New York Clubs where disco evolved into house music. Their debut instrumental B-side, 'UFO', was sampled by every early hip hop producer who knew his onions. And their family name was Scroggins. They are Emerald, Sapphire and Gold aka ESG, the greatest family band this side of The Jacksons.

ESG's music and geographical origins straddled the key musics in this book – punk, disco, post-punk, R&B, house, hip hop – at a crucial point in musical history, and became a secret, shadow influence on all of them, without ever making the band anything more than a cult among the sort of people who formed bands and became DJs. In many ways, hip hop was to blame. Renee (vocals, guitar), Deborah (bass), Marie (percussion) and Valerie (drums) Scroggins and their token male friend Tito Libran (percussion) were given instruments to learn to keep 'em out of street trouble, and, somehow stumbled on an avant-garde mixed-race dance that was overshadowed by the stridently black hip hop that was becoming their South Bronx neighbourhood's major cultural gift to the world. Moreover, one of the first global rap hits stalled their career at its peak. They were discovered by young entrepreneur Ed Bahlman at a New York talent show and signed to his independent label 99 Records. The similarly bass-heavy, punk-funk-inclined Liquid Liquid were 99's other great band. The bassline of Liquid Liquid's 'Optimo/Cavern' was copied by Grandmaster Flash And Melle Mel for their hit coke-anthem 'White Lines'. Bahlman

took the record's Sugar Hill label to court. But, by the time he'd won the case, Sugar Hill was bankrupt and took 99 down with it. The label-less ESG have spent most of the ensuing twenty-odd years tracking down the hundreds of samples of their 'UFO', a living example of both the travails of having your ideas stolen, and the lot of black musicians before hip hop's 'Paid In Full' ethic changed the rules forever.

All that, and we haven't even got to the music. Imagine a youth club disco band with a reggae bass-player and a punk producer, trying to play African dub versions of Motown's greatest hits, with a member of The Shangri-Las on lead vocals. Add jungle chants and girl-group harmonies, gritty, ghostly urban imagery and survivalist feminism, exhortations to dance and sultry invocations of steamy sex. If, at this point, you don't think that sounds like a dream cross between The Slits, The Supremes and Josie And The Pussycats, and you are not running to track down this album, then, man, I give up. Thankfully, although all now well into middle age, ESG haven't. They simply replace a tiring member with a baby Scroggins from time-to-time, passing on the family jewels, refusing to give up on being the world's most influential art-soul band that no one ever heard of.

STORIES FROM THE CITY, STORIES FROM THE SEA

PJ HARVEY

PRODUCED BY PJ HARVEY, ROB ELLIS AND MICK HARVEY
UNIVERSAL-ISLAND/OCTOBER 2000
UK CHART: 23
US CHART: 42
KEY TRACKS: 'Good Fortune'; 'A Place Called Home'; 'Big Exit'; 'This Is Love'; 'The Whores Hustle And The Hustlers Whore'

And more New York inspiration . . . so much so, that it's the best album Patti Smith never made. Indeed, the hairy androgene Queen of NY beat-punk warrior poetry must have heard the heavy, heady way Ms Harvey sang Little Italy – 'Leeduhl Eeduhleee!' – on the blissfully romantic 'Good Fortune' and wondered if someone had been sampling her singing in the bath. You suspect that PJ is kept from true greatness by just how in hock she is to her influences. But give the girl her due – this is a more consistent Patti Smith album than any the woman has made herself, apart from the unassailable masterpiece that is *Horses*.

Seen, at the time, as a pop surprise after Harvey's many apparently maverick soundscapes, the fact that it won a Mercury and still stalled at No. 23 is a salient reminder that, in 2000, a straightforward rock-pop album was far more alien to pop ears than the grunge or Cave-lite or trip hop that she'd had a go at before. What can't be denied is that *Stories* . . . took the raw and bloody sexual longing and disgust of her earlier work, refracted it through what appears to be a happy sexual/romantic encounter in New York, and used some neat city imagery to question whether this was love or lust, and whether the latter isn't the better, more life-affirming option. 'I can't believe life's so complex/When I just want to sit here and watch you undress,' she roars, with more than a hint of Chrissie Hynde's tough lover magic, on the punk rock stomp of 'This Is Love'. Throughout, she deliberately interrupts tributes to her lover with vivid descriptions of Manhattan's grandeur, chaos and buzz, neatly pointing out the two-way relationship between love's perfect moments and the place where they happen, questioning how much is real, and how much is the movie of our lives that we all play in our heads. A weird twist on that movie is Harvey's Mercury being awarded on, of all days, 11 September 2001, and her acceptance of it by telephone, as she watched events unfold first-hand, not in Manhattan, but in Washington DC.

Other than that, you have Thom Yorke guesting, cloyingly, on 'The Mess We're In', a bracing overall feel of me and you against the world, and a memorable set of rockin' guitar melodies which further prepared the way for people to accept some rock 'n' roll back into their pop lives in the twenty-first century. It reminded you of music that you didn't know you'd missed.

AMERICAN III: SOLITARY MAN

JOHNNY CASH

PRODUCED BY RICK RUBIN
AMERICAN/OCTOBER 2000
UK CHART: DID NOT CHART
US CHART: 88
KEY TRACKS: 'I See A Darkness'; 'One'; 'That Lucky Old Sun (Just Rolls Around Heaven All Day)'; 'Wayfaring Stranger'; 'I Won't Back Down'

The rep of Cash's American recordings is strikingly undercut by how few bought them upon release. They are extraordinary records, under the circumstances of career failures, illness, imminent death and a market unsympathetic to septuagenarian country singers, but their legend as life-defining epitaphs was set by the subversive, chilling video for Cash's version of Trent Reznor's 'Hurt', by the death of his wife June Carter, and his own demise in September 2003. But Cash's mentor Rick Rubin understood the myth he was creating, saw it as a long game. The opener on Cash's third Rubin-produced album of covers ancient and contemporary, 'I Won't Back Down', always sounded, out of the vocal cords of its writer Tom Petty, like the laziest form of middle-class bloke-rawk survivalism: I won't back down from . . . erm . . . wearing jeans. On a Sunday! In front of Mom! In Cash's thunderous yet waning baritone, it grows into nothing less than a vision of a flawed but proud man standing at the gates of Heaven, saying take me as I am, or I'll take my chances below. As for what Cash's wavering vocals do to U2's 'One' – the guy chews almost casually on a slice of old sub-

AMERICAN III: SOLITARY MAN/JOHNNY CASH

Lennon/Marley hugging-and-learning pap and makes you feel every last ounce of what it might take for us all to 'carry each other . . . carry each other'.

And on it goes. Cash's fellow country renegade veteran Merle Haggard, bringing a friend's joy to 'I'm Leavin' Now'. A version of alt-country cult figure Will Oldham's definitive 'I See A Darkness' that I'd demand to be played at my funeral if I didn't think it would be just too bleak and too self-aggrandising for anyone who cared about me to take. And a take on Nick Cave's 'The Mercy Seat' – I can only assume that old Nick felt he'd done it all once the spiritual father of his entire muse had given his blessing – that sometimes strikes me as genius (largely because of the saloon-bar melodrama of Benmont Tench's piano), and sometimes as a complete misfire, as if Cash simply couldn't relate to the ambivalence of Cave's Death Row con, in the face of eternal judgement. But what always strikes, no matter what mood this album finds you in, is Rubin's dry production, putting Johnny Cash and his boom-chicka guitar in your space, your head, your blood. It was a visionary thing that this metal-loving hip hop producer did for Cash, and for American music. It stands.

STANKONIA

OUTKAST
PRODUCED BY EARTHTONE III, ORGANIZED NOISE AND ANTONIO 'LA' REID
LAFACE/ARISTA/NOVEMBER 2000
UK CHART: 10
US CHART: 2
KEY TRACKS: 'Ms Jackson'; 'Toilet Tisha'; 'So Fresh, So Clean'; 'B.O.B.'; 'Red Velvet'

If you've read everything up to now, you might have noticed my love/hate relationship with hip hop. It's the greatest cultural innovation of my lifetime, and the one most abused by commerce and the willingness of various rappers to exploit

the most damaging aspects of black stereotyping in order to make money. It thrills me, and repulses me, in equal measures, like nothing else.

So it's really hard for me to express how I felt when I heard *Stankonia* for the first time. Its breadth and depth of vision, its fearlessness, its respect for black music history, its balance between the pure pleasure it finds in women, sex and being male, and its disquiet about America, masculinity and politics, is what I always thought hip hop was capable of. It almost destroyed the straitjacket of 'keepin' it real' rap insularity overnight, and found a way to fuse George Clinton and Sly Stone's progressive funk-rock, Prince's black pop art, and the whole gangsta-pimp culture shebang without ever lurching into either self-righteousness or macho defensiveness. It matched US rap's bright muscularity with the kind of stoned, eclectic experiment that had defined Massive Attack, Tricky and Portishead. It was rough and rude and pungent as anything called Stank (as in stink, because that's what the word 'funk' means) onia should be, and as avant-garde as a whole herd of Brian Enos locked in a performance art space.

Andre 'Andre 3000' Benjamin and Antwan 'Big Boi' Patton hail from Atlanta, Georgia, and named their duo in relation to the outcast nature of southern states hip hop, in an era dominated by the east and west coast. After their first three, increasingly adventurous albums had, along with the successes of Missy Elliott (see p.295) and the up-and-coming Neptunes, established 'The Dirty South' as hip hop's hot new wave, they scored their first global pop hit with the best track from *Stankonia*, 'Ms Jackson', a strange, subversive ballad, which was essentially an open apology to Erykah Badu's mother for splitting from her daughter and leaving her holding the baby. Ms Badu guests on 'Humble Mumble'. Cake-and-eat-it times, as I think I might have mentioned.

The rest of this seventy-five-minute album (and, for once, it isn't too long, not one second) spins from Cypress Hill's B-Real rhyming over harpsichord ('Xplosion') to high-speed drum 'n' bass ('B.O.B.'), from lo-fi electronica ('I'll Call Before I Come') to funk metal ('Gasoline Dreams'). There was an obvious split, an artistic and lifestyle tension, between Benjamin (freak throwback to Hendrix, occasionally wears dresses, doesn't care if you think he's queer, writes heartfelt paeans to his baby's famous mama's mama) and Patton, who built a lap-dancing club in his basement, had a dog-breeding business, and contributed dribbling misogyny to a good tune like 'We Love Deez Hoez'. The divide would be formalised on their next album, which was essentially two solo records in one sleeve (see p.362). But, on *Stankonia*, it felt like unlikely alchemy, the attraction of opposites, with a left-field maverick dragging his bullish partner into jungle-rock fusions about bombs over Baghdad ('B.O.B.'), which appeared to have nothing whatsoever to do with any Gulf except the one between the two of them. Yet it was Big Boi who wrote the spoken-word interlude for 'Toilet Tisha', a horrified funkadelic epic about a pregnant fourteen-year-old, drenched in shame, deciding whether she and her baby should live or die.

The album had shades of Public Enemy, inasmuch that the sheer density – and amount – of musical ideas is bewildering. But what PE's The Bomb Squad did with samples, Earthtone III (the OutKast duo, plus production partner Mr DJ) replicated with 'proper' instruments, played by themselves and session men. Outside of that, it's sex, violence, dancing, social commentary, gibberish, bad girls and badder (bing!) boys all the way. It wasn't just the best hip hop album of 2000, but the best rock 'n' roll album in years, too. The vague unifying theme is the idea of *Stankonia*, a place at the centre of the Earth from which all things funky derive. It just sounded like America.

THE W

WU-TANG CLAN
PRODUCED BY THE RZA
LOUD/RCA/NOVEMBER 2000
UK CHART: 19
US CHART: 5
KEY TRACKS: 'I Can't Go To Sleep'; 'Gravel Pit'; 'One Blood Under W'; 'Hollow Bones'; 'Jah World'

A launch party for the Wu-Tang Clan collective's third album proper had a surprise guest. Wu-Tang member Russell 'Ol' Dirty Bastard' Jones arrived to make a personal appearance in support of *The W*, on which he'd duetted with Snoop Dogg for 'Conditional'. He'd been serving time for parole violation, and had been on the run for a month. Somehow, he got away from the party without re-arrest, but was caught a few days later in the car park of a McDonalds, signing autographs. The group photo on the back of *The W* featured the group's leader and producer Robert 'The RZA' Diggs holding a bandana with the acronym O.D.B. embossed in yellow letters. Four years later Jones died at a Wu-Tang recording session, the result of an accidental overdose of cocaine and a painkiller called Tramadol. In terms of drug-induced chaos, drama and inevitable tragedy, Peter Doherty has a way to go yet.

All of this overshadowed the best of the Staten Island cast-of-thousands' long-players. By this time, the impact of their rough, gruff, over-rated debut *Enter The Wu-Tang (36 Chambers)* had been dispersed by an avalanche of Wu spin-off records, of which only the Method Man and ODB sets had truly stood out. What's more, *The W*'s host of guests – Snoop, Redman, the ubiquitous Busta Rhymes, Nas, Isaac Hayes, and roots reggae singer Junior Reid – suggested desperation, lack of focus. But the focus was all in the musical genius of The RZA, fresh from scoring (and guesting in) Jim Jarmusch's *Ghost Dog: The Way Of The Samurai*, a virtual visualisation of the Wu-Tang world, where the fusion of legends from martial arts movies and superhero comics, 'Five Per Cent nation'-derived (see D'Angelo, p.331 mystical numerology and bleak street reportage re-created New York's Staten Island as Shaolin, an almost mystical ghetto where black heroes battle the white power structure, where the scar of slavery informs every gunshot and gang-fight, where ancient Zen warriors provide invisible support to those trapped by poverty, racism and black-on-black violence.

On *The W*, this reaches a peak of weeping protest on the stunning 'I Can't Get To Sleep', which uses Isaac Hayes's booming speaking voice and his grandiose orchestral version of 'Walk On By' to dramatise the neurosis of a person who simply can't walk on by when slavery still feels real, the Afro-American leaders have all been murdered or exiled, and children die in ghetto streets. It's RZA himself who rages:

'They got me trapped up in a metal gate
Just stressed out with hate
And just give me no time to relax
And use my mind to meditate
What should I do? Grab a blunt or a brew?
Grab a two-two and run out there and put this fuckin' violence in you?'

It's the deep, authoritative voice of Hayes who issues the tough love in response to RZA and Ghostface Killah's angst: 'The power is in your hands/Stop all this cryin'/And be a man.' But the song fades, quickly, suggesting that this fatherly soldierism is easier said than done. Later, for the soul-and-spy-thriller-flecked hit 'Gravel Pit', Method Man presents the distraction from all this pain, The Wu-Tang party, as a bacchanal so far underground it's Stone Age. Yet, after literally rocking that party, 'Jah World' is another blasted dirge lament, where 'I'm still pickin' cotton/And my back is hottin'.

The Wu-Tang view of living may be hell on Earth, but RZA's unique meldings of soul samples, funk guitar riffs, oriental motifs, snatches of dubbed martial arts movie dialogue, and an overall, opiated depiction of the ghetto as a woozy supernatural universe is the way forward, the hope that lies in black art, in imagination and commitment to ideas, in reinventing yourself as a stronger entity, in order to get that sleep, and cope with days ahead. Tarantino heard it, hired The RZA for the *Kill Bill* movies, and, you suspect, set him off down a long path as the foremost soundtrack musician of his age, a master of sonic drama.

2001

STEPHEN MALKMUS

STEPHEN MALKMUS
PRODUCED BY JOHN LECKIE
VIRGIN/FEBRUARY 2001
UK CHART: 49
US CHART: DID NOT CHART
KEY TRACKS: 'Jo Jo's Jacket'; 'Jenny & The Ess-Dog';
'Phantasies'; 'Discretion Grove'; 'Vague Space'

One of the loveliest buried treasures of twenty-first-century indie rock. Santa Monica, California-born and Portland, Oregon-based singer/songwriter/guitarist Malkmus had been the head boy of cult US indie band Pavement, whose restless, obscurantist pop gems are often credited with inventing the 'lo-fi' genre of underground guitar music. After a somewhat acrimonious split, in which Malkmus chiefly and briefly became a minor celeb in England for his

friendship with Blur's Damon Albarn and Elastica's Justine Frischmann, and apparent influence on Blur's post-Britpop direction, Malkmus finally unveiled this lovely, warm, witty first solo album, recorded with his new band The Jicks, which kept Pavement's obtuse lyrical themes, but made the guitar-rock into something straighter, cleaner and more soulful. The dominant influence was undoubtedly Lou Reed, but the playful, folk-rock tunes mixed a host of '70s influences – Richard Thompson, Fairport Convention, Kevin Ayers, Steely Dan, Hunky Dory Bowie, early Brian Eno, and the twin guitar curlicues (all played by an overdubbed Malkmus) of Television's *Marquee Moon* (see p.11).

Malkmus always had the potential to be a big star. He looked the definitive indie-rock collegiate heart-throb, like a straight, slightly ruffled Rupert Everett, and had a unique way with lyric, tune, riff and offhand Lou Reed mumble. But you always felt that he was too lazy, or amused by celebrity, or maybe just too plain full of himself to do anything other than what came naturally. What came naturally was an unashamedly retro arm wrestle between arty glam and droning folk-rock, and songs about being a pirate ('The Hook'), being Yul Brynner ('Jo Jo's Jacket'), fishing in Alaskan ice-holes ('Phantasies') and about a middle-class couple, Jennifer (eighteen) and Sean (aka Ess-Dog, thirty-one) who smooch to Dire Straits albums and gradually grow apart, with no lessons particularly learnt ('Jenny & The Ess-Dog'). The music thrummed and endlessly delighted with its melodic twists and turns, performed and produced as if dance music and digital technology had never happened. On 'Jo Jo's Jacket', he breaks off from being an ironic version of Yul Brynner to attack some mysterious foe, Luddite tendencies revealed in all their glory: 'You're such monumental slime/Let the punishment fit the crime/Tie it to a chair/The house music will blare/And turn your ears into a medicinal jelly.' So there. A man forever doomed to look like a boy and want to be a folk-rock Lou Reed covering Elton's John's 'Island Girl' in a mythical 1973. I know how he feels, which is presumably why I have an unnatural affinity with this forty-minute gem of whimsical obfuscation.

ULTRAGLIDE IN BLACK

THE DIRTBOMBS

PRODUCED BY MICK COLLINS AND JIM DIAMOND
IN THE RED/MAY 2001
UK CHART: DID NOT CHART
US CHART: DID NOT CHART
KEY TRACKS: 'Ode To A Black Man'; 'Kung Fu'; 'Chains Of Love'; 'Underdog'; 'Your Love Belongs Under A Rock'

The new millennium inspired a new wave of back-to-basics worshippers at the altar of pre-punk rock and wheezing, rattling valve amplifiers. Making Malkmus sound like a laptop techno bod, Detroit's Mick Collins had been a key influence on his city's deluge of garage-rock revival bands, personified by The White Stripes. His first band, The Gories, had been a raw-as-fuck celebration of ham-fisted musicianship. The Dirtbombs were a different proposition, taking the '60s garage band ethos of legends such as The Sonics, ? And The Mysterions and The Count Five and overlaying a patina of prime Hendrix blues-rock. Being one of the few African-Americans playing basic rock 'n' roll in 2001, Collins came up with a logical idea: an album covering semi-obscure soul and funk gems by classic artists, covering different aspects of the black urban experience. The result was the best covers album a set of obscure multi-racial punk musicians could dredge from the primordial rockin' soul murk.

Collins has chutzpah too, taking on tunes by the likes of Curtis Mayfield, Sly Stone, Stevie Wonder and even Barry White. The Mayfield cover, 'Kung Fu', is despatched in the dub-goth style of early Bauhaus single 'Bela Lugosi's Dead', while they approach the funk of Stevie Wonder's 'Livin' For The City' and Marvin Gaye's 'Got To Give It Up' like disco-punk hooligans, making the imperious social commentary

of Wonder's anthem into a testimony from the gutter, all metallic riffage and off-key fuzz guitar. The keynote though, is a cover of an '80s B-side by Phil Lynott, the late leader of Thin Lizzy. 'Ode To A Black Man' is a lost gem, and The Dirtbombs deliver it with a driving swamp-pop relish, Lynott's lyrical tributes to Hendrix and Robert Johnson and his right to be a black rock 'n' roller chanted with warm sincerity by a multi-tracked Collins.

A cheap party in an illegal basement, all beers, high-school hormones, and a northern soul DJ following the rough-arsed band, *Ultraglide In Black* is the most spontaneous, live album in this book, a world where everyone good from the '60s is boiled down to high-concentrate garage rock 'n' roll, and where Mick Collins is a punk rock version of Isaac Hayes's chef from *South Park*, the big black uncle dispensing musical wisdom to the snotty white kids. In many ways, it's as punk-funk as any music gets.

10,000 HZ LEGEND

AIR

PRODUCED BY AIR
SOURCE/VIRGIN/MAY 2001
UK CHART: 7
US CHART: 88
KEY TRACKS: 'How Does It Make You Feel?'; 'Radio #1'; 'Lucky And Unhappy'; 'Sex Born Poison'; 'Don't Be Light'

The second Air album proper was a tribute to Kraftwerk by way of a Beach Boys sonic palette, as they sought to comment on the details of being deliberately synthetic while making music of ambitious, club-friendly elegance. It provoked a mini-backlash, accusations of self-indulgence, and that increasingly familiar media antipathy when an artist dares to laugh at certain aspects of their art. The quest for authenticity in pop, where even manufactured teeny popsters are forced to talk, in interviews, of 'keeping it real', whatever 'it' is, is the enemy of pop's major USP – its quick wit. Nicolas Godin and Jean-Benoît Dunckel were no more self-conscious about their contrivances in this album's opener, 'Electronic Performers', than the parade of drab singer-songwriters and sub-Radiohead choirboys routinely bought and praised for being 'emotional'. They simply figured that being obvious about it was both more honest, and funnier. Apparently, delight in a good joke doesn't count as an emotion these days.

The tune that dragged me right inside this blissful marriage of the pop-historical and the postmodern impulses is 'How Does It Make You Feel?' Over an ultra-lounge wash of Serge Gainsbourgian trip hop, a robot voice – you know, that Stephen Hawking, *OK Computer* voice – begins an earnest conversation with its lady-love. He is trying to explain his feelings. To throw off the bonds of machismo that keep men from expressing their true feelings about things. Every time the testimony reaches a peak of hysterical new-man vulnerability, the chorus glides in, slowly, from a celestial place. 'How does it make you feel?', the massed crowd of creamy male falsetto harmonies plead, taking you right back to that more childish take on the same theme, 10CC's 1975 No. 1 'I'm Not In Love'. Finally, Robot Boy's choir of angels asks one last time, 'How does this make you feel?' 'Well,' Robot Girl replies, with a thoughtful, distracted pause, 'I really think you should give up smoking.'

The lyrics and the robot voices give a get-out clause, of course. That it's all sci-fi, the ghosts in the machines negotiating love. But . . . screw that. It's a couple of typical French guys saying that, if you make yourself emotionally vulnerable to siren woman, she'll trample on your soul and fill your life with petty domestic rules. Don't agree, exactly, but the music is space and meadows and twinkling stars, and the joke exquisitely delivered. It fits neatly before the Brian Wilson-esque single, 'Radio #1', which was essentially a dare to Radio 1 not to play the new Air single, and a guest appearance from Beck on 'The Vagabond', where he essays some lost American road angst, perfectly out of place, and utterly in keeping.

America has definitely tainted the Air here, where they often seem to be travelling by car, on 'freeways', dispassionately observing 'sidewalks'. But the music is Europe, an old Europe of stately rhythms and frosty strings, where even the most synthetic squelch sounds '70s-ancient, reminding us how far music has travelled to design all these machines that sound like real instruments, killing our science-fiction dreams. There is great sadness here, even in the jokes, even in the satire of desire for natural woman – 'You don't wear cosmetic/You don't like arithmetic' – that calls itself 'Wonder Milky Bitch'.

Its most ambitious song – an attempt to cover just about every art-rock style in six minutes by way of Beck, again – implored us: 'Don't Be Light'. Too late. Their next album was some pleasant chill-out wine bar thing. I forget the name. People liked that one.

AMNESIAC

RADIOHEAD
PRODUCED BY NIGEL GODRICH AND RADIOHEAD
PARLOPHONE/JUNE 2001
UK CHART: 1
US CHART: 2
KEY TRACKS: 'Pyramid Song'; 'Life In A Glasshouse'; 'You And Whose Army?'; 'Knives Out'; 'Morning Bell/Amnesiac'

From the same experimental, tortuous, *OK Computer*-rejecting sessions as the courageous *Kid A*, *Amnesiac* is an album like a disturbed waking dream, where your subconscious arm-wrestles with the day's coming, turning rest into nightmare, and back again. Yorke is a somnambulist here, his scattershot references to cannibalism ('Knives Out'), divorce ('Morning Bell/Amnesiac') and the inevitable fall of the western military-industrial complex ('You And Whose Army?') emerging through a lazy sleep-talk fog, the very essence of resignation. That's why bands who copy

Radiohead are both useless and immensely popular – the ideal soundtrack for our surrender to market forces, a vague, gutless ennui. What makes Radiohead so much better – apart from a breadth of reference that enables them to tribute The Smiths on 'Knives Out' as imaginatively as they refashion the baroque blues of Charles Mingus for the unlikely hit 'Pyramid Song' and New Orleans funeral jazz on 'Life In A Glasshouse' – is not lyrical insight, but the fact that they are the best rock musicians on God's green Earth and, in Godrich, have a producer willing and able to give what could feel distant and lofty an air of horizontal intimacy, a series of whispers from a sad but true friend. No one else on Radiohead's creative and commercial level makes music like *Amnesiac* and *Kid A*, that felt so open to individual interpretation, gave so much credit to their fans for an adventurous ear, and was so generous in its refusal to bludgeon the listener with what are, in Yorke's case, pretty predictable, even bland, contemporary paranoias.

If Radiohead had a sense of humour, and their own ridiculousness, they'd be as good as people think they are. But *Amnesiac* forgets more about the unexpected twist of texture or melody than ninety-nine per cent of rock bands are even interested in knowing. Its more than enough.

TOXICITY

SYSTEM OF A DOWN
PRODUCED BY RICK RUBIN AND DARON MALAKIAN
AMERICAN-COLUMBIA/AUGUST 2001
UK CHART: 13
US CHART: 1
KEY TRACKS: 'Prison Song'; 'Needles'; 'Science'; 'Jet Pilot'; 'Aerials'

A measure of how much the radical impulse in rock 'n' roll had collapsed in Britain was our ignorance of this band. Californian Armenian-Americans System Of A Down were not only recklessly anti-establishment, and huge, and co-produced by Rick Rubin, but had this astonishing album at No. 1 in the US album charts as the planes hit the Twin Towers on 11 September 2001. 'All our taxes paying for your wars/Against the new non-rich,' this crushing, violent, melodramatic noise raged against the machine on the opening anthem 'Prison Song'. While the liberal thirty- and forty-somethings that set the British media agenda celebrated the trust-fund ennui of The Strokes, a million supposedly vacant, materialistic American kids went right on buying and listening to this hysterical assault on corporate American power, defying bans and patriotic clampdowns, empathising with the pissed-off immigrants. So Serj Tankian, Daron Malakian, Shavo Odadjian and John Dolmayan didn't need Cool Britannia's approval. It just seems ironic that their music sounds like Killing Joke and Napalm Death, and thinks like The Clash and the Gang Of Four, and yet the generation of Brits who first encouraged those bands ignores their spiritual heirs.

System Of A Down's noise borders on the utterly ridiculous. Like some bizarre wrestling match between death metal, Frank Zappa, Asian and north African devotional music, Zorba The Greek and a passing boy band. It's definitely not scared of attracting ridicule, which is why it attracts a global fanbase of children who intrinsically understand that their parents' clinging to the cool of good-taste rock is inseparable from our inability to organise and agitate against a planet that turns children into debt-ridden wage slaves before they've barely had time to understand that we've allowed them no choices. With the master producer Rubin's help, their portents of doom and their insistence that, if you know the facts and fight, that doom is avoidable, are loud and clear yet still rush through in an exhilarating blur. The torrent of ideas in the music, its frantic restlessness, define the terms of re-engagement with punk rock's crucial, crazed and joyful 'No!' It believes that America is being re-made into a giant prison and that, 'When you lose small mind/You free your life.' It makes me laugh, play air

TOXICITY/SYSTEM OF A DOWN

guitar, and realise that our children have more balls and brains than us. Not that they could possibly have had less.

IS THIS IT

THE STROKES
PRODUCED BY GORDON RAPHAEL
ROUGH TRADE/AUGUST 2001
UK CHART: 2
US CHART: 33
KEY TRACKS: 'Hard To Explain'; 'Last Nite'; 'Someday';
'Barely Legal'; 'Take It Or Leave It'

But trust-fund ennui can be very attractive. I get that. The Strokes, apart from changing the course of 'indie' rock, sounded like New York carrying on (self) regardless, arrogant and elegantly bored, existential and dirty. Julian Casablancas crooned druggily and years spun back to times when rock might change the world, if it could be arsed to get up and find its comb.

The spindly, sepia-tinted opening riff of, say, 'Alone, Together' comes in and I struggle to remember a new indie-rock record that doesn't sound exactly like this. Franz Ferdinand and The Libertines sound completely different to each other, but are both completely in hock to this sound. You knew, immediately, that it was a formula, worked out with Bunsen burners and an Etch-a-Sketch by Casablancas and their producer Gordon Raphael. But you didn't care. *Is This It* had all the sex and disease, the offhand method mumble and the insouciant strut, the perfect pop out of lo-fi, youth club sound, that had been missing in rock 'n' roll since *Bummed* by Happy Mondays . . . and that had been an aberration of its times. It was the revenge of the Less Than Zero generation, an effortless evocation of being too rich to live, too cool to die. It implied that class differences faded and died in the face of a rubbery retro bassline, an arch conversation about fuck all, and a scratchy wall of Velvet Underground/Television-lite guitars, and it was, of course, absolutely right.

Most of all, it was honest. These men did not care, and they weren't going to fake it. 'He's gonna let you down,' Casablancas growled on the closing 'Take It Or Leave It', with thrice as much commitment as he sang any other line. An upfront get-out clause, the ultimate cake-and-eat-it. When someone called on them to remove the mildly snotty 'New York City Cops' from the album in the wake of 9/11 (as well as, bizarrely, the British Spinal Tap-parodying Smell The Glove sleeve), they meekly complied. We don't want any trouble, officer. It's just a little rebellion, for personal use. Don't you play golf with my daddy?

The album's title asked a question and our response supplied the answer. We wanted our rock to be manufactured as efficiently and painlessly as Westlife. I tried to resist but their noise was everything I wanted and nothing I needed. Who wouldn't want to pull a Stroke?

2002

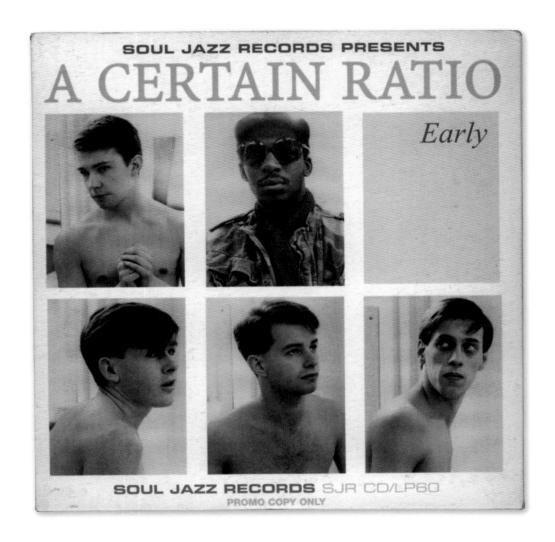

EARLY/A CERTAIN RATIO

EARLY

A CERTAIN RATIO

PRODUCED BY MARTIN HANNETT AND A CERTAIN
RATIO
SOUL JAZZ/JANUARY 2002
UK CHART: DID NOT CHART
US CHART: DID NOT CHART
KEY TRACKS: 'Knife Slits Water'; 'Shack Up'; 'Waterline';
'Flight'; 'Gum'

Owners of the most ironic shorts and whistles in pop, A
Certain Ratio were the Factory label's very own disco band.
Admittedly, this was a disco band featuring Simon Topping's
hilariously dolorous, sub-Ian Curtis vocals, blankets of
spooky bush of ghosts effects, echoey disorientating production, further occasional vocals from Martha Tillson that
sang in every tune but the right one, and that starred an
extraordinary black drummer backing the palest, least
funky-looking white boys in the whole of Manchester. But,
in their early '80s heyday, they were the hippest band in New
York, headlining over The Slits, Grandmaster Flash, even
Madonna. The shorts and whistles came from their live
shows, and their Latin and jazz-funk-worshipping attempts
to transform a room full of British students in grey over-
coats into a bleak, industrial take on Rio De Janeiro. ACR,
perhaps more than any other band, defined punk funk, and
provide the missing-link between post-punk's agitated
gloom and the Manc-derived hedonism of New Order, the
Hacienda, Happy Mondays and the whole late-'80s indie-
dance wave. This, as the title suggests, is a compilation of
their best early work, released by the same London Soul Jazz
label that, under their Universal Sound imprint, had also
compiled New York's similarly inclined and unlikely ESG
(see p.337 for a twenty-first-century dance/indie crossover
market becoming increasingly curious about the fusion pop
adventures of the late '70s/early '80s.

Pitched musically somewhere between Joy Division, Can,

Eno and Bowie's white labcoat-funk, and Man With The
Horn-era Miles Davis, Topping, Jeremy Kerr, Donald
Johnson, Martin Moscrop and Peter Terrel were among the
most progressive musicians of their day. Johnson's drums
were pure, taut and technical jazz-funk; Kerr's bass veered
between techno-funk thumb-plunking and doomy dub
drops; Topping's percussion and Moscrop's guitar scratched
and rattled at the sound's edges, while drones, whistles,
whoops, chants and those grim, avant-minimalist vocals
captured an essence that lent a title to their first, tape-only
album, *The Graveyard And The Ballroom*. The music's
triumph was that, even when sucking all black 'soul' from a
cover of Banbarra's US underground funk classic 'Shack Up',
the music was as hip-shakingly and feet-flailingly funky as
it was murky, enigmatic, arty and disquieting.

The reason that ACR have been left out until now is not
because this is a Greatest Hits – hits, they did not have – but
because none of their albums were entirely focused, as they
disappointingly sailed off into bland beige-funk waters with
indecent haste, as 'Life's A Scream' and 'Touch' reveal here.
But the group recorded nine tunes that are as multi-layered,
propulsive, strange and breathtaking as anything by PiL or
Talking Heads, and all nine are on *Early*, headed up by the
five deathlessly brilliant key tracks above. The brief exchange
of mutant disco ideas between Manchester and New York in
the early '80s are at their most exciting and maverick here,
and ACR played a hidden, crucial role in the marriage
between disco, electro and left-field synth-pop that begat
house and techno. They were gothic disco, I guess. New
Order owe them.

IS A WOMAN

LAMBCHOP

PRODUCED BY MARK NEVERS AND KURT WAGNER
CITY SLANG (MERGE IN USA)/FEBRUARY 2002
UK CHART: 38

2002 produced few good albums. At least, not in the part of the world where my awareness reaches. Music seemed to reel in the face of recent events, guilty about its frivolity in the face of an authentic horror, and deathly history made. The rest of the book also lives with the biggest threat to the commercial and critical primacy of the long-playing album since it became pop's major M.O. in the late '60s. The MP3 jukebox and its facility to play thousands of individual slices of your favourite music at random, twins with online file-sharing, and sees me, yet again, writing a book about a musical format that's facing extinction. But something tells me the album will survive. Artists – at least the ones for whom there may still be something more to all this than maximum profit – have rallied and made great coherent LPs in the last two years. In case you're interested, if albums from 2004 and 2005 had been covered here, I would almost certainly have included The Futureheads, Kanye West and The Streets from 2004, and LCD Soundsystem, Bright Eyes, Antony And The Johnsons, Roots Manuva, Gorillaz, Kanye again, and The Beta Band compilation from 2005.

And you're right. I am stalling . . .

This, the seventh Lambchop album, knocks me flat, every time, and I feel somewhat at a loss to define exactly why. It is samey, largely based on the slow, ruminatory piano lines of Tony Crow, presented as a cosmic desert shimmer by producer Mark Nevers. Unlike past Lambchop albums, it seems to have little to do with either country or soul. It has found its own tune. I ended up making a case, in a magazine review, for it being our generation's *Astral Weeks*. I stand by that, because I don't have a clue what Van Morrison's most famous album is about either. I just meant that Morrison found a music that seemed to drift, and float, and dive, like the ups and downs of a single, ordinary day. And that *Is A Woman* was like that; that organic, that natural, that magical.

It feels, apart from the playful, almost Stephen Malkmus-like (see p.345) 'D. Scott Parsley', like a set of dreamy internal conversations you might have when deciding whether to divorce your wife or not. On 'D. Scott Parsley', it's all gone badly wrong: 'This won't change the lonely life you see/This is not the life I thought would be.' But on the following 'Bugs', a song made of crickets rubbing legs randily and gossamer wings brushing sticky grass, it's all going to turn out just fine: 'A whispered comment or a compliment is said/And you take her hand as you gesture toward the bed/I can't believe this feels this good.' And the reason, perhaps, for the wondering whether to stay at all, comes early, with a typically Kurt Wagner-esque, friendly, grumbly sigh: 'I guess it's right/To love the girls who fight/Off our manly acts of desperation.'

So, I don't know, I am defeated by why I worship at the altar of a song called 'The New Cobweb Summer', and its intimations of simultaneous decay and rebirth, and by the bit in the closing title track when its softly treading folk becomes Bob Marley being played by librarians. They just slay me, and convince me that this is one of the most secretly sad records ever made, inspired by an awful event in Wagner's life that he has no intention of telling us about. It's just a guess. *Is A Woman* is so beautiful, modestly, humanly beautiful that I'm much happier to be wrong.

SONGS FOR THE DEAF

QUEENS OF THE STONE AGE
PRODUCED BY ADAM KASPER, JOSH HOMME AND ERIC VALENTINE
INTERSCOPE/AUGUST 2002
UK CHART: 4
US CHART: 17
KEY TRACKS: 'No One Knows'; 'You Think I Ain't Worth A Dollar But I Feel Like A Millionaire'; 'Go With The Flow'; 'The Sky Is Fallin'; 'A Song For The Deaf'

The best heavy metal album since Led Zeppelin's *Physical Graffiti*. Josh Homme is the only guitar hero worth having in the twenty-first century, apart from Blur's Graham Coxon, but that's different. Homme's art is narcotically sexy, his choice of guest band members (Dave Grohl of Foo Fighters/Nirvana on drums, Mark Lanegan of Screaming Trees on vocals) impeccable. He makes rock sound as if it never had any other point but to replicate the feeling of riding a boss hog through a desert to see your bay-bee and take drugs until you drool like a dog. As someone who has done that many times, I can verify this record's authenticity. For 'No One Knows', a masterpiece, he invents heavy metal Bavarian Oompah. Because someone had to. And the album ends with a proper Mariachi cowboy song called 'Mosquito Song'. Plus, he sort of plays like a cross between Tony Iommi of Black Sabbath and (early!) Brian May, and looks like Elvis, and John Reis of Rocket From The Crypt (see p.280), and Greg Dulli of The Afghan Whigs (see p.310), which makes him too many true rock heroes in one glassy eyed package to be anything other than hailed as rock's Messiah.

Actually, now the album's finished, I think that's going a bit far. But ... I'm putting it on again ... here we go ... OOOH!!! Josh! I LOVE YEWWW!!! Take me roughly!

He knows what boys like.

UP THE BRACKET

THE LIBERTINES
PRODUCED BY MICK JONES
ROUGH TRADE/OCTOBER 2002
UK CHART: 35
US CHART: DID NOT CHART
KEY TRACKS: 'What A Waster'; 'Boys In The Band'; 'Time For Heroes'; 'Up The Bracket'; 'I Get Along'

The first Libertines album staggers beneath the burden of Peter Doherty's tabloid life. You want ten years of distance between listening, and smack and crack and Kate and burgling Carl's flat and court case and prison and the man who began his public life on a mission to damn modern England and make a space for his band and their friends and their fans built on self-made myths of Arcadia and The Good Ship Albion, and has ended up selling his story countless times to papers that represent everything he seemed to despise in order to generate drug money, and who appears to drag everyone around him into the bad faith and ugliness. Yet this is the guy who wrote this: 'There are fewer more distressing sights than that/Of an Englishman in a baseball cap/Yeah we'll die in the class we were born/That's a class of our own, my love.' And that is an absolute distillation of the dreams of exclusivity, social mobility, bohemian intellect and loathing of conformity that inspire the greatest rock 'n' roll – not to mention the recurring British despair at the insidious spread of Americanisation. 'Time For Heroes', with its 'stylish kids in the riot ... shovelled up like muck', breathed a kind of life into a supine, moribund British pop culture. But the breath smelled of junk and the self-justifying elitism behind which the junkie hides, refusing to accept the truth: which is that addiction to Class A drugs is a retreat from facing the world, because, as the Au Pairs (see p.111) put it, plain and simple, on their 1981 'Headache': 'You're no threat when you're out of your head.'

So, with all that out of the way, what do you have if you hear *Up The Bracket* and have been blissfully unaware of the increasingly tedious and depressing story of the band's split and Doherty's travails? Well, you have a very fine punk/rock/pop group, owing much to The Strokes but managing to Anglicise the New Yorkers' demi-monde insouciance, bringing a pain and heroically doomed sense of damaged youth to those mutant Motown riffs, not to mention echoes of The Clash, The Jam, The Kinks, The Smiths, The Beatles, early Manic Street Preachers, Blur and punk-generation English junkie band The Only Ones, even Happy Mondays on the neatly funky opening of 'The Good Old Days' without ever sounding exactly like any one of those groups. You hear self-belief, and a reckless disregard for sounding cool and contained, in opposition to what British pop had become by 2002. You hear their obsessions with books and an English past of Tony Hancock and Sid James, *A Clockwork Orange* and music hall, of Merseybeat and well-dressed youth tribes. You hear Gary Powell's incongruously funky drumming preventing it from descending into faux-cockney thrash, and producer Jones allowing guitarists Doherty and Carl Barât's bickering jangles and unfinished cattle-prod whines to remain unresolved, messy and romantically doubtful. You hear a keen sense of location, in an east London remade as an art and cultural centre by cheap – well, cheaper – property, but dealing with problems of decay and poverty rubbing up against gentrification, a place of uneasy truce between black and white, flooded with drugs, bohemian outsiders and abused youth. You hear Barât's suave, rich voice and Doherty's drunk, childlike voice, and their strange love/hate affair, and their 'Two cold fingers . . .

these crooked fingers' raised to a world of murderous men on 'Up The Bracket', and their willingness to be beaten to a pulp for the greater good . . . a lie, on Doherty's part, perhaps. But this is the rock dream being peddled, after all, and kids love that lie, because we all want to believe we'd take the broken bones to protect someone/something else. The Libertines dramatised death or glory better than any band since The Clash, and made it seem easily accessible because they were easily accessible.

But, in hindsight, you don't hear a band in it for the long haul, not really. 'I Get Along' is a wry confession that they don't, with each other, with the world, despite that wonderfully delivered 'Fuck 'em'. And their very first single 'What A Waster', with its brilliant excavation of white trash gutter language (the 'divvy' and 'two-bob cunt'), sounds like an admission of defeat before anything's begun. It's extraordinary and it was all downhill from there. This album is the saddest rabble-rouser in existence. A loser's lament, drowning not waving.

HITS

PULP
PRODUCED BY ED BULLER, PHIL VINALL, CHRIS THOMAS, SCOTT WALKER, CAMERON CRAIG AND PULP
UNIVERSAL ISLAND/NOVEMBER 2002
UK CHART: 71
US CHART: DID NOT CHART
KEY TRACKS: 'Help The Aged'; 'Common People'; 'Sorted For E's And Wizz'; 'Babies'; 'Something Changed'

Possibly the least triumphant Greatest Hits album ever released – just clock that chart position! – *Hits* appeared just as a new kind of Britpop was poised to revive so successfully that even American bands – the children of 'Second British Invasion' '80s synth-pop – have started to all sound English.

PULP HITS

HITS/PULP

Sheffield's Pulp, a band that had existed for over twenty years, with eleven of those struggling on the margins throughout the 1980s, had fizzled out so quietly that no one's really sure if they ever officially split. Their leader, Jarvis Cocker, settled in the same east London area that The Libertines represented, occasionally playing with a low-key band called Relaxed Muscle. Whether he smiles wryly or seethes at the way bands such as The Kaiser Chiefs and The Killers have diluted his music to suit public taste, who knows? What is for sure is that Cocker is one of British pop's most acute and darkly comic writers, and that, sometimes, Pulp's kitschy, plastic pop was as good as he was. And that *Hits* is the best place to sample Pulp's sour subversions.

Commercially, Pulp were the victims of their own ironies. 'Common People' remains the best class-war song in British pop. But those who pogoed it into student disco infamy were, in many cases, the very privileged kids who it threw darts at. One of pop's key traits, from Dylan and The Beatles onwards, is that the pop buyer never sees themselves as the object of an accusatory hit's scorn. Everyone saw themselves as Jarvis in that song, and when Pulp began to make darker music to explore their themes of societal hypocrisy, consumers of 1995's Britpop-defining *Different Class* revealed that they'd never been interested in Cocker's attacks on their integrity. 'This Is Hardcore' and 'Help The Aged' made connections between sex, lies and porn on videotape that were guilt-inducing, uncomfortable, diseased. The Libertines were not just young, raucous and rockist, but there were no separations between themselves, the songs and their audience. They made their listeners feel like heroes, simply for listening. Cocker implicated the listener in the increasing emptiness of celeb/award ceremony/youth/cool/New Labour Britain, with its submission to hegemony and consumerism. It's the defining difference between rock and pop. Rock fools you into believing that you're part of its gang. Pop refuses to pretend that there's no gap between star and fan, and makes the best of its art from an exploration of that gap.

So *Hits* is a delight, and marks the territory of a group who did what smart pop groups should, as it points out that 'Different Class' itself moved easily from the sarcastic, glam-rock and '80s FM pop-derived triumphs of 'Common People' and 'Disco 2000' to the sincere loveliness of 'Something Changed' and the brilliant dissection of Britpop/Glasto/hedonist predictability (*Is This It* wasn't just a bushy-headed New York theme) that is 'Sorted For E's And Wizz'. The later singles, whether being ironic Bowie for 'Party Hard', or pulling off the coup of persuading legendary art-crooner recluse Scott Walker to produce the material from 2001's *We Love Life* album and finding a subtle musicality that only partly suited them, are surprisingly easy-listening sweet. The final, previously unreleased track, 'Last Day Of The Miner's Strike' laments the '80s defeat of socialism with a weariness that no amount of electro-clashing in the climax can obscure, and which fits the crime. I miss Jarvis.

2003

ELEPHANT/THE WHITE STRIPES

ELEPHANT

THE WHITE STRIPES

PRODUCED BY JACK WHITE
XL/MARCH 2003
UK CHART: 1
US CHART: 6
KEY TRACKS: 'Girl, You Have No Faith In Medicine'; 'There's
No Home For You Here'; 'The Hardest Button To Button';
'Black Math'; 'Ball And Biscuit'

What to say about an album recorded in east London's
Hackney on prehistoric equipment that embraces a song
about Scottish futurist genius/madman John Kane's impossibly complex theory of 'Black Math', a 'Seven Nation Army'
bassline that swallowed the planet and sounded like ESG
(see p.337) and wasn't played on a bass, a Detroit radio host
called Mort Crim getting all huggy and learny, references to
the ancient blues legend of 'the seventh son' for 'Ball And
Biscuit', a cult female garage-pop singer called Holly
Golightly demanding a cup of tea, and which somehow
became the most ubiquitous pop album in Britain in 2003.
Elephant was the fourth and most charismatic album from
Detroit's John Anthony Gillis and Megan Martha White, former partners who tried to convince the world they were the
secretly incestuous brother and sister Jack and Meg White.
Drums, guitar and voice, a strange variety of retro red and
white clothes, a slew of blues, folk, punk and indie influences
that all came out sounding like Led Zeppelin slumming it
with the Pixies, and a voodoo rock 'n' roll weirdness that
came all the way from all those pre-Elvis rockabillies, filtered
through a postmodern art-punk filter. What to say, indeed.

I'll start by saying that 'Seven Nation Army' isn't in the
key tracks because I got pig sick of hearing it, and haven't
recovered. And by also saying that the White Stripes magic
lies in the unlikely tension between the rock-historical guitar virtuosity and blues-metal bitch-baiting sneers of Jack
White, and an equal commitment to the twee end of the

lapel-badge and hairgrip, post-riot grrl bohemian-indie
netherworld, represented by Ms Golightly and the
Neanderthal thump of Meg's drums. Jack's bitchy love songs
and redneck testimonies inject mid-'60s Kinks, Sonics and
Stones boy-rock arrogance into a place they shouldn't be,
and classic rock 'n' roll is made, from simultaneously celebrating the old world in true Modern Lovers style (see p.4)
while refusing, like Jonathan Richman, to grow up. Sparks
fly from their conflict between intellect and naivety, and
emerge as shards of screeching, whizzing gee-tar and sexual
howling that seems oddly asexual, like an inversion of rock's
macho strut. It made *Elephant* fun, more than anything, but
dark with something occult and perverse, that leaves a dank
smell and a bloody trail.

BOY IN DA CORNER

DIZZEE RASCAL

PRODUCED BY DIZZEE RASCAL
XL/JULY 2003
UK CHART: 23
US CHART: DID NOT CHART
KEY TRACKS: 'Fix Up, Look Sharp'; 'I Luv U'; 'Jus' A Rascal';
'Wot U On?'; 'Jezebel'

It's all gone East End. 'Sittin' Here', the opening track from
eighteen-year-old Dylan 'Dizzee Rascal' Mills' explosive
debut, contains a spot-on summing-up of what twenty-
first-century London's human overload does to the introspective: 'I think too deep/I think too long/Yes I think I'm
getting weak/'Cos my thoughts are too strong.'

Dizzie reports from a Bow and Hackney black community where 'less bobbies on the beat' is a good thing, and
where a teenager is already looking back to an innocent
childhood with anxious nostalgia. His rapid-fire, London-
to-the-core vocals balance the machismo required for street
survival with the vulnerable fear lurking beneath.

Meanwhile, the brittle, broken, lurching synthetic beats meld the city's constant din – sirens, alarms, mobile ringtones, arcade machines – with decaying versions of all the musics of all the capital's cultures. The music was named 'grime', a science fiction derivation of hip hop, garage, dancehall and techno, uncompromising and exhilarating – just like the London town I finally fled in 2004, too old to deal with the stress and conflict illuminated by this album and 'Up The Bracket'.

'I Luv U' set the terms: an underground hit on a thriving, hustling, pirate radio-led British 'urban' scene that got Mills a record deal, the Holy Grail of album crossover without compromise, and a stabbing in Ayia Napa, the price it appears young black Britons pay for daring to rise from their environment. The battleground in 'I Luv U' is the gender trenches, Jeanine Jacques getting some, but not much, right to reply to Mills's terror of responsibility to girls who do nothing but grasp. It's as bleak a scenario as any in this book, because it feels true, no pose, no laddish rabble-rousing. 'Round We Go' and 'Wot U On?' make black comedy of the same nepotism and trash-talk, the endless he-say-she-say and suspicion and loathing. 'Jezebel's cautionary tale treads an uneasy line between contempt for and empathy with the song's promiscuous single-mother. The claustrophobia of this world renders love impossible, a romantic ideal that only the middle classes can afford. 'Love talks to everyone/Money talks more,' he and femme MC Caramel drawl, gleefully, on 'Wot U On?'

Elsewhere, it's violence, everywhere, among beats that nod to classical, metal, music from east and far east. 'I love raising conscience/But there's just too much violence,' he shouts on '2 Far', pure Jamaican-London aggro, glottal stops and daring curses, utilising a slew of London underclass slang terms. Yet there's regret, fear, an understanding of economic realities and a desire for a better life, all over these unhappy triumphs, and a vital element of cartoon that gives *Boy In Da Corner* more in common with *Cypress Hill* (see p.247) than the majority of British rap. The music feels like it can go anywhere, embrace any atonal noise London's streets have to offer. It's the restless genius of a hustler who admits he was saved from crime, prison and worse by his way with words and a laptop computer. The album ends with 'Do It', all poetry bets off, as straight and true a testimony of stress-related depression as he can muster. But he doesn't die, or kill, and it's not all about Dylan Mills. He ends his first album by imploring the youth of Bow, London E3, to stay in school, recalling and crashing right through the nihilism of Eminem's 'Don't do drugs' sneer (see p.313). His final line? 'And you need to talk more.' In the milieu that he's from, that line takes more guts and strength than every threat of violence he musters. This man – and he sure ain't no boy – is something special.

GALLOWSBIRD'S BARK

THE FIERY FURNACES
PRODUCED BY THE FIERY FURNACES AND NICHOLAS VERNHES
ROUGH TRADE/SEPTEMBER 2003
UK CHART: DID NOT CHART
US CHART: DID NOT CHART
KEY TRACKS: 'Worry Worry'; 'Bright Blue Tie'; 'I'm Gonna Run'; 'Tropical Ice-Land'; 'Asthma Attack'

The debut album from the alternative White Stripes, as if Meg and Jack weren't alternative enough.

Eleanor and Matthew Friedberger are real brother and sister, born in Oak Hill, Illinois, based in art-house Brooklyn, New York, and obsessed with Europe and the frozen North. Eleanor is, so I hear, girlfriend of Alex from Franz Ferdinand and the inspiration behind 'Eleanor, Put Your Boots On'. He has good taste, because she is the best female pop singer in America right now. She and her brother make music out of The Velvet Underground, fairgrounds, woodland animals, Captain Beefheart, sea shanties and mis-